THRIVING IN COLLEGE and BEYOND

Joseph B. Cuseo | Aaron Thompson | Michele Campagna | Viki Sox Fecas

Research-Based Strategies for Academic Success and Personal Development

CONCISE VERSION

Kendall Hunt
publishing company

Cover image © Shutterstock, Inc.

Kendall Hunt
publishing company

www.kendallhunt.com
Send all inquiries to:
4050 Westmark Drive
Dubuque, IA 52004-1840

Brief Contents

Contents

Chapter 8: Higher-Level Thinking

MOVING BEYOND BASIC KNOWLEDGE TO
CRITICAL AND CREATIVE THINKING   **165**

Chapter 9: Social and Emotional Intelligence

RELATING TO OTHERS AND REGULATING
EMOTIONS   **187**

Chapter 10: Diversity

LEARNING ABOUT AND FROM HUMAN
DIFFERENCES   **209**

Chapter 11: Financial Literacy

MANAGING MONEY AND MINIMIZING DEBT   **241**

Chapter 12: Physical Wellness

MAINTAINING BODILY HEALTH AND ATTAINING
PEAK PERFORMANCE   **263**

Preface

Plan and Purpose of This Book

This book is designed to help you make a smooth transition to college and equip you with strategies for success that can be used throughout your college experience and in life beyond college. Its goal is to promote the academic excellence and personal development of all students—whether they be students (a) transitioning to college directly from high school or from full-time employment, (b) living on or off campus, or (c) attending college on a full- or part-time basis. Whatever your previous level of academic performance may have been, or how many AP and dual-credit courses you have already taken, college is a new ball game played on a different field with new rules and expectations. If you have been an academically strong student prior to college, this book will make you an even stronger student in college. If you have not been a particularly successful student in the past, this book will help you become a successful student in the future.

One of the book's major goals is to equip you with one of the most powerful principles of human learning and personal success: *self-awareness*. Self-awareness is the critical first step toward personal growth and development in any endeavor. College students who are self-aware learners, aware of *how* they are learning and *if* they are learning strategically and deeply, rather than mindlessly and superficially. If you maintain self-awareness about whether you're "doing college" effectively (e.g., by using the research-based strategies identified in this book), you will have taken a huge step toward college success.

Practical, action-oriented strategies make up the heart of this book. Rather than trying to figure out how to do college on your own through random trial-and-error, this book provides you with a game plan for doing it right from the start, equipping you with a comprehensive set of strategies for doing college well. These strategies are not presented as a laundry list of things you should do (and should not do) dispensed arbitrarily and pontifically by authority figures who think they know what's best for you. Instead, the book's recommendations are accompanied by research-based reasons why they are effective and worthy of your consideration. If you have a deep understanding of the underlying principle that makes a strategy effective, you're more likely to put that strategy into practice. Furthermore, when you understand the principle behind the practice, it empowers you to create specific strategies of your own that are built on the same principle.

"Important achievements require a clear focus, all-out-effort, and a bottomless trunk full of strategies.

—*Carol Dweck, Stanford professor, and author of* Mindset: The New Psychology of Success

"The man who also knows why will be his own boss. As to methods there may be a million and then some, but principles are few. The man who grasps principles can successfully select his own methods.

—*Ralph Waldo Emerson, 19th-century author, poet, and philosopher*

ix

Specific and complete references for the research findings and action strategies cited in this book are included in the full-length version of the text, titled *Thriving in College & Beyond: Research-Based Strategies for Academic Success and Personal Development* (2020).

Preview of Content

Introduction

The Power of College and the First-Year Experience

In the introduction to this book, you will learn why college has the power to change your life and benefit you throughout life. The first year of college, in particular, is a crucial transitional stage characterized by significant change, challenge, and growth. It is the year of college during which students typically experience the most academic difficulties and highest risk of dropping out; however, it is also the year when college students report experiencing the most learning and greatest personal growth. Students who take a first-year experience or college success course (like the one you're likely enrolled in now) are more likely to make a smooth transition to college, experience a successful first year, and make the most of their college experience.

Chapter 1

Touching All the Bases

Using Powerful Principles of Student Success and Key Campus Resources

Like any journey, the journey through college begins with knowing what to bring with you and what resources to rely on along the way. This chapter supplies you with (a) an overview and preview of four powerful student-success principles that you can use throughout your college experience, (b) key campus resources to capitalize on, and (c) snapshot summaries of important things to do during the first weeks of college to get off to a smooth and successful start.

Chapter 2

Liberal Arts and General Education

What it Means to be a Well-Educated Person in the 21st Century

The liberal arts and general education are often misunderstood and underestimated components of a college education and career preparation. In this chapter, you will gain a deeper understanding and appreciation of the meaning, purpose, and benefits of the liberal arts and general education. You will learn how the liberal arts curriculum and general education courses equip you with a broad base of knowledge and a set of versatile skills that can be used to promote success in all college majors, careers, and life roles.

Chapter 3

Goal Setting and Motivation

Moving from Intention to Action

Achieving your goals is one definition of success. Studies show that people are more likely to be successful when they set specific goals for themselves and identify the means (succession of steps) needed to reach those goals. This chapter supplies you with practical strategies for setting specific, realistic goals and for maintaining motivation until you reach your goals.

Chapter 4

Time Management

Prioritizing Tasks, Preventing Procrastination, and Promoting Productivity

Setting goals is an important first step toward achieving success, but managing time and completing the tasks needed to reach those goals is a critical second step. Time is a valuable personal resource—when we gain greater control of it, we gain greater control of our lives. This chapter supplies a comprehensive set of strategies for managing time, establishing priorities, combating procrastination, and completing tasks.

Chapter 5

Deep Learning

Strategic Note-Taking, Reading, and Studying

The key academic tasks you're expected to perform in college include: taking lecture notes, completing reading assignments, studying, and test-taking. This chapter provides specific research-based and brain-based strategies for tackling these tasks. Implementing these strategies will enable you to learn at a much deeper level than rote memorization across all your college courses and throughout life.

Chapter 6

Test-Taking Skills and Strategies

What to do Before, During, and After Exams

Effective test-taking is both an art and a science. This chapter supplies you with a systematic set of strategies for improving your performance on both multiple-choice and essay exams. It identifies strategies that can be used before, during, and after exams, as well as practical tips for becoming more "test wise" and less "test anxious."

Chapter 7

Three Key Academic Success and Lifelong Learning Skills

Information Literacy, Writing, and Speaking

Researching, writing, and speaking effectively are flexible skills that can be transferred and applied to all majors and careers. In this chapter, you will acquire strategies to locate and evaluate information, write papers and reports, and use writing as a tool to learn deeply and think critically. The chapter also includes specific, practical tips for making effective oral presentations, overcoming speech anxiety, and becoming a more self-confident public speaker.

Chapter 8

Higher-Level Thinking

Moving Beyond Basic Knowledge to Critical and Creative Thinking

National surveys of college professors consistently show that their number one educational goal is developing students' critical thinking skills. In this chapter you will

"In high school, a lot of the work was done while in school, but in college all of your work is done on your time. You really have to organize yourself in order to get everything done.

—*First-year student's response to a question about what was most surprising about college life*

learn what critical thinking actually is, how it relates to creative thinking and other forms of higher-level thinking, and how to demonstrate different forms of higher-level thinking on your college exams and assignments. You will also learn how to use higher-level thinking skills to draw valid conclusions and to make sound judgments and personal decisions.

Chapter 9

Social and Emotional Intelligence

Relating to Others and Regulating Emotions

Communicating and interacting effectively with others are important life skills and essential elements of "social intelligence." Similarly, being aware of, and being able to manage, one's own emotions and the emotions of others are critical components of "emotional intelligence." This chapter identifies specific ways in which social and emotional intelligence can be developed and demonstrated; it also supplies interpersonal communication and human relations strategies that promote positive interactions with others and enhance your leadership potential.

Chapter 10

Diversity

Learning about and from Human Differences

Today's college students will experience more diversity on campus than at any other time in American history. This chapter defines "diversity", delineates its major forms, and documents how experiencing diversity deepens learning, enhances critical and creative thinking, and contributes to career success. The chapter also includes specific strategies for breaking down barriers and biases that often block humans from experiencing the full benefits of diversity, and supplies specific strategies for initiating and sustaining rewarding relationships with members of diverse groups.

Chapter 11

Financial Literacy

Managing Money and Minimizing Debt

Research shows that students who accumulate high amounts of debt in college are more likely to experience higher levels of stress, lower levels of academic performance, and higher risk of withdrawing from college. However, research also shows that students who use effective money-borrowing and money-management strategies are able to minimize debt, save money while in college, and increase the likelihood they will complete college and enter a productive career. This chapter identifies research-based strategies for making wise decisions about student loans and managing debt, tracking personal income and expenses, and striking a healthy balance between working for grades and working for pay.

Chapter 12

Physical Wellness

Maintaining Bodily Health and Attaining Peak Performance

Peak levels of performance, including academic performance, cannot be attained until physical wellness is maintained. Physical wellness involves being mindful of what we put into our body (healthy food), what we keep out of it (unhealthy substances), how we move it (regular exercise), and how well we restore and rejuvenate it (quality sleep). This chapter identifies strategies for attaining optimal physical wellness by (a) maintaining a balanced, performance-enhancing diet, (b) getting high-quality sleep, (c) exercising for total fitness, and (d) avoiding risky behaviors that undermine personal health, threaten physical safety, and impair human performance.

Chapter 13

Psychological Wellness

Preserving and Promoting Mental Health

Physical and mental health represent the "twin towers" of personal wellness; this chapter focuses on the latter tower—psychological well-being. Academic achievement in college and the ability to persist to college completion depend on students' ability to maintain their mental health and cope effectively with psychological stressors, particularly anxiety, depression, unhealthy relationships, and substance abuse. This chapter supplies specific strategies for preserving self-esteem, coping with college stressors, maintaining mental health, and attaining optimal psychological wellness.

Chapter 14

Educational Planning and Decision–Making

Making Wise Choices about Your College Courses, College Major, and Academic Pathway

Achieving your educational goals requires making strategic choices about your college courses and your college major. Having an educational plan in mind (and in hand) early in your college experience will enable you to explore your academic options and make well-informed decisions about your college major. Your major field of study should reflect who you are—your personal strengths, talents, interests and values. This chapter will supply you with strategies for deepening awareness of your personal attributes and connect them with your educational options and goals, and will help you design a strategic plan for reaching your chosen educational goal.

Chapter 15

Career Exploration, Preparation, and Development

Finding a Path to Your Future Profession

It may be surprising to find a chapter on career development in a book written for first-term college students. Certainly, entering college and entering a career are events taking place at different points in time and represent different life transitions. However, the process of exploring career options and developing career-entry skills should begin in the first year of college. Early career planning gives beginning college students a practical, long-term goal to strive for and gets them thinking about how the skills they are developing in college will contribute to their success beyond college. Thus, career planning is a form of *life* planning; the sooner you start the process, the sooner you start gaining control of your future and start steering it in the direction you want it to go.

Chapter Sequence

The chapters in this book are ordered in a way that positions you to ask and answer the following sequence of questions:

1. Why am I here?
2. Where do I want to go?
3. What must I do to get there?
4. How do I know when I've arrived?

Early chapters in the book are designed to orient you to the college environment, excite you about the college experience, and help you see where college can take you. Once you having a clear sense of why college is worth it, and how it can help you achieve your goals and brighten your future, you are then positioned (and motivated) to act on the strategies suggested throughout the remainder of the book. The middle chapters provide you with strategies for handling the day-to-day academic challenges, practical tasks, and interpersonal interactions that characterize the college experience. The book's final chapters help you make connections between your current first-year experience, your remaining years in college, and your future career and life goals.

Process and Style of Presentation

The impact of a book depends not only on the information it contains (its content); it also depends on how its information is delivered (the process). This book's information is delivered with learning and motivational features built into the delivery process that are designed to: (a) stimulate your motivation to learn, (b) deepen your understanding of what you are learning, and (c) strengthen your retention (memory) for what you have learned. These features are described below.

Chapter Purpose and Preview

At the very start of each chapter, a short summary of the chapter's primary purpose and key content is provided to supply you with an overview and sneak preview of what you are about to read. This feature highlights the chapter's relevance, giving you a reason (and motivation) to read it. Educational research indicates that when students see the reason or relevance of what they are about to learn, the more motivated they are about learning it and they learn it more deeply.

Reflections

At the beginning of each chapter, a question is posed to activate your thoughts and feelings about the chapter topic. This pre-reading exercise is designed to "warm up" or "tune up" your brain, preparing it to connect the ideas you will encounter in the chapter with the ideas about the topic that you already have in your head. This mental warm-up feature implements one of the most powerful principles of learning: Humans learn more deeply when they activate their prior knowledge and connect it to what they're about to learn.

Reflections are also included throughout the chapter to give you time to think about the material you're reading. These timely pauses keep you mentally active throughout the reading process, break up reading time with thinking time, and break down "attention drift" that typically takes place when the brain continues to engage in the same mental task for an extended period of time—such as continuous reading.

Another way in which these reflections strengthen your understanding of the material is by asking you to respond *in writing* to what you're reading. Unlike the simple and passive process of highlighting what you're reading, writing in reaction to what you read promotes active involvement, deepens learning, and stimulates higher-level thinking. Because writing supports learning, we recommend keeping a record of your written responses to the textbook's reflection questions in a *learning journal*.

Multiple Modes of Information Input

The information contained in this book is delivered through a variety of formats, including visual images (diagrams, pictures, cartoons), sidebar quotes, and personal stories drawn from the authors' experiences. These different forms of informational input infuse variety and change of pace into the learning process, which improves concentration and motivation by combating "habituation"—the tendency for humans to lose interest in (and attention to) information that's delivered to them repeatedly through the same perceptual modality.

Concept Maps

Most chapters include concept maps that organize and depict ideas in visual formats (diagrams and figures). When ideas are organized and represented in a visual-spatial format, they're more likely to be retained because two different memory traces (tracks) are recorded in the brain: a verbal memory trace and a visual memory trace. (This memory improvement principle is known as "dual coding.")

Summary Boxes

Boxes containing summaries of key concepts and strategies appear regularly throughout the text. These boxed summaries are designed to pull together major strategies relating to the same concept and get them organized in the same place. When related ideas are connected in the same place on a page, they're more likely to get connected in the same place in your brain and are better retained.

Highlighted Passages

Within each chapter of the book, certain passages are highlighted to emphasize that the ideas contained in these highlighted passages contain high-impact, high-priority points. Research on human memory indicates that information that stands out in some distinctive way is more likely to be attended to and remembered. (This memory principle is known as the "Von Restorff effect.")

Sidebar Quotes

In the side margins, quotes from successful and influential people appear that relate to and reinforce ideas just discussed in the body of the chapter. The words of these people can serve as sources of inspiration and resources for learning. You will find quotes from successful and influential people living in different historical periods and representing a wide variety of fields, such as politics, philosophy, religion, science, business, music, art, and athletics. The wide range of timeframes, cultures, and occupations of the notable people quoted throughout the book suggests that their words of wisdom are timeless and universal.

You can also learn a lot from the first-hand experiences of current students and recent college graduates. Throughout the book, you will find comments and advice from students at different stages of the college experience, and from college alumni. Studies show that students can learn a great deal from other students—especially from more experienced students who've "been there, done that." By reading about their success stories and stumbling blocks, you can learn from their college experiences to enhance your own college experience.

Authors' Experiences

Relevant personal stories drawn from the authors' experiences appear throughout the book. Studies show that when students hear personal stories shared by others, their understanding of and memory for key ideas contained in those stories is deepened and strengthened. We share our stories for the purpose of personalizing the book and with the hope that you will learn from our experiences—including our mistakes!

Cartoons: Visual–Emotional Aids

You will find cartoons sprinkled throughout the text to add some levity to your reading and provide an occasional change of pace. More importantly, the content of these cartoons relate to concepts covered in the text. Viewing the cartoons should strengthen your retention of the concepts you're reading about by reinforcing them with a visual image (drawing) and an emotional experience (humor). Studies show that learning and memory of a concept improves when the concept is delivered with humor.

Internet Resources

At the conclusion of each chapter, websites are recommended where you can find additional information relating to the chapter's major ideas. If the chapter ignites your interest in the topic that it has covered, you can use these online resources to learn more about it.

Exercises

At the end of each chapter are exercises designed to help you think more deeply about the material and *apply* it to your college experience. Acquiring knowledge is just the first step to effective performance. Knowledge acquisition needs to be followed by knowledge *application*—taking the knowledge acquired and putting it into practice. When you move beyond simply acquiring knowledge to applying your knowledge for positive and productive purposes, you exhibit *wisdom*.

Online Self–Assessments

In some chapters, you are directed to electronic self-assessment instruments that accompany the book. After completing these instruments, a set of personalized strategies are recommended for you. These self-assessments will help you deepen your self-awareness and supply you with personalized strategies for implementing key concepts covered in the chapter.

> "I've gotten a better sense of how to manage my life."
>
> "I know that I have a lot to learn, but this class has given me the stepping stones to help me become the person that I want to be."
>
> —*Comments made by first-year students in a course that used this book*

We sincerely hope and strongly believe that the ideas contained in this book, and the manner in which they are delivered, will do more than help you adjust to and survive in college; they will enable you to *thrive* in college and beyond. The skills and strategies you will read about are relevant to both success in college and success in life. Self-awareness, planning and decision-making, learning deeply and remembering longer, thinking critically and creatively, speaking and writing persuasively, managing time and money effectively, communicating and relating effectively with others, and maintaining health and wellness are more than just college success skills—they are *life* success skills.

> *Learning doesn't stop after college; it's a lifelong process. If you strive to apply the ideas in this book, you will thrive in college and beyond.*

Enjoy the journey!
Sincerely,
Joe Cuseo, Aaron Thompson, Michele Campagna, and Viki Sox Fecas

Acknowledgments

I'd like to take this opportunity to thank several people who have played an important role in my life and whose positive influence made this book possible. My parents, Mildred (nee Carmela) and Blase (nee Biaggio) Cuseo, for the many sacrifices they made to support my education. My wife, Mary, for her patience, love, and meticulous editorial feedback. My uncle, Jim Vigilis, for being a second father and life coach to me during my formative years. Jim Cooper, my best friend, for being a mentor to me in graduate school. My students, who taught me a lot and permitted me to share their insightful perspectives, poignant poems, and illustrations in this book. Finally, thanks to all the author-centered professionals at Kendall Hunt who gave me the freedom to write a book that reflects who I am and what I believe.

—Joe Cuseo

I would first of all thank those in my family and communities that had and still have faith in me being more than what society stereotyped me to be. I want to thank my children for making me more humble than I want to be. Thanks to the wonderful employees at Eastern Kentucky University and the KY Council on Postsecondary that have nourished me. Special thanks go out to colleagues and mentors such as Dr. Reid Luhman, Dr. Russ Enzie, Dr. Steve Savage, and Mr. Bob King for having my back. Thanks to all the students that have passed through my doors and those yet to come that have helped me to understand the value of learning versus the value of teaching. Last but not least, thanks to my Kendall Hunt friends especially Paul Carty and my co-authors Joe Cuseo, Michele Campagna, and Viki Fecas. I am truly blessed having you as friends and colleagues.

—Aaron Thompson

My thanks to my husband Dominic, and my children Nicolas and Brianna, for their continuous support and love. I would also like to express my gratitude to my parents, Sal and Yolanda, who despite their very limited education taught me the importance of *educación y ganas* (education and desire/drive). These values have stayed with me over the years, shaping my work and inspiring my contributions to this book. I also thank the many colleagues and students who have motivated me and have supported my efforts. I am especially grateful to my coauthors, Aaron and Joe, and to Paul at Kendall Hunt for their sharing and collaboration.

—Michele Campagna

If not for the love and support of my parents, Wyman and Fae Sox, and son, Matt Fecas, my involvement in this project would never have happened. Thanks also to Kendall Hunt's Paul Carty's wisdom in assembling the writing team and assigning a crackerjack editorial team. I also tremendously value my colleagues for their encouragement and feedback through the writing and review process.

—Viki Sox Fecas

About the Authors

Joe Cuseo holds a doctoral degree in Educational Psychology and Assessment from the University of Iowa and is Professor Emeritus of Psychology. For more than 25 years, he directed the first-year seminar—a core college success course required of all new students.

He's a 14-time recipient of the "faculty member of the year award" on his home campus—a student-driven award based on effective teaching and academic advising; a recipient of the "Outstanding First-Year Student Advocate Award" from the National Resource Center for The First-Year Experience and Students in Transition; and a recipient of the "Diamond Honoree Award" from the American College Personnel Association (ACPA) for contributions made to student development and the Student Affairs profession.

Currently, Joe serves as an educational advisor and consultant for AVID—a nonprofit organization whose mission is to promote the college access and success of underserved student populations. He has delivered hundreds of campus workshops and conference presentations across North America, as well as Europe, Asia, Australia, and the Middle East.

© The Kentucky Council on Postsecondary Education

Aaron Thompson is a nationally recognized leader in higher education with a focus on policy, student success and organizational leadership and design. He currently serves as the President of the Council on Postsecondary Education in Kentucky. He has served in many faculty and higher education administrative capacities such as Interim President of Kentucky State University, Executive Vice-President and Chief Academic Officer, Vice President of Academic Affairs, Associate VP for University Programs, Associate VP for Enrollment Management, and Executive Director of the Student Success Institute to mention a few. Many of these roles were served at Eastern Kentucky University where he also held the positioned as a tenured full professor.

His leadership experience spans 27 years across higher education, business, and numerous non-profit boards. Thompson has researched, taught and consulted in areas of diversity, leadership, ethics, multicultural families, race and ethnic relations, student success, first-year students, retention, cultural competence, and organizational design throughout his career.

As a highly sought after national speaker, Thompson has presented more than 800 workshops, seminars, and invited lectures in areas of race and gender diversity, living an unbiased life, overcoming obstacles to gain success, creating a school environment for academic success, cultural competence, workplace interaction, leadership, organizational goal setting, building relationships, the first-year seminar, and a variety of other topics. He continues to serve as a consultant to educational institutions (elementary, secondary, and postsecondary), corporations, non-profit organizations, police departments, and other governmental agencies. Thompson has published more than 30 publications and numerous research and peer reviewed presentations. He has authored or co-authored the following books: *The Sociological Outlook*, *Infusing Diversity and Cultural Competence into Teacher Education*, and *Peer to Peer Leadership: Changing Student Culture from the Ground Up*. He also co-authored *Thriving in College and Beyond: Research-Based Strategies for Academic Success*, *Thriving in the Community College and Beyond: Research-Based Strategies for Academic Success and Personal Development*, *Diversity and the College Experience*, *Focus on Success* and *Black Men and Divorce*.

Michele Campagna, Ed.D., is the Assistant Dean of Student Success/Title V Coordinator at Westchester Community College. Dr. Campagna has nearly 30 years experience teaching and designing first-year seminar courses and leading programs and services to promote student learning and success at 2-and 4-year institutions.

Dr. Campagna holds an Ed.D. in higher education and is a recipient of the "Outstanding First-Year Student Advocate Award" from the National Resource Center for the First-Year Experience and Students in Transition. She is the author of "New Student Experience: A Holistic and Collaborative Approach to First-Year Retention" in *Exploring the Evidence: Campus-Wide Initiatives in the First College Year*, published by the National Resource Center for the First-Year Experience and Students in Transition. Dr. Campagna has facilitated numerous faculty development workshops, served as consultant to several college campuses, and has presented at many statewide and national conferences on designing and implementing student engagement and retention initiatives, academic advising, strategic planning, assessment, and diversity.

Viki Sox Fecas has a Ph.D. in educational administration from the University of South Carolina (USC). In her role as program manager for freshman and pre-freshman programs, she coordinated the career component for all 150+ sections of the number one-ranked University 101 program in the country. She served as a career resource for international scholars visiting the National Resource Center (NRC).

Viki has served as an adjunct professor in the Higher Education and Student Affairs graduate program at USC. She was recognized as the *Outstanding Freshman Advocate* in 1996. She took University 101 as a freshman at USC, and has been teaching for over 20 years, including sections dedicated to transfer students. Her research interests center around the transition of college students, with a special interest in transfer students. She has written career chapters for the U101 *Transitions* book and *Your College Experience*. She has been a regular presenter at both national First-Year Experience and Students in Transition Conferences.

Introduction

The Power of College and the First-Year Experience

Congratulations on your decision to continue your education! Prior to college, education was required of you, but your enrollment in college is a choice made by you. You're about to begin an exciting and challenging journey that will transform your life. Compared with your previous school experiences, the college experience will provide you with a broader range of courses and learning opportunities, more resources to capitalize on, and more educational choices. This wider range of options and opportunities means that your college experience can be different than that of any other college student. You have the freedom to actively shape and create it in a way that's uniquely your own.

 Reflection I.1

Why have you decided to attend college?

What are you most *looking forward to* most about college?

It's probably safe to say that after college you will never again be part of any other organization or community with so many resources and opportunities available to you that have been intentionally designed to promote your personal development and future success. If you capitalize on your campus resources and utilize effective college-going strategies—such as those suggested in this book—your college experience should be a life-changing experience that will enrich the quality of your life for the rest of your life. **Box I.1** contains a summary of the multiple, lifelong benefits of a college education and college degree.

Box I.1

Why College Is Worth It: The Economic and Personal Benefits of a College Education

Despite the belief that earning a college degree is as common as earning a high school diploma, only 31% of Americans have a four-year college diploma. Comparing college graduates compared to others with similar social and economic backgrounds who did not continue their education beyond high school, research shows that a college degree is well worth the time and effort invested to achieve it. Summarized below are positive outcomes associated with a college education and a college degree. As you can see from the length of this list, the college experience benefits graduates in multiple ways at multiple stages of life.

1. Economic and Career Benefits

- Job Security and Job Stability—college graduates have higher rates of employment and are less likely to be laid off work.
- Higher Income—the gap between the earnings of high school and college graduates is large and *growing*. Individuals holding a bachelor's degree earn an average weekly salary that's approximately $18,900 higher than high school graduates. When these differences are calculated over 40 years of work, the average income of college graduates is about 65% higher than high school graduates, which adds up to more than a million dollars over the course of their lifetime. (See Figures I.1 and I.2)

FIGURE I.1

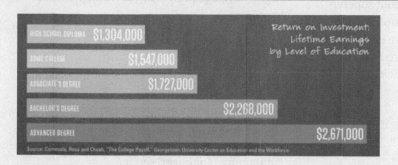

©Kendall Hunt Publishing Company

> The benefit of attending college in material terms remains at historically high levels."
> —*Commission on the Future of Undergraduate Education*

FIGURE I.2

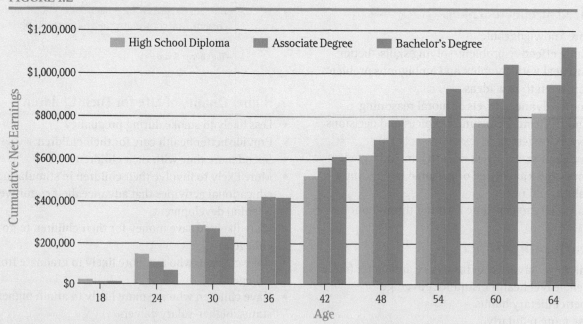

©Kendall Hunt Publishing Company

> It's an irrefutable fact that college gives you a significant and persistent advantage decade after decade."
>
> —*Mary C. Daly, Vice President of the Federal Reserve Bank of San Francisco*

- More likely to live in their own apartment or home (rather than with their parents)
- Career Versatility and Mobility—greater ability to move from one position and to another. (College graduates have more job options.)
- Career Advancement—greater opportunity to move up to higher-level positions. (College graduates have more opportunities for job promotions.)
- Career Satisfaction—college graduates are more likely to find themselves in careers that interest them and in positions they find stimulating, challenging, and personally fulfilling
- Career Autonomy—college graduates have more opportunities to work independently (without supervision) and make their own on-the-job decisions
- Career Prestige—college graduates are more likely to hold higher-status jobs (positions considered to be highly desirable and highly regarded by society)
- Better retirement and pension benefits

> The bachelor's degree recipient doesn't just have a bachelor's degree. He [or she] has the option of entering a variety of professions that require this credential and continuing for a graduate degree"
>
> —The College Board, *How College Shapes Lives*

2. Advanced Intellectual Skills

- Are more knowledgeable
- Have more effective problem-solving skills—better ability to deal with complex and ambiguous problems
- Are more open to new ideas
- Have more advanced levels of moral reasoning
- Make more effective consumer choices and decisions
- Make wiser long-term investments
- Have a clearer sense of self-identity, including self-awareness and knowledge of personal talents, interests, values, and needs
- Are more likely to continue learning throughout life

3. Physical Health Benefits

- More likely to have health insurance and better (more comprehensive) health insurance coverage
- Have better dietary habits
- Exercise more regularly

- Have lower rates of smoking and obesity
- Live longer and healthier lives

4. Social Benefits

- More social self-confidence
- Stronger interpersonal and human relations skills
- Better leadership skills
- Greater popularity
- Higher levels of marital satisfaction

5. Emotional Benefits

- Lower levels of anxiety
- Higher levels of self-esteem
- Greater sense of self-efficacy—belief that they can influence or control the outcomes of their life
- Higher levels of psychological well-being and mental health
- Higher levels of life satisfaction and personal happiness

6. Effective Citizenship

- More interest in national issues—both social and political
- Greater knowledge of current events
- Higher voting participation rates
- Higher rates of participation in civic affairs and community (volunteer) service
- Less likely to be incarcerated

> The evidence is overwhelming that higher education improves people's lives, makes our economy more efficient, and contributes to a more equitable society."
>
> —The College Board

7. Higher Quality of Life for Their Children

- Less likely to smoke during pregnancy
- Provide better health care for their children
- Spend more time with their children
- More likely to involve their children in stimulating educational activities that advance their cognitive (mental) development
- More likely to save money for their children to go to college
- Have children who are more likely to graduate from college
- Have children who are more likely to attain higher-status, higher-salary careers

Reflection I.2

Glance back at the seven major benefits or positive outcomes of a college education listed in Box I.1. If you were to rank them in terms of their importance to you, which three would rank at the top your list? Why?

The Importance of the First-Year Experience

Your transition into higher education represents a major life transition. Similar to an immigrant transitioning to a new country, you're an educational immigrant transitioning to a new culture with a different language, expectations, regulations, and customs. (For definitions and "translations" of this new language spoken in college, see the Glossary and Dictionary of College Vocabulary, pp. 367–373.)

The *first* year of college is likely to be the most important year of your college experience because it's a *transitional* stage in your life. Research shows that college students experience more personal change, learning, and development during their first year than during any other year of their college experience. Other research suggests that the academic habits students develop in their first year are likely to persist throughout their remaining years of college. When graduating seniors look back at their college experience, many of them say that their first year was the time of greatest challenge and the time when they made the most significant improvements in their approach to learning. Here's how one senior put it during a personal interview:

> **Interviewer:** What have you learned about your approach to learning [in college]?
>
> **Student:** I had to learn how to study. I went through high school with a 4.0 average. I didn't have to study. It was a breeze. I got to the university and there was no structure. No one took attendance to make sure I was in class. No one checked my homework. No one told me I had to do something. There were no quizzes on the readings. I did not work well with this lack of structure. It took my first year and a half to learn to deal with it. But I had to teach myself to manage my time. I had to teach myself how to study. I had to teach myself how to learn in a different environment.

In some ways, the first-year experience in college is similar to downhill skiing: It can be filled with exciting thrills, such as the thrill of meeting new people, experiencing new challenges, and making remarkable gains in learning and development; however, it's also the year fraught with the most spills—for example, when students tend to experience the most stress, the most academic difficulties, and the highest withdrawal (dropout) rates. Like downhill skiing, the goal of your first-year of college should be to experience the thrills, avoid the spills, and finish the run (year) on your feet, feeling exhilarated and excited about making your next run (your sophomore year). Studies show that if students complete their first-year experience in good standing, their chances for successfully completing college increase dramatically.

As you read this book, you will find that the research it cites and the advice it provides point to the same conclusion: Success in college depends on what you do—the strategies you use and the resources you utilize. Take charge of your college experience—don't let college happen *to* you; make it happen *for* you.

"My three-month-old boy is very important to me, and it is important I graduate from college so my son, as well as I, live a better life.

—*First-year student's response to the question: "What is most important to you?"*

"For the individual, having access to and successfully graduating from an institution of higher education has proved to be the path to a better job, to better health and to a better life.

—*The College Board*

"One of the major transitions from high school to college involves the unlearning of past attitudes, values, and behaviors and the learning of new ones. This represents a major social and psychological transition and a time when students may be more ready to change than at any other point in their college career.

—Ernest Pascarella & Patrick Terenzini, *How College Affects Students*

"What students do during college counts more than who they are or where they go to college.

—George Kuh, author, *Student Success in College*

After reviewing 40 years of research on how college affects students, two distinguished researchers reached the following conclusion:

> *The impact of college is largely determined by individual effort and involvement in the academic, interpersonal, and extracurricular [co-curricular] offerings on a campus. Students are not passive recipients of institutional efforts to "educate" or "change" them, but rather bear major responsibility for any gains they derive from their postsecondary [college] experience.*

> "When it comes to finding the secret to success, it's not 'where you go.' It's 'how you do it' that makes all the difference in higher education."
>
> —*Great jobs, great lives. The 2014 Gallup-Purdue Index Report: A study of more than 30,000 college graduates across the U.S.*

Reflection I.3

Why have you decided to attend the particular college or university you're enrolled in now?

Are you happy to be here? Why?

The Benefits of a First-Year Experience Course (a.k.a. College Success Course)

If you are reading this book, you are already beginning to take charge of your college experience because you are enrolled in a course that's designed to promote your college success. Research strongly indicates that new students who participate in first-year experience courses are more likely to earn higher first-year grades, return for their sophomore year, and go on complete their college degree. These positive outcomes of first-year experience courses have been found for:

> "Being in this class has helped me a lot. What I learned I will apply to all my other classes."

- All types of students (under-prepared and well-prepared, minority and majority, residential and commuter, male and female),
- Students at all types of colleges and universities (two-year and four-year, public and private),
- Students attending colleges of all sizes (small, mid-sized, and large)
- Students attending colleges in all locations (urban, suburban, and rural).

> "I am now one of the peer counselors on campus, and without this class my first semester, I don't think I could have done as well, and by participating in this class again (as a teaching assistant), it reinforced this belief."
>
> — *Comment made by a student when evaluating his first-year experience course*

More research has been conducted on the first-year experience course and more evidence supports its positive impact on student success than any other course in the college curriculum. If you have had a history of academic success before college and have earned college credits while in high school, the first-year experience course will still help you handle the variety of challenges associated with the college experience. Remember that these challenges not only include adjusting to the academic demands of college, such as deep learning and critical thinking, but also social and emotional adjustments, and decision-making challenges related to your future educational, career, and life plans. By giving a first-year experience course your best effort and taking full advantage of all that it has to offer, you will be taking an important first step toward achieving success in your first year of college and beyond.

AUTHOR'S EXPERIENCE

I've learned a lot from my many years of teaching a first-year experience (college success) course and from the years I've put into writing a book for this course. Even as a college graduate, I didn't have a clear understanding of the meaning, purpose, and value of a college education, or why general education was so important for achieving personal and professional success. By preparing for and teaching this course, I developed a deeper understanding and appreciation of what the college experience is and what it did for me. I also learned new strategies for improving my memory and my writing, as well as for managing my time, money, and health. I continue to use these strategies in my personal and professional life. My only regret is that I didn't take a course like this when I began college. If I had, I would have been able to get even more out of my college experience and could have applied these life-success skills much earlier in my life.

—*Joe Cuseo*

Touching All the Bases

USING POWERFUL PRINCIPLES OF STUDENT SUCCESS AND KEY CAMPUS RESOURCES

Like any journey, the journey through college begins with knowing what to bring with you and what resources to rely on along the way. This chapter supplies you with (a) an overview and preview of four powerful student-success principles you can use throughout your college experience, (b) key campus resources to capitalize on, and (c) snapshot summaries of important things to do during the first weeks of your college journey to get off to a smooth and successful start.

Acquire knowledge of powerful college-success principles and valuable campus resources, understand why they are important, and learn how to capitalize on them.

 Reflection 1.1

To excel in college, what do you think you will need to do differently than you did in high school?

Powerful Principles of College Success

Research points to the following four factors as being key principles of college success. These principles are covered in the opening chapter of this book because they provide the foundational bases for all success strategies discussed throughout the book (See **Figure 1.1**).

1. Active Involvement (Engagement)
2. Effective Use of Campus Resources (Resourcefulness)
3. Interpersonal Interaction and Collaboration (Social Integration)
4. Reflection and Self-Awareness (Mindfulness)

FIGURE 1.1: The Four Bases of College Success

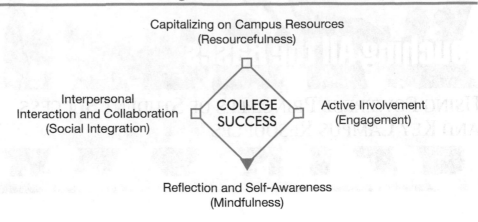

©Kendall Hunt Publishing Company

Principle 1. Active Involvement (Engagement)

Many years of research indicate that active involvement (engagement) is the most powerful principle of human learning and college. To succeed in college, students cannot be passive spectators; they need to be actively engaged in the game. Active involvement has two key components:

- The amount of *time* devoted to the college experience—inside and outside the classroom
- The degree of *effort or energy* (mental and physical) invested in the learning process.

Think of something you do with intensity, passion, and commitment. If you do college that way, you would be faithfully implementing the principle of active involvement. Here's how you can apply both key components of active involvement—time and energy—to the college experience.

Time Spent in Class

Not surprisingly, the more time students devote to the task of learning, the more they learn and the deeper they learn. This relationship leads to a straightforward recommendation: Get to all classes in all courses. It's tempting for new students to skip or cut classes because, unlike the teachers they had in high school, college professors are less likely to call roll or monitor class attendance. Don't let this lack of attendance monitoring lead you to thinking that missing classes will not affect your course grades.

Over the past 75 years, numerous studies have shown a direct relationship between class attendance and course grades—as one goes up or down, so does the other. **Figure 1.2** depicts the results of one major study that clearly shows the relationship between students' class attendance during the first 5 weeks of the term and their final course grades.

Look at going to class like going to work. If you miss work days, it lowers your pay; if you miss classes, it lowers your grades. Keep in mind that a full load of college courses (15 units) only requires that a student to be in class about 13 hours per week. If going to college full time were viewed as a full-time job, it would be a job that only required students to show up at work about 13 hours a week. That's a pretty sweet deal that leaves college students with much more educational freedom than they had in high school. For students to miss class when they're being asked to spend such a

> "Tell me and I'll listen. Show me and I'll understand. Involve me and I'll learn."
> —*Teton Lakota Indian saying*

> "My biggest recommendation: GO TO CLASS. I learned this the hard way my first semester. You'll be surprised what you pick up just by being there. I wish someone would have informed me of this before I started school."
> —*Advice to new students from a college sophomore*

FIGURE 1.2: Relationship between Class Attendance Rate and Course Final Grades

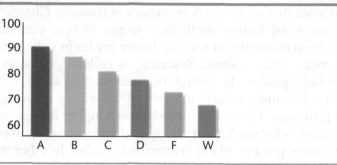

©Kendall Hunt Publishing Company

limited time in class is a real abuse of this freedom. It's also an abuse of the money that they, their family, and taxpaying citizens are paying for their college education.

> College students who stop attending classes in a course are not automatically dropped from the course—even if they stop attending during the first few weeks of the term. To withdraw from a class, see an academic advisor.

Time Spent on Coursework Outside of Class

Less than 40% of beginning college students report that they studied at least 6 hours per week during their final year in high school and only one-third of them expect to spend more than 20 hours per week preparing for class in college. When they get their first schedule of classes, first-year students are often pleasantly surprised by how much "free time" they have. However, college students are expected to spend much more time outside of class on their courses than they did in high school and this "homework" doesn't involve simply turning in assignments on a daily or weekly basis. Out-of-class work assigned in college may not even be collected and graded. Instead, it's expected that students do it on their own and for their own benefit—to prepare for upcoming exams and larger assignments. Rather than formally collecting homework, college professors expect students to do assigned work without close supervision or enforced accountability.

A common "rule of thumb" used by college faculty is that students are expected to students to spend at least 2 hours on coursework outside of class for each hour they spend in class. For example, in a three-credit course that meets 3 hours per week, students should devote at least 6 hours of out-of-class work each week. Unfortunately, less than 10% of beginning college students report putting in at least 2 hours of work out of class for every hour spent in class. This must change if first-year students are to thrive in college. Just as successful athletes put in a significant amount of practice time to excel athletically, successful students do the same to excel academically.

Approach college like it's a full-time job. If you're taking a full load of courses, you're in class about 13 hours per week, which means you should spend about 26 hours a week working on those courses outside of class time. This adds up to a 40-hour work week—similar to a full-time job. In one study of more than 25,000 college students, it was found that the percentage of students who spent 40 or more hours per week on academic work received "A" grades at a rate that was almost three times higher than for students who spent between 20 and 40 hours per week on academic work. For students who spent 20 or fewer hours per week on academic work outside of class, twice as many of them received grades of "C" or below than did students who spent 40 or more hours on out-of-class work. (For tips on the type of course-related work that should be done outside of class, see Chapter 4, pp. 75–76.)

If you need further motivation to put in time outside of class to earn good grades, keep in mind that earning better grades in college translates into better career benefits after college. Research on college graduates shows that the higher their college grades, the higher: (a) their starting salary, (b) the status (prestige) of their first job, and (c) their career mobility—ability to change jobs or move into different positions. This relationship between higher college grades and greater career benefits exists for students at all types of colleges and universities, regardless of the reputation or prestige of the institution attended. In other words, how well students do in college matters more than the name of the college on their diploma.

> "I thought I would get a better education if the school had a really good reputation. Now, I think one's education depends on how much effort you put into it."
>
> —First-year college student

Reflection 1.2

During your senior year in high school, about how many hours per week did you spend on schoolwork outside of class? How many hours do you plan to spend on out-of-class schoolwork in college?

Active Involvement in the Learning Process

College success will require that you work harder—put in more time than high school and work smarter—learn more strategically and deeply. Perhaps the most powerful principle of deep learning is active involvement (engagement); there's simply no such thing as "passive learning." When you learn actively, you act (engage in some action) on what you're learning. You can be sure you're learning actively by engaging in one or more of the following *actions* while learning:

> "All genuine learning is active, not passive. It is a process in which the student is the main agent, not the teacher."
>
> —Mortimer Adler, American professor of philosophy and educational theorist

- Writing—write about what you're learning (e.g., take notes on what you're reading rather than passively highlight sentences).
- Speaking—state aloud what you're learning (e.g., discuss what you're reading with a study partner rather than just looking over the material silently).
- Organizing—connect (integrate) the ideas you're learning onto index cards, diagrams, or maps.

Active Classroom Listening and Note-Taking

You will find that many college professors rely heavily on the lecture method—they dispense knowledge by speaking for long stretches of time, and they expect students to listen and take notes on the knowledge they dispense. This method of instruction places great demands on your ability to listen actively and take notes accurately and completely. Research consistently shows that most test questions on college exams come from professors' lectures; students who take better lecture notes earn better grades.

> "I never had a class before where the teacher just stands up and talks to you. He says something and you're writing it down, but then he says something else."
>
> —First-year college student

The best way you can apply the principle of active involvement to a class lecture is to actively take (write) notes on the lecture. Writing down what your instructor is saying essentially "forces" you to pay closer attention to what is being said and reinforces your retention of what has been said. By taking notes, you not only hear the information (auditory memory), you also see it on paper (visual memory) and feel it in the muscles of your hand as you write it (motor memory).

Box 1.1 contains a summary of top strategies for active classroom listening and note-taking that you can put into action right now.

Your role in the college classroom is not to be an absorbent sponge or passive spectator who simply sits back and soaks up information. Instead, it should be that of a detective or investigative reporter on a search-and-record mission. Actively search for knowledge, pick the instructor's brain, pick out the instructor's key points, and record your "pickings" in your notebook (or on your laptop).

Box 1.1

Top Tips for Active Listening and Note-Taking in the College Classroom

One task that you'll be expected to perform during the very first week of college is taking lecture notes. Studies show that professors' lecture notes are the number one source of test questions (and answers) on college exams. You can improve the quality of your note-taking and earn higher course grades by using the following strategies.

1.   Get to every class. There is a clear connection between class attendance and course grades; as one goes up (or down), so does the other.
2.   Get to every class on time. During the first few minutes of a class session, instructors often share valuable information—such as important announcement, reviews, and previews.
3.   Get organized. Bring the right equipment to class. Get a separate notebook for each class, write your name on it, date each class session, and store all class handouts in it.
4.   Get in the right position.
     • The ideal place to sit is the front and center of the room—where you're in the best position to hear and see what's going on.
     • The ideal posture to adopt is sitting upright and leaning forward—because your body influences your mind; if your body is in an alert and ready position, your mind is likely to follow.
     • The ideal social position to occupy in class is to sit by motivated classmates who will not distract you but motivate you to listen actively and take notes aggressively.

The previous three strategies are particularly important in large classes where you're likely to feel more anonymous, less accountable, and less engaged.

5.   Get in the right frame of mind. Come to class with the attitude that you're there to pick your instructor's brain, pick up answers to test questions, and pick up points to raise your course grade.
6.   Get it down (in writing). Actively look, listen, and take notes throughout the entire class period. Pay special attention to whatever information instructors put in writing, whether it appears on the board, on a slide, or in a handout.

Most college professors will not write all important information for you on the board or on Power Point slides; instead, they expect you to listen carefully and write it down yourself. When in doubt, write it out (or type it out); it's better to have it and not need it than to need it and not have it.

7.   Finish strong. During the last few minutes of class, instructors often share valuable information, such as timely reminders, reviews, and previews.
8.   Stick around. When class ends, don't bolt out; instead, hang out and quickly review your notes (by yourself or with a classmate). This quick end-of-class review will help your brain retain the information it just received. If you detect any gaps or confusing points in your notes, try to clear them with the instructor or a classmate immediately after class.

For more detailed information and strategies on active listening and effective note-taking, see Chapter 5, pp. 89-97.

Reflection 1.3

Do you feel confident about meeting the challenge of taking effective lecture notes in college classes? Will you need to make adjustments or changes in your previous classroom learning habits to meet this challenge? If yes, in what way(s)?

Finish class with a rush of attention, not a rush out the door!

Active Class Participation

You can implement the principle of active involvement in the college classroom not only by actively taking lecture notes, but also by being an engaged class participant who comes to class well prepared (e.g., having done the assigned reading), who asks relevant questions in class, and who contributes thoughtful comments during class discussions. Being an active class participant increases your ability to stay alert and attentive in class; it also sends a clear message to the instructor that you are a motivated student who wants to learn. Furthermore, class participation is likely to account for a portion of your final grade in many courses, so your attentiveness and involvement in class can have a direct effect on your course grades.

AUTHOR'S EXPERIENCE

I worked many hours each week while in college to pay for basic needs, such as housing, my meal plan, and my books. I was stretched so thin and was terribly exhausted every day. These circumstances meant that not only did I have to carefully decide how I spent my time outside of class, I also had to pay careful attention to how my time was spent in class. I knew that class time was my opportunity to take in all the material that I could (and to do everything possible to stay awake!) so I forced myself to sit in the front of the room, participate in discussions, and take notes vigorously. I used highlighters to emphasize important points that I wrote down and to remind myself of points I needed to review further. These active learning strategies helped me all though my college years.

—*Michele Campagna*

Active Reading

Note-taking not only contributes to active listening in class, it also contributes to active reading outside of class. Taking notes on what you read (or on information you've highlighted while reading) is the best way to stay actively involved in the reading process because it requires more mental and physical energy than simply reading the material or passively highlighting sentences.

College professors also expect you to relate or connect what they talk about in class to your reading assignments. Thus, it's important to start developing good reading habits right now. You can do so by using the top tips listed in **Box 1.2**.

Box 1.2

Top Tips for Strengthening Textbook Reading Comprehension and Retention

"I recommend that you read the first chapters right away because college professors get started promptly with assigning certain readings. Classes in college move very fast because, unlike high school, you do not attend class five times a week but two or three times a week."

—Advice to new college students from a first-year student

1. **Get the textbooks required for your courses as soon as possible and get your reading assignments done on time.** Information from reading assignments ranks right behind lecture notes as a source of test questions on college exams. Many professors deliver their lectures with the expectation that you've done the assigned reading and assume that you will build on the information you've read to help you understand their lectures. If you haven't done the reading, you're likely to have more difficulty following what the instructor is saying in class. Thus, by not doing the assigned reading, you pay a double penalty: you miss information contained in the reading that's not covered in class (which is likely to appear on exams) and you miss ideas presented in class that build on the assigned reading.

2. **Read with the right equipment.**
   - Bring a writing tool (pen, pencil, or keyboard) to record important information and a storage space (notebook or computer) in which you can save the information you recorded and use it to prepare for tests and complete assignments (e.g., use ideas obtained from your reading by incorporating into term papers and other out-of-class assignments).
   - Have a dictionary nearby (electronic or paper) to quickly find the meaning of unfamiliar words that may interfere with your ability to comprehend what you're reading. Looking up definitions of unfamiliar words not only helps you understand what you're currently reading; it also builds your overall vocabulary. A strong vocabulary will improve your reading comprehension in all your courses as well as your performance on standardized tests, such as those required for admission to graduate and professional schools.
   - Check the back of your textbook for a glossary (list) of key terms included in the book. Each college subject or academic discipline has its own special language, and decoding that language is often the key to understanding the concepts covered in your courses in that subject. The glossary at the end of your textbook is more than an ancillary frill; it's a valuable tool that can be used to improve your comprehension of course concepts. Consider making a photocopy of the glossary at the back of your textbook and have it next to you while reading so you don't have to stop reading, hold your place, and go to the back of the text to find terms in the glossary.

3. **Get in the right position.** Sit upright to maximize attention and position yourself so that light is coming from behind you and over the side of your body that's opposite your writing hand. (This will minimize the amount of glare and shadows that appear on the pages you're reading, which can be distracting and fatiguing.)

4. **Get a sneak preview.** Start a book chapter by first reading its boldface headings and any chapter outline, summary, or end-of-chapter questions that are provided. This will supply you with a mental map of the chapter's important ideas before you start your trip through it. By first getting an overview of the chapter, it's easier to keep track of its major ideas (the "big picture") and it reduces your risk of getting lost in all the smaller details that you encounter along the way. (In other words, you're less likely to "lose the forest for the trees.")

5. **Finish each of your reading sessions with a short review.** Rather than using the last few minutes of a reading session to try to cover a few more pages, end it with a review of the information have already highlighted or noted as important. We forget most of the information we take in immediately after we have stopped processing that information and start doing something else. Thus, it's best to use your last minutes of reading time to "lock in" the most important information you have just been read.

> *The goal of reading is not just to cover the assigned pages, but to discover the most important ideas on those pages, and then review (lock in) those ideas.*

Note: For a more detailed discussion of reading comprehension and retention strategies, see Chapter 5 (pp. 97-103).

Principle 2. Capitalizing on Campus Resources (Resourcefulness)

Successful students (and successful people) are *resourceful*—they seek out and use resources to help them reach their goals. College and university campuses are chock full of resources that have been intentionally designed to support students' quest for educational and personal success. Studies show that students who use campus resources report higher levels of satisfaction with college and get more out of the college experience.

> *Your use of campus resources comes free of charge—the cost of these services is already covered by your tuition. By investing time and energy in campus resources, you're not only increasing your prospects for college success, you're also maximizing the return on your financial investment in college. In other words, you get a bigger bang for your buck!*

The college-success principle of capitalizing on campus resources is a natural extension of the principle of active involvement. Successful students get *involved* both inside and outside the classroom, and involvement outside of class includes involvement with campus resources.

The first step to effectively capitalizing on campus resources is becoming aware of the full range of resources available to you and what they can do for you. Listed below are key college services you're likely to find on campus, accompanied by their purposes and benefits. The specific names given to these resources may differ from one college campus to another, but their purposes are the same, as are their benefits for students who capitalize on them.

Learning Center (a.k.a. Academic Resource Center or Academic Success Center)

You can use this campus resource to strengthen your academic performance in any course or field of study. The individual and group tutoring provided at the Center can help you master difficult course concepts and assignments, and the people working there are professionals whose expertise is helping students learn *how to learn*. Just as professors are experts in the subjects they teach, learning resource professionals are experts on how students learn. They are professionally prepared to equip college students with effective learning strategies for handling the unique challenges posed by different subjects and teaching styles.

Learning Centers also employ trained peer tutors who can be especially effective learning coaches for college students because (a) they are close in age and experience to the students seeking help, which enables them to explain concepts in a language that is easier for students to understand and (b) they have recently learned the material that students are currently trying to learn.

Despite the powerful advantages associated with the use of academic support services, these services are typically underused by college students—especially by students who need them the most. Unfortunately, some college students believe that seeking academic help is an admission that they're not smart, self-reliant, or capable of succeeding on their own. Don't buy into this myth. In high school, students may have only gone to a campus office if they were *required* to, if they had forgotten to do something, or if they had done something wrong. In college, students *choose* to use campus offices to enhance their success by taking advantage of the personalized support these offices and programs provide.

> "Do not be a PCP (Parking Lot → Classroom → Parking Lot) student. The time you spend on campus will be a sound investment in your academic and professional success."
>
> —Dr. Drew Appleby, professor emeritus, psychology

> "Where I learn the material best is [from] tutoring because they go over it and if you have questions, you can ask. They have time for you or will make time for you."
>
> —First-year college student

> "At colleges where I've taught, the grade-point averages of students who used the Learning Center were higher than the college average, and honors students were more likely to use the Center than other students."
>
> —Joe Cuseo, Professor Emeritus, Psychology

When a student uses academic support services, it doesn't mean that the student has a "problem" or deficiency that needs to be repaired or remediated, is on the brink of failure, or needs academic life support. Using these services isn't a sign of weakness but an indication of motivation, resourcefulness, and pursuit of academic excellence. Both struggling and successful students can and do benefit from academic support services.

Writing Center

Writing is an academic skill that you will use in virtually all your courses, freshman through senior year. Thus, if you strengthen your writing skills, you will strengthen your overall academic performance in college. Many college campuses offer specialized support for students seeking to improve their writing. Sometimes this support is delivered in a Writing Center—a place on campus where students can receive assistance at any stage of the writing process, whether it be initially collecting and organizing their ideas, composing their first draft, or proofreading their final draft. Take advantage of this resource to improve your writing, your overall academic performance in college, and your career performance after college.

 Reflection 1.4

How much writing did you typically do in high school?

How would you rate writing skills right now?

Campus Library

Librarians are professional educators who develop students' ability to search for, find, and evaluate information. These are lifelong learning skills that promote success throughout college and in life beyond college.

"The next best thing to knowing something is knowing where to find it.

—Dr. Samuel Johnson, English literary figure and original author of the *Dictionary of the English Language* (1747)

Disability Services (a.k.a. Disability Resource Center)

If students have a documented physical or learning disability that's interfering with their performance in college, or if they think they might have a disability, the Office of Disability Services is the place on campus where they can receive assistance and support. Programs and services typically provided by this office include:

- Assessment for learning disabilities,
- Verification of eligibility for disability support services,
- Authorization of academic accommodations for disabilities, and
- Specialized counseling, advising, and tutoring.

Financial Aid Office

If you have any concerns about your ability to pay for college, do not hesitate to consult this office. The process of applying (and reapplying) for financial aid can be a complicated and intimidating process. Don't let the complexity of the process prevent you from capitalizing on the fiscal support that you're eligible to receive. Professional financial aid counselors can walk you through the process and help you find:

- Low-interest student loans
- Grants or scholarships
- Part-time campus employment (as a work–study student).

Check your e-mail regularly for messages from the Financial Aid Office, especially messages pertaining to financial-aid application and renewal deadlines. If you have any doubt about whether you're using the most effective plan to finance your college education, make an appointment to see a professional in this office. (For more detailed information on financial aid, see Chapter 11.)

Academic Advisement

The Academic Advisement Center is the place on campus where students can get help with course selection, educational planning, and how to choose or change a major. Studies show that students who have clear educational and career goals are more likely to persist in college and complete their degree. Research also shows that most new students need assistance to help them clarify their educational goals, decide on a college major, and identify their career options.

As a first-year student, it's perfectly understandable and acceptable to be undecided about a college major. However, the process of thinking about and planning for a major should begin in the first term of college. Connect early and often with an academic advisor to help you think through your educational options and find a college major that best matches your interests, talents, values, and goals. (For more detailed information on educational planning and decision-making, see Chapter 14.)

Career Development Center (a.k.a. Career Center)

As a first-year student, a career might seem like something's that light-years away. However, just as educational planning should begin in the first year of college, so should career exploration and planning. Research indicates that students are more likely to stay in college and complete their degree when they see a connection between their current college experience and their future career goals. However, most first-year college students are uncertain about their career goals and vocational plans. The Career Development Center is the place on campus that can help you can explore different career options and clarify your career plans through such services as personal career counseling, workshops on career exploration and development, and on-campus career fairs. (For more detailed information on career exploration and development, see Chapter 15.)

Health and Wellness Center

The transition from high school to college often requires students to take more personal responsibility for decisions that affect their health and well-being, particularly if they are living away from home. Students who develop good health habits early in their college experience are better equipped to cope with college stress and better positioned to achieve peak levels of academic performance. The Health Center is the campus resource where students can get help to maintain physical health and attain optimal wellness. It's also the place where students can receive medical care and advice for physical illnesses and sexually transmitted diseases (For more detailed information on physical health and wellness, see Chapter 12.)

Personal Counseling Center

This is the campus resource where students can acquire ideas and develop strategies for coping with anxiety, depression, and other emotional challenges. However, personal counselors are not only professionals who deal with psychological "problems," they are also professionally prepared to help any students who want to gain greater self-awareness, improve their relationships, develop social and emotional intelligence, and reach their full potential. (For more detailed information on mental health and psychological wellness, see Chapter 13.)

> *Personal counseling is not just for students experiencing emotional problems. It's for all students who want to enrich their quality of life.*

Office of Student Life (Student Development)

This is your campus resource for getting involved in student life outside the classroom, including student clubs and organizations, recreational programs, leadership activities, and volunteer experiences. Research consistently reveals that learning experiences outside the classroom contribute as much to students' personal and career development as their coursework. This is one reason why most campuses no longer refer to these out-of-class experiences as "extracurricular" activities, but as "co-curricular" experiences—to convey the message that they combine with academics to educate the student as a whole person. Studies show that students who become actively involved in campus life are more likely to:

- Enjoy their college experience
- Graduate from college
- Develop leadership skills that enhance their career performance beyond college.

> *Co-curricular experiences are résumé-building experiences and the campus professionals with whom you interact while engaging in these experiences (e.g., Director of Student Life or Dean of Students) can serve as valuable personal references and resources for letters of recommendation.*

Devoting a reasonable amount of time to co-curricular experiences should not interfere with your academic performance and lower your grades. Since college students spend considerably less time inside the classroom than they did in high school, they're left with more time to engage in learning experiences outside the classroom. Research indicates that college students' academic performance and progress to degree completion are not impaired if they spend 20 or fewer hours outside of class on co-curricular experiences and part-time work. In fact, students who get involved in co-curricular experiences tend to earn higher grades than students who do not get involved at all.

Co-curricular experiences also include participation in student success workshops offered on campus (e.g., workshops on time management and study strategies); take advantage of these opportunities. Also, take advantage of student clubs or organizations whose activities relate to your educational, personal, or career plans. If there are none, see the Director of Student Activities and ask if you can start one of your own.

One caveat: Although co-curricular involvement is valuable, limit yourself to no more than two or three major campus organizations at a time. Restricting the number of co-curricular experiences you engage in will not only enable you to keep up

"Just a [long] list of club memberships is meaningless; it's a fake front. Remember that quality, not quantity, is what counts.

—*Lauren Pope, former director of the National Bureau for College Placement*

with your studies, it will also be a more impressive résumé-builder. A long list of involvement in numerous out-of-class activities can send the message that you're trying to impress others by padding your résumé. People reading your résumé may conclude that your involvement in all these activities was superficial, short-lived, and lacked sustained commitment.

 Reflection 1.5

What campus clubs or student organizations do you think would align most closely with your personal interests or educational and career goals? Do you intend to join any of them? (If not, why?)

Principle 3. Interpersonal Interaction and Collaboration (Social Integration)

Students who become socially integrated or connected with other members of the college community are more likely to complete their first year of college and go on to complete their college degree. Listed below are key interpersonal connections you could and should make in college. Start making these connections in your first year so you can begin building a social-support network that you can rely on throughout your college experience.

- Connect with a student development professional you may have met during orientation.
- Connect with a peer leader who has been selected and trained to support first-year students (e.g., orientation week leader or peer mentor).
- Connect with classmates by teaming up with them to take notes, complete reading assignments, and study for exams together. (For more detailed information on forming collaborative learning teams, see Chapter 5, pp. 112-115.)
- Connect with peers who live near you or who commute to campus from the same area in which you live. If your schedules are similar, consider carpooling together.
- Connect with faculty members—particularly in a field that you're considering as a major. Visit with faculty during their office hours, converse briefly with them after class, and communicate with them via e-mail.
- Join a college club, student organization, campus committee, intramural team, or a community service (volunteer) group whose members share the same interests or goals as you do. If you don't see a club or organization on campus that you were hoping to join, ask the Director of Student Activities or Student Life if you can start one of your own, especially one that relates to your educational or career goals. For example, if you are an English major, start a Writing Club or a Book Club. If you plan to pursue a career in law, start a pre-law club.
- Connect with an academic advisor to develop an educational plan.
- Connect with academic support professionals in the Learning Resource Center or Academic Success Center for tutoring related in any course that you would like to improve your performance and achieve academic excellence.
- Connect with a college librarian to get early assistance and a head start on any research projects you've been assigned.

- Connect with a personal counselor to discuss any questions or personal issues relating to college adjustment, interpersonal relationships, or psychological wellness and growth.

Research points to four particular forms of interpersonal interaction as being especially important for promoting student learning and development in college:

1. Student–faculty interaction
2. Student–advisor interaction
3. Student–mentor interaction
4. Student–student (peer) interaction.

Student–Faculty Interaction

The frequency and quality of student–faculty interaction *outside the classroom* is strongly associated with college success. Out-of-class contact with faculty has been found to promote the following positive student outcomes:

- Improved academic performance
- Increased critical thinking skills
- Greater satisfaction with the college experience
- Increased likelihood of completing a college degree
- Stronger desire to pursue education beyond a four-year degree.

Because the positive outcomes of student-faculty contact outside the classroom are so powerful and prevalent, try to initiate this contact as soon as possible. Here are three ways to do so.

1. **Interact with your instructors immediately after class.** Interacting briefly with instructors after class can help them get to know you as an individual and help you gain the confidence to approach them during office hours. If something covered in class captures your interest, approach your instructor to discuss it further. You could also ask a quick question about a point made in class that you weren't sure you understood, or to have a short conversation about how the material covered in class relates to something you have experienced personally or learned in another course.

2. **Connect with course instructors during their office hours.** One of the most important pieces of information contained in a course syllabus is your instructor's office hours. College professors reserve times in their weekly schedule to make themselves available to students in their offices. Make note of these times and make an earnest attempt to capitalize on them. Don't wait until late in the term when major exams and assignments start piling up, which is when most students start rushing to see their instructors for extra help. Try to schedule an office visit with your instructors early in the term, when quality time is easier to find. Even if your early contact with instructors is only for a few minutes, it can be a valuable icebreaker that helps them get to know you as a person and makes you feel more comfortable interacting with them in the future.

   Another way to engage in out-of-class contact with faculty is by making office visits with a small team of classmates to help prepare for upcoming exams and assignments. Visiting an instructor with other students has the following advantages:

"[In high school] the teacher knows your name. But in college they don't know your name; they might see your face, but it means nothing to them unless you make yourself known.

—*First-year college student*

"I wish that I would have taken advantage of professors' open-door policies when I had questions, because actually understanding what I was doing, instead of guessing, would have saved me a lot of stress and re-doing what I did wrong the first time.

—*College sophomore*

- You're more likely to feel comfortable about venturing onto your instructor's "turf" in the company of peers than flying solo. As the old expression goes, "There's safety in numbers."
- When you make an office visit as a team, the information shared by the instructor is heard by more than one student, so your teammates may pick up useful information that you may have missed (and vice versa).
- You save time for your instructors by enabling them to help more than one student at a time. This saves your instructor from having to engage in multiple "repeat performances" for individual students seeking help at separate times.
- By taking time—ahead of time—to connect with your peers and prepare for the office visit, you send a clear message to the instructor that you're a motivated student who's serious about the course.

> "Two heads are better than one, not because either is infallible, but because they are unlikely to go wrong in the same direction."
>
> —C.S. Lewis, English novelist and essayist

AUTHOR'S EXPERIENCE

I tell first-year students to see their course instructors during their office hours at least three times during the term. In fact, I've made this a requirement for students in my college success course.

At the end of the term, my students complete a course evaluation. Almost always, the number-one positive statement they make about the course was how helpful the faculty office visits were. They tell me that those visits not only helped them learn the course material, but also enabled them to interact with their instructors in a different, more personal way.

—*Aaron Thompson*

3. **Connect with your instructors via e-mail.** Electronic communication is another effective tool for experiencing the benefits of student–faculty interaction outside the classroom, particularly if your professor's office hours conflict with your class schedule, work responsibilities, or family commitments. If you're a commuter student who doesn't live on campus, or if you're an adult student juggling family and work commitments along with your academic schedule, e-mail communication may be an especially effective and efficient way to interact with faculty.

   E-mail is also a good way to become more comfortable about eventually seeking out face-to-face interaction with your instructors. In one national survey, almost half of college students surveyed reported that e-mail enabled them to communicate their ideas with professors on subjects they would not have discussed in person.

   E-mail communication is a good way to make connections with your instructors. However, if you miss class, do *not* use e-mail to ask an instructor the following questions:
   - Did I miss anything important in class today?
   - Could you send me your PowerPoint slides from the class I missed?

   Also, when communicating with your instructors via email, be sure to do it sensitively and professionally by:
   - Including your full name in the message.
   - Mentioning the class or course in which you're enrolled.

©Kendall Hunt Publishing Company

Did I miss anything important in class today?

Probably the worst question you could ever ask a college professor.

- Using complete sentences, correct grammar, and "hip" but unprofessional expressions (e.g., "Yo!", "Whatup?").
- Spell checking and proofreading your message before sending it.
- Including your full contact information. (If you're communicating via Facebook, choose an appropriate screen name; for example, names like "Sexsea" or "Studly" wouldn't be appropriate.)
- Giving your instructor time to reply. (Don't expect an immediate response, particularly if you send your message in the evening or on a weekend.)

In addition to using electronic technology responsibly for out-of-class communication with your instructors, use it responsibly an sensitively in class by adhering to the guidelines provided in **Box 1.3**.

Box 1.3

Guidelines for Civil and Responsible Use of Personal Technology in the College Classroom

> "The right to do something does not mean that doing it is right."
>
> —William Safire, American author, journalist, and presidential speech writer

Classroom behavior that interferes with the right of others to learn or teach is referred to as *classroom incivility*. Listed below are forms of classroom incivility that involve student use of personal technology. Be sure to avoid them.

Using Cell Phones

Keeping a cell phone on in class is a form of classroom incivility because its ringing can interfere with the teaching and learning process. In one study of college students, the researchers arranged for a cell phone to be deliberately rung during class and the students were later tested on information presented in class at the time the phone rang. These students scored approximately 25% lower for this information than did students who were not exposed to the ringing cell phone. Their drop in performance occurred even when the material was covered by the professor just before the cell phone rang and even when it was projected on a slide while the phone rang. The study also showed that students' attention to information presented in class is significantly reduced if a nearby classmate searches through a handbag or pocket to find and silence a vibrating phone. These findings clearly show that cell phone use in class disrupts the learning process and the civil thing for students to do is:

- Turn their cell phone off before entering class or keep it out of the classroom altogether. (The app *studiousapp.*

com can be used to automatically silence a phone at times of the day when a student is in class.) In rare cases when students think they may need to leave class to respond to an emergency, they should seek the instructor's permission in advance.

- Don't check their cell phone during the class period by turning it off and on.
- Don't look at their cell phone at any time during an exam because the instructor may think that they are looking up answers to test questions.

Text Messaging

Although this form of electronic communication is silent, it still can distract or disturb classmates. It's also discourteous to the instructor when students turn their head down and their attention away from the person who is speaking to them. The bottom line: Students should respect their instructors' right to teach and their classmates' right to learn—no texting in class!

Surfing the Web

Although this can be done without creating distracting sounds, it still can create visual distractions. Studies show that use of a laptop during class for reasons unrelated to the class not only distracts the laptop user, but also classmates seated nearby. Unless students are doing class-related work on their laptop, they should keep it closed to avoid distracting their classmates and their instructor.

Final Note: In addition to technological incivilities, other forms of classroom incivility include personal grooming, holding side conversations, and doing homework for other classes. Even if a student's attendance is perfect, "little things" the student does in class that signal inattention or disinterest can send a strong message to the instructor that the student lacks motivation (and civility).

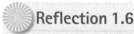

Reflection 1.6

Have you observed any recent examples of classroom incivility that you thought were particularly distracting or discourteous? What was the uncivil behavior and what consequences did it have on others?

Interacting with Academic Advisors

If you need assistance understanding college policies and procedures or navigating course options and requirements, an academic advisor is the person to see. Too often, students view academic advisors as someone to go to only for class scheduling. Yes, advisors do that, but they do much more. Advisors are professionals who also:

- Help students choose or change majors.
- Advise students about whether to drop a class.
- Alert students to educational and career opportunities relating to their chosen major.
- Refer students to campus resources and off-campus opportunities.
- Help students construct an educational plan that will enable them to graduate in a timely manner.
- Assist students with exploring educational options after college graduation (e.g., attending graduate or professional school).

In short, academic advisors are much more than course schedulers; they are student-support agents, mentors, and partners with whom students can collaborate to promote their success in college and beyond. Your academic advisor should be someone whom you feel comfortable speaking with, who knows your name, and who is familiar with your personal interests and goals. Give advisors the opportunity to get to know you personally, and seek their advice on courses, majors, and any academic challenges you may be experiencing. If you have been assigned a specific advisor and are not able to develop a good relationship with this person, ask the director of advising or academic dean if you could make a change. If you're unsure about who to change to, seek recommendations from a trusted peer or a peer leader.

If your college does not assign you to a personal advisor but offers advising services in an Advising Center on a drop-by or drop-in basis, you could end up seeing a different advisor each time you visit the center. If you would prefer not to work with different advisors from one visit to the next, find one you that you relate well to, and make that person your advisor by scheduling appointments in advance. This will enable you to connect consistently with the same advisor and develop a close, ongoing relationship. Unlike your course instructors—who change from term to term—your academic advisor can be your steady "go to" professional on campus with whom you have continuous contact throughout your college experience.

 **Reflection 1.7**

Do you have a personally assigned advisor?

If yes, do you know who this person is and where he or she can be found?

If you don't have a personally assigned advisor, who will you see for help with class scheduling and educational planning?

Interacting with a Mentor

A mentor may be described as an experienced guide who takes a personal interest in you, motivates you, and helps you reach your goals. (For example, in the movie *Star Wars*, Yoda served as a mentor for Luke Skywalker.) Research demonstrates that when first-year college students have a mentor, they feel more valued and are motivated to complete their degree. A mentor can help you anticipate challenges, resolve problems, and serve as a sounding board—someone to bounce ideas off, and someone with whom you can share your personal struggles and success stories. Keep an eye out for a person on campus who can be a mentor to you. Here are some potential candidates:

- Your instructor in a first-year experience course
- Your academic advisor
- A faculty member in your major field of interest
- A peer mentor or peer leader
- An academic support professional (e.g., a professional working in the Learning Center)
- A career counselor
- A personal counselor
- A student development professional (e.g., the director of student life or residential life)
- Campus minister or chaplain
- A financial aid counselor
- A professional working in a career you're interested in pursuing

 Reflection 1.8

Think about the first interactions you had on campus. Did you meet anyone at that time who impressed you, took an interest in you, and who might be a potential mentor for you?

Interaction with Peers (Student–Student Interaction)

Your peers can be more than competitors or sources of negative peer pressure; they can also be collaborators, provide positive social influence, and serve as resources for college success. Peer support is important at all stages of the college experience, but it's especially valuable during the first term of college because it is a transitional stage

FIGURE 1.3: Abraham Maslow's Hierarchy of Belonging

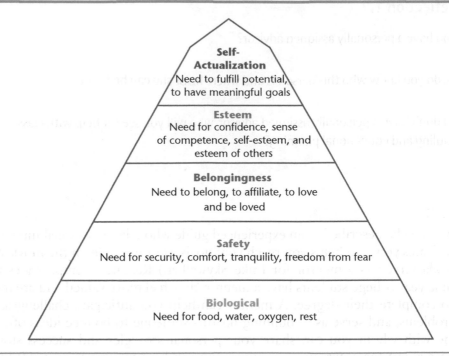

of life during which students are encountering a new, more diverse social community and are likely to have strong needs for belonging and social acceptance. It may be useful to view the first-year college experience through the lens of psychologist Abraham Maslow's hierarchy of human needs (see **Figure 1.3**). According to Maslow, humans only reach their full potential and achieve peak performance *after* their more basic social and emotional needs have been met (e.g., needs for social acceptance and self-esteem). Making early connections with your peers helps you fulfill these basic human needs, provides you with a base of social support to ease your integration into the college community, and enables you to move up to higher levels of Maslow's need hierarchy (e.g., achieving academic excellence and reaching your educational goals).

Getting involved with campus organizations or activities is one way to connect with other students and fulfill your social and emotional needs. Interacting with students who have more college experience than you (e.g., sophomores, juniors, and seniors) can supply you with valuable social support, especially those who have been selected and trained as peer leaders and peer mentors.

Research clearly demonstrates that college students learn as much from peers as they do from instructors and textbooks. One study of more than 25,000 college students revealed that when peers interact with one another while learning, they achieve higher levels of academic performance and are more likely to persist to college graduation.

Be observant—keep an eye out for peers who are successful. Ask yourself: Are these peers going to make me a more successful student (and person)? Start building your social support network by surrounding yourself with success-seeking and successful peers. Learn from them, emulate their productive habits and strategies, and use them as a social resource to promote your own success.

Your campus may offer opportunities for students to participate in a *learning community*, in which the same group of students takes the same block of courses together during the same term. If this opportunity is available to you, take advantage

> "Surround yourself with only people who are going to lift you higher."
>
> —*Oprah Winfrey, actress and talk-show host*

of it because research suggests that students who participate in learning communities are more likely to:

- Become actively involved in classroom learning
- Form their own learning groups outside of class
- Experience greater intellectual growth
- Continue their college education.

If a learning community program isn't offered on your campus, consider creating informal learning communities on your own by finding other students who are enrolling in the same courses as you (e.g., the same general education or pre-major courses). Connect with these students prior to registration and see if you can enroll in the same two or three courses together. This will allow you to reap the benefits of a learning community, even though your college may not offer a formal learning community program.

Reflection 1.9

Think about the classmates in your courses this term. Would you consider joining up with any of them to form a learning team? Why?

Principle 4. Reflection and Self-Awareness (Mindfulness)

The final step in the learning process, whether it be learning in the classroom or learning from experience, is to step back from it, thoughtfully review it, and connect it to what you already know. Reflection is the flip side of active involvement; these two processes complement one another and are necessary for learning to become complete and deep. Active involvement ensures *attention*—it enables information to enter your brain, and reflection ensures *consolidation*—it converts that information into knowledge, enabling your brain to retain it by moving it from short-term to long-term memory.

Research reveals that active involvement and reflection are two different mental states, each of which generates a unique type of electrical activity in the brain. In **Figure 1.4**, the electrical pattern on the left shows the brain waves of someone *actively involved* in the learning process—indicating that information is being attended to and processed by the brain. The electrical pattern on the right shows the brain waves of a person *reflecting on* information and moving it into long-term memory. The brain wave patterns in these two different stages of the learning process

FIGURE 1.4

Beta Waves: High-Amplitude Brain Waves
Associated with a Mental State
of *Active Involvement*.

Alpha Waves: High-Frequency Brain Waves
Associated with a Mental State
of *Reflective Thinking*.

suggests that deep, long-lasting learning takes place through a combination of two mental states: (a) active involvement—characterized by high-amplitude "beta" brain waves—and (b) thoughtful reflection—characterized by high-frequency "alpha" brain waves (similar to someone in a meditative state).

Self-Awareness

It's not only important to reflect on the information you're learning, it's also important to reflect on *yourself*. Self-reflection involves gaining greater self-awareness of *who* you are and *what* you are doing. Two forms of self-awareness are particularly important for academic success in college: (a) self-monitoring and (b) self-assessment.

Self-Monitoring

One characteristic of successful learners is that they self-monitor (check themselves) while they're learning to remain aware of: (a) whether they're using effective learning strategies—for example, if they are giving their undivided attention to what they are learning, (b) whether they're truly comprehending what they are learning—for example, if they're understanding it at a deep level, not memorizing it at a surface level, and (c) whether they need to regulate or adjust their learning strategies to learn different subjects—for example, if they're reading technical material in a science textbook, they read at a slower rate and check their understanding more frequently than when reading a novel.

You can begin to establish good self-monitoring habits by getting in the routine of periodically pausing to reflect on how you're learning and doing college. You can do so by asking yourself the following questions:

> "We learn neither by thinking nor by doing; we learn by thinking about what we are doing."
>
> —*George Stoddard, Professor Emeritus, University of Iowa*

- Am I listening attentively to what my instructor is saying in class?
- Am I comprehending what I'm reading outside of class?
- Am I effectively using campus resources designed to support my success?
- Am I interacting with campus professionals who can contribute to my current success and future development?
- Am I interacting and collaborating with peers who will support (not sabotage) my learning and development?
- Am I effectively implementing college-success strategies (such as those identified in this book)?

> *Successful students and successful people are mindful—they don't mindlessly "go through the motions" without reflecting on what and how they're doing; instead, they remain aware of whether they're doing it effectively and how they can do it better.*

Self-Assessment

Another way to gain self-awareness is through self-assessment. Simply defined, self-assessment is the process of reflecting on and evaluating your personal characteristics. The following personal characteristics are especially important to self-assess because gaining deep awareness of them is essential for making effective decisions about your educational and career goals:

- **Personal interests.** What you like to do. (What you really enjoy doing.)
- **Personal values.** What's important to you. (What you really care about doing.)
- **Personal talents.** What you do well. (Or are capable of doing well.)

- **Personality traits.** Your temperament, emotional characteristics, and social tendencies (e.g., whether you tend to be an introvert or extrovert).

(To help you get a better understanding of your personality type and how it connects to your learning preferences, your personality type, and your academic and career interests, log into AchieveWORKS and complete the Personality self-assessment.)

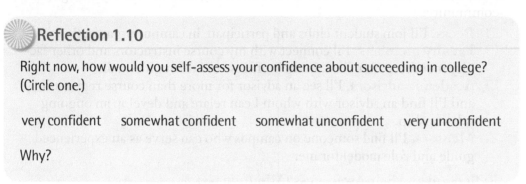

Reflection 1.10

Right now, how would you self-assess your confidence about succeeding in college? (Circle one.)

very confident   somewhat confident   somewhat unconfident   very unconfident

Why?

Summary and Conclusion

In short, research on college students indicates that successful students are:

- **Involved.** They *get into* it by investing time and effort in the college experience
- **Interactive.** They *team up* for it by interacting and collaborating with others
- **Resourceful.** They *get help* with it by capitalizing on campus resources
- **Reflective.** They *step back* from it to think about their performance and themselves.

The following self-assessment checklist summarizes the success-promoting principles and practices discussed in this chapter. You may use this checklist as a guide to maintain self-awareness of what you could (and should) do to thrive in college.

A Checklist of Success-Promoting Principles and Practices

1. **Active Involvement (Engagement)**
   I will:

   - ☐ *Get to class.* I'll treat it like a job and be there on all days that I am expected.
   - ☐ *Get involved in class.* I'll come prepared, listen actively, take notes, and participate.
   - ☐ *Read actively.* I'll take notes while I read to increase attention and retention.
   - ☐ *Double up.* I'll spend twice as much time on academic work outside of class as I spend in class. If I'm a full-time student, I'll make it a full-time job and put in a 40-hour workweek (with occasional "overtime" as needed).

2. **Capitalizing on Campus Resources (Resourcefulness)**
   I will take advantage of the academic and student support services available to me, such as the:

   - ☐ Learning Center
   - ☐ Writing Center
   - ☐ College Library
   - ☐ Academic Advisement Center

    ☐ Office of Student Life
    ☐ Financial Aid Office
    ☐ Counseling Center
    ☐ Health Center
    ☐ Career Development Center

3. **Interpersonal Interaction and Collaboration (Social Integration)**
I will interact and collaborate with the following members of my college community:

    ☐ **Peers.** I'll join student clubs and participate in campus organizations.
    ☐ **Faculty members.** I'll connect with my course instructors and other faculty members after class, in their offices, and through e-mail.
    ☐ **Academic advisors.** I'll see an advisor for more than course registration, and I'll find an advisor with whom I can relate and develop an ongoing relationship.
    ☐ **Mentors.** I'll find someone on campus who can serve as an experienced guide and role model for me.

4. **Reflection and Self-Awareness (Mindfulness)**
I will engage in:

    ☐ **Reflective Learning.** I'll step back from what I'm learning, review it, and connect it to what I already know.
    ☐ **Self-Monitoring.** I'll maintain self-awareness of whether I'm using effective learning and college-success strategies.
    ☐ **Self-Assessment.** I'll reflect on and evaluate my personal talents, interests, and values, and be mindful of them when making educational and career decisions.

✺ Reflection 1.11

Identify one way you will put each of the following four principles of college success into practice during the next few weeks:

1. Active Involvement (Engagement)

2. Capitalizing on Campus Resources (Resourcefulness)

3. Interpersonal Interaction and Collaboration (Social Integration)

4. Reflection and Self-Awareness (Mindfulness)

Internet-Based Resources

For additional information on concepts contained in this chapter, consult the following websites.

www.smu.edu/alec/transition.asp

https://students.dartmouth.edu/academic-skills/learning-resources/learning-strategies/strategic-learning-videos-and-books

www.studygs.net

https://www.csn.edu/advising/generalACSresources

Chapter 1 Exercises

1.1 Quote Reflections

Review the sidebar quotes contained in this chapter and select two that were especially meaningful or inspirational to you.

For each quote you selected, provide an explanation of why you chose it.

1.2 Strategy Reflections

Review the top tips for *active listening* and *note-taking* on p. 5. Select three strategies you think are most important and intend to put into practice right now.

1.3 Reality Bite

Alone and Disconnected: Feeling Like Calling It Quits

Josephine is a first-year student in her second week of college. She doesn't feel like she's fitting in with other students on campus. She also feels a little guilty about the time she's spending away from family and friends back home, and she fears that her ties with them will be weakened or broken if she continues spending so much time at school and on schoolwork. Josephine is feeling so torn between college, her family, and her hometown friends that she's beginning to have second thoughts about whether she should leave college at the end of this term.

Reflection and Discussion Questions

1. What would you say to Josephine to persuade or motivate her to stay in college?

2. What could Josephine do for herself right now to minimize the conflict she's experiencing between her commitment to college and her commitment to family and high school friends?

3. What could Josephine do to get more connected with her college community and feel less disconnected from her family and hometown friends?

4. Can you relate to Josephine's situation? If yes, in what way? If no, why not?

1.4 Birds of a Different Feather: High School vs. College

The following list identifies 12 key differences between high school and college. Rate each difference on a scale from 1 to 4 in terms of how aware you were of this difference when you began college:

1 = totally unaware
2 = not fully aware
3 = somewhat aware
4 = totally aware.

a) In high school, class schedules are typically made for students.

b) In college, students make their own class schedules—either on their own or in consultation with an academic advisor.
Awareness Rating _____

a) In high school, classes are scheduled back-to-back at the same time every day with short breaks in between.

b) In college, courses are scheduled at various times throughout the day (and night) and larger time gaps can exist between successive classes in a student's schedule.
Awareness Rating _____

a) In high school, class attendance is mandatory and checked regularly.

b) In college, class attendance is not always mandatory; in many classes, attendance isn't taken at all.

   Awareness Rating _____

> "In college, if you don't go to class, that's up to you. Your professor doesn't care really if you pass or fail.
> —*First-year student*

a) In high school, teachers often write all the important information they cover in class on the board or on PowerPoint slides .

b) In college, professors frequently expect students to write down important information contained in their lectures without explicitly writing it on the board or including it on PowerPoint slides.

   Awareness Rating _____

a) In high school, teachers often re-teach material in class that students were assigned to read.

b) In college, professors often do not cover the same material in class that's covered in the assigned reading, yet information from the assigned reading still appears on exams.

   Awareness Rating _____

a) In high school, teachers often take class time to remind students of assignments and their due dates.

b) In college, professors list their assignments and due dates on the course syllabus and expect students to keep track of them on their own.

   Awareness Rating _____

> "College teachers don't tell you what you're supposed to do. They just expect you to do it. High school teachers tell you about five times what you're supposed to do.
> —*College sophomore*

a) In high school, homework assignments (e.g., math problems) are typically turned into the teacher who checks and grades the student's work.

b) In college, assigned work is often not turned in to be checked or graded; students are expected to have the self-discipline to do the work on their own.

   Awareness Rating _____

a) In high school, students spend most of their learning time in class; they spend much less time studying outside of class than they spend learning in class.

b) In college, students typically spend no more than 15 hours per week in class and are expected to spend at least twice as much time studying out of class for every hour they spend in class.

   Awareness Rating _____

a) In high school, tests are given frequently and cover limited amounts of material.

b) In college, exams are given less frequently (e.g., midterm and final) and tend to cover large amounts of material.

   Awareness Rating _____

a) In high school, make-up tests and extra-credit opportunities are often available to students.

b) In college, if an exam or assignment is missed, rarely do students have a chance to make it up or recapture lost points by doing extra-credit work.

   Awareness Rating _____

> "In high school, they're like, 'Okay, well, I'll give you another day to do it.' In college, you have to do it that day . . . teachers are like, 'If you don't do it, that's your problem.
> —*First-year student*

a) A grade of "D" in high school is still passing.

b) In college, a grade-point average below "C" puts a student on academic probation, and if it doesn't improve to C or higher, the student may be academically dismissed.

   Awareness Rating _____

a) In high school, students go to campus offices only if they must, or if they're required to (e.g., if they forgot to do something or did something wrong).

b) In college, students go to campus offices because they want to, and they use the support services provided by these offices to enhance their success, even if they are already doing well.

Awareness Rating _____

1.5 Syllabus Review

Review the syllabus (course outline) for all classes you're enrolled in this term and answer the following questions.

Self-Assessment Questions

1. Is the overall workload what you expected? Are you surprised by the amount of work required in any particular course(s)?

2. At this point in the term, what do you see as your most challenging or demanding course(s)? Why?

3. Do you think you can handle the total workload required by the full set of courses you're enrolled in this term?

4. What adjustments or changes do you think you may need to make to your previous learning and study habits to handle your course workload this term?

1.6 Creating a Master List of Resources on Your Campus

1. Construct a master list of all support services that are available to you on your campus by consulting the following sources:
   - Information published in your college catalog and student handbook
   - Information posted on your college's website
   - Information obtained by visiting different offices or centers on campus

2. Your final product will be a comprehensive list that includes the following:

Campus Support Service	Type of Support Provided	Contact Person	Campus Location
_____	_____	_____	_____
_____	_____	_____	_____
_____	_____	_____	_____
_____	_____	_____	_____

etc.

Note:
- You can team up with other classmates to work collaboratively on this assignment. Different members of your team could divide the labor by identifying different campus resources to research and then your team can come back together to integrate their separate work.
- After completing this assignment, save your master list of support services for future use.

1.7 Using Campus Resources in Your First Term

Look back at the campus resources you identified in the previous exercise, or those described on pp. 8-11 of this chapter.

Which of these resources do you think would be most beneficial to you? Why?

Is there anything that would prevent you, or make you feel reluctant to, use these resources?

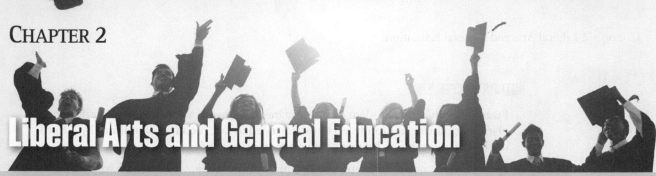

CHAPTER 2

Liberal Arts and General Education

WHAT IT MEANS TO BE A WELL-EDUCATED PERSON IN THE 21ST CENTURY

The liberal arts and general education are often misunderstood and underestimated elements of college education and career preparation. In this chapter, you will gain a deeper understanding and appreciation of the meaning, purpose, and benefits of the liberal arts and general education. You will learn how the liberal arts empower you with a broad base of knowledge and a set of versatile skills that are relevant to all college majors, careers fields, and life roles.

Chapter Purpose & Preview

Appreciate the meaning, purpose, and value of the liberal arts and general education for promoting personal development and professional success.

Learning Goal

Ignite Your Thinking

 Reflection 2.1

Before diving into this chapter, answer the following question:
Which one of the following statements best captures the meaning and purpose of the term *liberal arts*?
1. Learning to be more artistic
2. Learning about things that are theoretical rather than practical
3. Learning to be less politically conservative
4. Learning to be a liberal spender
5. Learning skills for freedom
(The answer to this question appears on p. 28.)

The *Meaning* and *Purpose* of the Liberal Arts

Whether or not you're enrolled at a liberal arts college, all college students take courses in the liberal arts. If you are uncertain about what "liberal arts" means, you're not alone. National surveys show that the vast majority of college students do not have a clear idea (or even the foggiest idea) about what the liberal arts stand for and why they're valuable. Many students think it refers to "learning for its own sake" and has no practical application, or that it has something to do with liberal politics—as illustrated by the following true story.

Laura probably would have picked option (1) as her answer to the multiple-choice question posed to you at the start of this chapter; she would have been wrong because the correct choice is option (5). Literally translated, the term "liberal arts" derives from two Latin roots: *liberalis*—meaning to "liberate" or "free," and *artes*—meaning "skills." Thus, the liberal arts represent and develop "skills for freedom."

The roots of the liberal arts date back to the roots of modern civilization—to the ancient Greek and Roman democracies—where citizens were given the freedom to elect their own leaders, thus "liberating" them from uncritical dependence on autocrats or dictators. Thus, one of the goals of a liberal arts education is to empower students with breadth of knowledge and critical thinking skills to vote wisely and participate effectively in a democracy.

The political ideals of the ancient Greeks and Romans were shared by the founding fathers of the United States who believed that an educated citizenry was essential for sustaining America's new democracy. As Thomas Jefferson, principal author of the U.S. Declaration of Independence, put it: "If a nation expects to be ignorant and free, it expects what never was and never will be."

Thus, the liberal arts are rooted in the belief that education and freedom are inescapably intertwined. To this day, the liberal arts continue to be a hallmark of the American college and university system and a feature that distinguishes it from other systems of higher education around the world.

> *The original purpose of college education in America was not just career preparation; it was preparation for citizenship and leadership in a democratic nation.*

> "I want knowledge so I don't get taken advantage of in life."
> —*First-year college student*

Over time, the concept of the liberal arts evolved into a broader educational process that is designed to liberate students to become self-directed thinkers capable of making decisions and taking actions based on well-reasoned ideas and values, rather than blind obedience to authority or social conformity. In addition to resisting manipulation by political dictators, self-directed critical thinkers are also able to withstand manipulation by other societal forces, including:

- **Peers**—resisting negative forms of social conformity and peer pressure
- **Media**—detecting and rejecting manipulative advertisements and misleading propaganda

> "Advertisers rely on a half-educated public ... because such people are easy to deceive with an effective set of logical and psychological tricks."
> —Robert Harris, *On the Purposes of a Liberal Arts Education*

In short, the liberal arts empower you to become a well-informed citizen and critical thinker who is armed and ready to ask the question: "Why?" You're equipped and empowered with an inquiring mind and the mental tools to think independently.

The Liberal Arts Curriculum

Based on the educational philosophy of the ancient Greeks and Romans, the first liberal arts *curriculum* (collection of courses) originated during the Middle Ages and consisted of the following subjects: Logic, Language, Rhetoric (the art of argumentation and persuasion), Music, Mathematics, and Astronomy. This curriculum was designed to: (a) supply students with a broad base of knowledge so they would be well-informed in a variety of subjects and (b) equip them with a flexible set of reasoning skills to think deeply and critically about any subject.

The liberal arts curriculum of today's colleges and universities consists of a wider range of courses than the original seven subjects that made up the medieval curriculum. However, the goal of the liberal arts curriculum has withstood the test of time: Its purpose continues to be that of supplying college students with a broad base of knowledge and equipping them with a versatile set of thinking and communication skills that can be applied across different subjects and situations.

Today, the liberal arts curriculum is often referred to as *general education* because it supplies students with general knowledge and skills rather than specialized knowledge tied narrowly to one field of study or professional occupation. General education is what all college students experience, no matter what their college major or career path may be.

> The liberal arts are what distinguish a college education from vocational training; they define what it means to be a well-rounded, well-educated person.

On some campuses, general education is also referred to as: (a) the *core curriculum*—what's central or essential for all students to learn, (b) *breadth requirements*—the broad range of subject areas and skill sets that every college graduate should possess, or (c) *distribution requirements*—courses that are distributed across a variety of subjects and fields of study.

 Reflection 2.2

On your campus, what term is used to refer to the fields of study that all students are required to experience in order to graduate?

Whatever term is used to describe general education on your campus, the bottom line is that it provides the foundation of a college education on which all academic specializations (majors) are built. It represents what every college graduate should know and be able to do in order to be an effective person, citizen, and professional—in whatever occupation he or she may choose to pursue.

Major Bodies of Knowledge in the General Education Curriculum

The divisions of knowledge that constitute the general education curriculum vary somewhat from campus to campus, and there may be some campus-to-campus differences in terms of the specific courses students are required to take within each of these divisions of knowledge. What follows is a description of the typical divisions of knowledge that comprise the general education curriculum on most campuses today. As you read through the specific fields of study within each of these divisions of knowledge, make note of the subjects in which you never had a course.

Humanities

Courses in this division of general education focus on the human experience and the "big questions" humans have always tried to answer, such as: "Why are we here?" "What is the purpose of our existence?" "What does it mean to be human?" "What constitutes a 'good life'?" "Is there life after death?" Listed below are the primary subjects in the Humanities, followed by the type of skills these subjects are designed to develop.

- **Literature.** Critical reading, literary interpretation, and appreciation of different literary genres—e.g., novels, short stories, poems, plays, and essays.
- **Philosophy.** Rational thinking, acquiring wisdom (the ability to use knowledge prudently), and living an ethical life.
- **Theology.** Appreciating the ways in which humans believe and express their faith in a transcendent (supreme) being.
- **English Composition.** Writing clearly, thoughtfully, and convincingly.
- **Speech.** Communicating orally in a clear, articulate, and persuasive manner.
- **Languages.** Understanding and communicating in languages other than one's native tongue.

Fine Arts

Courses in this division of general education focus largely on the art of human expression, asking and seeking answers to such questions as: "How do humans create, and appreciate beauty?" and "How do humans express themselves aesthetically (through the senses), imaginatively, and stylistically?" Listed below are the primary subdivisions of the Fine Arts and the type of skills these subjects are designed to develop.

- **Visual Arts.** Expression and appreciation of creativity through visual representation (drawing, painting, sculpture, photography, and graphic design).
- **Musical Arts.** Expression and appreciation of creativity through rhythmical arrangement of sounds.
- **Performing Arts.** Expression and appreciation of creativity through drama and dance.

Mathematics

Courses in this division of general education develop skills relating to quantitative reasoning, numerical calculations, and data analysis. Listed below are the subjects that typically comprise the general education curriculum in mathematics, accompanied by the type of skills these subjects are designed to develop.

- **Algebra.** Mathematical reasoning and logical thinking expressed in symbols which represent numbers in the language of letters.
- **Statistics.** Summarizing quantitative data; estimating probabilities; representing and understanding numerical information in the form of graphs, charts, and tables; drawing accurate inferences from statistical information.

"Challenging the meaning of life is the truest expression of the state of being human."
—*Viktor Frankl, Austrian neurologist and Holocaust survivor*

"It was books that taught me that the things that tormented me the most were the very things that connected me with all the people who were alive, and who have ever been alive."
—*James Baldwin, African-American novelist, essayist, playwright, and poet*

"Dancing is silent poetry."
—*Simonides, ancient Greek poet*

"The universe is a grand book which cannot be read until one learns to comprehend the language of which it is composed. It is written in the language of mathematics."
—*Galileo Galilei, 17th-century Italian physicist, mathematician, astronomer, and philosopher*

- **Calculus.** Advanced mathematical skills used to calculate areas enclosed by curves and the rate at which the quantity of one entity changes in relation to another.

Natural Sciences

Courses in this division of the liberal arts curriculum focus on systematic observation of the physical world and underlying explanations of natural phenomena, seeking answers to such questions as: "What causes the physical events that take place in the natural world?", "How can we predict and control natural events?", and "How do we promote harmonious interaction between humans and the natural environment in ways that support their mutual survival and well-being?" Listed below are the primary subject areas in the Natural Sciences and the type of skills these subjects are designed to develop.

- **Biology.** Understanding the structures and processes of all forms of life.
- **Chemistry.** Understanding the composition of natural and synthetic substances, how these substances can be altered, and how new substances may be synthesized.
- **Physics.** Understanding the properties of physical matter, their principles of energy and motion, and how they are affected by electrical and magnetic forces.
- **Geology.** Examining the composition of the earth and the natural processes that shaped its development.
- **Astronomy.** Exploring the makeup and motion of celestial bodies that compose the cosmos.

Social and Behavioral Sciences

Courses in this division of general education focus on the systematic observation of human behavior, both individually and in groups, asking and seeking answers to such questions as: "What causes humans to behave the way they do?" and "How can we predict, control, and improve human behavior and social interaction?" Listed below are subjects that typically comprise the Social and Behavioral Sciences curriculum and the type of skills these courses are designed to develop.

- **History.** Understanding past events, their causes, and their influence on current events.
- **Political Science.** Understanding how societal authority is organized and used to govern people, make collective decisions and maintain social order.
- **Psychology.** Understanding the human mind, its conscious and subconscious processes, and the underlying causes of human behavior.
- **Sociology.** Understanding the behavior of human groups, social organizations, and institutions that comprise society (e.g., families, schools, hospitals, and corporations).
- **Anthropology.** Understanding the cultural origins, physical origins, and development of the human species.
- **Geography.** Understanding how the place (physical location) where humans live can shape, and be shaped by, their culture.
- **Economics.** Examining how society's material needs are met through allocation of limited resources and how monetary wealth generated by society's production of goods and services are distributed, priced, and consumed.

"The media through which we get our information about the world are full of charts, graphs, and statistical information. Important decisions you will make about such matters as a medical treatment, home buying or voting will depend on your math skills."

—*Robert Shoenberg, Senior Fellow, Association of American Colleges and Universities*

"There are in fact two things, science and opinion; the former begets knowledge, the latter ignorance.

—*Hippocrates, ancient Greek philosopher, physician, and the "father of western medicine"*

"Man, the molecule of society, is the subject of social science.

—*Henry Charles Carey, 19th-century American economist*

AUTHOR'S EXPERIENCE

I majored in anthropology as an undergraduate and I am very thankful to have done so. As the daughter of immigrant parents, studying anthropology helped me better understand my culture and the cultural communities that surrounded me where I grew up (Brooklyn, New York). More importantly, studying anthropology contributed to my appreciation of the rich human diversity that makes up the world in which we live.

—*Michele Campagna*

Physical Health and Wellness

Courses in this division of general education focus on how humans maintain optimal health and attain peak levels of human performance, asking and seeking answers to such questions as: "How does the body function most effectively?" and "What can humans do to minimize illness, maximize wellness, and improve the overall quality of their lives?" Listed below are the primary subject areas in this division of the college curriculum and the type of skills they're designed to develop.

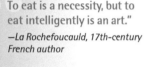

"To eat is a necessity, but to eat intelligently is an art."
—*La Rochefoucauld, 17th-century French author*

- **Physical Education.** Understanding the benefits of, and engaging in, exercise to enhance health and human performance.
- **Nutrition.** Understanding what and how foods nourish the body, maintain health, and generate energy.
- **Sexuality.** Understanding the biology and psychology of sexual relationships.
- **Drug Education.** Understanding how chemical substances alter the body and mind, and affect physical health, mental health, and human behavior.

 Reflection 2.3

Look back at the subject areas that comprise general education. In subject areas where you've never had a course, identify one subject that strikes you as particularly interesting or potentially useful. Provide a brief explanation of why you chose it.

Most general education requirements are likely to be taken during your first two years of college. Interestingly, research reveals that students make their greatest gains in learning and thinking during their first two years of college—the time when most general education requirements are taken. Don't be dismayed if some of these requirements look similar to courses you've had in high school. They will not be videotape replays of your high school courses; you will dive deeper into these subjects, learn them in greater depth and apply higher levels of thinking to the concepts they cover.

General education deepens learning not only by equipping you with a broad base of knowledge spanning multiple subjects, it also disciplines your mind to *think* in multiple ways. This is why the subject areas that comprise general education are referred to as academic *disciplines*—by studying them, you develop the "mental discipline" needed to do the type of thinking required by these different fields of study. For instance, when you study history, algebra, biology, and art, you discipline your mind to think chronologically, symbolically, scientifically, and aesthetically.

The Liberal Arts Liberate You from Narrowness and Broaden Your Perspectives

The liberal arts empower you to think *comprehensively*. The wide range of subjects encountered during your journey through the general education curriculum equips you with a wide-angle lens through which to view the world from a panoramic perspective. The key vantage points supplied by this broader perspective are illustrated in **Figure 2.1**. The center circle represents the self. Fanning out to the right of the self are increasingly wider arches representing the progressively broader social–spatial perspective developed by the liberal arts. This expanded *social–spatial perspective* provides you with a "world view" that enables you to step beyond yourself to view the world in terms of successively larger social groups and more distant places; it moves you from the micro to the macro, from the narrowest perspective (the individual) to the broadest perspective (the universe).

To the left of the self in **Figure 2.1** are three arches that comprise the *chronological perspective* developed by the liberal arts. Each of these perspectives represents a key dimension of time: the *past* (historical perspective), the *present* (contemporary perspective), and the *future* (futuristic perspective). The liberal arts equip you with a chronological perspective that includes hindsight to see where the world has been, insight to see where the word is now, and foresight to see where the world is going. By stretching your perspective beyond the here and now, you're able to view the world through the eyes of humans who have lived before you and who will live after you.

> "Truly educated persons move beyond themselves, gain social perspective, see themselves in relation to other people and times.
>
> *—Ernest Boyer and Martin Kaplan, in "Educating for Survival: A Call for a Core Curriculum"*

FIGURE 2.1: Broadening Perspectives Developed by the Liberal Arts

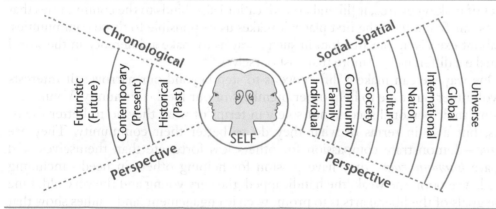

©Kendall Hunt Publishing Company

In a nutshell, the liberal arts supply you with a social–spatial perspective that widens your frame of reference and a chronological perspective that lengthens it. Together, these two broadening perspectives enable you to appreciate the experiences of humans living long ago and far away.

The Social–Spatial Perspective: Moving Beyond the Self to the Wider World

The Perspective of *Family*

One of the ways in which the liberal arts broaden your social perspective is by deepening your understanding of how the family influences development of the individual. Those who raised you and with whom you were raised have shaped the person you are today. Moreover, your family members have not only influenced you, you have influenced them. For example, your decision to go to college may influence your parents' view of you and may influence whether other members of your family decide to attend college. If you have children, your college experience will likely impact their development because research shows that children of college graduates experience improved intellectual development, better physical health, and greater economic security.

The Perspective of *Community*

In addition to being nested in a family, you're also nested in a larger social unit—your community. A community may be defined as a group of people that share the same environment, interests, beliefs, and values. This circle of community members includes your friends as well as people in the communities where you live, work, and go to school. If you want to make the world a better place, the place to start is to engage in service and leadership in the communities in which you are a member. As William Cronon notes in his famous essay, *"Only Connect:" The Goals of a Liberal Education*, "In the act of making us free, it [liberal arts education] also binds to the communities that gave us our freedom in the first place; it makes us responsible to those communities. It is about exercising our freedom in such a way as to make a difference in the world and make a difference for more than just ourselves."

One way we can make a difference is to step beyond our narrow self-interests and volunteer our time to help other members of our local community. Volunteers measure their personal success not solely in terms of what they do to better themselves, but also in terms of what they do to better their community. They are *humane*—demonstrate compassion for others less fortunate than themselves, and they are *humanitarian*—they have passion for helping others in need—including the sick, the poor, the weak, the handicapped, the very young and the very old. One of the goals of the liberal arts is to promote civic engagement, and studies show that compared with other citizens, college graduates have higher rates of engagement in civic affairs and community service.

> *The purpose of a college education is not only to learn how to earn a better living; it's also about learning to be a better human being.*

The Perspective of *Society*

In addition to being members of our local communities, we are members of *society*—a larger group of people organized under the same social system. This larger society includes social subgroups organized into different geographical regions (e.g., north, south, east, west), different states, and different population densities (e.g., urban, suburban, rural). Society is also stratified into groups of people with different socioeconomic status—based on their income, education and job status, which is accompanied by different (and unequal) social privileges and economic resources. For instance, in the United States, the wealthiest 20% of Americans controls approximately 85% of America's wealth, and this wealth gap is widening.

In addition to lower income, groups with lower socioeconomic status also have poorer educational and social-networking opportunities. For instance, young adults from high-income families are more than seven times more likely to have earned a college degree and hold prestigious jobs than those from low-income families. These differences may be explained, at least in part, by the fact that young adults raised in families with higher socioeconomic status are privileged with two forms of capital, each of which contributes to their higher rates of college attendance and college completion: (a) *economic* capital—the *material* resources their family possesses—such as higher income, better health benefits, discretionary income for travel, technology, tutors, and other enriching educational experiences; and (b) *social* capital—*who* they know—such as contacts with employers, college counselors, college admissions officials, and "power players" in the legal and political system.

The broader societal perspective developed by the liberal arts helps us understand how such stratification advantages or disadvantages different groups of people and increases our empathy for less privileged members of society.

The *National* Perspective

In addition to being members of a society, we are also members (citizens) of a nation. The signers of the Declaration of Independence believed that the pursuit of personal happiness was not possible without pursuit of the national good; the well-being of the individual and the nation were inescapably interrelated. The hallmark of a *democratic* nation is its citizens' right to participate in, the national good and contribute to through the voting process. The right to vote is both a privilege and a responsibility of citizens in a democratic nation. In a democracy, voting is more than a political choice; it's a patriotic act.

When voter turnout rates are low, citizens with more moderate political views are often the ones who fail to vote, which results in people holding more extreme views getting a larger percentage of the total vote. Thus, low voter turnouts result in a more polarized political system that's less conducive to balanced, bipartisan representation and negotiation. Also, when voter turnouts are low, political candidates are more likely to use extreme media tactics—such as attack ads and smear campaigns—to instill public fear of the opposing candidate.

Disappointingly, American citizens between the ages of 18 and 24 continue to display the lowest voter-turnout rate of any age group that's eligible to vote. Also disappointing are the results of national surveys revealing that first-year college students rank preparation for citizenship and civic engagement among the least important reasons for attending college. Hoping to combat this voter apathy among young Americans, the "March for Our Lives" movement (organized by a high school senior from a school that experienced a mass murder) has registered more than 50,000 voters, most of them between the ages of 18 and 29.

Having the privilege of citizenship in a free nation brings with it the responsibility of learning about political candidates and participating in the country's governance through the voting process. As Derek Bok, former president of Harvard University puts it: "Civic responsibility must be learned, for it is neither natural nor effortless. It takes work to inform oneself sufficiently to cast an intelligent vote." National surveys show that employers of college graduates feel the same way: 83% agree that college students should take classes that build civic knowledge and judgment.

> "Get involved. Don't gripe about things unless you are making an effort to change them. You can make a difference if you dare.
>
> —*Richard C. Holbrooke, former director of the Peace Corps and American ambassador to the United Nations*

Your investment in a college education is not just an investment in yourself, it's an investment in your country.

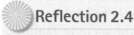 **Reflection 2.4**

Did you vote in the last presidential election? If yes, why? If no, why not?

The *International* Perspective

Beyond being citizens of a nation, we're also members of a larger international community that includes close to 200 other nations worldwide. In today's internationally interdependent world, citizens of all nations are affected by events taking place in other nations. Traditional boundaries between countries are blurring or disappearing altogether due to increasing international travel, international trading, and the growth of international corporations. The information technology explosion has also brought with it the capacity for citizens of different nations to communicate more frequently and rapidly than at any time in human history. The Internet (originally called the "worldwide web") has truly made today's world a "small world after all," and success in it requires an international perspective—one of the broadening perspectives developed by the liberal arts.

You can begin developing an international perspective by taking internationally-focused courses (e.g., international relations) and partaking in international experiential-learning opportunities (e.g., study abroad or study travel). Research on college students who study abroad indicates that it transforms their perspective on the world, promotes greater appreciation of international and cross-cultural differences, increases their interest in world affairs, and elevates their awareness of the importance of international cooperation for preserving international peace. Research also shows that students who study abroad experience personal benefits, such as increased self-confidence, a stronger sense of independence, and the ability to function effectively in complex or unfamiliar environments.

When you learn about and from people of other countries, you extend your sense of citizenship beyond the boundaries of your own nation—you become cosmopolitan—*a citizen of the world.*

The *Global* Perspective

Even broader than an international perspective is a global perspective—it transcends nations to embrace all forms of human and nonhuman life on planet earth and examines how these diverse life forms interface with natural resources (minerals, air, and water). Humans share the earth with approximately 10 million animal species and more than 300,000 forms of vegetative life, all of which have needs that must be met and balanced to ensure the health and sustainability of our planet. Just as individuals should avoid egocentrism—viewing the self as the center of the universe—humans should avoid *anthropocentrism*—viewing the human species as the only significant life form on the planet while ignoring (or abusing) other elements of the natural world. According to Howard Gardner, internationally acclaimed psy-

> "A liberal [arts] education frees a person from the prison-house of class, race, time, place, background, family, and nation."
>
> —*Robert Hutchins, former dean of Yale Law School and president of the University of Chicago*

chologist, for today's young people to thrive in the communities of the future, they will need to demonstrate "ethical" commitment—which includes empathy for the needs of others, the capacity to move beyond narrow self-interests, and take the initiative to become actively involved in broader societal and global issues.

A global perspective includes mindfulness of how our industrial and economic pursuits impact the earth's sustainability. As "global citizens" occupying the same planet, we have the collective responsibility to protect Earth's natural resources and the life forms that depend on those resources for their current and future survival. Scientists across the globe have reached strong consensus that man-made pollution is building up levels of carbon dioxide in the atmosphere, causing temperatures to rise (and sometimes fall) around the world. These changing temperatures are creating more extreme weather conditions and more frequent natural disasters—such as droughts, wildfires, hurricanes, and dust storms. Addressing the problem of climate change requires a global perspective and appreciation of how waste emissions generated in all countries around the world need to be held to environmentally sustainable levels in order to preserve the future health of the planet and the health of future generations of humans who will depend on its resources. Developing such a global perspective is one of the educational goals of the liberal arts.

> "[College] graduates need to develop a sense of global citizenship . . . to care about people in distant places, to understand the nature of global economic integration, to appreciate the interconnectedness and interdependence of people, and to protect planet Earth.
>
> —*Yong Zhao, noted Chinese painter, calligrapher, and poet*

> "Treat the Earth well. It was not given to you by your parents. It was loaned to you by your children.
>
> —*Kenyan proverb*

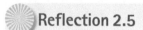

Reflection 2.5

Other than climate change (a.k.a. global warming), what would you say is another worldwide issue that requires a global perspective to understand and solve?

The Perspective of the *Universe* (*Cosmos*)

Beyond the global perspective is the broadest of all perspectives—the universe. Gaining this cosmic perspective positions us to view planet Earth as sharing a solar system with other planets and as one celestial body sharing a galaxy with millions of other celestial bodies including stars, moons, meteorites, and asteroids.

It is noteworthy that the original liberal arts curriculum developed during the Middle Ages included astronomy as one of its seven essential subjects. The timeless intrigue of the cosmos continues today in a field of study known as cosmology. Reflecting on the massive, mysterious nature of the universe, how it began, where it may be going, and whether it will ever end, are considered by some to be spiritual questions. For example, some astronauts who have travelled beyond the earth's force of gravity to view the universe from a cosmic perspective have referred to their journey as a "spiritual experience."

Whether the universe is viewed from the perspective of astronomy or spirituality, it is the broadest of all social–spatial perspectives developed by the liberal arts.

> "In astronomy, you must get used to viewing the earth as just one planet in the larger context of the universe.
>
> —*Physics professor*

> "Man must rise above the Earth—to the top of the atmosphere and beyond—for only thus will he fully understand the world in which he lives.
>
> —*Socrates, classic Greek (Athenian) philosopher and founding father of Western philosophy*

The Chronological Perspective: Embracing the Past, Present, and Future

In addition to broadening your perspective of the social and physical world by equipping you with knowledge about other people and places, the liberal arts also stretch your perspective of time by learning about the past and its relationship to the present and future. Thus, a chronological perspective consists of three key components: historical, contemporary, and futuristic.

> "We all inherit the past. We all confront the challenges of the present. We all participate in the making of the future.
>
> —*Ernest Boyer & Martin Kaplan, in "Educating for Survival: A Call for a Core Curriculum"*

Historical Perspective

The liberal arts deepen your understanding of the historical roots of the current human condition and world situation. Humanity today is a product or byproduct of many years of social and natural history. The earth is estimated to be more than 4.5 billion years old and our human ancestors date back more than 250,000 years. Viewed from this historical perspective, a human lifespan represents a very small frame of time in a very long chronological reel. Every modern convenience we now enjoy reflects the collective knowledge and cumulative efforts humanity amassed over thousands of years of history. For instance, we build on the knowledge and efforts of the ancient Egyptian pyramid makers to build today's skyscrapers, and we build on our knowledge of the causes and consequences of the Holocaust to reduce the risk that an atrocity of such magnitude ever happens again. By studying the past, we learn from both the successes and mistakes of our ancestors.

> "Those who cannot remember the past are damned to repeat it."
>
> —*George Santayana, Spanish-born American philosopher*

Reflection 2.6

What historical event or development do you think is having the most impact on today's world?

Contemporary Perspective

Today's news is tomorrow's history. A contemporary perspective gives us insight into current issues and events that are affecting us now and will continue to affect us in the future. Being able to take a critical perspective on current events is particularly important in today's world because the news reporting by contemporary media may be more politically biased than at any other time in history. Political campaigns today employ manipulative media advertisements, rely on short one-sided sound bites, and deploy sensational visual images designed to stoke emotions rather than appeal to logic and reason. It could be said that the original goal of the liberal arts—to develop a well-informed, critical-thinking citizenry—is more important than ever. Your exposure to the liberal arts will strengthen your contemporary perspective by supplying you with the mental skills and wisdom to make discerning choices and decisions in today's increasingly complex and polarized world.

> "Yesterday is gone. Tomorrow has not yet come. We have only today. Let us begin."
>
> —*Mother Teresa of Calcutta, Albanian, Catholic nun and winner of the Nobel Peace Prize*

Reflection 2.7

Do you keep up with current events? If yes, what news source(s) do you rely on?

Futuristic Perspective

A futuristic perspective frees us from the here and now, allowing us to envision what our world will be like in the years and decades ahead. This perspective allows us to anticipate the challenges facing humankind in the future by asking and seeking answers to such questions as: "Will we leave the world a better place for our children and grandchildren?" and "How can we avoid short-term, shortsighted thinking and adopt a long-range perspective that enables us to anticipate and control the consequences of our current actions on future generations of humans?"

The liberal arts help us remain mindful that an individual's lifespan is incredibly short when compared with the lifespan of humanity. Viewing the world from this extended perspective underscores our moral responsibility to use the limited time we have on earth to promote the quality and preserve the sustainability of life on our planet.

In summary, the chronological perspective developed by the liberal arts brings the past, present, and future into focus on a single screen. It enables you to see how the current world is just one link in a long chain of time that has been shaped by past events and will be shaped by future events. When the past-present-future dimensions of a chronological perspective are combined with the progressively wider dimensions of a social–spatial perspective, you're positioned to understand how humanity is interconnected and nested within multiple layers of context—as illustrated in **Figures 2.2** and **2.3**.

FIGURE 2.2: Nested *Social–Spatial* Perspectives Developed by the Liberal Arts: Interconnecting People and Places

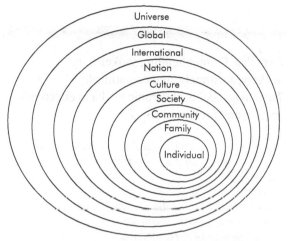

©Kendall Hunt Publishing Company

FIGURE 2.3: Nested *Chronological* Perspectives Developed by the Liberal Arts: Interconnecting Periods of Time

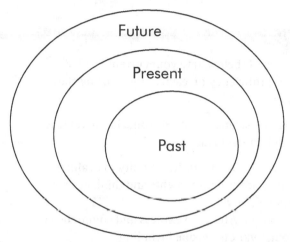

©Kendall Hunt Publishing Company

The Synoptic Perspective: Integrating Multiple Perspectives into a Coherent Whole

The liberal arts do not only supply you with multiple perspectives, they also position you to integrate those perspectives into a meaningful whole. When you're able to see how the perspectives of time, place, and person intersect to form the "big picture," you're equipped with a *synoptic* perspective. The word derives from a combination of two roots: *syn*—meaning "together" (as in the word "synthesize")—and *optic*—meaning "to see." Thus, a "synoptic" perspective literally means to "see things together" or "see the whole." It's a panoramic perspective that allows us to "connect the dots" and see how the trees form the forest.

A synoptic perspective enables us to see how we, as individuals, fit into the larger scheme of things. When we see ourselves as nested within an interconnected web of other people, places, and times, we become aware of our shared humanity. This connection with humankind reduces our sense of isolation and alienation; it increases our ability to empathize and identify with people whose life experiences differ radically from our own. In his book, *The Perfect Education*, Kenneth Eble eloquently describes the benefits of the synoptic perspective developed by a liberal arts education:

"It can provide that overarching life of a people, a community, a world that was going on before the individual came onto the scene and that will continue on after [s]he departs. By such means we come to see the world not alone. Our joys are more intense for being shared. Our sorrows are less destructive for our knowing universal sorrow. Our fears of death fade before the commonness of the occurrence."

The Liberal Arts Develop Transferable Skills that Can be Applied across Different Contexts and Situations

In addition to providing you with a broad base of knowledge and multiple perspectives for viewing yourself and the world around you, the liberal arts equip you with a set of skills that can be adapted for use in a wide variety of settings. This is another way in which the liberal arts "liberate" you—by empowering you with a set of versatile skills that are not tied to one particular subject area or career field, but are transferable across the curriculum and throughout life. **Box 2.1** contains a sample of these transferable skills.

Box 2.1

As you read the skills below, rate your current level of development or proficiency on each of them, using the following scale:

4 = very strong, 3 = strong, 2 = needs some improvement, 1 = needs much improvement

1. Critical and Creative Thinking. Ability to evaluate the validity of ideas or arguments and think innovatively or imaginatively.
2. Communication. Ability to express and comprehend ideas through various media, including:
    *   *Written Communication.* Writing in a clear, creative, and persuasive manner
    *   *Oral Communication.* Speaking concisely, confidently, and eloquently
    *   *Reading.* Comprehending, interpreting, and evaluating the literal and figurative meaning of language written in various styles and subjects

*   *Listening.* Comprehending spoken language actively, accurately, and empathically
*   *Technology.* Using electronic media to effectively acquire and present ideas

> Effectively managing personal affairs, from shopping for household products to electing health care providers to making financial decisions, often requires people to acquire new knowledge from a variety of media, use different types of technologies and process complex information."
> —*The Partnership for 21st Century Skills*

3. Quantitative Skills. Ability to calculate, analyze, summarize, interpret, and evaluate quantitative information and statistical data.
4. Information Literacy Skills. Ability to access, retrieve, and evaluate information from various sources, including in-print and online (technology-based) systems.

 Reflection 2.8

Reflect on the above transferable skills developed by general education (communication, information literacy, computation, and higher-level thinking). Which of these skills do you need the most improvement? How do you plan to improve them?

The liberal arts skills listed in **Box 2.1** have two powerful qualities:

1. **Flexibility:** they are *nimble, portable* skills that "travel well"—you can carry them with you and apply them across a wide range of subject areas, work situations, and life roles.
2. **Durability:** they are *sustainable, enduring* skills with "staying power" that can be used continually throughout life.

What the liberal arts do for the mind is comparable to what cross-training does for the body. Cross-training engages the body in a range of different exercises that promotes total physical fitness and develops a broad set of physical skills—strength, endurance, flexibility, and agility—which can be applied to improve performance in any sport or athletic endeavor. Similarly, general education engages the mind in a wide range of mental skills that can be used to improve performance in any major or career. As Robert Harris articulates it:

> *"Good learning habits can be transferred from one subject to another. When a basketball player lifts weights or plays handball in preparation for basketball, no one asks, "What good is weightlifting or handball for a basketball player?" because it is clear that these exercises build muscles, reflexes, and coordination that can be transferred to basketball—building them perhaps better than endless hours of basketball practice would. The same is true of the mind. Exercise in various areas builds brainpower for whatever endeavor you plan to pursue."*

"You know you've got to exercise your brain just like your muscles.
—*Will Rogers, Native American humorist and actor*

AUTHOR'S EXPERIENCE

I must confess that I graduated from college without really understanding the true meaning and purpose of general education. When I became a college professor, two of my colleagues from the Office of Student Affairs asked me to help them create a first-year experience (college success) course. I agreed and volunteered to teach the course, which included a unit on the Meaning and Value of General Education. When I was preparing to teach this unit, I began to realize what general education represented and what it did for me. It became clear that the lasting power of my college education didn't come from all the factual information I had studied (and forgotten), but the transferable skills and "habits of mind" that I developed in college and continue to use throughout my professional and personal life.

—*Joe Cuseo*

> *Much of the specialized, factual information you learn in college may be forgotten. However, what will be remembered are the ways of thinking, habits of mind, and communication skills developed by general education, which will continue to be used in multiple life roles throughout life.*

The Liberal Arts Develop the *Whole Person*

Socrates, the ancient and influential Greek philosopher, issued the famous proclamation: "Know thyself." This proclamation is a primary goal of the liberal arts. In addition to expanding your knowledge of the world around you, the liberal arts expand your knowledge of the world within you by encouraging you to look inward and learn about yourself. Scholars consider introspection (the ability to inspect oneself and gain self-awareness) to be a major form of human intelligence—referred to as "intrapersonal intelligence."

"A liberal arts education can help us develop a more comprehensive understanding of the universe and ourselves.
—Spencer Mc Williams, in *Liberal Arts Education: What Does it Mean? What is it Worth?*

> "The unexamined life is not worth living."
>
> —Socrates, ancient Greek philosopher and a founding father of Western philosophy

To know thyself—to be fully self-aware—requires knowledge of the *whole* self. The liberal arts liberate you from a narrow or single-dimensional view of yourself, helping you become aware of all the key components that make up the "self" and make you "whole." National surveys reveal that the number one reason why students go to college is to get a good job. Although finding a job and earning a decent living are certainly important, vocational development is just one slice of a larger pie of holistic (whole person) development. A college education should not just enrich you economically; it should enrich you holistically, enabling you to become a well-rounded and fully developed human being.

As can be seen in **Figure 2.4**, the different dimensions of self are interrelated. They do not operate independently, but interdependently—they intersect and interact with one another to affect our overall development and total well-being. Our intellectual performance can be influenced by our emotional state (e.g., whether we're enthusiastic or anxious); our emotional state can be influenced by our social relationships (e.g., whether we feel socially accepted or isolated); and our social relationships can be influenced by our physical state (e.g., whether we have a positive or negative physical self-image). If one link in this interconnected chain of selves is strengthened or weakened, other links in the chain are likely to be simultaneously strengthened or weakened. For instance, when college students make gains in intellectual development, research shows that they also make gains in social self-confidence and self-esteem.

Holistic self-awareness and self-growth encompass the following key forms of development.

Know Thyself

Self-awareness (self-knowledge) is one of the most important outcomes of a liberal arts and general education.

1. *Intellectual* Development: acquiring a broad base of knowledge, learning how to learn, and developing critical thinking skills.
2. *Emotional* Development: understanding, managing, and expressing emotions.
3. *Social* Development: improving the quality and depth of interpersonal relationships.
4. *Ethical* Development: building moral character—making sound ethical judgments, developing a clear value system for guiding personal decision-making, and demonstrating consistency between convictions (beliefs) and commitments (actions).
5. *Physical* Development: acquiring knowledge about one's body and applying that knowledge to prevent disease, promote wellness, and achieve peak performance.
6. *Spiritual* Development: pondering the "big questions", such as the meaning and purpose of life, the inevitability of death, and the origins of human life and the universe.
7. *Vocational* Development: exploring career options and pursuing a career path that is consistent with one's true talents, interests, and values.
8. *Personal* Development: developing a sense of personal identity, a coherent and positive self-concept, and the capacity to effectively manage personal resources (e.g., time and money).

> "Everyone is a house with four rooms: a physical, a mental, an emotional, and a spiritual. Most of us tend to live in one room most of the time but unless we go into every room every day, even if only to keep it aired, we are not complete."
>
> —Native American proverb

(For a more detailed description of these eight elements of self-development, see **Exercise 2.5,** pp. 49-52.)

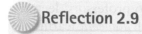

Reflection 2.9

Which one of the eight dimensions of self listed above are you most interested in developing or improving while you're in college? Why?

FIGURE 2.4: Key Elements of Holistic (Whole-Person) Development

©Kendall Hunt Publishing Company

"I want to see how all the pieces of me come together to make me.

—*College sophomore*

AUTHOR'S EXPERIENCE

On my office door, I post a picture of the holistic-development wheel to remind myself to keep my life balanced. Every Sunday night I reflect on the previous week and ask myself if I've ignored any particular component(s) of self-development. If I have, I try to make an earnest attempt to pay more attention to that aspect of my life during the upcoming week. For instance, if my previous week's activities reveal that I've neglected to spend enough time on my social self, I plan to spend more time the following week with family and friends. If I've neglected to attend to my physical self, I plan to exercise more consistently and eat more healthily the next week. The picture of the holistic self-development wheel on my door supplies me with a continual visual reminder to strive for "wholeness" and "balance" in my life.

—*Joe Cuseo*

The Co-Curriculum: Using Your *Whole Campus* to Develop Yourself as a *Whole Person*

The power of the liberal arts is magnified when college students take advantage of their total campus environment. A college education involves more than just enrolling in courses and piling up credits; it also involves capitalizing on the learning opportunities available to you outside the classroom—the *co-curriculum*. Co-curricular experiences include educational discussions with peers and professors outside of class, as well as participation in campus events, programs, and organizations sponsored by the Office of Student Life or Student Development.

Learning from courses (the curriculum) is primarily vicarious—it involves learning from or through somebody else—namely, listening to professors' lectures in class and by reading scholarly materials outside of class. Such *academic* learning is important but needs to be complemented by *experiential* learning—that is, learning that takes place directly from first-hand experiences. For example, leadership cannot be learned solely by listening to lectures and reading books about leadership. Developing leadership skills also requires engaging in actual leadership experiences, such as holding office in student government or serving as captain of a sports team.

> *General education involves learning through the curriculum and co-curriculum. Together, they combine to create a college graduate who is both well-rounded and globally minded.*

Listed in **Box 2.3** are some of the major out-of-class, co-curricular programs and services offered on colleges and university campuses; they are organized according to the primary dimension of self-development they're designed to promote.

> *The power of general education is magnified when you learn from both the breadth of courses in the liberal arts curriculum and the diversity of experiences available through the co-curriculum. By combining the two, you use the whole college to develop yourself as a whole person.*

Box 2.3

Dimensions of Holistic (Whole-Person) Development Promoted by Out-of-Class Experiences and Co-Curricular Programs

Intellectual Development

- Learning center
- College library
- Academic advising
- Tutoring services
- Information technology services
- Campus speakers
- Academic skills-development workshops
- Concerts, theater productions, and art shows

Ethical Development

- Judicial review board
- Student government
- Integrity committees and task forces

Physical Development

- Student health services
- Wellness programs
- Campus athletic activities and intramural sports

Spiritual Development

- Campus ministry
- Peer ministry
- Religious services

Vocational Development

- Career development services
- Internships
- Service learning experiences
- Work-study programs
- Major and career fairs

Personal Development

- Financial aid services and workshops
- Self-management workshops (e.g., managing time and money)
- Student development workshops and retreats

Reflection 2.10

What student club or organization on your campus most interests you?

Which element(s) of the self would this club or organization help you develop?

The Liberal Arts Develop Skills for Success in Your College Major

Despite the multiple benefits of general education, studies show that students often view liberal arts courses as something to "get out of the way" or "get behind them" so they can get into their major. Don't buy into the belief that general education is nothing more than a series of hoops and hurdles that must be surmounted or circumnavigated before you get to do what really matters. Instead of just getting these courses "out of the way," get "into them" and take away from them the essential skills you need to succeed in your major and to help you choose a major that best reflects your interests, talents, and values.

Remember the story at the very start of this chapter about Laura, the business major, who questioned why she had to take a course in philosophy. By taking that philosophy course, Laura didn't just check off a general-education requirement box, she acquired critical thinking and ethical reasoning skills that she could apply to understand business issues more deeply and respond to them more humanely. That general education course helped her gain greater awareness of important philosophical issues related to her major, such as: (a) underlying philosophical assumptions and values of capitalism and how they differ from other economic systems, (b) business ethics—philosophical principles that could serve as guidelines for ethical hiring and advertising practices, and (c) business justice—how the philosophical tenet of "distributive justice" ensures equitable distribution of profits among workers, executives, and shareholders.

Similarly, other subjects in the liberal arts curriculum provide business majors (and the many non-business majors who end up working in business organizations) with logical thinking and ethical reasoning skills needed to function effectively in the corporate world, such as:

- **History and Political Science:** how governmental policies impact business operations and regulations.
- **Psychology and Sociology:** how different motivational forces affect worker productivity and consumer purchasing habits, both individually and in groups.
- **Speech, English Composition, and Literature:** how to speak confidently and persuasively at meetings, write clear and concise memos, and read business reports analytically and critically.
- **Mathematics:** how to analyze, summarize, and interpret statistical data from marketing surveys.
- **Natural Science:** how to evaluate effective and efficient ways for companies to conserve energy and sustain natural resources.
- **Fine Arts:** how to create visually engaging advertisements and innovative marketing designs.

"Virtually all occupational endeavors require a working appreciation of the historical, cultural, ethical, and global environments that surround the application of skilled work.

—Robert Jones, author, *Liberal Education for the Twenty-first Century: Business Expectations*

The liberal arts also contribute to a successful performance in fields other than business. For instance, historical perspectives and ethical principles learned through the liberal arts are relevant to all majors because all of them have a history and none of them are value-free.

The Liberal Arts Enhance Career Preparation and Career Success

The world has changed dramatically during the 21st century, and along with it, so has the world of work. Today's employers are seeking employees with different skill sets than they have in the past; they are now looking for job candidates who are able to adapt to a variety of environments, who can problem-solve and manage projects, who have strong communication and interpersonal skills, and who can work effectively in teams.

In particular, employers report that the following skills and perspectives are essential for college graduates to have in order to be prepared for work in the twenty-first century:

> "From Utah to the Ukraine and from Milwaukee to Manila, industry is demanding that our graduates have better teamwork skills, communication abilities, and an understanding of the socioeconomic context in which engineering is practiced."
>
> —Ernest Smerdon, president of the American Society for Engineering Education

1. Knowledge of human cultures, the physical world, and the natural world, including understanding of:
   - Concepts and new developments in science and technology
   - Global issues and developments and their implications for the future
   - The role of the United States in the world
   - Cultural values and traditions in America and other countries
2. Intellectual and practical skills, such as the ability to:
   - Communicate orally and in writing
   - Think critically and analytically
   - Locate, organize, and evaluate information from multiple sources
   - Innovate and think creatively
   - Solve complex problems
   - Work with numbers and statistics
3. Integrative learning: the ability to connect (apply) knowledge and skills to real-world settings
4. Personal and social responsibility:
   - Teamwork skills and the ability to collaborate with others in diverse group settings
   - A sense of integrity and ethics

Reflection 2.11

Review the above four areas of knowledge and skills emphasized by today's employers. Which of them were you most surprised to see? Why?

The skills and qualities now being sought by employers are best developed by a well-rounded education that combines general education through the liberal arts and specialized education in a specific major. Interviews with hundreds of recent college graduates and their employers indicate that both believe the best preparation for career entry is an education which provides career-specific preparation *plus* broad-based knowledge and flexible skills. In fact, 93% of employers report that a candidate's capacity to think critically, communicate clearly, and solve complex problems is *more* important than his or her undergraduate major.

> *Preparing for a career involves more than just specialized education (a major); it also requires general education (the liberal arts). Remember: general education is career preparation.*

The Liberal Arts Prepare You for Lifelong Learning

The world's economy has progressed from agrarian (farm-based) to industrial (machine-based) to technological (information-based). The current technological revolution is generating information and new knowledge at a faster rate than at any other time in human history. When new knowledge is produced and communicated at a fast rate, existing knowledge and jobs become obsolete at a fast rate.

Studies show that today's college graduates change jobs 12 times during their first 20 years of work following graduation, and the job-changing rate is highest for younger workers. These findings point strongly to the conclusion that college graduates need transferable skills and a broad knowledge base so they can adapt to the changing work positions and job responsibilities they will encounter during their career(s). This conclusion is supported by a national survey of 1000 executives and employers who reported that most college graduates have adequate entry-level job skills, but do not possess skills needed for promotion and advancement in their careers. Many of the key skills they thought college graduates lacked to progress in their careers were the very skills promoted by the liberal arts, namely: oral and written communication skills, critical thinking and analytical reasoning, and ethical judgment and decision-making.

To advance in their careers, workers in today's complex, fast-changing world must continually update their skills and learn new ones. This need for lifelong learning is creating demand for workers who have *learned how to learn* and who can learn continually throughout life. This is not only a characteristic of a successful worker, it's also a signature feature of the liberal arts and a key attribute of a well-educated person.

> *College graduation is also called* commencement *because it's not the end of learning for college graduates, but the start of applying the skills they have learned to continue learning throughout life.*

AUTHOR'S EXPERIENCE

One role in life that the liberal arts helped prepare me for was that of a parent. Courses I took in psychology and sociology proved to be useful in helping me understand my son's development and how I could best support him at different stages of his life. There was another course I took that I never expected would help me as a parent, but it turned out to be critical. That course was statistics, which I took merely to complete my general education requirements in mathematics. It was not a particularly enjoyable course (in fact, some of my classmates sarcastically referred to it as "sadistics"), but what I learned in that course proved very valuable to me many years later when my 14-year-old son (Tony) developed leukemia—a cancer that attacks blood cells. Tony had a particularly perilous form of leukemia—one that 65% died from within 7 years. This statistical average was based on patients treated with chemotherapy, which was the type of treatment that my son's doctors began using when his cancer was first detected.

Another set of doctors strongly recommended that Tony's cancer be treated with a bone marrow transplant, which involved using radiation to destroy all his existing bone marrow and replacing it with bone marrow from a matched donor. My wife and I got opinions from doctors at two major cancer centers—one from a center that specialized in chemotherapy

continued...

and one from a center specializing in bone marrow transplants. The chemotherapy doctors felt strongly that drug treatment would be the better way to treat and cure my son; however, the bone marrow transplant doctors felt just as strongly that his chances of survival would be much better if he had a transplant. Thus, my wife and I had to decide between two opposing recommendations, each made by a respected group of doctors.

To help us reach a decision, I sought out research findings on the effectiveness of chemotherapy and bone marrow transplants for treating my son's particular type of cancer. While carefully reviewing all the statistical results, I remembered from my college statistics course that when an average is calculated for a group of people (e.g., average cure rate for people with leukemia), individuals from different subgroups are included among the general group studied (e.g., males and females; children, teenagers, and adults). Any differences in the results for these different subgroups are masked (hidden) in the overall average. In other words, the overall statistical average for a large group may not accurately reflect the averages of different subgroups embedded within it. With this in mind, I dug deeper to see if there were any subgroup statistics contained in the reports. I found two subgroups of patients with my son's form of cancer that had a higher rate of cure with chemotherapy than the general (whole-group) average of 35%. One subgroup included patients with a low number of abnormal cells at the time their cancer was first diagnosed, and the other subgroup consisted of patients whose cancer cells dropped rapidly after their first week of chemotherapy. My son belonged to both of these subgroups, which meant that his chance for cure with chemotherapy was higher than the overall 35% average. Furthermore, I found that the statistics for successful bone marrow transplants were based only on patients whose body accepted the donor's bone marrow. The bone marrow statistics didn't include the subgroup of patients who died from the transplant rather than from the cancer itself, so the success rate for bone marrow patients wasn't as high as it appeared to be at first glance. Based on my interpretation of these statistics, my wife and I decided to have my son treated with chemotherapy instead of a bone marrow transplant.

It looks like we made the right decision because my son has now been cancer free for over 10 years. I never imagined, however, that a statistics course, which I took many years ago merely to fulfill a general education requirement, would play such a critical role in helping me fulfill my role as a parent and make a successful life-or-death decision about my only son.

—*Joe Cuseo*

General education is not just "learning for its own sake." The skills developed by the liberal arts are more than "academic" skills; they are also practical skills that can be applied to different roles throughout life. They are a mental gift that keeps on giving.

Internet-Based Resources

For additional information on liberal arts and general education, see the following websites.

"What is a liberal arts education?"
http://www.iseek.org/education/liberalarts.html

Understanding Liberal Education:
https://www.aacu.org/leap/what-is-a-liberal-education

The Value of the Liberal Arts in the Global Economy:
http://www.huffingtonpost.com/edward-j-ray/the-value-of-a-liberal-arts-education_b_3647765.html

Skills for Success in the 21st Century:
http://edglossary.org/21st-century-skills/

Chapter 2 Exercises

2.1 Quote Reflections

Review the sidebar quotes contained in this chapter and select two that you found to be especially meaningful or inspirational.

For each quote you selected, provide an explanation of why you chose it.

2.2 Strategy Reflections

Review the four *skills and perspectives* that employers report are essential for college graduates to have in order to be prepared for work in the twenty-first century on p. 46. Select two you think are the most important and intend to develop.

2.3 Reality Bite

Dazed and Confused: General Education "versus" Career Specialization

Joe Tech was really looking forward to college because he thought he would have the freedom to select the courses he wanted and immediately start working on the major of his choice (computer science). However, he is shocked and disappointed with his first-term schedule of classes because it consists mostly of required general education courses that seem totally unrelated to his major. He's also frustrated because some of these courses are about subjects he already had in high school (English, History, and Biology). He's beginning to think he would be better off quitting college and going to a technical school for a year or two so he can get right into computer science and immediately begin to acquire the skills he'll need to work in the field of computer technology.

Reflection and Discussion Questions

1. If Joe decides to get a technical certificate and not pursue a college degree, how do you see it affecting his future:
   a) in the short run?
   b) in the long run?

2. Do you see any way Joe might strike a balance between pursuing his career interest and obtaining a college degree so that he could work toward achieving both goals at the same time?

3. Can you relate to Joe's story in any way, or do you know anyone else having a similar experience?

2.4 Your AchieveWORKS Personality Assessment

The AchieveWORKS Personality assessment produced a report exclusively for you.

What do those results tell you about yourself?

Which areas of the liberal arts can bolster your strengths and which can help you uncover your blind spots?

2.5 Holistic Development: Self-Assessment

Development of the whole self is an essential goal of the liberal arts and general education. As you read through the objectives and outcomes associated with the following dimensions of holistic ("whole person") development, rate each one in terms of its *importance to you* on a scale of 1 (lowest) to 5 (highest).

1. **Intellectual Development:** Acquiring a broad base of knowledge, learning how to learn deeply and how to think critically and creatively.

   Objectives and Outcomes:

   ____ Becoming aware of your intellectual abilities, interests, and learning strategies

   ____ Improving your focus of attention and concentration

   ____ Moving beyond memorizing to learning at a deeper level

   ____ Improving your ability to retain knowledge on a long-term basis

   ____ Acquiring effective research skills to access information from a variety of sources and systems

   ____ Learning how to view issues from multiple angles or perspectives (cultural, historical, political, economic, etc.)

   ____ Responding constructively to differing viewpoints and opposing positions

   ____ Critically evaluating the truth and value of ideas and arguments

   ____ Detecting and rejecting propaganda that appeals to emotion rather than reason

   ____ Thinking creatively and innovatively

   > "Intellectual growth should commence at birth and cease only at death.
   >
   > —*Albert Einstein, Nobel Prize-winning physicist*

2. **Emotional Development:** Understanding, managing, and expressing emotions.

   Objectives and Outcomes:

   ____ Becoming emotionally self-aware

   ____ Maintaining a healthy balance between emotional control and emotional expression

   ____ Responding with empathy and sensitivity to emotions experienced by others

   ____ Accepting feedback from others in an open, non-defensive manner

   ____ Maintaining a sense of optimism and enthusiasm

   ____ Responding constructively to setbacks and feelings of frustration

   ____ Managing anger effectively

   ____ Overcoming fear of failure and lack of self-confidence

   ____ Using effective stress-management strategies to control anxiety and reduce tension

   ____ Coping effectively with depression

   > "It's not stress that kills us, it is our reaction to it.
   >
   > —*Hans Selye, Canadian endocrinologist and author of* Stress Without Distress

3. **Social Development:** Improving the quality and depth of interpersonal relationships.

   Objectives and Outcomes:

   ____ Increasing social self-confidence

   ____ Improving listening and conversational skills

   ____ Overcoming shyness

   ____ Relating to others in an open, non-judgmental manner

   ____ Forming meaningful and supportive friendships

   ____ Learning how to resolve interpersonal conflicts

   ____ Developing greater empathy for others

   ____ Relating effectively to people from different cultural backgrounds and lifestyles

   ____ Collaborating effectively with others while working in groups or teams

   ____ Becoming an effective leader capable of positively influencing others

   > "Chi rispetta sara rippetato." ("Respect others and you will be respected.")
   >
   > —*Italian proverb*

4. **Ethical (Character) Development:** Developing a clear value system for guiding personal decisions, making sound ethical judgments, and demonstrating consistency between convictions (beliefs) and commitments (actions).

   Objectives and Outcomes:

   ____ Gaining deeper awareness of one's most strongly held values and ethical priorities

   ____ Making personal choices and life decisions based on a meaningful value system

   ____ Developing the capacity to think and act with integrity and authenticity

   ____ Resisting social pressure to behave in ways that are inconsistent with one's personal values

   ____ Treating others in a fair and just manner

   ____ Exercising freedom responsibly without infringing on the rights of others

   > "If you don't stand for something you will fall for anything.
   >
   > —*Malcolm X, African-American Muslim minister, public speaker, and human rights activist*

___ Using information technology and social media in a civil and ethical manner
___ Becoming an engaged and responsible citizen
___ Increasing awareness of and commitment to human rights and social justice
___ Developing the courage to challenge or confront others who violate human rights and obstruct social justice

5. **Physical Development:** Acquiring knowledge about the human body and how to apply that knowledge to prevent disease, preserve wellness, and promote peak performance.

   Objectives and Outcomes:

   ___ Becoming more aware of one's physical condition and state of health
   ___ Applying knowledge about exercise and fitness to maximize physical and mental energy
   ___ Developing sleep habits that optimize physical and mental well-being
   ___ Maintaining a healthy balance between work, recreation, and relaxation
   ___ Applying knowledge about nutrition to reduce risk of illness and achieve peak levels of performance
   ___ Understanding the causes and cures of eating disorders
   ___ Developing a positive physical self-image
   ___ Becoming more knowledgeable about how drugs affect the body and mind
   ___ Gaining knowledge about human sexuality and sexual diversity
   ___ Understanding how biological differences between the sexes affect male–female communication and relationships

   > "A man too busy to take care of his health is like a mechanic too busy to take care of his tools."
   > —*Spanish proverb*

6. **Spiritual Development:** Pondering the "big questions" about the meaning and purpose of life, the inevitability of death, and the origins of human life and the natural world.

   Objectives and Outcomes:

   ___ Developing a meaningful philosophy of life
   ___ Exploring the unknown or what cannot be completely understood scientifically
   ___ Appreciating the mysteries associated with the origin of the universe (cosmos)
   ___ Seeking meaningful connections between the self and the larger world
   ___ Searching for the mystical or supernatural—what transcends the boundaries of the natural world
   ___ Examining questions relating to death and life after death
   ___ Exploring questions about the existence of a Supreme Being or higher power
   ___ Gaining knowledge about different approaches to spirituality and their underlying beliefs or assumptions
   ___ Understanding the relationship between faith and reason
   ___ Becoming more aware of, and accepting of, religious diversity

   > "We are not human beings having a spiritual experience. We are spiritual beings having a human experience.
   > —*Pierre Teilhard de Chardin, French philosopher, geologist, paleontologist, and Jesuit priest*

7. **Vocational Development:** Exploring career options and pursuing a career path that's congruent with one's interests, talents, and values.

   Objectives and Outcomes:

   ___ Understanding the relationship between majors and careers
   ___ Using effective strategies for exploring and identifying potential career options
   ___ Discovering career options that are most compatible with one's personal interests, talents, needs, and values
   ___ Acquiring work experience related to one's career interests
   ___ Building an effective resume or portfolio
   ___ Identifying personal references and securing letters of recommendation
   ___ Implementing effective job-search strategies
   ___ Writing effective letters of inquiry and letters of application for positions of employment or acceptance to graduate school
   ___ Acquiring networking skills for connecting with potential employers
   ___ Developing strategies for improving performance in job interviews

   > "Your work is to discover your work and then with all your heart to give yourself to it.
   > —*Hindu Siddhartha Prince Gautama Siddharta, a.k.a. Buddha, founder of the philosophy and religion of Buddhism*

8. **Personal Development:** Developing a strong sense of personal identity, a coherent self-concept, and the ability to manage personal affairs and resources.

Objectives and Outcomes:

____ Developing a clear sense of personal identity (Answering the question: Who am I?)

____ Finding purpose and direction in life. (Answering the question: Who will I become?)

____ Developing self-respect and self-esteem

____ Increasing self-confidence

____ Acquiring a strong sense self-efficacy—belief that the outcomes of one's life are within one's control and can be influenced by personal initiative and effort

____ Strengthening skills for managing personal resources (e.g., time and money)

____ Becoming more independent, self-directed, and self-reliant

____ Setting realistic goals and priorities

____ Developing self-motivation and self-discipline needed to reach personal goals

____ Developing resiliency to overcome obstacles and roadblocks, ability to bounce back from setbacks, and the capability of converting setbacks into comebacks

> "Remember, no one can make you feel inferior without your consent.
>
> —*Eleanor Roosevelt, former United Nations diplomat and humanitarian*

- Based on your total score in each of the eight above areas of holistic development, what aspect(s) of self-development appear to be most and least important to you? How would you explain (or what do you think accounts for) this discrepancy?
- Add up your score in each of the eight areas of holistic development.
  a) Do your totals in each area suggest that all aspects of self-development are equally important to you and that you're striving to become a well-rounded person?
  b) If yes, why? If no, why not?

2.6 Identifying Courses that Broaden Your Perspectives

Using your *College Catalog* or *University Bulletin*, identify one course you could take that would develop each of the broadening perspectives of the liberal arts listed in the grid below.

Broadening Social–Spatial Perspectives	Course Developing this Perspective
See pages 34-37 for specific descriptions of these perspectives.	*Read the course descriptions in your Catalog or Bulletin to identify a general education requirement that develops this perspective.*
Self	
Family	
Community	
Society	
Nation	
International	
Global	
Universe	
Broadening Chronological Perspectives	Course Developing this Perspective
See pages 38-39 for detailed descriptions of these perspectives.	*Read the course descriptions in your Catalog or Bulletin to identify a general education requirement that develops this perspective.*
Historical	
Contemporary	
Futuristic	

2.7 Identifying Co-Curricular Experiences that Develop the Whole Self

Using your *Student Handbook,* identify a co-curricular program or experience you could engage in that would contribute to each of the key dimensions of holistic (whole person) development listed in the grid below.

Dimensions of Self	Co-Curricular Experience Developing this Dimension of Self
See page 42 for a description of these dimensions of self-development.	*Consult your Student Handbook to identify a co-curricular experience that contributes to this dimension of self-development.*
Intellectual	
Emotional	
Social	
Ethical	
Physical	
Spiritual	
Vocational	
Personal	

Using your Student Handbook, identify a co-curricular program or experience you could engage in that would contribute to each of the key dimensions of holistic (whole person) development listed in the grid below.

See page 42 for a description of these dimensions of self-development.	Consult your Student Handbook to identify a co-curricular experience that contributes to this dimension of self-development.
Intellectual	
Emotional	
Social	
Ethical	
Physical	
Spiritual	
Vocational	
Personal	

Goal Setting and Motivation

MOVING FROM INTENTION TO ACTION

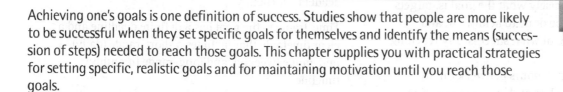

Achieving one's goals is one definition of success. Studies show that people are more likely to be successful when they set specific goals for themselves and identify the means (succession of steps) needed to reach those goals. This chapter supplies you with practical strategies for setting specific, realistic goals and for maintaining motivation until you reach those goals.

Chapter Purpose & Preview

Acquire knowledge on setting meaningful personal goals and apply self-motivational strategies to persist to goal attainment.

Learning Goal

 **Reflection 3.1**

What does being "successful" mean to you?

Ignite Your Thinking

"What keeps me going is goals.

—*Muhammad Ali, philanthropist, social activist, and Hall of Fame boxer who was crowned "Sportsman of the 20th Century" by* Sports Illustrated

The Relationship between Goal Setting and Success

The word "success" derives from the Latin root "*successus*"—meaning "to follow or come after" (as in the word "successive"). Thus, by definition, success involves a succession or sequence of actions that leads to a desired outcome. The process of attaining success starts with identifying an end (goal) then identifying the means (sequence of steps) to reach that goal. Research shows that successful people set goals on a regular basis and develop specific plans for reaching the goals they set. As Angela Duckworth notes in her study of individuals who overcame setbacks and went on to achieve success: "They not only had determination, they had *direction*." Effective goal setting provides direction through a process known as *means-end analysis*, which involves working backward from a long-range goal (the end) and identifying mid-range and short-range subgoals (the means) that must be reached to eventually achieve that long-range goal. Engaging in this means-end analysis doesn't mean you're locking yourself into a premature plan that will restrict your flexibility or options. It's just a process that gets you to: (a) think about where you want to go, (b) provides some sense of direction about how to get there, and (c) starts moving you in the right direction.

"Stopping a long pattern of bad decision-making and setting positive, productive priorities and goals.

—*College sophomore's answer to the question: "What does being successful mean to you?"*

"The tragedy of life doesn't lie in not reaching your goal. The tragedy of life lies in having no goal to reach.

—*Benjamin Mays, minister, scholar, activist, and former president of Morehouse College*

Characteristics of a Well-Designed Goal

Studies show that people who set specific, well-designed goals are more likely to achieve them than those who simply tell themselves they're going to try hard and do their best. The acronym "SMART" is a well-known mnemonic device (memory strategy) for recalling all the key components of a well-designed goal. **Box 3.1** describes the key components of a SMART goal. You can use this goal-setting strategy to help you define and design goals that are both meaningful and achievable.

Box 3.1

The SMART Method of Goal Setting

A *SMART* goal is one that is:

- Specific—it defines precisely what the goal is, targets exactly what needs to be done to achieve it, and provides a clear picture of what successfully reaching the goal looks like.
  Example: By spending 25 hours per week on my coursework outside of class and by using effective learning strategies (such as those recommended in chapter 5), I will achieve at least a 3.0 grade-point average this term. (Note how this goal is much more specific than saying, "I'm really going to work hard this term.")

- Meaningful (and Measurable)—the goal I'm pursuing is personally important to me (meaningful) and I can clearly measure the progress I'm making to achieve it.
  Example: Achieving at least a 3.0 grade-point average this term is important to me because it will enable me to get into the field I'd like to major in, and I'll measure my progress toward this goal by calculating the grade I'm earning in each of my courses at regular intervals throughout the term. (Note: At www. futureme.org, you can set up a program to send yourself e-mails that remind you to check your progress on the goals you've set for yourself.)

- Actionable (i.e., Action-Oriented)—the actions or behaviors to be taken to reach my goal are concrete and specific.
  Example: I will achieve at least a 3.0 grade-point average this term by (a) attending all classes in all my courses,(b) taking detailed notes in all my classes, (c) completing all my reading assignments by their due dates, and (d) studying in advance (rather than cramming) for my exams.

- Realistic—the time, effort, and skills needed to reach my goal are reasonable and manageable, so the goal is within my reach.
  Example: Achieving a 3.0 grade-point average this term is a realistic goal because (a) I have a reasonable

course load, (b) I will work no more than 15 hours per week at my part-time job, and (c) I will be able to get help from campus support services if I run into academic difficulty.

- Time-framed—the goal has a definite deadline and a clear timetable that includes a short-range (daily), mid-range (weekly), and long-range (monthly) timeline.
  Example: To achieve at least a 3.0 grade-point average this term, I'll first acquire all the information I need to learn by taking complete lecture notes in my classes and completing all my reading assignments (short-range step). Second, I'll learn the information I've acquired from my lecture notes and readings by breaking it into manageable parts and studying these parts in separate sessions in advance of major exams (mid-range step). Third, the day before exams I'll review all information I previously studied in parts, get a good night's sleep, and be well rested on exam days (long-range step).

This SMART goal-setting process can be used to set goals in any area of your life and for any aspect of personal development, such as:

- self-management (e.g., setting goals for managing time and money)
- physical development (e.g., setting health and fitness goals)
- social development (e.g., setting relationship goals)
- emotional development (e.g., setting goals for managing stress or frustration)
- intellectual development (e.g., setting goals for learning and academic achievement)

The SMART process may also be used to set career-development goals relating to the three key skills that today's employers are seeking in college graduates: *professional* skills, *problem-solving* skills, and *people* skills. (For more specific details about these skills, see Chapter 15, pp. ___.)

> *Goal setting is a strategic and systematic process that could (and should) be applied to achieve any goal you set for yourself at any stage of your life.*

 **Reflection 3.2**

If you were to set a goal for yourself right now, what would you choose and why would you choose it?

In addition to setting well-designed goals that are consistent with the SMART method, research reveals that the following practices and attributes characterize people who successfully set and achieve goals. Be mindful of these qualities and practices when you set and pursue your own goals.

Rather than setting perfection (be-good) goals, successful goal setters set *self-improvement* **(***get-better***)** *goals* **that focus on personal progress and growth.** Studies show that when people set get-better goals, they pursue them with greater interest, intensity, and joy. This is probably because get-better goals give us a sense of progress by focusing on how far we've come. In contrast, perfection (be-good) goals focus on how far we still have to go.

Successful goal setters focus on outcomes they can *influence or control.* For instance, for an aspiring actress, a controllable goal would be to increase her acting skills and professional acting opportunities, not to become a famous movie star—a desirable outcome but not something that's totally within her control.

Successful goal setters set goals that are *challenging and effortful.* Goals worth achieving make us stretch and break a sweat; they call for endurance, persistence, and resiliency. Studies of successful people in all occupations indicate that if they set goals that are attainable but also *challenging*, they pursue those goals more strategically, with more intensity, and with greater commitment. There's an additional advantage of setting a challenging goal: When it's achieved, the person achieving it experiences a strong sense of personal satisfaction and accomplishment, and a boost in self-esteem.

Successful goal setters anticipate *obstacles* **they may encounter along the path to their goals and have a plan for dealing with these potential obstacles.** One characteristic of successful people is that they imagine what their life would be like if they didn't reach their goals. Imagining this scenario drives them to prepare for events or circumstances that might interfere with their aspirations and plans. They remain optimistic about succeeding, but they're not blind optimists; they realize that the road may be tough so they have a plan in place to deal with rough spots and roadblocks they anticipate experiencing along the way. Thus, effective goal-setters have both a plan for reaching their goal and a plan for surmounting potential obstacles or impediments.

"Accomplishing something hard to do.

—*First-year student's response to the question: "What does being successful mean to you?"*

"Nothing ever comes that is worth having, except as a result of hard work.

—*Booker T. Washington, born-in-slavery Black educator, author, and advisor to Republican presidents*

Reflection 3.3

Think about possible obstacles you may encounter along the path to completing college.

What resources could you use (on or off campus) to help you overcome these obstacles?

Research indicates that success in college involves a combination of what students do for themselves (personal responsibility) and how well students capitalize on available resources designed to promote their success.

> *Successful people are resourceful—they're aware of, and take advantage of, resources to help them reach their goals.*

Remember that peers are a social resource for achieving goals. The motivational power of social-support groups is well documented by research conducted in multiple fields of study. You can harness the power of social support by surrounding yourself with peers who are committed to achieving their educational goals and distancing yourself from "toxic" people who can poison your plans and dampen your dreams.

Find motivated peers and make mutual-support "pacts" with them to reach your respective goals. These peer-support pacts may be viewed as "social contracts" signed by "co-witnesses" who hold each other accountable for fulfilling their goal commitments. Studies show that when people commit to a goal in the presence of others, their goal commitment is strengthened because it makes it both a personal commitment *and* an interpersonal commitment.

> "Develop an inner circle of close associations in which the mutual attraction is not sharing problems or needs. The mutual attraction should be values and goals."
>
> —*Denis Waitley, former mental trainer for U.S. Olympic athletes and author of* Seeds of Greatness

Strategies for Maintaining Motivation and Making Progress Toward Goals

The word "motivation" derives from the Latin root "movere," meaning "to move." As its root meaning implies, motivation involves overcoming inertia. Motivated people get off their butts and get moving, and once they get moving, they maintain momentum and keep moving until their goals are reached. Studies show that goal setting is just the first step in a success-seeking process; it must be followed by a strong, effortful commitment to that goal until it is reached. Goal setting establishes the intention to act, but motivation transforms that intention into action.

> "You can lead a horse to water, but you can't make him drink."
>
> —*Author unknown*

Thus, challenging goals requires maintaining motivation and sustaining effort over an extended period of time. Listed below are strategies you can use to stay motivated and continue progressing toward your goals.

Put your goals in writing and keep them visible. A written goal can operate like a written contract—a formal statement that holds us accountable for following through on our commitment. Placing a written goal in a place where we cannot help but see it on a daily basis (e.g., on our laptop cover, refrigerator door, or bathroom mirror) ensures that we don't "lose sight" of it and are continually reminded to pursue it. Said in another way: what stays in our sight, stays on our mind.

> *The next best thing to actually doing something is to write down our intention to do it, which keeps our intention visible (and memorable).*

Visualize reaching your long-range goals. To maintain motivation over time, we need to keep the "big picture" in mind and keep our "eye on the prize." One way to do so is by creating vivid mental images or pictures of reaching our goal and experiencing its positive consequences. As a beginning college student, your long-rage goal is graduating from college, so you could visualize a crowd of cheering family, friends, and faculty at your graduation ceremony. (You could even add musical accompaniment to your visualization by playing a motivational song in your head—e.g., "We are the Champions" by Queen).

AUTHOR'S EXPERIENCE

My father, who spent 50 years working in the coal mines of eastern Kentucky, always had a simple, motivating statement to encourage me to gain more education than he had. He would always say, "Son, I did not have the chance to go to school, so I have to write my name with an X and work in the coal mines. You have the opportunity to get an education and not break your back in those mines." What my father was telling me was that education would give me options in life that he did not have and that I should take advantage of those options by going to college. My dad's lack of education supplied me with the drive and dedication to pursue education. My experience suggests that when you are setting your goals and motivating yourself to achieve them, it may be as important to visualize what you don't want your future to be as it is to visualize what you want it to be.

—*Aaron Thompson*

Visualize completing all the key steps leading up to your goal. For visualization to be an effective motivator, it's important not only to visualize the success itself (the end goal), but also the successive steps you'll be taking along the way. As motivational researcher and author, Heidi Grant Halvorson, puts it: "Just picturing yourself crossing the finish line doesn't actually help you get there—but visualizing how you run the race (the strategies you will use, the choices you will make, the obstacles you will face) not only will give you greater confidence, but also leave you better prepared for the task ahead."

Yes, reaching a long-term goal requires focusing on the prize—the dream and why fulfilling the dream is important. Such "big picture" thinking serves to inspire us. However, we also need to focus on the little things that need to be done to get there—the to-do lists, the day-to-day tasks, the due dates, etc. (For specific strategies on managing time, combating procrastination and completing tasks, see chapter 4.) This is the nitty-gritty stuff—the effortful perspiration that converts inspiration into action, and enables us to plug away and persist until our goals (and dreams) and are realized.

It could be said that successfully achieving a long-term goal requires that we use two lenses, each with a different focus point. We need a wide-angle lens that gives us a big-picture view of the future far ahead of us (our ultimate goal) and a narrow-angle lens that zooms in and focuses on the here and now—the steps that lie immediately ahead of us. As a first-year college student, alternating between these two perspectives allows you to view your smaller, short-term chores and challenges (e.g., completing an assignment that's due next week) in light of the larger, long-range picture (e.g., college graduation and a successful future).

> "You've got to think about 'big things' while you're doing small things, so that all the small things go in the right direction.
>
> —*Alvin Toffler, American futurologist and author who predicted the future effects of technology on our society*

AUTHOR'S EXPERIENCE

I once coached a youth soccer team (5- to 6-year-old boys) and noticed that many of the less successful players tended to make either of two mistakes when trying to advance the ball down the field.

Some of them spent too much time looking down, focusing on the ball at their feet and trying to make sure they didn't lose control of it. By not occasionally lifting their heads up and looking ahead, these players often missed open territory, open teammates, or an open goal.

Other unsuccessful players made the opposite mistake: They spent too much time with their heads up, trying to see where they were headed. By not periodically glancing down to see the ball right in front of them, these players often lost control of it, moved ahead without it, or sometimes stumbled over it and fell flat on their face. In contrast, the more successful players had developed the habit of shifting their focus between looking down to maintain control of the ball in front of them and lifting their eyes to see where they were headed.

The more I thought about how the successful soccer players alternated between these two perspectives, it struck me that this was a metaphor for success in life. Successful people alternate between long- and short-range perspectives; they remain mindful of both the long-term goal far ahead of them and the short-term tasks right in front of them.

—*Joe Cuseo*

We need to keep our future dreams and current tasks in dual focus. Integrating these two perspectives provides us with both the inspiration to set goals and the determination to reach them.

Keep a record of your personal progress. Highly effective people reflect regularly on their daily progress to ensure they're on track and making progress toward their goals. Research indicates that even the simple act of monitoring and recording progress toward our goals increases our motivation to continue pursuing them. Keeping a regular record of our personal progress increases our motivation because it supplies us with frequent *feedback* about whether we're on track and provides us with positive *reinforcement* for staying on track.

You can keep a record of your short- and mid-range goal achievements in a calendar or journal. These recordings can serve as benchmarks that provide you with visible markers (and reminders) of your progress. You could also mark your progress on a chart or graph, or list them as achievements in a personal portfolio. By placing these progress markers where they can be seen on a daily basis, you will have a visible record of your short-term accomplishments that can motivate you to continue striving toward your long-term goal.

Reward yourself for completing the stepping-stones along the road to your long-range goal. Not only should we document our progress, we should celebrate our success. Reaching a long-range goal is clearly cause for celebration because it marks the end of the trip and the thrill of reaching our desired destination. Reaching short- and mid-range goals, however, are not as obviously rewarding because they're merely steps along the way. If we reward ourselves for making these steps, we're more likely to continue climbing these stepping stones until we reach our long-range goal. This is a simple yet powerful self-motivational strategy for maintaining momentum over an extended period of time, which is exactly what's needed to achieve a long-term goal.

Reflection 3.4

To reach your ultimate goal of becoming a college graduate, what key stepping-stones or sub-goals would you need to complete along the way? How would you reward yourself for completing them?

Characteristics of Successful People

Achieving success involves effective use of goal-setting and motivational strategies, but it takes something more. Ultimately, success emerges from the inside out—it flows from personal qualities and attributes found within a person. Studies of successful people who achieve their goals reveal that they typically possess the personal characteristics discussed below. Keep these characteristics in mind and do your very best to exhibit them.

(Take a look at the results of your AchieveWORKS Personality report. What does it say about your strengths and challenges when it comes to goal setting and motivation? Any surprises? Any areas you've identified for self-improvement?)

> "If you do not find it within yourself, where will you go to get it?
>
> —Zen saying (Zen is a branch of Buddhism that emphasizes seeing deeply into the nature of things and ongoing self-awareness.)

Self-Efficacy

Self-efficacy is the belief that you can positively influence the *outcomes* of your life. People with self-efficacy have what psychologists call an "internal locus of control"—they believe that the locus (location or source) of control for events in their life is primarily *internal*—"inside" them and within their control, rather than *external*—outside them and beyond their control. They believe that success is influenced more by attitude, effort, and commitment than by luck, chance, or fate. In contrast, people with low self-efficacy tend to feel helpless and powerless; they think (and allow) things to happen to them rather than taking charge and making things happen for them.

College students with a strong sense of self-efficacy believe they're in control of their educational success and can shape their future—regardless of what their past experience or current circumstances happen to be. Research on students with a strong sense of *academic self-efficacy* shows that these students:

> "Whether you think you can or you can't, you're right.
>
> —Henry Ford, founder of Ford Motor Co. and one of the wealthiest men of his generation.

1. Put considerable effort into their studies
2. Use active-learning strategies
3. Capitalize on campus resources
4. Persist in the face of obstacles.

Students with a strong sense of self-efficacy also possess a strong sense of personal responsibility. As the breakdown of the word "responsible" suggests, they believe they are "response-able"—able to respond effectively to personal and educational challenges.

> "I'm a great believer in luck, and I find the harder I work the more I have of it.
>
> —Thomas Jefferson, third President of the United States

Reflection 3.5

In what area of your life do you think you have the strongest sense of self-efficacy? Is there anything you can take from the strong self-efficacy you have in this area and apply it to help you succeed in college?

Growth Mindset

A *mindset* is a strong belief. People with a "*growth mindset*" believe that intelligence and other positive qualities can be grown or developed. In contrast, people with a "fixed mindset" believe that intelligence and other abilities are permanent, inborn traits that cannot be modified or acquired. The power of a growth mindset is supported by studies indicating that a person's IQ score is not fixed but can change significantly over time. Research also shows that the human brain isn't immutable; it changes with experience and parts of the brain responsible for learning a particular skill (e.g., math) grow and develop when those skills are practiced and developed.

Listed below are opposing pairs of traits—one representing a fixed mindset (FM) and the other a growth mindset (GM). As you read through these pairings, honestly assess yourself in terms of whether you lean more toward a fixed or growth mindset by circling either the FM or GM option.

* I try to get better at what I do. (GM)
* I try to show others (including myself) how good I am. (FM)

* I try to validate myself by proving how smart or talented I am. (FM)
* I validate myself by trying to become smarter and more talented than I am now. (GM)

* If I cannot learn something easily or quickly, I think that means I'm not smart or good at it. (FM)
* I believe I can get good at something even if it doesn't come easily to me at first. (GM)

* I evaluate my performance by comparing it to my past performances. (GM)
* I evaluate my performance by comparing it to the performance of others. (FM)

* I believe the amount of intelligence people start with doesn't predict the amount they'll end up with. (GM)
* I believe people are born with a certain amount of intelligence and not much can be done to change it. (FM)

* I think success is a matter of having ability. (FM)
* I think success is a matter of getting ability. (GM)

* I focus on demonstrating my skills to others. (FM)
* I focus on developing my skills for myself. (GM)

* I like to improve myself (by getting better). (GM)
* I like to prove myself (as being good or smart). (FM)

* I feel smart when I complete tasks quickly and without mistakes. (FM)
* I feel smart when I struggle with tasks at first, but then succeed at them eventually. (GM)

* I seek out feedback from others to improve myself. (GM)
* I avoid seeking feedback from others for fear it will expose my weaknesses. (FM)

> "No matter what your ability is, effort is what ignites that ability and turns it into accomplishment."
>
> —*Carol Dweck, Stanford psychologist and author of* Mindset: The New Psychology of Success

* I tend to show progressive improvement in my performance over time. (GM)
* I tend to peak early and don't progress to higher levels of performance. (FM)

* I think success should be effortless. (FM)
* I think success should be effortful. (GM)

* I view challenges as opportunities to develop new skills. (GM)
* I view challenges as threatening because they may prove I'm not smart. (FM)

* I believe effort creates talent. (GM)
* I believe effort is for those who can't make it on talent. (FM)

* I focus on self-improvement—about becoming the best I can be. (GM)
* I focus on self-validation—about proving I'm already good. (FM)

* I look at grades as labels that judge or measure my intelligence. (FM)
* I look at grades as feedback that I can use to improve my skills. (GM)

Reflection 3.6

Look back at the previous pairs of statements and compare the total number of fixed mindset (FM) and growth mindset (GM) statements you circled.

a) Do your totals suggest that, in general, you lean more toward a growth or fixed mindset?

b) Do you see any patterns in your responses that suggest you're more likely to have a growth mindset for certain characteristics or situations and a fixed mindset for others?

c) How do you think your responses would compare with other students?

Numerous studies show that a growth mindset is strongly associated with goal achievement and academic success. For example, when growth-mindset students do poorly on a test, they improve on the next one. In contrast, fixed-mindset students' show no pattern of improvement (or show decline) over time, particularly if their first exam score is low. It's also been found that students can have different mindsets for different subjects and situations. Some students may have a fixed mindset for math, but a growth mindset for English.

The most important thing to remember about mindset is that although it plays a powerful role in motivation and success, it's just a belief and it can be changed from "fixed" to "growth" for any academic subject or personal challenge. If your belief about what makes someone intelligent or talented suggests a fixed mindset, you may need to change that mindset to reach the goals you've set for yourself and realize your full potential. Even if you lack self-confidence, you can still develop a growth mindset. As growth-mindset guru, Carol Dweck, notes: "A remarkable thing I've learned from my research is that even when you think you're not good at something, you can still plunge into it wholeheartedly and stick to it. Actually, sometimes you plunge into something *because* you're not good at it."

You can develop a growth mindset by controlling the language or self-talk you use in reaction to your successes and setbacks. Listed below are examples of how self-talk that associated with a fixed mindset (FM) can be changed into language that promotes a growth mindset (GM).

1. After unsuccessful performance:

    "Well, at least I tried." (FM)   →   "I know that wasn't the outcome I was hoping for. What went wrong and how might it be corrected?" (GM)

    "That was hard. I shouldn't feel bad about → "That was hard. I shouldn't feel not being able to do it." (FM)   bad about not being able to do it *yet*." (GM)

2. After successful performance:

    "I'm so talented!" (FM) → "I learn so well!" (GM)

    "Great job! (FM) → "Great job! If I were to do it over again, is there anything I could have done even better?" (GM)

Self-talk that focuses on talent and intelligence focuses on traits that are fixed or unalterable. In contrast, self-talk that focuses on the effort you expend and the strategies you use, focuses on behavior you can change and continually improve.

> "Our words have a far greater motivational impact than most of us realize, and that's a responsibility that should be taken seriously."
>
> —Heidi Grant Halvorson, social psychologist, and author of *Succeed: How We Can Reach Your Goals*

Grit

When a person sustains significant effort, energy, and perseverance over an extended period to achieve a goal, that person is demonstrating *grit*. People with grit have been found to possess the following qualities.

Passion. Many people associate passion with intensity, infatuation, or obsession. However, for high achievers, when asked about what it takes to be successful, they refer to passion as *consistency over time*. It's more about stamina than intensity. As grit guru, Angela Duckworth puts it: "Grit is about working on something you care about so much that you're willing to stay loyal to it. It's doing what you love, but not just falling in love—staying in love."

Perseverance. Gritty people pursue goals with relentless determination. If they encounter something along the way that's hard to do, they work harder to do it. Studies of highly successful people—whether they be scientists, musicians, writers, chess masters, or basketball stars—consistently show that achieving excellence requires repeated effort and dedicated practice. This is even true for famous people that are often viewed as being naturally talented, brilliant, or gifted. For example, before they burst into musical stardom, the Beatles performed live an estimated 1,200 times over a 4-year period, and many of these performances lasted five hours or more per night. They performed (practiced) for more hours during their first four years together than most bands perform during their entire career. Similarly, before Bill Gates became a computer software giant and creator of Microsoft, he logged almost 1,600 hours of computer time during one seven-month period alone, averaging eight hours a day, seven days a week.

These extraordinary success stories point strongly to the conclusion that reaching goals and achieving success takes dedication, determination, and perseverance. Being successful is not just an inborn gift; it takes a lot of grit.

Reflection 3.7

Think about something you achieved in your life that involved considerable dedication, determination, and perseverance. Do you see ways in which you could apply the same qualities to achieve success in college?

Resilience. Grit involves hanging in there, sustaining effort until a goal is reached, and displaying the fortitude to push forward in the face of frustration or adversity. It takes courage not to get discouraged. A gritty person bounces back from setbacks and turns them into comebacks.

How we initially react (mentally and emotionally) to a setback can determine the action we take in response to it. For instance, if you react to a poor test grade by knocking yourself down with self-putdowns ("I'm a loser" or "I screw up everything"), you're likely to become discouraged and give up. Notice that these reactions have two resilience-destroying characteristics: they're *permanent*—a "loser" is always a loser and *pervasive*—screwing up "everything" means not screwing up one thing, but all things. A permanent and pervasive explanation for a setback turns a molehill into a mountain. Be mindful about how you react to setbacks. If you catch yourself engaging in negative self-talk, put an immediate stop to it. Replace it with positive self-talk that reacts to the setback as *temporary* (not permanent) and *specific* (not pervasive). For instance, respond to a setback by saying: "I'm going to let this one disappointment define who I am; I'll learn from it and use it as motivation to get it right next time."

Research shows that when people think they can learn from mistakes, their brain reacts to mistakes by responding with two consecutive electrical responses—the first one indicating that they're paying attention to the mistake, followed immediately by a second electrical response indicating that they're consciously figuring out how to correct it.

Interestingly, the root of the word *failure* is "faller"—to "trip" or "fall." Thus, failing doesn't mean we've been defeated; it just means we've stumbled and taken a temporary spill. Similarly, the word "problem" derives from the Greek root "proballein"—"to throw forward"—suggesting that a problem is an opportunity to move ahead. You can take this positive approach to a problem or setback by rewording it in terms of a positive goal statement. (For example, "I'm flunking math" can be reworded as: "My goal is to get a grade of C or better on the next exam to pull my overall course grade into passing territory.") Another way to respond positively to a current setback is to think about previous setbacks from which you bounced back. Ask yourself what you did to bounce back from that setback and how you might use similar strategies or resources to deal with your current setback.

Remember that the root of the word *success* is "*successus*"—meaning "to follow or come after." This suggests that success can still be achieved after a fall—if we don't give up but get up and continue taking steps toward our goal. In the movies, a clipboard is used to signal the next "take" (shooting) if the previous take was unsuccess-

> "How smart you are will influence the extent to which you experience something as difficult (for example, how hard a math problem is), but it says nothing about how you will deal with difficulty when it happens. It says nothing about whether you will be persistent and determined or feel overwhelmed and helpless.
>
> —Heidi Grant Halvorson, social psychologist, and author of *Succeed: How We Can Reach Your Goals*

> "What happens is not as important as how you react to what happens.
>
> —Thaddeus Goals, *Lazy Man's Guide to Enlightenment*

> "The harder you fall, the higher you bounce.
>
> —*Chinese proverb*

ful. You can use this as a metaphor to remind yourself that if I make early mistakes in college, it's my "first take"; I can learn from it, improve my performance on the next take, and achieve success on my final take.

Try to view any poor academic performances or other setbacks (particularly those occurring early in their college experience) not as failures but as opportunities for learning and growth; and when you overcome setbacks, be sure to recognize and reinforce your resilient behavior with self-*affirmations*, such as: "I demonstrated a lot of grit when I overcame . . ." and "I showed a lot of perseverance by sticking with . . ."

Reflection 3.8

What is the most significant setback or obstacle you've encountered in college thus far?

How did you overcome it? (What actions did you take to get past it or prevent it from holding you back?)

What did you learn from this experience that you might use again to help you handle future obstacles or challenges?

Internet-Based Resources

For additional information on goal setting and motivation, consult the following websites:

Goal Setting
https://itsallyouboo.com/examples-of-smart-goals-for-college-students/

Self-Motivational Strategies
https://positivepsychologyprogram.com/self-motivation/

Self-Efficacy:
https://positivepsychologyprogram.com/3-ways-build-self-efficacy/

Grit and Resilience
https://learningconnection.stanford.edu/resilience-project

Growth Mindset
https://www.mindsetworks.com/

Chapter 3 Exercises

3.1 Quote Reflections

Review the sidebar quotes contained in this chapter and select two that were especially meaningful or inspirational to you.

For each quote, provide an explanation of why you chose it.

3.2 Strategy Reflections

Review the strategies for *maintaining motivation and progress toward your goals* on pp. 58-60. Select three strategies you think are most important and intend to put into practice right now.

3.3 Clarifying My Goals

Take a moment to answer the following questions honestly.

- What are my highest priorities?
- What competing needs and priorities do I need to keep in check?
- How will I maintain balance across different aspects of my life?
- What am I willing or able to give up to achieve success?
- How will I maintain motivation on a day-to-day basis?
- Who can I collaborate with to reach my goals?

3.4 Reducing the Gap between Your Ideal Future and Current Reality

Think of an aspect of your life where there's a significant gap between what you would like it to be (the ideal) and what it is (the reality).

Create a goal statement for reducing this gap that includes:

- The specific *actions* to be taken.
- *When* the actions will be taken.
- Anticipated *obstacles* or *roadblocks*.
- *Resources* that could be used to overcome anticipated obstacles or roadblocks.
- How you will *measure your progress*.
- How you will know when you *reached or achieved* your goal.

3.5 Converting Setbacks into Comebacks

In *Hamlet*, Shakespeare wrote: "There is nothing good or bad, but thinking makes it so." His point was that experiences have the potential to be positive or negative, depending on how people interpret them and react to them. Listed below is a list of negative reaction statements that people often make in response to personal setbacks. For each of these self-defeating statements, reword or rephrase it to make a more positive, self-motivating statement. (For examples, see the section on resilience, pp. 65-66.)

a) "I'm just not good at this."
b) "There's nothing I can do about it."
c) "Nothing is going to change."
d) "This always happens to me."
e) "Everybody is going to think I'm a loser."

3.6 Self–Assessment of Hope

Studies of people who have changed their lives in positive and productive ways indicate they exhibit "high hope" behaviors that enable them to find the will and the way to reach their personal goals. A sample of hopeful behaviors is listed below. Assess yourself on these behaviors, using the following scale:

1 = Never

2 = Rarely

3 = Frequently

4 = Almost Always

Behavior Exhibited by People Possessing High Levels of Hope

_____ When I think of goals, I think of challenges, rather than setbacks and failures.

_____ I seek out stories about how other people have succeeded to inspire me and give me new ideas on how to be successful.

_____ I find role models I can emulate and who can advise, guide, or mentor me.

_____ I tell my friends about my goals and seek their support to help me reach my goals.

_____ I use positive self-talk to help me succeed.

_____ I think that mistakes I make along the way to my goals are usually the result of using a wrong strategy or making a poor decision, rather than lack of talent or ability on my part.

_____ When I struggle, I remember past successes and things I did that worked.

_____ I reward myself when reaching smaller, short-term goals I accomplish along the way to larger, long-term goals.

Self-Assessment Reflections

For any item you rated "1" or "2," explain:

a) *Why* you "rarely" or "never" engage in the practice.

b) *If* you intend to engage in the practice more frequently in the future.

c) *How likely* is it that you will engage in the practice more frequently in the future.

d) *When* you plan to begin engaging in the practice.

Adapted from: Snyder, C. R. 1995. Conceptualizing, measuring, and nurturing hope. *Journal of Counseling and Development,* 73(January/February), 355–360.

CHAPTER 4

Time Management

PRIORITIZING TASKS, PREVENTING PROCRASTINATION, AND PROMOTING PRODUCTIVITY

Chapter Purpose & Preview

Setting goals is an important first step toward achieving success, but managing time and completing the tasks needed to reach those goals is a critical second step. Time is a valuable personal resource—when we gain greater control of it, we gain greater control of our lives. This chapter supplies a comprehensive set of strategies for managing time, establishing priorities, combating procrastination, and completing tasks.

Learning Goal

Develop an effective set of strategies for setting priorities, planning time, combating procrastination, and completing tasks in a timely and effective manner.

Ignite Your Thinking

 Reflection 4.1

Complete the following sentence with the first thought that comes to your mind:

For me, time is . . .

The Relationship between Goal Setting, Managing Time, and Managing Tasks

To have a realistic chance of achieving our goals, we need a plan for spending our time in a way that aligns with our goals and enables us to progress toward them. Thus, setting goals, managing time and completing tasks are interrelated skills. They involve asking and answering the following questions: How should my big goals be broken down into smaller, more manageable steps? What specific tasks need to be completed at each of these steps? How do I ensure that I have enough time to complete all the tasks associated with each step?

Reaching goals involves step-by-step accomplishments made on a day-by-day basis. Each day, whether we plan to or not, we make decisions about how our time will be spent. To reach our goals, we need to remain mindful of whether the things we're spending time on are moving us in the direction of our goals. This practice of ongoing (daily) assessment of how our time is being spent is a simple yet important form of self-reflection. Research on highly effective people reveals that they plan

> "Ultimately, a student (and all of us) should craft a 'dream' but the dream must be broken down into bite-size pieces.
> —*Brad Johnson & Charles Ridley,* The Elements of Mentoring

their time and tasks and reflect regularly on their daily progress to be sure they're on track and making steady progress toward their goals. For instance, in a study of 150 highly creative and productive people in the arts and sciences, it was found that one thing these innovative artists and scientists had in common was daily rituals—they developed day-by-day work routines and habits.

AUTHOR'S EXPERIENCE

I started the process of earning my doctorate a little later in life than other graduate students. I was a married father with a preschool daughter (Sara). Since my wife left for work early in the morning, it was always my duty to get up and get Sara's day going in the right direction. In addition, I had to do the same for myself. Three days of my week were spent on campus, either in class or in the library. (We didn't have quick access to research on home computers back then as you do now.) The other two days of the workweek and the weekend were spent on household chores, family time, and studying.

I knew that to have any chance of finishing my Ph.D. in a reasonable amount of time, I had to adopt an effective schedule for managing my time. Each day of the week, I held to a strict routine. I got up in the morning, ate breakfast while reading the paper, got Sara ready for school and got her to school. Once I returned home, I put a load of laundry in the washer, studied, wrote, and spent time concentrating on what I needed to do to be successful from 8:30 a.m. to 12:00 p.m. every day. At lunch, I had a pastrami and cheese sandwich and a soft drink while rewarding myself by watching *Perry Mason* reruns until 1:00 p.m. I then continued to study until it was time to pick up Sara from school. Each night I spent some time with my wife and daughter and then prepared for the next day. I lived a life that had a preset schedule. By following that schedule, I was able to successfully complete my doctorate in a reasonable amount of time while giving my family the time they needed. (By the way, I still watch *Perry Mason* reruns.)

—*Aaron Thompson*

The Importance of Time Management for College Students

Research indicates that managing time is a significant challenge for college students. National surveys reveal that almost 50% of first-year college students report difficulty managing their time effectively. Time management is particularly challenging for students transitioning directly from the lockstep schedule of high school to the less tightly controlled schedule of college—where they spend less "seat time" in class per week, leaving them with much more "free time" to manage outside of class.

Simply stated, students who have difficulty managing their time in college have difficulty succeeding in college. Studies show that first-year students who manage their time well earn higher grades. In a national study of college sophomores who were interviewed about their first-year experience, one key difference was found between students who had an outstanding first year (both academically and personally) and those who struggled during their first year: The successful students frequently brought up the topic of time management during the interviews. They said they had to think carefully about how to spend time and intentionally budgeted their time. In contrast, sophomores who had had trouble during their first year of college hardly talked about the topic of time at all during their interviews, even when they were specifically asked about it.

People of all stages of life report that managing time is a critical aspect of their life and setting priorities and balancing work with other responsibilities (e.g., work and family) is often a stressful juggling act. In fact, national surveys of employers re-

> "The major difference [between high school and college] is time. You have so much free time on your hands that you don't know what to do with most of your time."
>
> —First-year college student, quoted in Erickson & Strommer, *Teaching College Freshmen*

veal that the ability to manage time and work productively is one of the top-ranked professional skills they seek in college graduates. These findings suggest that time management is more than just a college-success skill; it's also a life-management and career-success skill. When people improve their ability to manage time, other aspects of their life also improve, including their level of stress. Studies show that people who have good time-management skills report higher levels of life satisfaction and personal happiness.

"Time = Life. Therefore waste your time and waste your life, or master your time and master your life.

—Alan Lakein, international expert on time management and author of the best-selling book *How to Get Control of Your Time and Your Life*

Reflection 4.2

What do you think will be the biggest time-management challenge you will face in college?

You can be more successful in college (and life) by remaining mindful of the importance of how you're spending your time and by consistently employing effective time- and task-management strategies, such as those discussed in this chapter. These strategies may seem obvious and simple, but it's probably because they look so simple, they're often simply overlooked.

Strategies for Managing Time and Tasks

Effective time- and task-management involves three key steps:

1. **Analysis**—breaking down time to see *where* it's going
2. **Itemization**—listing *what* tasks need to be done and *when* they need to get done
3. **Prioritization**—ordering tasks in terms of their importance or urgency and tackling them in that order.

The following strategies can be used to execute these three steps.

Analysis: breaking down time into smaller units to gain greater awareness of how it's being spent. How often have you heard someone say, "Where did all the time go?" or "I just can't seem to find the time!" One way to determine where time goes and discover more time for getting things done is by doing a *time analysis*— a detailed examination of how much total time we have and what we're spending it on, including patches of wasted time when little gets done or nothing gets accomplished. A time analysis only needs to be done for a week or two to give us a pretty good idea of where our time is going and help us find ways to use our time more productively.

"Doesn't thou love life? Then do not squander time, for that is the stuff life is made of.

—Benjamin Franklin, 18th-century inventor, newspaper writer, and cosigner of the Declaration of Independence

> *What we spend our time on is often a true test of who we are and what we value. Taking time to reflect on how we're spending our time is more than a clerical activity; it's a tool for promoting self-awareness and gaining deeper insight into our priorities and values.*

Itemization: listing *what* tasks are to be done and *when* they are to get done. Just as we make lists to remember items to buy at a grocery store or people to invite to a party, we can make lists of tasks to complete. One characteristic of highly successful people is that they are list makers; they create daily lists for things they want to accomplish each day.

> *Whenever you find yourself saying, "I gotta do this" or "I need to do this," get it on a to-do list and just do it!*

 Reflection 4.3

Do you make daily to-do lists of things you need to get done? If not, why?

The following time-planning and task-management tools can be used to help manage your time and tasks.

- **Small, portable planner.** This can be used to list all course assignments and exams, along with their due dates. (It can also be used in sync with the same calendar programs available on your desktop or laptop.) Pulling together all work tasks required in each of your courses and getting them in the same place makes it much easier to keep track of what needs to be done and when it needs to get done.

- **Large, stable calendar.** In the calendar's date boxes, record major assignments that need to be completed throughout the term. Post the calendar in a place where you can't help but see it every day (e.g., bedroom or refrigerator door). By repeatedly seeing the things you must do, you're less likely to overlook them, forget about them, or subconsciously repress them because you'd rather not do them.

- **Smartphone.** This device can be used for purposes other than checking social networking sites and sending or receiving text messages. It can be used as a calendar tool to record due dates and set up alert functions to remind you of deadlines. Many smartphones also allow you to set up task or "to-do" lists and set priorities for each item entered. A variety of apps are also available for planning tasks and tracking the amount of time you spend on them (for example, see: http://www.rememberthemilk.com).

Take advantage of these cutting-edge, high-tech tools, but at the same time, remember that planners don't plan time, people do. Ultimately, the effectiveness of any time-management strategy depends on making a strong personal commitment to our goals and to completing the tasks required to reach our goals.

AUTHOR'S EXPERIENCE

When I entered college in the mid-1970s, I was a first-generation student from an extremely impoverished background. Not only did I have to work to support my education, I also needed to assist my family financially. I stocked grocery store shelves at night during the week and waited tables at a local country club on the weekends. Managing my time, school, work, and life required a lot of self-discipline. However, I always understood that my goal was to graduate from college and all of my other commitments supported that goal. One of my greatest achievements in life was to keep my mind focused on the ultimate goal of earning a college degree. That achievement has paid off for me many times over the course of my life.

—Aaron Thompson

Time management is rooted in goal commitment. When the roots of goal commitment are strong, they provide fertile soil for time-management skills to grow into productive lifelong habits.

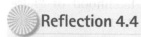 **Reflection 4.4**

a) Do you use a paper calendar or an electronic calendar tool on your cell phone?

b) If you don't use either of these tools, why not?

c) How do you think most students would answer the above two questions?

Prioritization: ordering tasks in terms of their importance and tackling them in that order. After itemizing tasks we need to get done, the next step is *prioritizing* them—determining the *order or sequence* in which they will get done. Prioritizing is basically a process of ranking tasks in terms of their importance and tackling high-priority tasks first. Here are two key criteria (standards of judgment) you can use to determine high-priority tasks:

- **Urgency.** Unfinished tasks that are close to their deadline or due date should receive high priority. Starting an assignment that's due next week takes precedence over starting an assignment that's due next month (even if the latter assignment may be more interesting or stimulating).

- **Gravity.** Tasks that carry greater weight (count more) should receive higher priority. If an assignment worth 100 points and an assignment worth 10 points are due at the same time, the 100-point task should receive higher priority. Simply stated, tasks that matter more should receive higher priority. Similar to investing money, time should be invested on tasks that yield the greatest dividends.

A simple and effective strategy for prioritizing tasks is to divide them into "A," "B," and "C" lists. The "A" list is for *essential* (non-negotiable) tasks that *must* be done now. List "B" is for *important* tasks that *should* be done soon. List "C" is for *optional* tasks that *could* be done if there's time remaining after the more important tasks on lists A and B have been completed. Organizing tasks into these three lists can help us make rational decisions about how to divide our labor and tackle our tasks. We shouldn't be wasting time on less important things and convince ourselves that we're "getting stuff done"—when, in reality, all we're doing is "keeping busy" and distracting ourselves (and subtracting time) from the more important things we should be doing.

Developing a Time–Management Plan

Don't buy into the myth that planning time is wasting time that could be spent getting started and getting things done. Like successful chess players, successful time managers plan and anticipate their next moves.

You've probably heard of the old proverb: "A stitch in time saves nine." Planning time represents a "stitch" (one unit of time) that saves "nine" (additional units of time). Actually, time-management experts estimate that taking time to plan our work reduces our total work time by a factor of three; in other words, for every one unit of time we spend planning, we save ourselves three times as much work time.

"First things first.
—*An old proverb*

"Things that matter most must never be at the mercy of things that matter least.
—*Johann Wolfgang von Goethe, German poet, dramatist, and author of the epic* Faust

"When I have lots of homework to do, I suddenly go through this urge to clean up and organize the house. I'm thinking, 'I'm not wasting my time. I'm cleaning up the house and that's something I have to do.' But all I'm really doing is avoiding schoolwork.
—*College sophomore*

"If you fail to plan, you plan to fail.
—*Benjamin Franklin*

Thus, 5 minutes of planning time saves us about 15 minutes of total work time, and 10 minutes of planning time saves us 30 minutes of work time.

Taking time to plan our work saves work time in the long run because it gives us a map of where we're going, reducing the risk of our veering off track or getting sidetracked. Developing a plan of attack also reduces the likelihood of "false starts"—starting our work and discovering later that we didn't start off on the right track, forcing us to backtrack and start all over again.

Key Elements of an Effective Time-Management Plan

Once we let go of the belief that taking time to plan is a waste of time and realize that it will save us time in the long run, we can take some time to develop a time-management plan. Listed below are components of a well-designed plan for managing time and tasks.

An effective time-management plan transforms goal-setting into action-taking. The first step is to plan the work; second step is to work the plan. Studies show that setting goals and getting motivated are important, but completing the tasks needed to achieve those goals requires more than motivation; it requires an action plan.

You can transform a plan on paper (or on a computer screen) into an action plan by: (a) previewing what you intend to do, (b) reviewing whether you actually did what you intended to do, and (c) closing any gaps between your intentions and actions. This process includes having a *daily to-do list* at the start of the day, carrying it with you throughout the day, and checking off (not putting off) items you intend to accomplish during the day. At the end of the day, review the list and determine what you did and didn't get done. Things that didn't get done become high-priority tasks for the next day's to-do list.

If you frequently find lots of unchecked (uncompleted) items on your to-do list at the end of the day, this probably means you're spreading yourself too thin and trying to accomplish too much too soon. You may need to be more conservative about what you can get done in a single day and reduce the number of items on your daily to-do list.

Having difficulty completing all tasks on our daily to-do lists may also mean that we need to adjust our overall time-management plan by substituting work time for time spent on other activities (e.g., Facebook, text messaging, or phone calls). If we consistently fail to complete our daily tasks, we may have to ask ourselves if we're truly committed to investing the time and effort needed to reach our goals.

An effective time-management plan reserves time for the unexpected. We should plan for the best, but also prepare for the worst. A good plan includes a buffer zone or safety net of extra (unscheduled) time to accommodate unforeseen developments and unexpected emergencies. Just as we should have extra funds in our savings account to accommodate unexpected expenses (e.g., car repairs or medical care), we should reserve extra time in our schedule to accommodate tasks that end up taking more time than we budgeted for, and for tasks that may unexpectedly crop up (e.g., a family emergency).

An effective time-management plan should include scheduling time for both work and play. A time-management plan should not turn us into robotic workaholics. It shouldn't be just a dry and daunting list of work tasks we must do; it should also include things that we want to do, creating a balanced blend of work

> "
> Murphy's Laws:
> 1. Nothing is as simple as it looks.
> 2. Everything takes longer than it should.
> 3. If anything can go wrong, it will.
>
> —Murphy's Laws (named after Captain Edward Murphy, a naval engineer)

tasks and fun activities that allow us to relax, recreate, refuel, and recharge. This balance may be created by following a daily "8- 8-8 rule": 8 hours for sleep, 8 hours for school work, and 8 hours for other activities. We are more likely to faithfully execute a time-management plan that includes play time along with work time, and if we schedule play time as a reward for putting in our work time.

> If a time-management plan includes things we <u>like</u> to do, we're more likely to do the things we <u>have</u> to do.

Reflection 4.5

What relaxing and recreational activities do you engage in to maintain work-play balance in your life? Do you develop an intentional plan for engaging in these activities on a regular basis? (If not, why?)

An effective time-management plan should have some flexibility. The plan shouldn't be so rigid that it enslaves you; it should be flexible enough to allow you the freedom to modify it if necessary. Just as work commitments and family responsibilities can pop up unexpectedly, so, too, can fun activities. A good time-management plan should allow you some freedom and spontaneity to take advantage of enjoyable opportunities that may emerge unexpectedly. You should be able to *bend* your plan, as long as you don't *break* it. If you substitute play time for work time, the work time needs to be rescheduled for another time. In other words, you shouldn't steal work time from your plan, but you can borrow it and pay it back later.

Making Productive Use of "Free Time" Outside the Classroom

Compared with high school, college students are expected to put in much more independent work outside of class. Thus, using out-of-class time strategically and productively is critical to college success. Listed below are strategies for working on your own outside the classroom to prepare (in advance) for exams and assignments. Building time for each of these activities into your time-management plan will enable you to make more productive use of your time outside the classroom, reduce your level of stress, and strengthen your overall academic performance.

• **Review lecture notes** from the last class before the next class. After taking notes in class students often don't look at those notes again until they study them just before test time. Don't fall into this habit; instead, review your notes regularly between class sessions, rewrite any notes that may have been sloppily written the first time, and reorganize your notes to get different pieces of information relating to the same point in the same place. If you find any information gaps or confusing points in your notes, seek out the course instructor or a trusted classmate to clear them up before the next class session. If you take some time to review and refine your course notes between class sessions, you can build mental bridges between successive lectures and connect information to be learned in the upcoming class with information you learned in the previous class.

- Complete reading assignments pertaining to an upcoming lecture topic *before* that topic is discussed in class. This will make lectures easier to understand and enable you to participate more effectively in class by asking meaningful questions and making well-informed contributions to class discussions.
- Review and take notes on information highlighted in assigned readings. Students often do not review reading material they have highlighted until they're about to be tested on it. Avoid this habit by reviewing and taking notes on your reading highlights in advance of exams. This will reduce the need to engage in last-minute cramming and give you ample time before exams to clear up confusing information found in the reading with a fellow classmate or the course instructor.
- Integrate class notes and reading notes relating to the same point or concept. Connect information in your lecture notes with information in your reading notes that pertain to the same idea and get them in the same place (e.g., on the same index card).
- Use a "part-to-whole" study method. Study in advance of (not just the night before) exams by breaking the material you need to know into small parts (pieces) and study these parts in short, separate study sessions. This strategy will enable you to avoid last-minute cramming and enable them to use your last study session right before the exam to review the "whole"—all the parts you previously studied. (For more details about the part-to-whole study method, see Chapter 5, pp. 107-108.)
- Work on large, long-term assignments due at the end of the term by breaking them into smaller short-term tasks and complete them in successive stages throughout the term. For instance, if you have a large term paper to turn in by the last week of class, divide your work on it into the following smaller tasks and complete each of these tasks in separate installments.
  1. Search for and decide on a topic.
  2. Locate sources of information on the topic.
  3. Organize information obtained from your sources into categories.
  4. Develop an outline of your paper's major points, including the order or sequence in which they'll be covered.
  5. Construct a first draft of the paper.
  6. Review and refine the first draft (and, if necessary, write additional drafts).
  7. Complete a final draft.
  8. Proofread the final draft for spelling and grammatical errors before turning it in.

Reflection 4.6

Are you currently making productive use of your time between classes? If not, what could (or should) you do instead of what you're currently doing?

> Take portable *schoolwork with you during the day—work that can be carried with you and worked on anywhere at any time. This will enable you to take "dead time"—time spent being bored or doing nothing (such as waiting for appointments or transportation)—and transform it into "live" (productive) time.*

Combating Procrastination

A major enemy of effective time management is procrastination. Research indicates that 80% to 95% of college students procrastinate and almost 50% report they procrastinate consistently. Procrastination is such a serious issue that some college campuses have opened "procrastination centers" especially for students struggling with this problem.

Instead of abiding by the proverb, "Why put off till tomorrow what can be done today?" the procrastinator's philosophy is just the opposite: "Why do today what can be put off till tomorrow?" Adopting this philosophy leads to a perpetual pattern of postponing what needs to be done until the last possible moment, forcing the procrastinator to rush frantically to finish work just before the deadline, and then turning in work that is inferior or incomplete (or turning in nothing at all).

"Many people take no care of their money 'til they come nearly to the end of it, and others do just the same with their time
—Johann Wolfgang von Goethe, German poet, dramatist, and author of the epic Faust

©Kendall Hunt Publishing Company

List of Things To Do Today
1. Write Paper
2. Study for Math Test
3. Prepare Speech

List of Things Due Today
1. Turn in Paper
2. Take Math Test
3. Deliver Speech

Next time I'll start sooner!

A procrastinator's intention to work in advance often ends up with this scenario.

Myths That Promote Procrastination

To have any hope of putting a stop to procrastination, students need to let go of two popular myths (misconceptions) about time and performance. If you believe in either of the following myths, challenge yourself to think otherwise.

Myth 1. "I work better under pressure" (on the day or night before something is due). Procrastinators often confuse desperation with motivation. Their rationale for thinking that they work *better* under pressure really isn't a rationale at all; instead, it's a rationalization to justify the fact that they *only* work under pressure—when they're forced to, because they've run out of time and are under the gun of a looming deadline.

It's certainly true that when we're under the pressure of an immediate deadline, we're more likely to *start* working and work *faster*, but that doesn't mean we're working *smarter*, more *effectively*, or producing work of better *quality*. Because procrastinators repeatedly play "beat the clock," they focus more on beating the buzzer than delivering their best shot. The typical result is delivering a work product of poorer quality than what could have been produced if they started sooner.

Myth 2. "Studying in advance is a waste of time because I'll forget it all by test time." Procrastinators use this belief to justify putting off all studying until the night before an exam. As will be discussed in chapter 5, studying that's distributed (spread out) over time is more effective than massed (crammed) studying. Furthermore, last-minute studying can lead to pulling "late-nighters" or "all-nighters," depriving the brain of dream sleep (a.k.a. REM sleep) that's needed to retain information and manage stress.

Working under time pressure also increases performance pressure because it leaves procrastinators with little time to seek help with their work and no time to accommodate last-minute emergencies or random catastrophes.

Strategies for Preventing and Overcoming Procrastination

Listed below are strategies for reducing the tendency to procrastinate and preventing it from happening in the first place.

Consistently use effective time-management strategies. It's been found that procrastinators are less likely to procrastinate when they convert their intentions or vows ("I swear I'm going to start tomorrow") into concrete action plans. Studies show that if people consistently use effective time-management plans and practices (such as those discussed in this chapter) and apply them to tasks that they procrastinate on, their procrastination habit begins to fade and is replaced by more productive work habits.

Organization matters. Research indicates that disorganization contributes to procrastination. If our workspaces and work materials are well-organized and ready to go, we're more likely to get going and start working. Having the right materials in the right place at the right time not only makes it easier for us to begin work, it also helps us maintain momentum by reducing the need to stop, find stuff that's needed to continue working, and then have to restart the work process all over again. For procrastinators, anything that delays the start of their work, or interrupts their work once it's begun, can supply them with just enough time (and the right excuse) to postpone doing the work.

> *The less time and effort it takes to start working and continue working, the more likely it is that the work will be started, continued, and completed.*

A simple and effective way to organize college work materials is to develop a personal file system, in which materials from separate courses are filed (stored) in separate notebooks or folders—paper or electronic. This keeps all materials related to the same course in the same place and allows for immediate access to these materials when they're needed. A file system not only helps with organization, it also reduces the risk of procrastination by reducing the time (and effort) it takes to get started. Also, by having everything "in place," it reduces stress triggered by the unsettling feeling of having things "all over the place."

Location matters. Effective time and task management include effective management of one's work environment. *Where* work takes place can influence *whether* work is begun and gets done. Working in an environment that minimizes distractions and maximizes concentration reduces the risk of procrastination. Intentionally arrange your work environment to minimize social distractions (e.g., friends nearby who are not working) and social-media distractions (e.g., texting or tweeting). Better yet, remove everything from your work site that's not related to the work you're doing.

Procrastination can also be reduced by working in an environment that includes positive social-support networks; for example, working with a group of motivated students who make your work more attractive, less distractive, and more productive.

AUTHOR'S EXPERIENCE

Although my college friends and I had different majors, we found that if we all studied together we could help each other stay focused and avoid procrastination. Each night about five of us would meet up in one of our residence hall rooms with our coffee, snacks, and textbooks. We'd each find a spot somewhere in that room–either at a desk or on the floor–and hunker down to study for exams or to get our reading assignments done. These study sessions were both enjoyable and productive; we were able to keep up with the demands of our courses while also spending time together.

However, despite our best efforts, some of us would occasionally get distracted, start cracking jokes, or just lose steam. Since we were so committed to supporting each other, whenever this happened, we'd rein each other in and refocus. These evening sessions with my friends helped me stick to a regular study schedule, do well in my courses, and strengthened the friendships I made in college.

—Michele Campagna

Make the start of work as inviting or appealing as possible. For many procrastinators, initiating work—getting off the starting blocks—is their stumbling block. They experience what's known as "start-up stress"—when they're about to start working, they start having negative thoughts about the work they're about to do—expecting it to be difficult, stressful, or boring.

Start-up stress can be reduced by sequencing work tasks in a way that allows you to work first on tasks you find more interesting or are more likely to do successfully. Beginning with these tasks can give you a "jump-start," enabling you to overcome inertia and generate momentum. Once this initial momentum is created, you can ride it and use it as motivational energy to attack the less appealing work that comes later in your work sequence—which often turns out to be less onerous or anxiety-provoking than you thought it would be. Many times, the anticipation of a daunting task is worse than the task itself. In one major study of college students who didn't start a project until just before its due date, it was found that that they experienced anxiety and guilt while they were procrastinating, but once they began working, these negative emotions subsided and were replaced by more positive feelings of progress and accomplishment. Another study found that the areas of the brain where pain is experienced are active before procrastinating students began doing their work but became deactivated once they started working.

If you have trouble beginning your work due to start-up stress, try starting your work in an environment that you find pleasant and relaxing while doing something you find pleasant and relaxing (e.g., working in your favorite coffee shop while sipping your favorite beverage).

> "The secret to getting ahead is getting started.
> *—Mark Twain (Samuel Clemens), acclaimed American humorist and author*

> "Did you ever dread doing something, and then it turned out to take only about 20 minutes to do?
> *—Conversation between two college students overheard in a coffee shop*

If you don't have trouble starting your work but lose motivation before completing it, schedule easier and more interesting work tasks in the middle or toward the end of your planned work time. Some procrastinators have difficulty starting work; others have trouble continuing and finishing the work they've started. As previously mentioned, if you have trouble beginning your work, it might be best for you to start with tasks that you find easier or more interesting. On the other hand, if your procrastination involves stopping your work before completing it, then it might be better to attack easier and more interesting tasks at a later point in your work sequence—at a time when your interest and energy tends to fade. Knowing that there are more stimulating and manageable tasks ahead of you can also provide you with an incentive for completing the less enjoyable or more difficult tasks first.

> "I'm very good at starting things but often have trouble keeping a sustained effort."
> —First-year college student

If you are close to completing a task, "go for the kill"—finish it then and there—rather than stopping and going back to it later. As the old saying goes: "There's no time like the present." By continuing to work on a task that you already started, you capitalize on the momentum you've already generated. In contrast, postponing work on a task that's near completion and going back to it again later means that you have to overcome start-up inertia and regenerate momentum all over again.

There's another advantage of finishing a task that's already been started—it provides a sense of *closure*—a feeling of personal accomplishment and self-satisfaction that comes with knowing you've "closed the deal." Seeing a task checked off as completed supplies you with a visible sign of achievement that can motivate you to keep going and tackle the next task.

(Complete the AchieveWORKS Learning and Productivity Self-Assessment. Take a close look at these results and the results of your AchieveWORKSPersonality Self-Assessment. What do these two reports say about your inclination to finish tasks and activities? What suggestions offered by these two self-assessments could help you stay on task and increase productivity?)

Divide large work tasks into smaller, bite-sized pieces. Work becomes less overwhelming and less stressful when it's handled in small chunks or segments. Procrastinating about large work tasks can be reduced by using a "divide and conquer" strategy—divide the large task into smaller, more manageable subtasks, set deadlines for these smaller tasks just like you would the final product, and attack the small tasks one at a time. By breaking down the total task into smaller pieces, you can take quick jabs at the tall task, poke holes in it, and whittle down its size with each successive punch. This divide-and-conquer approach reduces the pressure of having to deliver one, big knockout punch right before the final bell (deadline or due date). Don't underestimate the power of short work sessions; they can be more productive than marathon sessions because it's easier to maintain motivation, concentration, and energy for shorter periods of time.

AUTHOR'S EXPERIENCE

The two biggest projects I've had to complete in my life were writing my doctoral thesis and this textbook. The strategy that enabled me to complete both of these large tasks was to set short-term deadlines for myself (e.g., complete 5-10 pages each week). I psyched myself into thinking that these little, self-imposed due dates were really drop-dead deadlines that I had to meet. This strategy allowed me to divide a monstrous chore into a series of smaller, more manageable mini-tasks. It was like taking a huge, hard-to-digest meal and breaking it into small, bite-sized pieces that I could easily ingest and gradually digest over time.

—Joe Cuseo

 **Reflection 4.7**

Would you say you're a procrastinator?

If yes, do you think you procrastinate to such a degree that it reduces the quality of your work or adds to your level of stress?

How do you think most students would answer the above two questions?

> "To eat an elephant, first cut it into small pieces.
> *—Author unknown*

Psychological Causes of Procrastination

In some cases, procrastination isn't the result of poor time-management habits but has deeper psychological roots. Procrastination can be used as a psychological strategy to protect one's self-image and self-esteem. Some procrastinators engage in a strategy called *self-handicapping*—they intentionally (or unconsciously) "handicap" themselves by limiting the amount of time they have to prepare for and complete tasks. So, if their performance turns out to be less than spectacular, they can always conclude (or rationalize) that it was because they were performing under a handicap—lack of time. For example, if self-handicapping procrastinators receive a low grade on a test, they can "save face" (self-esteem) by saying that they had the ability or intelligence to earn a high grade, but just didn't put in much time studying for the exam. Better yet, if they happen to get a good grade—despite the last-minute, last-ditch effort—it proves just how smart they were because they were able to earn a high grade without putting in much time at all! Thus, self-handicapping creates a fail-safe or win-win scenario that always protects the procrastinator's self-image.

> "Procrastinators would rather be seen as lacking in effort than lacking in ability.
> *—Joseph Ferrari, professor of psychology and procrastination researcher*

In addition to self-handicapping, there are other psychological factors that have been found to contribute to procrastination, such as the following:

- **Perfectionism.** The procrastinator has unrealistically high personal standards or expectations and believes that it's better to postpone work, or not do the work at all, than to risk doing it less than perfectly.
- **Fear of failure.** The procrastinator feels that it's worse to put in the time to do the work and fail or receive negative feedback, than to do the work at all.
- **Fear of success.** The procrastinator fears that doing well will show others that he can perform at a high level, which will create expectations from others that he maintain this high level of performance.
- **Indecisiveness.** The procrastinator has difficulty making decisions in general, including decisions about what to do first, when to do it, or whether to do it.

> "Striving for excellence motivates you; striving for perfection is demoralizing.
> *—Harriet Braiker, psychologist and bestselling author*

> "When you're given a positive label, you're afraid of losing it, and when you're hit with a negative label, you're afraid of deserving it.
> *—Carol Dweck, Professor of Psychology, Stanford University*

- **Thrill seeking.** The procrastinator loves the adrenaline rush associated with rushing to get things done just before a deadline.

If these psychological issues are the root of procrastination, they need to be uprooted and dealt with before the problem can be solved. This may require seeing a counseling psychologist (either on or off campus) who is professionally trained to deal with these issues.

Regardless of whether the cause is lack of time-management skills or deeper psychological factors, procrastination continues to be a problem for many students and one that can have significant impact on their ability to succeed in college. Be on the lookout for it, guard against it, and be willing to seek help if you're experiencing it.

Internet-Based Resources

For additional information on managing time and preventing procrastination, consult the following websites:

Time-Management Strategies:
http://www.studygs.net/timman.htm
https://pennstatelearning.psu.edu/time-management

Beating Procrastination:
https://www.mindtools.com/pages/article/newHTE_96.htm
https://success.oregonstate.edu/learning/stop-procrastinating

Chapter 4 Exercises

4.1 Quote Reflections

Review the sidebar quotes contained in this chapter and select two that you found to be especially meaningful or inspirational.

For each quote you selected, provide an explanation why you chose it.

4.2 Strategy Reflections

Review the strategies recommended for *preventing and overcoming procrastination* on pp. 78-80. Select three strategies that you think are most important and intend to put into practice.

4.3 Reality Bite

Procrastination: The Vicious Cycle

Delayla has a major paper due at the end of the term. It's now past midterm and she still hasn't started to work on it. She keeps telling herself, "I should have started sooner" and is now beginning to feel anxious and guilty. To relieve her anxiety and guilt, Delayla starts doing other tasks instead, such as cleaning her room and organizing files on her computer. These tasks keep her busy, take her mind off the term paper, and give her the feeling that she's getting something accomplished. Time continues to pass and the deadline for the paper is growing dangerously close. Delayla now finds herself in the stressful position of having lots of work still to do and very little time to do it.

Adapted from *Procrastination: Why You Do It, and What to Do About It* (Burka & Yuen)

Reflections:

1. What do you expect Delayla will do at this point? Why?
2. What grade do you think she will end up receiving on her paper?
3. Can you relate to this student's experience, or know students who have had this experience?
4. Other than simply starting sooner, what else could Delayla (and other procrastinators like her) have done to break this procrastination cycle?

4.4 Time Analysis Inventory

1. Go to the following website: http://tutorials.istudy.psu.edu/timemanagement/TimeEstimator.html
2. Complete the time management exercise at this site. The exercise asks you to estimate the hours per day or week that you engage in various activities (e.g., sleeping, employment, and commuting). When you enter the amount of time you devote to each activity, the website automatically computes the total number of remaining hours you have available in the week for schoolwork.
3. After completing your entries, answer the following questions (or provide your best estimate).
   a) How many hours per week do you have available for schoolwork?
   b) Do you have two hours available for schoolwork outside of class for each hour you spend in class? If you don't, what activities could be eliminated or reduced to create this 2:1 ratio?

4.5 Time Management Self-Awareness

Look at the results of your AchieveWORKSPersonality assessment report

Did the results provide you with helpful insights on how you organize your time and your approach to completing tasks? If yes, why? If no, why not?

4.6 Term at a Glance

Review the syllabus (course outline) for each course you're enrolled in this term, and complete the following information for each course:

Term _____ Year _____

Course	Professor	Exams	Projects & Papers	Other Assignments	Attendance Policy	Late & Makeup Assignment Policy

1. Is the overall workload what you expected? Are you surprised by the amount of work required in any particular course(s)?

2. At this point in the term, what do you see as your most challenging or demanding course(s)? Why?

3. Do you think you can handle the total workload required for the full set of courses you're enrolled in this term?

4. What adjustments or changes could you make to your personal schedule that would make it easier to accommodate your academic workload this term?

4.7 Developing a Weekly Time-Management Plan for Your First Term in College

Use the following *Week-at-a-Glance Grid* to map out your typical week looks like this term. Start by recording what you usually do on these days, including the times you're in class, at work, and when you relax or recreate. You can use abbreviations (e.g., CT for class time, HW for homework, J for job, and R&R for rest and relaxation). List the abbreviations you created at the bottom of the page so that you (and your instructor) can follow them.

If you're a *full-time* student, plan for 25 *hours* a week for homework (HW). (If you're a *part-time* student, find two *hours* you could devote to homework *for every hour* you're in class—for example, if you're in class nine hours per week, find 18 hours of homework time).

These homework hours could take place at any time during the week, including weekends. If you combine 25 hours per week of out-of-class school work with the amount of time you spend in class each week, you should end up with a 40-hour academic workweek—comparable to a full-time job—which is how college work should be viewed.

> "The amount of free time you have in college is much more than in high school. Always have a weekly study schedule to go by. Otherwise, time slips away and you will not be able to account for it.
>
> —Advice to new college students from a first-year student

Week-at-a-Glance Grid

	Sunday	Monday	Tuesday	Wednesday	Thursday	Friday	Saturday
7:00 a.m.							
8:00 a.m.							
9:00 a.m.							
10:00 a.m.							
11:00 a.m.							
12:00 p.m.							
1:00 p.m.							
2:00 p.m.							
3:00 p.m.							
4:00 p.m.							
5:00 p.m.							
6:00 p.m.							
7:00 p.m.							
8:00 p.m.							
9:00 p.m.							
10:00 p.m.							
11:00 p.m.							

Reflections

1. How likely are you to put this time-management plan into practice?
   Circle one: Definitely   Probably   Unlikely
2. What would *help* or *encourage* you to put this plan into practice?
3. What would *deter* or *discourage* you from putting this plan into practice?
4. How do you think other students would answer the above three questions?

7:00 a.m.

8:00 a.m.

9:00 a.m.

10:00 a.m.

11:00 a.m.

12:00 p.m.

1:00 p.m.

2:00 p.m.

3:00 p.m.

4:00 p.m.

5:00 p.m.

6:00 p.m.

7:00 p.m.

8:00 p.m.

9:00 p.m.

10:00 p.m.

11:00 p.m.

Reflections

1. How likely are you to put this time management plan into practice?

   Circle one: Definitely Probably Unlikely

2. What would help to move you to try this plan into practice?

3. What would delay or discourage you from putting this plan into practice?

4. How do you think other students would answer the above three questions?

CHAPTER 5

Deep Learning

STRATEGIC NOTE-TAKING, READING, AND STUDYING

The key academic tasks you're expected to perform in college include taking lecture notes, completing reading assignments, studying, and test taking. This chapter provides specific research- and brain-based strategies for tackling these tasks. Implementing these strategies will enable you to learn at a deeper level than simply memorizing information. You can apply these deep-learning strategies across all subjects and throughout life.

Acquire and apply a comprehensive set of strategies that will enable you to study smarter, learn more deeply, and retain what you learn longer.

 Reflection 5.1

What would you say is the key difference between learning and memorizing?

What is Deep Learning and Why is it Important?

Learning is the fundamental mission of all colleges and universities, and it's something that doesn't stop after graduation. It's a lifelong process that is important for personal and professional success but has become even more important in the 21st century. Currently the ongoing growth of information technology, coupled with a knowledge-based economy and increasing global interdependence, is creating a high demand for college graduates who have "learned how to learn" and who can apply their learning skills throughout life in different occupational roles and cultural contexts.

When college students learn deeply, they dive below the surface of shallow memorization to build mental bridges between what they are learning and what they already know. Deep learning doesn't take place if information is passively absorbed into the brain, as if it were a sponge. Instead, it involves actively building new ideas onto ideas that are already stored in the brain. When this happens, memorizing isolated facts and bits of information is transformed into a deeper learning process that builds conceptual knowledge—networks of connected ideas in the brain that involve actual physical (neurological) connections between brain cells. (See Figure **5.1**.)

> "When I have to do work, and I'm getting it. It's linking what I already know to what I didn't know.
>
> —*Student's description of a "good class"*

FIGURE 5.1: Network of Brain Cells

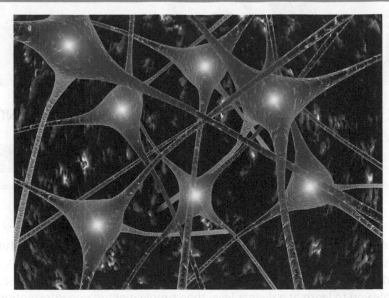

Deep learning involves making connections between what you're trying to learn and what you already know. When you learn something deeply, it's stored in the brain as a link in an interconnected network of brain cells.

©Jurgen Ziewe/Shutterstock.com

Studies suggest that most college students are not in the habit of engaging in deep learning. They show up for class most of the time, copy down some notes, highlight information in their textbooks, memorize what they think they'll be tested on, and regurgitate what they've memorized on exams. These practices may get students through high school, but different methods are needed to excel in college—methods that promote deep learning, long-term retention of what has been learned, and application of learning to life.

Stages in the Learning and Memory Process

Learning deeply and retaining what you've learned is a process that involves three key stages:

1. **Sensory input (perception).** Taking information into the brain
2. **Memory formation (storage).** Transforming that information into knowledge and storing it in the brain
3. **Memory recall (retrieval).** Bringing that knowledge back to mind when you need it.

These three stages are summarized visually in **Figure 5.2.** The stages are similar to the way information is processed by a computer: (1) information is first entered onto the screen (input), (2) then saved in a memory file (storage), and (3) later retrieved (recalled) when needed. This three-stage process can serve as a framework for using the two major routes through which you will acquire knowledge in college: lectures and readings.

FIGURE 5.2: **Key Stages in the Learning and Memory Process**

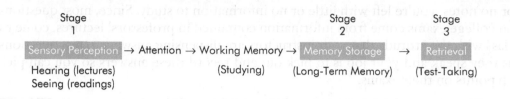

©Kendall Hunt Publishing Company

Effective Lecture-Listening and Note-Taking Strategies

The importance of listening skills for academic success was highlighted in a classic study of more than 400 students who were given a listening test at the start of their college experience. At the end of their first year in college, 49% of the students who scored low on the listening test were on academic probation, compared to only 4.4% of students who scored high on the listening test; furthermore, 68.5% of students who scored high on the listening test were eligible for the honors program, compared to only 4.17% of those students who had low listening test scores.

Reflection 5.2

Do you think writing notes in class helps or hinders your ability to pay attention to and understand lectures?

Why?

Studies show that information delivered during lectures is the number one source of test questions (and answers) on college exams. When lecture information is not recorded in students' notes and a question about it appears on a test, it has only a 5% chance of being recalled. Thus, as you would expect, students who take notes during lectures earn higher course grades than students who just listen to lectures, and students who take more complete lecture notes have higher overall grade-point averages.

Good college grades begin with good class notes.

Contrary to a popular belief that writing while listening interferes with listening, students report that taking notes in class increases their attention and concentration. Studies also show that when students write down information presented to them during lectures, they're more likely to remember that information when tested on it later. One study discovered that students with grade-point averages (GPAs) of 2.53 or higher recorded more information in their notes and retained a larger percentage of the most important information delivered in class than did students with GPAs of less than 2.53. These findings aren't surprising when you consider that taking notes involves *hearing* information, *writing* it, and then *seeing* it after it's been written. Thus, three different memory traces (tracks) for that information are recorded in the brain, which triples the likelihood it will be remembered.

In addition, when you take notes, you're left with a written record of lecture information that can be studied later to prepare for exams. In contrast, if you take few or no notes, you're left with little or no information to study. Since, most questions on college exams come from information contained in professors' lectures, come to class with the attitude that your instructors are dispensing answers to test questions as they speak and your job is to pick out and record these answers so you can pick up points on their exams.

> *Points your professors make in class that make it into your notes turn into points you earn on exams (and higher grades you earn in your courses).*

You can get the most out of class lectures by employing effective strategies at three key times: *before, during,* and *after* class.

Pre-Lecture Strategies: What to Do *Before* Class

Check your syllabus to see where you are in the course and how the upcoming class fits into the total course picture. By checking the course syllabus before each class session you're able to see how each part (class) relates to the whole (course). The brain's natural tendency is to look for patterns in the information it receives and integrate separate pieces of information into a meaningful whole. In **Figure 5.3**, notice how your brain naturally connects information to perceive a whole that is meaningful (a triangle).

FIGURE 5.3: Triangle Illusion

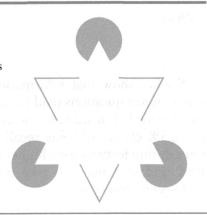

You perceive a white triangle in the middle of this figure. However, if you use three fingers to cover up the three corners of the white triangle that fall outside the other (green) triangle, the white triangle suddenly disappears. What your brain does is take these corners as starting points then fills in and connects the rest of the information on its own to create a complete or whole pattern (triangle) that is meaningful to you. Also, notice how you perceive the background (green) triangle as a whole triangle, even though parts of its three sides are missing. This triangle illusion illustrates how the human brain is naturally wired to make connections and seek patterns. You can learn more effectively and deeply by capitalizing on the brain's pattern-seeking, connection-making tendencies.

©Kendall Hunt Publishing Company

Before class, review your notes from the previous class session and from any reading assignments relating to the upcoming lecture topic. Research indicates that when students review information related to an upcoming lecture topic, they take more accurate and complete notes on that topic when it's discussed in class. Thus, one way to improve your ability to learn from lectures is to review your notes from the previous class session and read textbook information related to the lecture topic—*before* hearing the lecture. By reviewing previously acquired information, your prior knowledge is activated, which enables you to connect the upcoming lecture information with what you already know—a powerful way to promote deep learning.

Adopt a seating location that maximizes attention and minimizes distraction.
Many years of research show that students who sit in the front and center of class
get higher exam scores and earn higher course grades. This relationship has been
found even when students are assigned seats by their instructor, which proves that
it's not just due to the fact that more motivated and studious students tend to sit at
the front of the room. Instead, the better academic performance achieved by students sitting front and center stems from learning advantages they experience
when they sit in this location.

Front-and-center seating benefits academic performance by improving your
ability to see material written on the board or screen and your ability to hear what the
instructor is saying. It also means that you don't have to peer over or around the
heads of other students. This means you make more direct eye contact with the instructor, which increases your focus of attention, reduces your sense of anonymity,
and increases your level of involvement in class. In addition, sitting in the front of
class can reduce any anxiety you may have about speaking up in class because you will
not have a host of students turning around and looking at you when you speak.

> "I like to sit up front so I am not distracted by others and I don't have to look around people's heads to see the board.
>
> —*First-year college student*

© Kendall Hunt Publishing Company.

The evolution of student attention from the back to the front of class.

When you enter class, you have a choice about where you're going to sit. Choose wisely by selecting a location that will maximize your attentiveness to the instructor and your effectiveness as a note-taker.

The *bottom line:* When you walk into a classroom, get in the habit of heading
for a seat in the front and center of class. In your larger classes, it's especially important to get "up close and personal" with your instructors—not only to improve your
attention, note-taking, and class participation—but also to improve your instructors' ability to remember who you are and how you perform in class. This will work
to your advantage when it's time to ask instructors for letters of recommendation.

Sit by people who will enable (not disable) your ability to listen and learn.
Your ability to maintain attention in class and take good lecture notes depends not
only on *where* you are seated, but *who* is seated nearby you. Make an intentional attempt to sit near classmates who will not distract you and interfere with the quality
of your note-taking. Listening actively throughout a lecture is a demanding task
that requires undivided attention; your attention is less likely to be divided if you're
sitting near motivated students who are giving the lecture their undivided
attention.

Reflection 5.3

When you enter a classroom, where do you usually sit?

Why do you sit there? Is it a conscious choice or more like an automatic habit?

Do you think that the seat you usually occupy in class places you in the best possible position for listening and learning?

Adopt a seating posture that screams attention. Sitting upright and leaning forward is body language associated with alertness and attention. When these physical (postural) signs of alertness reach the brain, they stimulate mental alertness. Brain research shows that when humans are mentally alert and ready to learn, a greater amount of a brain chemical (C-kinase) is released at the connection point between brain cells, which increases the likelihood that neurological (learning) connections are formed between them.

If your body is in an alert and ready position, your mind picks up these physical cues and follows your body's lead. Similar to how baseball players get into a ready position before a pitch is delivered to prepare themselves to catch batted balls, students who get into a ready position in class put themselves in a better position to catch ideas delivered in class.

Another advantage to being attentive in class is that it sends a clear message to your instructors that you're a courteous and conscientious student. This can influence your instructor's perception and evaluation of your academic performance, and if at the end of the course you're on the border between a higher and lower grade, you're more likely to get the benefit of the doubt.

Listening and Note-Taking Strategies: What to Do *During* Class

Give lectures your undivided attention. As previously noted, research shows that in all subject areas, most test questions appearing on college exams come from the professor's lectures, and students who take better class notes get better course grades. Studies also show that the more time students spend surfing the web or using Facebook during lectures, the lower their scores on course exams. These results hold true for all students, regardless of how they scored on college admissions tests.

Like all human beings, all college professors are not created equal. Some are dynamic speakers who are easy to pay attention to; others are less dynamic and pose a greater challenge to your attention span. It's in classes taught by less-dynamic speakers that you will be more tempted to lose attention and stop taking notes. Resist this temptation. Instead, rise to the challenge, ramp up your attention, redouble your efforts to listen actively, and try even harder to take good notes. Don't let a less engaging or less entertaining lecturer lower your course grade. Stay self-engaged and finish the course with the self-satisfaction of earning a good grade.

Take your own notes in class. Don't rely on someone else to take notes for you. Taking notes in your own words focuses your attention and ensures the notes you take make sense to you. Taking your own notes in your own words makes them *meaningful to you*. Research shows that students who record and review their own notes on information presented to them earn higher scores on memory tests for that information than do students who review notes taken by others. Although it's a good idea to collaborate with classmates to compare notes for accuracy and to pick up information you may have missed, don't rely on someone else to do your note-taking for you.

Take notes in longhand rather than typing them on a laptop. Studies show that when students use a keyboard to type notes, they're more likely to mindlessly punch in the exact words used by the instructor instead of transforming the instructor's words into words that are meaningful to them. When tested for understanding and memory of key concepts presented in class, students who take notes in longhand tend to outperform those who type notes on a keyboard. This may be because the finger movements used for writing require greater attention and more varied, effortful movement than touch typing. These more effortful movements leave stronger motor (muscle) memory traces in the brain, which serve to deepen learning and strengthen memory.

Be alert to instructor cues about important information contained in lectures. Because the human attention span is limited, it's impossible to attend to and take notes on every single word a professor says. A listener's best alternative is to listen actively and *selectively* for information that matters most. Here are some strategies for detecting and recording the most important information delivered by professors during lectures:

- Pay attention to information your instructors put *in print*—on the board, on a slide, or in a handout. If an instructor has taken the time and energy to write it out or type it out, this is usually means that the information is important and you're likely to see it again—on an exam.
- Pay special attention to information presented at the very *beginning* and *end* of class. Instructors are most likely to provide valuable reminders, reviews, and previews at the very start and very end of class sessions.
- Look for *verbal and nonverbal cues* signalling that the instructor is delivering especially important information. Don't fall into the mindless habit routine of paying attention only to what the instructor is writing down on the board or has recorded on a PowerPoint slide and then mindlessly copying it down verbatim. It's been found that students record almost 90% of material written on the board or on PowerPoint slides, but less than 50% of important ideas that professors state aloud but don't write out.

Taking effective lecture notes involves more than just robotically recording what you see on the board or on a screen; it also involves actively listening to what the instructor is saying and selectively detecting key ideas to record in your notes. See **Box 5.1** for common clues to important information that your professors may be communicating orally to you, but not writing down for you.

Box 5.1

Clues for Detecting Important Information Delivered by Professors during Lectures

Verbal cues:

- Phrases that signal important information (e.g., "The point here is . . ." or "What's most significant about this is . . .").
- Information that's repeated or rephrased in a different way (e.g., "In other words, . . ." or "To put it another way . . .").
- Stated information that's followed by a question to check students' understanding (e.g., "Is that clear?" "Do you follow that?" "Does that make sense?" or "Are you with me?").

Vocal (tone of voice) cues:

- Information delivered in a louder tone or at a higher pitch—which may indicate excitement or emphasis.

- Information delivered at a slower rate or with longer pauses—which may be your instructor's way of giving you more time to write down these ideas because they're particularly important.

Nonverbal cues:

- Information delivered with:
  a) Facial expressiveness (e.g., raised or furrowed eyebrows);
  b) Body movement (e.g., gesticulation or animation);
  c) Eye contact (e.g., looking directly and intently at the faces of students to see if they're following or understanding what's being said).
- Moving toward the class (e.g., moving away from the podium or blackboard and closer to the students—as if to ensure they hear what's being said).
- Orienting their body directly toward the class (i.e., both shoulders squarely facing the class—as if to ensure that students see their face when they say it).

Keep taking notes during a lecture even if you don't immediately or fully understand what is being said. Your professors will often lecture on information that you may have little prior knowledge about, so it's unrealistic to expect that you'll understand everything being said the first time you hear it. When you're uncertain or confused about the material being presented, don't give up and stop taking notes. Having notes on that material will at least leave you with a record to review later—when you have more time to think about it and make sense of it. If the lecture material still doesn't make sense to you after you've taken time to review it, seek clarification from your instructor, a trusted classmate, or your textbook.

Take notes in organized form. When you keep separate ideas in separate paragraphs, you're left with a better organized and more understandable set of notes. If your instructor continues to make points relating to the same idea, keep taking notes on that idea in the same paragraph. When the instructor shifts to a new idea, skip a few lines and shift to a new paragraph.

Your instructors are likely to using certain phrases that signal a shift to a new or different idea (e.g., "Let's turn to . . ." or "In addition to . . ."). Use these phrases as cues to help you take notes in paragraph form. Be sure to leave extra space between paragraphs to give yourself room to later add information that you may have initially missed, or to take notes on your notes.

Consider using the *Cornell Note-Taking System.* This method of note-taking was first developed by a college professor at Cornell University. Frustrated by his students' poor test scores, he designed a system that students could use to take better notes in class and later use their notes to better prepare for exams. Because he taught at Cornell University, his method came to be called the Cornell Note-Taking System; it has become one of the most well known and most frequently recommended college note-taking method. Listed below are its key steps.

- On a single 8 ½ x 11 page of notepaper, draw a vertical line about 2 ½ inches from the left edge of the page and a horizontal line about 2 inches from the bottom edge of the page (as depicted in the scaled-down illustration below). This creates three separate spaces—labeled A, B, and C.
- Use area A (right side of the vertical line) to record notes during lectures.
- Use area B (bottom of page) to summarize the main points—which should be done as soon as possible after class.
- Use area C (left side of the page) to list questions about the material covered in class. Then use the lecture notes taken in areas A and B to answer the questions listed in area C.

After you have listed the questions and attempted to answer them from your notes, you can team up with a classmate to check whether the questions and answers are similar, or check with your professor to see if other questions should be added.

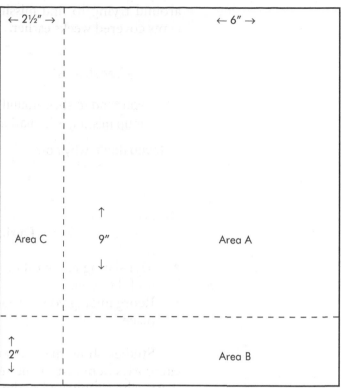

©Kendall Hunt Publishing Company

The Cornell method of note taking promotes deep learning by prompting you to reflect on your notes and by challenging you to restate the material in your own words—which ensures you're not memorizing it superficially but understanding it deeply.

Post-Lecture Strategies: What to Do *After* Class

Whatever note-taking method you choose to use, the most important thing is to use a method that (a) enables you to stay actively engaged *in class* and (b) allows you to reflectively review the notes you have taken *after class*. The following pair of strategies may be used to ensure that you don't forget to take the second key step in the note-taking process: reflective review.

As soon as class ends, quickly check your notes for missing information or incomplete thoughts. Information delivered during a lecture is likely to be fresh in your mind immediately after class, so a quick check of your notes at this time will allow you to take advantage of your short-term memory. Quickly reviewing and reflecting on the information you've recorded helps you move that information into long-term memory before it's forgotten. You can do this quick review alone, or better yet, with a motivated classmate. If you both find the same gaps in your notes, check them out with your instructor before he or she leaves the classroom. Even though it may be weeks before you will be tested on the material, the sooner you pick up missed points and clear up sources of confusion, the better, because it will put you in a better position to understand upcoming material that builds on what was previously covered. Catching confusion early in the game also enables you to avoid the last-minute scenario of being one of many students seeking help from the instructor just before test time. The critical time just before exams should be spent studying notes that you know are complete and accurate, rather than rushing around trying to find missing information and seeking last-minute help on concepts covered weeks earlier.

 Reflection 5.4

Do you tend to stick around a few minutes after class to review your notes and clear up missing information or confusing points before leaving the classroom?

If you don't, why not?

Before the next class session meets, reflect on and review your notes from the previous session. During this review process, take notes on your notes by:

- Translating technical information into your own words to make it more meaningful to you.
- Reorganizing your notes to get ideas related to the same point in the same place.

Studies show that students who organize their lecture notes into meaningful categories demonstrate better recall of that information on memory tests than students who simply review the notes they've taken in class.

> *Effective note taking is a two-stage process: Stage 1 involves actively taking notes in class and stage 2 takes place after class—when you take time to reflect on the notes you've taken and process them more deeply.*

AUTHOR'S EXPERIENCE

I spent my first year in college spending a lot of time trying to manipulate my schedule to create large blocks of free time. I took all of my classes in a row without a break to preserve some time at the end of the day for relaxing and socializing with friends. Seldom did I even look at my notes until it was time to be tested on them. Thus, on the day before a test I was in a panic trying to cram the lecture notes into my head for the upcoming exam. Needless to say, I didn't perform well on many of my first tests. Eventually, a professor told me that if I spent some time each day rewriting my notes I would retain the material longer, increase my grades, and decrease my stress at test time. I employed this system and it worked wonderfully.

—*Aaron Thompson*

Reflection 5.5

Rate yourself in terms of how frequently you engage in the note-taking strategies listed below, using the following scale:

4 = always, 3 = sometimes, 2 = rarely, 1 = never

1. I take notes aggressively in class.   4   3   2   1

2. I sit near the front of class.   4   3   2   1

3. I adopt an alert, active-listening posture when
    seated in class (e.g., I sit upright and lean forward).   4   3   2   1

4. I take notes on what my instructors say, not
    just what they write on the board.   4   3   2   1

5. I pay special attention to information presented
    at the start and end of class.   4   3   2   1

6. I take notes in paragraph form.   4   3   2   1

7. I review my notes immediately after class to
    check if they're accurate and complete.   4   3   2   1

8. If I miss class, I get notes from a motivated
    classmate.   4   3   2   1

Strategic Reading

Reading assignments in college are likely to be lengthier and more challenging than those assigned in high school and college students are expected to do the assigned reading without anyone checking to see if they have done it. Not surprisingly, research shows that college students who consistently complete their assigned readings earn higher course grades.

Information contained in assigned readings ranks right behind information from lectures as a source of test questions on college exams. College students are likely to find questions on exams about information contained in reading assignments that their professors didn't talk extensively about in class or didn't even mention in class. Professors are also likely to expect students to relate or connect information covered in their lectures with information contained in the readings they've assigned. Furthermore, professors often deliver information in their lectures with the expectation that students have completed the assigned reading on the topic they're lecturing about. Consequently, if students do not complete assigned readings by their due date, they are likely to have more difficulty understanding class lectures.

It's important to remember that assigned reading is not optional; it's required and should be done according to the schedule your instructor has established. By completing reading assignments in a timely manner, you will: (a) be better positioned to understand class lectures, (b) improve the quality of your participation in class, and (c) obtain information that may appear on exams that is not explicitly covered in class.

Your reading comprehension and retention can be strengthened by using the following research-based strategies.

"Employ your time in improving yourself by other men's writing so that you shall come easily by what others have labored for.

—*Socrates, classic Greek (Athenian) philosopher and founding father of Western philosophy*

Pre-Reading Strategies: What to Do *Before* Reading

Before starting a reading assignment, first get a sense of how what you're about to read will fit into the overall organizational structure of the book and course. If you're reading a textbook chapter, you can do this efficiently by taking a quick look at the book's table of contents to see how the chapter you're about to read is situated in the overall sequence of chapters. Look especially at the chapter's relationship to the chapter before it and after. This pre-reading strategy will give you a sense of how the part you're focusing on fits into the bigger picture. Research shows that when students see how the material they're about to learn is organized—if they see how the part relates to the whole—*before* they attempt to learn the specific part, they're better able to comprehend and retain that particular part. Thus, the first step toward improving reading comprehension and retention of a book chapter is to see how the chapter fits into the book or course as a whole.

Preview a chapter you're about to read by first reviewing its boldface headings and any chapter outline, objectives, summary, or end-of-chapter questions that may be included. Before tackling the chapter's specific content, preview what's in the chapter to get a general sense of its overall organization. If you dive into the specific details first, you may lose sight of how the smaller details connect with the larger picture. Because the brain's natural tendency is to perceive and comprehend whole patterns rather than isolated bits of information, start by taking a moment to see how the part you're working on fits into the bigger picture. Just as seeing the picture of a completed jigsaw puzzle can help see where the piece in your hand belongs, so, too, does getting a picture of the whole chapter help you connect (and understand) its particular parts.

Before beginning to read, take a moment to think about what ideas or knowledge you may already have that relates to the main topic. This short reflection will activate areas of the brain where your prior knowledge about that topic is stored, thereby preparing it to make meaningful connections with the material you're about to read.

 Reflection 5.6

When you open a textbook to read an assigned chapter, do you immediately start reading it sentence by sentence, or do you first scan the chapter to get a sense of its overall organization? If you don't, would you be willing to put this strategy into practice?

Strategies to Use *During* the Reading Process

Approach reading with the mindset that you're on a search and find mission—to detect and select the most important information. Described below are three key strategies that can be used while reading to help you determine what information should be focused on and retained.

Use boldface or dark-print headings and subheadings as guideposts to find important information. These headings organize the chapter's major points; you can use them as "traffic signs" to steer you toward the most important information contained in the chapter. Better yet, turn the chapter's headings into questions and read to find answers beneath them. This question-and-answer strategy will ensure that you read actively and with a purpose. Studies show that most students try to learn and remember material they've read by simply re-reading it; however, this practice is much less effective than reading with a purpose. Asking yourself questions about what you are reading while you are reading it is one way to read with a purpose. You can set up this strategy by previewing the chapter and placing a question mark after each heading contained in the chapter.

Creating and answering questions while reading also increases your motivation to read because the questions can stimulate your curiosity and desire to find answers to them. Creating and answering questions about what you're reading is also an effective way to prepare for exams because you're practicing exactly what you'll be expected to do on exams—answer questions.

Pay close attention to information that's italicized, underlined, or capitalized. These features are intentionally designed to call your attention to key terms that must be understood so that you can understand terms and concepts covered later in the reading. Don't simply highlight these words because their special appearance suggests they're important. Instead, slow down to read them carefully and be sure you understand them before moving on to read additional material.

> *Your goal when reading is not just to* cover *the assigned pages, but to* uncover *the most important ideas found on those pages.*

Pay special attention to the first and last sentences in each paragraph. These sentences provide an important introduction and conclusion to the key point made in the paragraph. In fact, it's a good idea to reread the first and last sentences of each paragraph before you move on to the next, particularly if you're reading subject matter in math and science which is highly technical and cumulative—sequenced in such a way that understanding upcoming concepts depends heavily on what was previously covered.

Take written notes on important information you find in your reading. Just as taking notes on information delivered during lectures improves performance on exams, so does taking notes on reading assignments. Research shows that the common student practice of just highlighting the text (the author's words) is not a particularly effective reading strategy. Highlighting is a passive process, whereas note-taking actively engages you in the reading process and enables you to transform the author's into words that are meaningful to you.

Don't slip into the habit of using your textbook simply as a coloring book in which the artistic process of highlighting information in spectacular, kaleidoscopic colors distracts you from the more important process of learning actively and thinking deeply about what you are reading. Highlighting is okay as long it's not the only thing you do while reading; instead, take time to make notes on the material you've highlighted—in your own words—to ensure that you reflect on it and make it personally meaningful. When you transform what someone else has written into words of your own, you're implementing a powerful principle of deep learning: Connecting what you're trying to learn to what you already know.

An ideal time to pause and write a brief summary of what you've read in your own words is when you encounter a boldface heading—this indicates that you're about to embark on a new topic or concept. Pausing to reflect on what you read prior to the new heading will deepen your knowledge of it and enable you to use that knowledge to help you understand what you're about to read next.

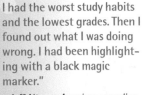

> "I had the worst study habits and the lowest grades. Then I found out what I was doing wrong. I had been highlighting with a black magic marker."
>
> —Jeff Altman, *American comedian*

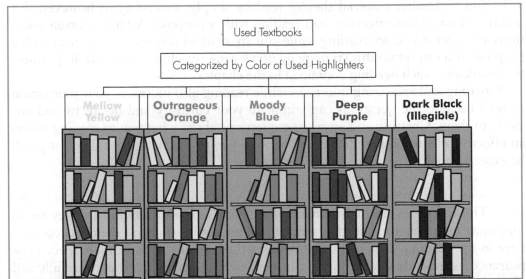

Highlighting textbooks in psychedelic colors is a very popular reading strategy among college students, but it's a less effective strategy for producing deep learning than taking written notes on what you've highlighted.

Reflection 5.7

When reading a textbook, do you usually have the following tools on hand?

Highlighter:	yes	no
Pen or pencil:	yes	no
Notebook:	yes	no
Class notes:	yes	no
Dictionary:	yes	no
Glossary:	yes	no

If you haven't used one or more of the above tools while reading, which one(s) do you plan to use in the future?

Use the visual aids that accompany the written text. Don't fall into the trap of thinking that visual aids can or should be skipped because they're merely supplemental or ornamental. Visual aids, such as charts, graphs, diagrams, and concept maps, are powerful learning and memory tools because: (a) they enable you to "see" the information in addition to reading (hearing) it, and (b) they organize separate ideas into a single snapshot.

Furthermore, periodically shifting from words to visuals adds variety and a change of pace to the learning process. Research shows that breaking up sustained periods of reading (verbal input) with other forms of sensory input, such as visual input, serves to stimulate motivation and sustain attention.

Regulate or adjust your reading speed to the type of subject matter you're reading. As you know, academic subjects vary in terms of their level of technicality and complexity. Reading material in a math or science textbook requires reading at a slower rate with more frequent pauses to check for understanding than reading a novel or short story.

Post-Reading Strategies: What to Do *After* Reading

End reading sessions with a short review of the key information you've highlighted and taken notes on. Instead of ending reading sessions by trying to cover a few more pages, reserve the last five minutes to review the key ideas you've already covered. Most forgetting of information taken into the brain takes place immediately after we stop focusing on that information and start turning our attention to something else. The graph in **Figure 5.4** depicts the results of a classic experiment that tested how well information is recalled at various times after it was taken in. As you can see on the far left of the graph, most forgetting occurs soon after information has been received (e.g., after 20 minutes, more than 60% of it was forgotten). The results of this classic study have been confirmed multiple times and underscore the importance of reviewing information *immediately* after it's been read. Doing so improves memory by intercepting the human "forgetting curve" at its steepest point of memory loss—just after the information has been processed (taken in).

So, before moving onto another task, take a few minutes at the end of your reading sessions to review the most important information you've just read to help your brain "lock" that information into long-term memory.

FIGURE 5.4: **The Forgetting Curve**

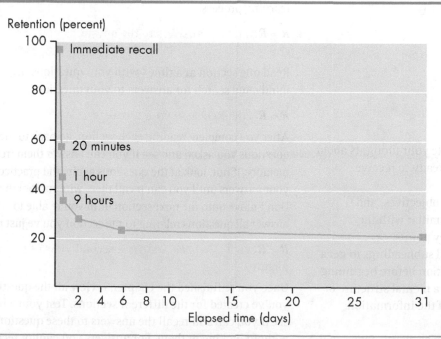

Source: Hermann Ebbinghaus, *Memory: A Contribution to Experimental Psychology*, 1885–1913.

After completing a reading assignment and reviewing what you've read, if there are important concepts that you still find confusing, seek clarification from another source. The problem may not be you; it may be the way in which the author presented or explained the concept. You may be able to quickly clear up your confusion by consulting another source or resource.

- **Look at how another book or an Internet site explains it.** Not all textbooks are created equal; some do a better job of explaining certain concepts than others. A different book or website may sometimes explain a hard-to-understand concept more clearly than your assigned textbook.
- **Seek help from your instructor.** If you completed the reading assignment and made every effort to understand the concepts contained in the reading, most instructors should be willing to help clear up any confusion you may have about a particular concept.
- **Seek help from learning assistance professionals or peer tutors in your Learning Center (Academic Support Center).** This is your key campus resource for assistance with learning, including learning from reading assignments.

Box 5.2

SQ3R: A Method for Improving Reading Comprehension and Retention

A popular system for organizing and remembering effective reading strategies is the *SQ3R* system. SQ3R is an acronym for key steps that should be taken when reading college textbooks. Research supports the effectiveness of the SQ3R system for improving reading comprehension and exam performance. The system consists of the following five-step sequence:

1. Survey
2. Question
3. Read
4. Recite
5. Review

S = *S*urvey: Get a preview and overview of what you're about to read.

1. Use the chapter's title to activate your thoughts about the subject and get your mind ready to receive information related to it.
2. Read the introduction, chapter objectives, and chapter summary to become familiar with the author's purpose, goals, and key points.
3. Note the boldface headings and subheadings to get a sense of the chapter's organization before beginning to read. This supplies you with a mental structure or framework for making sense of the information you're about to read.
4. Take note of any graphics—such as charts, maps, and diagrams; they provide valuable visual reinforcement for the verbal material contained in the text.

5. Pay special attention to reading aids (e.g., italics and boldface font); use these aids to help you identify, understand, and remember key concepts.

Q = *Q*uestion: Stay active and curious.

As you read, use boldface headings to formulate questions and read to find answers to those questions. Also, add any questions of your own that come to mind while you're reading. When your mind is actively searching for answers to questions, it becomes more engaged in the learning process.

R = *R*ead: Find answers to the questions you have created.

Read one section at a time—with your questions in mind—and search for answers to your questions.

R = *R*ecite: Rehearse your answers.

After you complete reading each section, go back to the questions you asked and see if you can answer them from memory. If not, look at the questions again and practice your answers until you can recall them without looking. Don't move onto the next section until you're able to answer all questions relating to the section you've just read.

R = *R*eview: Go back and get a second view of the whole picture.

Once you're finished the chapter, review all the questions you've created for the different sections. Test yourself to see if you can still recall the answers to these questions without looking at them. For answers you cannot recall, review the information in that section to refresh your memory.

Reflection 5.8

Rate yourself in terms of how frequently you engage in the reading strategies listed below, using the following scale:

4 = always, 3 = sometimes, 2 = rarely, 1 = never

1. I read chapter outlines and summaries before I start reading the chapter content.   4   3   2   1

2. I preview a chapter's boldface headings and subheadings before I begin to read the chapter.   4   3   2   1

3. I adjust my reading speed to the type of subject I am reading.   4   3   2   1

4. I try to relate what I'm reading to what I already know.   4   3   2   1

5. I look up the meaning of unfamiliar words and unknown terms that I come across before I continue reading.   4   3   2   1

6. I take written notes on information I read.   4   3   2   1

7. I use the visual aids included in my textbooks.   4   3   2   1

8. I finish reading sessions by reviewing important information that I noted or highlighted.   4   3   2   1

Strategic Studying: Learning Deeply and Remembering Longer

Studying shouldn't be a short and fast sprint that takes place just before test time; it should be a slower, long-distance run that's spread out over an extended period of time. The studying that's done the night before an exam should be the last step in a sequence of test-preparation steps that begins well before test time. These steps include: (a) taking accurate and complete notes in class, (b) completing assigned readings, and (c) seeking help from instructors, learning assistance professionals, or trusted peers to understand any concepts contained in lectures and readings that are unclear or confusing. Once these steps have been taken, you're then positioned to study the information you've acquired and learn it deeply.

Described below is a comprehensive set of study strategies you can use to ensure that your learning is deep and durable (long-lasting).

Give Studying Undivided Attention

The human attention span has limited capacity—we have only so much of it available to us at any point in time and we can give all or part of it to whatever task(s) we're working on. As the phrase "paying attention" suggests, it's like paying money; we don't have unlimited amounts of it to spend. When studying, if some attention is spent on other activities at the same time (e.g., watching TV or messaging friends), it's deducted from the total amount of attention paid to studying. Thus, studying receives "divided" rather than "undivided" (full) attention.

Research on multitasking reveals that when people engage in two or more tasks at the same time, they don't pay equal attention to the multiple tasks they're performing. Instead, attention is divided by shifting it back and forth between tasks, and performance on the task that demands the most concentration or deepest thinking suffers the most. Challenging or complex mental tasks cannot be done automatically or mindlessly. For deep learning to take place on these tasks, the brain needs quiet, internal reflection time for permanent connections to form between brain cells. If the brain is engaged in other tasks, or is receiving other sources of external stimulation at the same time, this connection-making process is interfered with and learning is impaired.

> "You can do several things at once, but only if they are easy and undemanding. You are probably safe carrying on a conversation with a passenger while driving on an empty highway [but] you could not compute the product of 17 x 24 while making a left turn into dense traffic, and you certainly should not try."
>
> —Daniel Kahneman, professor emeritus of Psychology, and author of *Thinking Fast and Slow*

Studies show that doing challenging academic work while multitasking divides up attention and drives down comprehension and retention.

To minimize the learning-interference effects of multitasking, unplug all electronic accessories while studying. You can even use apps to help you do so (e.g., a cell-phone silencer). If you cannot commit to going completely "unplugged," then set aside a short block of time to check electronic messages independent of study time. You can arrange this in a way that allows you to use social media as a reward *after* studying rather than as a distraction *while* studying.

Make Meaningful Associations

Deep learning doesn't take place through osmosis—by passively soaking up information in the same form as it appears in a textbook or lecture. Instead, it occurs when learners actively translate the information they receive into a form that's meaningful to them.

> *Deep learning does not take place through the simple <u>transmission</u> of information from teacher or textbook to learner; it involves effortful <u>transformation</u> of information into knowledge by the learner.*

The brain's natural learning tendency is to transform unfamiliar information into a familiar form that makes sense and is personally meaningful to the learner—as illustrated by the following experience.

AUTHOR'S EXPERIENCE

When my son was about 3 years old, we were riding in the car together and listening to a song by the Beatles, *Sergeant Pepper's Lonely Hearts Club Band*. You may be familiar with this tune, but in case you're not, there's a part in it where the following lyrics are sung repeatedly: "Sergeant Pepper's Lonely, Sergeant Pepper's Lonely, Sergeant Pepper's Lonely . . ."

When this part of the song was playing, I noticed that my 3-year-old son was singing along. I thought it was pretty amazing for a boy his age to be able to understand and repeat those tricky lyrics. However, when that part of the song came on again, I was listening to him more closely and noticed that he wasn't singing "Sergeant Pepper's Lonely, Sergeant Pepper's Lonely . . ." Instead, he was singing: "Sausage Pepperoni, Sausage Pepperoni . . ." (which were his two favorite pizza toppings).

My son's brain was doing what all human brains naturally do. It took unfamiliar information—song lyrics that didn't make any sense to him—and transformed it into a form that was meaningful to him.

—Joe Cuseo

You can experience the brain's natural inclination for meaning-making by reading the following passage, which once appeared anonymously on the Internet:

Aoccdrnig to rscheearch at Cmabridge Uinverstisy, it deos't mattaer in what order the ltteers in a word are, the only iprmoetnt thing is that the frist and lsat ltteer be at the rghit pclae. The rset can be a total mses and you can still raed it wouthit a porbelm. This is bcusae the human mind deos not raed ervey lteter by istlef, but the word as a wlohe. Amzanig huh?

Notice how natural it was for you to transform these meaningless, misspelled words into familiar, meaningful words that were already stored in your brain. This exercise illustrates how when we are learning something new or unfamiliar, the brain's natural tendency is to find meaning in it by relating it something we already know. You can capitalize on the brain's natural meaning-making tendency to learn more efficiently and effectively in college. For instance, if you're learning an unfamiliar academic term, before trying to beat the term into your brain through sheer repetition or brute memorization, first try to find something about the term that's meaningful to you. One way to do so is by looking up the etymology or "root" of the unfamiliar term. Suppose you're taking a biology course and studying the autonomic nervous system—the part of the nervous system that operates without our conscious awareness and voluntary control (e.g., heart and lungs). The meaning of this biological term is revealed by its prefix "auto," which means self-controlling or "automatic"—as in automatic transmission. Once you find meaning in abstract or academic terms, you can learn them faster and retain them longer than by trying to memorize them through sheer repetition.

If looking up the etymological root of an unfamiliar term still doesn't make it meaningful, you can make the term meaningful to you in other ways. For example, if looking up the root of "artery" (a blood vessel that carries blood *away* from the heart) doesn't reveal anything about its meaning or purpose, you can take its first letter, "a", make it stand for "*a*way," and make sense (meaning) out of this otherwise meaningless term. By so doing, you take an unfamiliar term that would require repeated rehearsal to be remembered and transform it into a meaningful term that's immediately and forever memorable.

Another way you can make learning meaningful is by *comparing* or *contrasting* what you're learning with something you already know. You can do this by getting in the habit of asking yourself the following questions when studying new concepts:

(a) How is this concept similar to something I have previously learned or experienced? (Compare)

(b) How is this concept different than something I previously learned or already know? (Contrast)

Research indicates that asking these questions is a very simple yet effective learning strategy. It works because the new idea being learned becomes more meaningful when it's related to something you already know.

Deep learners dive below the shallow surface of memorization by making the effort to connect what they're currently learning to what they've previously learned.

 Reflection 5.9

Think of a technical academic term or concept you're learning in a course this term and create a meaningful association you could use to remember it.

Try first to find meaning in what you're learning before memorizing it through sheer repetition. If you can connect what you're trying to learn to what you already know, the deeper you'll learn it and the longer you'll remember it.

> "The extent to which we remember a new experience has more to do with how it relates to existing memories than with how many times we experience it."
>
> —Morton Hunt, in *The Universe Within: A New Science Explores the Human Mind*

Integrate Information from Lectures and Readings

Try to find connections between ideas in your lecture notes and reading assignments that relate to the same concept. Get them in the same place under the same category heading. Index cards can be used for this purpose. They can function like a portable file cabinet, with a card representing a separate category and functioning like the hub of a wheel, around which individual pieces of related information can be attached like spokes. In contrast, when ideas pertaining to the same point or concept are spread all over the place, they're likely to be spread all over the place in your mind—leaving them mentally disconnected and leaving you confused, overwhelmed, or stressed out.

Deep learners ask questions like: How can this specific piece of information be categorized or classified into a larger concept? How does this idea relate to or "fit into" something bigger?

Distribute Study Time across Separate Study Sessions

Deep learning depends not only on *how* you learn (your method), but also on *when* you learn (your timing). The way in which you distribute or spread out your study time is as important as the total time you spend studying. For students of all abilities and ages, research consistently shows that distributing study time over several shorter sessions results in deeper learning and longer retention than loading all study time into one long session.

Although cramming before exams is better than not studying at all, it's far less effective than spacing out studying across time. Instead of frantically jamming all your study time into a massive, one-shot session ("massed practice"), use *distributed practice*—"distribute" or spread out your study time across several shorter sessions. Distributed practice improves learning and memory in two major ways:

- It minimizes loss of attention due to fatigue and boredom that can set in during a long study session.
- It reduces mental interference by giving the brain some downtime, allowing it to cool down and lock in information it has just processed (taken in) without having to process a lot of additional incoming information. The brain works like a muscle: After it's been exercised, if given some "cool down" time before it's exercised again, it builds greater strength (memory) for information it just worked on. On the other hand, if the brain's downtime is interfered with by the arrival of a new wave of information, it gets overloaded and is less able to retain information it previously took in. That's exactly what cramming does—it overloads the brain with lots of information in a limited period. In contrast, distributed study does just the opposite—it uses shorter sessions with downtime in between sessions, which gives the brain time to slow down and retain the information it previously processed (studied) and gives it the opportunity to move that information from short-term to long-term memory.

> "Hurriedly jam-packing a brain is akin to speed-packing a cheap suitcase—it holds its new load for a while, then most everything falls out.
>
> —Benedict Carey, in *How We Learn: Throw Out the Rule Book and Unlock Your Brain's Potential*

Lastly, distributed study has emotional advantages: it's more motivating and less stressful than cramming. Your motivation to begin and continue studying is likely to be stronger if you know you're going to be doing it for a short, manageable segment of time than for a long, exhausting stretch of time.

 **Reflection 5.10**

Do you study in advance of exams or cram just before exams?

How do you think most students would answer this question?

Use the "Part-to-Whole" Study Method

This method of learning is a natural extension of the distributed practice strategy. It involves breaking up the material to be learned into smaller parts, studying those parts in separate sessions in advance of an exam, and using the very last study session just before the exam to review (restudy) "the whole"—all the parts that were studied previously in separate sessions. Thus, the final session isn't a cram session or a study-something-new session; it's a review session.

Research shows that college students of all ability levels learn material more effectively when they study it in small units and move on to the next unit only after material from the previous unit has been learned and understood. Dividing up material into smaller parts and studying those parts in advance of an exam gives you a chance to check your understanding of each part before moving on to learn the next part. This is particularly advantageous in cumulative courses where learning the next unit builds on understanding the previous unit (e.g., math and science courses).

Don't buy into the myth that studying in advance is a waste of time because you'll forget everything you previously studied near test time. (As discussed in chapter 4, procrastinators often use this argument to rationalize their habit of putting off studying until the very last moment.) Memory research demonstrates that information studied previously may be temporarily forgotten, but once it's reviewed, it can be relearned and retained much faster than it was the first time. Thus, if we cannot recall previously studied information right away, it doesn't mean it's completely forgotten; there's still a memory trace of it in the brain and all it takes is a quick review to strengthen that memory trace and enable us to recall the previously studied information. This disproves the myth that studying ahead of time is a waste of time and supports the idea that reviewing previously studied information just before test time is an effective learning strategy.

Capitalize on the Power of Visual Learning

The human brain consists of two hemispheres (half spheres)—a left and right hemisphere (see **Figure 5.5**). Each of these hemispheres specializes in different types of learning. Typically, the left hemisphere specializes in verbal learning; it primarily processes words, both spoken and written. In contrast, the right hemisphere specializes in visual–spatial learning, dealing primarily with perceiving and learning from images, patterns, and objects that occupy physical space. If you engage both hemispheres while studying, two different memory traces are recorded in the brain—one in each hemisphere. This process of laying down both verbal and visual memory traces is referred to by learning scholars as *dual coding*. Because two memory traces are better than one, when information is dual coded, it's learned more deeply and retained longer.

FIGURE 5.5

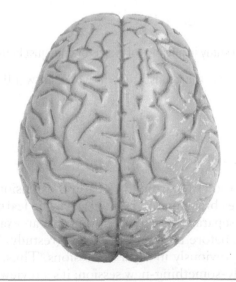

The human brain is comprised of two half spheres (hemispheres): the left hemisphere specializes in verbal learning, and the right hemisphere specializes in visual learning.

You can capitalize on the power of dual coding when processing verbal information by using all the visual aids available to you, including those used by your instructors in class and those supplied by the textbooks you're reading outside of class. Research shows that visual images are powerful aids to learning. You can also create your own visual aids by representing the verbal information you're learning in the form of pictures, symbols, or concept maps—such as flowcharts, timelines, spider webs, wheels (with hubs and spokes), or branching tree diagrams. (For an example of a concept map, see **Figure 5.6**. For additional examples and ideas for creating your own concept maps, go to: https://coggle.it/?lang=en-US). Research indicates that students who make drawings of what they're learning outperform students who do not or who just look at drawings provided for them. As previously mentioned, when you represent verbal information in visual form, it doubles the number of memory traces recorded in your brain. (As the old saying goes, "A picture is worth a thousand words.")

FIGURE 5.6: Concept Map for the Human Nervous System

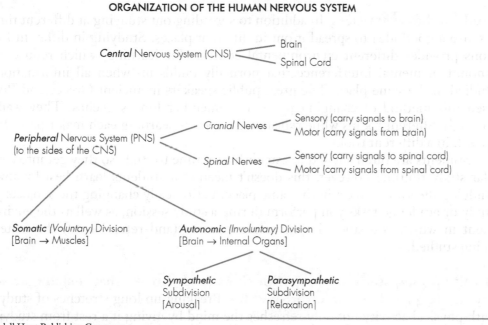

ORGANIZATION OF THE HUMAN NERVOUS SYSTEM

Central Nervous System (CNS) — Brain / Spinal Cord

Peripheral Nervous System (PNS) (to the sides of the CNS)

Cranial Nerves — Sensory (carry signals to brain) / Motor (carry signals from brain)

Spinal Nerves — Sensory (carry signals to spinal cord) / Motor (carry signals from spinal cord)

Somatic (Voluntary) Division [Brain → Muscles]

Autonomic (Involuntary) Division [Brain → Internal Organs]

Sympathetic Subdivision [Arousal]

Parasympathetic Subdivision [Relaxation]

©Kendall Hunt Publishing Company

Drawings and visual illustrations can be much more than forms of artistic expression; they can also be powerful learning tools—you can draw to learn!

 Reflection 5.11

Think of a course you're taking this term in which related pieces of information could be joined together to form a concept map. Make a rough sketch of this map that includes the information you're trying to learn and remember.

Build Variety into the Study Process

Infusing variety and change of pace into your study routine can increase your motivation to study and your concentration while studying. Here are some practical strategies for doing so.

Mix it up: periodically shift the type of academic tasks you engage in during a single study session. Changing the nature of the academic work you're doing while studying increases your alertness and concentration by reducing *habituation*—attention loss that typically takes place after engaging in the same type of mental task over and over again. You can combat attention loss due to habituation by varying the type of tasks you perform during a study session. For instance, you can shift periodically between tasks that involve reading, writing by hand, typing on a keyboard, reviewing, reciting, or solving problems. Similar to how athletes benefit from mixing different types of drills into their workouts (e.g., separate drills for building strength, speed, and endurance), studies show that "interleaving" (mixing) different academic subjects or academic skills during a single study session results in deeper learning and stronger memory.

Study in different places. In addition to spreading out studying at different times, it's also a good idea to spread it out in different places. Studying in different locations provides different environmental contexts for learning, which reduces the amount of mental interference that normally builds up when all information is studied in the same place. The great public speakers in ancient Greece and Rome used this method of changing places to remember long speeches. They walked through different rooms while rehearsing a speech, learning each major part of the speech in a different room.

Students are often advised to establish a set time to study so they get into a regular study routine; however, this doesn't mean that students learn best by always studying the same subject in the same place. Periodically changing the subjects you study or academic tasks you perform during a study session, as well as the environment in which you study, improves attention to (and retention of) the material being studied.

Break up long study sessions with short study breaks that include physical activity (e.g., a short jog or brisk walk). Breaking up long stretches of studying with physical activity not only refreshes the mind by giving it a rest from studying, it also gets stimulates the mind by increasing blood flow to the brain, which increases retention of what has been studied and concentration for what will be studied next.

Learn with and through multiple sensory channels. Different senses channel information into different centers of the brain. When we see something, it may start with our eyes, but we don't actually "see" it until that sensory input reaches the visual center of the brain. Similarly, input from other senses, such as hearing and touch, reach areas of the brain specialized for receiving information from these particular senses. **Figure 5.7** contains a map of the outer surface of the human brain that shows where different areas specialize in receiving input from different sensory modalities. Learning through multiple sensory channels results in deeper learning and stronger memory because: (a) interconnections are formed across multiple areas of the brain, allowing the information to be stored in more than one place, and (b) more routes or avenues are created through which we can retrieve (recall) the information that's been stored.

FIGURE 5.7: A Map of the Functions Performed by the Outer Surface of the Human Brain

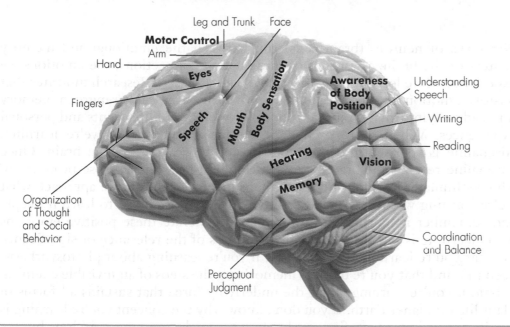

Brain image modified from ©David Huntley/Shutterstock.com

Remember that movement is also a sensory channel. When we move, our brain receives kinesthetic stimulation—sensory signals generated by our muscles. Memory traces for movement are stored in an area of the brain that involved in all types of learning and memory. Thus, incorporating movement into the learning process can improve your ability to retain what's being learned by adding a powerful motor (muscle) memory trace of it to your brain. You can capitalize on movement to enhance your ability to learn and retain academic information by using your body to act out what you're studying or to symbolize it with your hands. For instance, if you're trying to remember five points relating to a topic or concept, your memory of those points can be strengthened by counting them out on your fingers while studying them.

> "When I have to remember something, it's better for me to do something with my hands so I could physically see it happening.
>
> —First-year college student

AUTHOR'S EXPERIENCE

I was talking about memory in class one day and told my students that when I have trouble remembering how to spell a word, its correct spelling often comes back to me as soon as I start to write out the word. One of my students raised her hand and said the same thing happens to her when she forgets a phone number—it comes back to her when she begins to punch it in. Both of these experiences point to the power of movement for improving learning and memory

—*Joe Cuseo*

Also, remember that talking involves movement—moving your lips and tongue. Thus, talking aloud about what you're studying, either to a friend or to oneself, improves memory not only by supplying the brain with auditory (sound) input, but also supplying it with kinesthetic (motor) input.

(Complete Exercise 5.5 at the end of this chapter. If your results on the Achieve-WORKSLearning and Productivity Report indicate that you have kinesthetic

> "I have to hear it, see it, write it, and talk about it.
>
> —First-year college student responding to the question: "How do you learn best?"

and tactile preferences, these learning-through-movement activities may be particularly effective ways to strengthen your learning.)

Learn with Emotion

Networks of neurons (brain cells) run between the emotional and memory centers of the brain; as a result of these neural connections, the emotions we experience while learning can affect how well we learn. Research indicates that positive emotions, such as excitement and enthusiasm, can strengthen memory for academic information just as it does for memory of life events and personal experiences. When we're excited or enthused about what we're learning, adrenaline is released into the bloodstream and carried to the brain. Once adrenaline reaches the brain, it increases blood flow and glucose production, which stimulates learning and strengthens memory. Thus, if we approach what we're learning with passion and positivity, we're more likely to learn it deeply and remember it longer. One way you can generate these positive emotions while learning is by increasing your awareness of the relevance or significance of what you're learning. For instance, if you're learning about photosynthesis, keep in mind that you're not just memorizing the steps of an invisible chemical reaction; you're learning about the underlying force that sustains all forms of plant life on planet Earth. If you don't know why the concept you're learning is significant or important, find out by doing a quick computer search or by discussing it with your instructor or an advanced student majoring in the field.

> *You learn more deeply and retain what you learn much longer when it's a "total body experience"—when you put your whole self into it—your mind (thinking), body (movement), and heart (emotion).*

Learn Collaboratively

In contrast to working independently or competitively, collaborative learning involves two or more students work *interdependently* to advance each other's success. Learning is strengthened when it takes place in a social context that includes interpersonal interaction. As learning scholars put it, human knowledge is "socially constructed" or built up through dialogue and exchange of ideas. When students who are learning the same concepts talk to each other about what they're learning, the ideas they exchange verbally get combined mentally and are incorporated into one another's thinking. Thus, by having frequent, intelligent conversations with other learners, you broaden your knowledge base, deepen your learning, and elevate the quality of your thinking.

In a national study involving in-depth interviews with more than 1,600 college students, it was discovered that almost all students who were struggling academically had one particular learning habit in common: They always studied alone. In contrast, research from kindergarten through college shows that when students learn collaboratively in teams, they experience significant gains in academic achievement. When seniors at Harvard University were interviewed, nearly every one of them who had participated in learning teams considered the experience to be crucial to their academic progress and success. The ability to collaborate and work in teams is also one of the top skills sought by employers of college graduates.

> "If you want to go quickly, go by yourself—if you want to go farther, go in a group."
> —*African proverb*

The power of teamwork is magnified further when students make wise choices about what other students to include on their learning teams. Listed below are some guidelines for making wise choices about learning teammates and study partners.

- Keep a keen eye out for classmates who are motivated, who attend class consistently, come to class prepared, and participate actively in class. These students are likely to be significant contributors to your learning team, not hitchhikers or freeloaders looking for a free ride.

- Include members on your learning team whose personal characteristics, backgrounds, and experiences differ from your own. When teams are composed solely of students with similar characteristics and experiences, or students who are very familiar with one another, they often end up being the least productive teams. Because of their similarity and familiarity, their work group can quickly turn into a social group or gabfest, which take them off task and onto topics that have nothing to do with the learning task (e.g., what they did last weekend or what they're planning to do next weekend). Instead, include at least some members on your learning team who are not friends or close acquaintances and who differ from you in age, gender, race or ethnicity, and cultural or geographical background. Such variety brings different life experiences, thinking strategies, and learning approaches to the team, which not only increases its social diversity, but also its learning capacity.

> "TEAM = Together Everyone Achieves More
> —Author unknown

Maximize the benefits of collaborative learning by teaming up with peers from different backgrounds and cultures. Studies consistently show that we learn more from people who differ from us than from people like us.

Keep in mind that learning teams are more than just study groups formed the night before an exam. You can team-up with classmates earlier and more frequently to collaborate on a number of different academic tasks, such as those listed below.

Note-Taking Teams. Immediately after class, take a couple of minutes to team-up with a motivated classmate to compare and share notes. Because listening to lectures is a demanding task, it's likely that one of you will miss a point that your partner picked up and vice-versa. You could use a two-step procedure called "cooperative note-taking pairs," in which one partner summarizes his or her notes for the other—who adds any information to the notes that he or she may have missed; then partners reverse roles—the summarizer becomes the listener and adds information missing from the notes that the partner picked up. During this cooperative note-taking process, you and your teammate could ask each other questions such as: "What do you think were the main ideas or most important points covered?", "What points did you find most challenging or confusing"?, and "What test questions might be asked of us that are based on these notes?"

AUTHOR'S EXPERIENCE

During my first term in college, I was having difficulty taking complete notes in my biology course because the instructor spoke rapidly and with an unfamiliar accent. I noticed another student (Alex) sitting in the front row who was trying the best he could to take notes but seemed to be experiencing the same difficulty as me. Following one particularly fast and complex lecture, we looked at each other and started shaking our heads in frustration. We got together, talked about how difficult it was to take notes in this class, and decided to join forces after every class to compare notes and identify points we missed or found confusing. First, we helped each other by quickly comparing and sharing our notes in case one of us got something the other missed. If there were points we both missed or couldn't figure out, we immediately went to the front of class together to consult with the instructor before he left the room. At the end of the course, Alex and I finished with the highest grades in the course.

—*Joe Cuseo*

Reading Teams. After completing reading assignments, team up with another student to compare your highlighting and margin notes and identify information you think should be studied for upcoming exams.

Writing Teams. Collaborate with other students to provide one another with feedback on your writing. Studies show that when peers review each other's writing, the quality of their individual writing improves and they develop more positive attitudes about writing. You can form peer-writing teams to improve your writing at any or all of the following stages in the writing process:

- **Topic selection and refinement**—collaborate to come up with a list of possible topics and subtopics to write about
- **Pre-writing**—collaborate to clarify your writing purpose, thesis statement, and reading audience
- **First draft**—collaborate to improve the organization, style, or tone of your writing
- **Final draft**—collaborate to proofread your writing, detect technical errors, and correct clerical mistakes before turning in your final product.

Library Research Teams. First-year students are often unfamiliar with how to navigate a college or university library and conduct academic research. Some students actually experience "library anxiety" and will go to great lengths to avoid even stepping foot into the library, particularly if it's a large and intimidating place. By forming a library research team, you can create a social support group to make library research less intimidating and transform it from a solitary experience done alone to a collaborative venture done together. Such collaboration not only can reduce library anxiety, it can also generate collective energy that results in a better work than library research done alone.

It's perfectly acceptable and ethical to team up with others to search for information and share resources. This isn't cheating or plagiarizing—as long as your final products are completed individually and what you turn into the instructor is your own written work.

Study Teams. Research on study groups indicates that they are most effective when each member has done all required course work prior to the group meetings—for example, each teammate has attended class, taken notes, and completed all the required readings. The power of study teams is also magnified when its members: (a) study *individually* before meeting as a group, (b) come to group meetings prepared with answers or ideas to share with teammates, and (c) come armed with specific questions to ask. This ensures that all team members are both individually accountable for their own learning and collectively responsible for contributing to the learning of their teammates.

> *Don't forget that team learning means more than late-night study groups. Students can form learning teams in advance of exams to help each other with other academic tasks—such as note-taking, reading, writing, and library research.*

Test-Review Teams. After receiving your results on course examinations (and assignments), you can join others to review your results as a team. By comparing your answers with those of your teammates, you can get a clearer idea about how you lost and earned points. Having the opportunity to view the work of teammates who received the maximum number of points on certain test questions can also provide work models you can emulate to improve your future performance. It's especially effective to team-up with peers to review tests and assignments *early in the term* because you are then left with ample time to use their feedback to improve your final course grade.

Reflection 5.12

Think about the students in your classes this term. Are there classmates you would feel comfortable connecting with after exams to form test-review teams?

If yes, why? If no, why not?

Self-Monitoring: Self-Assessment for Deep Learning

Deep learners are *reflective* learners—they reflect on *how* they go about learning (their learning habits and strategies) and *if* they are learning deeply. They self-monitor (self-check) and self-assess whether they're really getting it by asking themselves questions such as: "Am I actually understanding this?" and "Do I really know it, or am I just memorizing it?"

How do you know if you really know it? Probably the best answer to this question is if you can say: "I find *meaning* in it—I can relate to it personally or put it in terms that make sense to me." Listed below are self-assessment questions you can use to check to see if you have moved beyond memorization to deeper, more meaningful learning. By answering these specific questions, it will help you answer the bigger question: "How do I know if I really know it?"

Can you *paraphrase* (restate or translate) what you're learning in your own words? One way to check if you really know something is to see if you can state it differently than the way your instructor or textbook stated it. If you can, it's a good sign that you've moved beyond surface memorization (mental regurgitation) to a deeper level of comprehension. For example, by taking what you're learning and completing the following sentence: "In other words . . .", it shows you've transformed it into a form that's meaningful to you.

Can you explain what you're learning to someone else? Another way to gain awareness of how well you know or don't know something is by trying to explain it to someone who doesn't know it (just ask any teacher). Studies confirm that students gain a deeper level of understanding of what they're learning when they're asked to explain it to another person. If you can translate what you're learning into language that's understandable to a peer, it's a good sign that you've learned it deeply.

Can you think of an *example* of what you are trying to learn? If you can come up with a specific instance or illustration of an academic concept, it shows you're able to take an abstract concept and convert it into a concrete experience.

Can you think of an *analogy* between the concept you're learning and something you already know or have previously experienced? If you can say that this concept is "similar to" or "works the same way as", it indicates that you have connected what you're learning to what you already know—a sign of deep learning.

Can you *transfer* what you're learning to a new situation or problem that you haven't seen before? The ability to apply what you've learned in a different situation or context is a good indicator of deep learning. Learning specialists refer to this mental process as *decontextualization*—taking what's been learned in one context and transferring it to a different context. For instance, you know you've learned a mathematical concept deeply when you can take that concept and use it to solve math problems that are different from those solved by your instructor in class or used by the author of your textbook. This is why math instructors rarely include the same problems on exams that they solved in class or in the textbook. They're not trying to "trick" students at test time; they're trying to determine whether students have learned deeply really learned to solve problems (deep learning), rather than just memorize solutions.

> "You do not really understand something unless you can explain it to your grandmother."
>
> —*Albert Einstein, the "father of modern physics"*

> "Most things used to be external to me—out of a lecture or textbook. It makes learning a lot more interesting and memorable when you can bring your experiences into it. It makes you want to learn."
>
> —*Returning adult student*

Reflection 5.13

Rate yourself in terms of how frequently you use the following learning strategies:

4 = always, 3 = sometimes, 2 = rarely, 1 = never

1. I avoid multitasking while studying.   4   3   2   1

2. I try to make connections between what I'm currently studying and what I've previously learned.   4   3   2   1

3. Before I start memorizing unfamiliar terms, I first try to discover their meaning from their prefix, suffix, or word origin.   4   3   2   1

4. I pull together information from my class notes and readings that relate to the same concept and get it in the same place.   4   3   2   1

5. I use as many senses as possible while studying (e.g., say it aloud, map it out, act it out).   4   3   2   1

6. I self-monitor (check myself) while studying to be sure I'm
    learning deeply, not just memorizing.   4   3   2   1

7. I distribute (spread out) my study time over several short
    sessions in advance of exams and use my last study session
    before exams to review the information I studied previously.   4   3   2   1

8. I participate in learning teams or study groups
    with classmates.   4   3   2   1

Which of the above study strategies have you not used in the past but plan to use in
the future?

Internet-Based Resources

For additional information on how to learn deeply and strategically, see the following websites:

Strategic Learning & Study Strategies:
https://students.dartmouth.edu/academic-skills/learning-resources/
learning-strategies
https://www.uh.edu/ussc/launch/services/handouts/

Brain-Based Learning:
http://www.brainrules.net/the-rules
https://www.middleweb.com/37519/7-brain-based-ways-to-make-learning-stick/

Learning Math and Overcoming Math Anxiety:
http://platonicrealms.com/minitexts/Coping-With-Math-Anxiety
https://www.cowley.edu/academics/skills/math_anxiety.html
https://www.sheffield.ac.uk/polopoly_fs/1.753619!/file/Maths_anxiety_strategies.
pdf

Chapter 5 Exercises

5.1 Quote Reflections

Review the sidebar quotes contained in this chapter and select two that were especially meaningful or inspirational to you.

For each of the quotes you selected, provide an explanation of why you chose it.

5.2 Strategy Reflections

Review the strategies for *strategic studying, learning deeply,* and *remembering longer* discussed on pp. 103-116. Select three strategies that you think would be most useful and intend to put into practice.

5.3 Reality Bite

Too Fast, Too Frustrating: A Note-Taking Nightmare

Susan Scribe is a first-year student majoring in journalism. She's currently enrolled in an introductory course required for her major (Introduction to Mass Media). The instructor for this course lectures at a rapid rate and uses vocabulary that goes right over her head. Because she cannot get all her instructor's words in her notes and cannot understand half the words she does manage to write down, she's become so frustrated that she's stopped taking notes. She really wants to do well in this course because it's the first course in her major, but she's afraid she'll fail it because her class notes are so pitiful.

Reflection and Discussion Questions

1. Can you relate to this case personally, or do know any students who are in a similar situation as Susan?

2. What would you recommend that Susan do at this point? Why?

5.4 Self-Assessment of Learning Habits

Look back at the ratings you gave yourself for strategic *note-taking* (Reflection 5.5, p. 97), *reading* (Reflection 5.8, p. 103), and *studying* (Reflection 5.13, pp. 116-117). Add up your total score for these three sets of learning strategies:

Note Taking = _____

Reading = _____

Studying = _____

Total Learning Strategy Score = _____

Self-Assessment Questions

1. In which learning-strategy area did you score lowest?

2. Do you think the area in which you scored lowest may be contributing to your lowest course grade at this point in the term?

3. Of the eight strategies listed in the area that you scored lowest, which one could you put into practice immediately to improve your performance in a course you're having the most difficulty with this term?

4. What's the likelihood that you will put the preceding strategy into practice?

5.5 Consulting a Learning Specialist

Make an appointment to visit the Learning Center or Academic Support Center on campus to discuss the results of your note-taking, reading, and studying self-assessment in Exercise 5.3 (or any other learning self-assessment you may have taken). Ask for recommendations about how you can improve your learning habits in your lowest score area. After your visit, answer the following questions.

1. Who did you meet with in the Learning Center?

2. What steps were recommended to you for improving your academic performance?

3. How likely is it that you will take the steps recommended to you?

   a) definitely

   b) probably

   c) possibly

   d) unlikely

   Why?

4. Do you plan to see a learning specialist again? (If yes, why? If no, why not?)

5.6 Learning Style Assessment

Take the *AchieveWORKS Personality* assessment review in the *Learning and Productivity Report.*

What do the results suggest are your strongest learning preferences?

For which classes this term would the suggestions offered be most helpful?

CHAPTER 6

Test-Taking Skills and Strategies

WHAT TO DO BEFORE, DURING, AND AFTER EXAMS

Effective test-taking is both an art and a science. This chapter supplies you with a systematic set of research-based strategies for improving your performance on both multiple-choice and essay exams. It identifies strategies that can be used before, during, and after exams, as well as practical tips for becoming more "test wise" and less "test anxious."

Apply effective strategies to prepare for and improve performance on college exams and standardized tests, and as strategies for using past test results to improve future test performance.

 Reflection 6.1

Which one of the following types of tests do you prefer to take, or do you tend to perform better on?

a) Multiple-choice tests

b) Essay tests

Why?

Learning in college typically takes place in a three-stage process: (1) students acquire information from lectures and readings; (2) study that information; and (3) attempt to recall the information they study at test time. This chapter focuses on strategies relating to the third stage of this learning process and are organized into three key categories:

- Strategies to use *in advance* of a test
- Strategies to use *during* a test
- Strategies to use *after* test results are received.

Pre-Test Strategies: What to Do *in Advance* of Exams

Your ability to remember material on an exam depends not only on how well you studied, but also on how the way you studied matches the way you're tested. For

121

instance, you may be able to remember what you studied if you're tested in a multiple-choice format, but not if you're tested in an essay format, because these two types of test questions require different types of memory. Test questions can be classified into two major categories, depending on the type of memory required to answer them:

1. *Recognition* test questions: these questions ask you to select or choose the correct answer from choices that are provided for you. Falling into this category are multiple-choice, true–false, and matching questions. Such questions do not require you to supply or produce the correct answer on your own; instead, you're asked to identify or pick out the correct answer, similar to how a witness is asked to identify the "correct" criminal from a lineup of suspects.

2. *Recall* test questions: these questions ask you to retrieve information and produce it on your own. As the word "recall" implies, you have to re-call ("call back") information and supply it yourself—as opposed to picking it out from information supplied for you. Recall test questions include essay and short-answer questions, which require you to generate your own answer—in writing.

Because recognition test questions (e.g., multiple-choice or true–false) ask you to recognize or pick out the correct answer from answers provided for you, studying that involves carefully reading over your class notes and textbook highlights and selecting important information may be an effective strategy because it matches the type of mental activity you will be using on the test—reading test questions and selecting the correct answer.

On the other hand, recall test questions, such as essay questions, do not involve answer selection; they require answer *production*—you produce the answer on your own. Studying for essay tests by just looking over your class notes and reviewing your reading highlights would not be an effective study strategy because it doesn't match what you're expected to do on the test—which is to supply the correct information yourself rather than recognize information provided for you. To prepare for essay test questions, study time needs to be spent on memory *retrieval*—recalling the information on your own—without looking at it.

You can practice memory retrieval while studying for essay tests by using the following strategies: (1) recitation and (2) creating retrieval cues.

Recitation

Stating aloud the information you're trying to remember—without looking at it—is a memory-improvement strategy known as *recitation*. Research consistently shows that recitation is a self-testing study strategy that may be the most powerful of all test-preparation strategies. Recitation strengthens memory and prepares you well for essay tests because:

- It requires *more mental effort* to dig out (retrieve) the answer on your own and enables the brain to practice exactly what it's expected to do on an essay test.
- It gives you clear *feedback* about whether or not you know the material. If you're unable to retrieve and recite information without looking at it when you're studying, you know for sure that you will not be able to recall it at test time and need to study it further. You can supply yourself with this type of feedback by putting questions on an index cards and their answers on the flip side. If you find yourself flipping over the index card to look at the answer, it's a clear sign that you cannot retrieve the information and need to study it again. (To create electronic flash cards, go to: https://www.studystack.com/)

- It encourages you to express what you're learning *in your own words*. If you can paraphrase what you're studying—rephrase it in your own words—that's a good indicator you really understand it. If you really understand it, you're more likely to remember it because you've made it more meaningful.

Recitation can be done silently, by speaking aloud, or by writing out what you're reciting. Speaking aloud or writing out what you're reciting are particularly effective essay test-preparation strategies because they involve physical activity, which ensures that you're actively involved and engaged in the learning process. (Check the results of your AchieveWORKS Personality assessment. How does the recitation technique match up with your auditory preference? What recommendations would work best for you?)

Creating Retrieval Cues

Have you ever had the experience of trying to remember the name of someone, and you know you know it, but just can't bring it to mind? If you were given a hint (e.g., the first letter of the person's name or a name that rhymes with the name you can't remember), you're likely to suddenly recall the name. The hint you were given is called a retrieval cue. A *retrieval cue* is a type of memory trigger (like a string tied around your finger) that helps trigger your memory of something that you know but may have temporarily forgotten.

Research shows that students who are unable to remember previously studied information are better able to recall that information if they're given a retrieval cue. In one classic study, students studied a long list of items, some of which were animals (e.g., giraffe, coyote, and turkey); other items on the list fell into different categories (vegetables, minerals, etc.). After the students finished studying the list, they were given a blank sheet of paper and asked to write down all the items on the list that they could recall. None of the students were able to recall the names of all the items on the list. However, when the word "animals" was written on top of the answer sheet given to some of the students, they were able to recall the names of more animals from the list they studied than did students who were just given a blank answer sheet. This experiment confirmed that *category names* can serve as powerful retrieval cues. By taking pieces of information you need to recall on an essay test and organizing it into categories, you can then use these category names as retrieval cues at test time. Retrieval cues work to improve memory because memories are stored in the brain as part of an interconnected network. If you're able to recall one piece or segment of the network (the retrieval cue), it can trigger memory of other pieces of information related to it that are stored in the same network.

Reflection 6.2

Think about important items of information you need to remember in a course you're taking this term. Group these items into a category that may be used as a retrieval cue to help you remember them.

1. What's the course?

2. What's the category you've created as a retrieval cue?

3. What items of information would this retrieval cue help you recall?

Another way to create retrieval cues is to come up with your own *catchword or catchphrase* to "catch" (batch together) related ideas you're trying to remember. Acronyms can serve as catchwords, with each letter acting as a retrieval cue for a batch of related ideas. For instance, suppose you're studying for an essay test in abnormal psychology that will test your knowledge of different forms of mental illness. You could create the acronym SCOT as a retrieval cue to help you remember to include the following key elements of mental illness in your essay answers: Symptoms (S), Causes (C), Outcomes (O), and Treatments (T).

Strategies to Use *Immediately Before* a Test

If possible, take a brisk walk or light jog prior to the exam. Physical activity increases mental alertness by increasing oxygen flow to the brain; it also decreases tension by increasing your brain's production of emotionally "mellowing" brain chemicals (e.g., serotonin and endorphins).

Come to the test fully armed with all the test-taking tools you need. In addition to the basic supplies (e.g., no. 2 pencil, pen, blue book, Scantron, calculator, etc.), bring backup equipment in case you experience equipment failure (e.g., an extra pen in case your first one runs out of ink or extra pencils in case your original one breaks).

> "Avoid flipping through notes (cramming) immediately before a test. Instead, do some breathing exercises and think about something other than the test."
>
> —*Advice to first-year students from a college sophomore*

Get to the classroom as early as possible. Arriving early allows you to take a few minutes before the exam and get into a relaxed pre-test state of mind by thinking positive thoughts, taking slow, deep breaths, and stretching your muscles.

(Take a look at your AchieveWORKS Personality assessment report. What do the results suggest you do when starting an exam?)

Sit in the same seat you normally occupy in class. Research indicates that memory is improved when information is recalled in the same place where it was originally received. For example, research shows that when students take a test on material in the same environment where they studied the material, they tend to remember more of it at test time than do students who study the material in one place and take a test on it in a different place. Although it's unlikely you can do all your studying in the same room where your test will be taken, it may be possible to do a short, final review session in your classroom or in an empty classroom with similar features. This strategy can strengthen your memory by enabling you to associate the physical features of the room with the material you're trying to remember. Seeing these features again at test time can help trigger your memory of that material.

A fascinating study supporting this recommendation was once conducted on a group of deep sea divers. Some of these divers learned a list of words on a beach, while the others learned the list underwater. They were later tested for their memory of the words on the list. Half the divers who learned the words on the beach remained there to take the test; the other half were tested underwater. Half the divers who studied the words underwater took the test in the same place; the other half took the test on the beach. The results showed that the divers who took the test in the same place where they learned the list recalled 40% more of the items than divers who did their learning and testing in different places. This study provides strong evidence that memory is strengthened when studying and testing takes place in the same location.

Other intriguing studies have shown that if students are exposed to a certain aroma while studying (e.g., the smell of chocolate) and are later exposed to that same smell when tested, they're better able to recall what they studied. One way to apply this finding to improve your memory of previously studied information at test time is to put on a particular cologne or perfume while studying, and put in on again on the day of the test. This strategy may improve your memory for the information you studied by matching the scent of the study environment with the scent of the test environment. Although this strategy may seem silly, keep in mind that the area of the brain where humans perceive smell has many connections with the brain's memory centers. These neurological connections probably explain why people often report that certain smells trigger long-ago memories (e.g., the smell of a summer breeze may trigger memories of summer games played during childhood). Because smell and memory are neurologically linked in the brain, smell has the potential to serve as a memory-retrieval cue. It certainly wouldn't hurt to give it a try. You might also consider trying the nutritional strategies described in **Box 6.1.**

Box 6.1

Nutritional Strategies for Strengthening Academic Performance

Is there a "brain food" that can enhance test performance? Can we "eat to learn" or "eat to remember"? Some animal studies suggest that memory can be improved by consuming foods containing lecithin—a substance that helps the brain produce acetylcholine—a chemical that plays an important role in the formation of memories. High amounts of lecithin, which explains why fish is sometimes called "brain food."

Despite the results of some animal studies, not enough human research evidence exists to conclude that certain foods significantly improve our ability to acquire, retain, or recall knowledge. However, the following nutritional strategies are likely to improve your mental performance on days when your knowledge is being tested.

Eat breakfast on the day of the exam. Studies show that when students eat a nutritious breakfast on test day, they achieve higher test scores. Breakfast on test day should include grains (e.g., whole wheat toast, whole grain cereal, oatmeal, or bran) because these foods contain complex carbohydrates that deliver a steady stream of energy to the body throughout the day. Complex carbohydrates also help the brain produce a steady stream of serotonin—a brain chemical that reduces tension and anxiety.

> "No man can be wise on an empty stomach."
> —George Eliot, 19th-century English novelist

Make the meal you eat before an exam a light meal. Eating a heavy meal near test time will elevate your blood sugar to an especially high level, causing your body to release large amounts of insulin into the bloodstream to reduce the high blood-sugar level. This draws blood sugar away from the brain, causing mental fatigue—which is the last thing you want to experience during an exam.

If you need an energy boost prior to an exam, eat a piece of fruit rather than a candy bar. Candy bars are processed sweets that infuse synthetic sugar into the bloodstream, providing a short, sudden burst of energy. That's the good news; the bad news is that this short-term rush of blood sugar and sudden jolt of energy is accompanied by increased bodily tension, followed by a sharp drop in energy and feelings of sluggishness. The key is to find a food that elevates energy without elevating tension and supplies a high level of energy over an extended period of time. The best nutritional option for producing such a steady, sustained state of higher energy is consuming natural sugar contained organically in a piece of fruit, not processed sugar slipped artificially into a candy bar.

Avoid consuming caffeine before an exam. Although caffeine stimulates alertness, it also elevates bodily tension and nervousness. These are feelings you don't want to experience during a test, particularly if you're prone to test anxiety. Also, because caffeine is a diuretic, it increases the urge to urinate—an urge you want to avoid during an exam because you're confined to a classroom and can't afford to lose time to leave the room to tend to urinary needs (or stay in the room and be distracted by them).

©Kendall Hunt Publishing Company

Consuming large doses of caffeine or other stimulants before exams is likely to increase your alertness, but it's also likely to increase your level of stress and test anxiety.

Strategies to Use *During* Exams

As soon as you receive a copy of the test, write down any hard-to-remember terms, formulas, equations, and any memory-retrieval cues you may have created. You want to be sure not to forget this important information once you start focusing your attention on the test itself.

Answer first the questions you know well and carry the most points. Before automatically answering questions in the order they appear on the test, take a moment to check out the overall layout of the test and note the questions that carry the most points and the questions you're best prepared to answer. Tackle these questions first. Put a checkmark next to questions whose answers you're unsure of and come back to them later after you've answered the questions you know well. This strategy will ensure that you earn points for the answers you know before you run out of test time.

If you experience "memory block" for information you know that you know, use the following strategies to unlock it.

- Mentally put yourself back in the environment in which you studied. Re-create the situation by mentally picturing the place where you first heard or saw the information and where you studied it—including sights, sounds, smells, and time of day. This memory-improvement strategy is referred to as *guided retrieval*, and research supports its effectiveness for recalling information of all kinds, including information recalled by eyewitnesses to a crime.
- Think of any idea or piece of information that relates to the information you can't remember. Studies show that when students forget something they studied, they're more likely to suddenly remember it if they first recall something related to it.
- Take your mind off the question for awhile and answer another question. This frees up your subconscious to focus on the forgotten information, which can later trigger your conscious memory of it. Moving on to other test questions might also enable you to find information included in those questions that triggers recall of the answer to the earlier question that you temporarily forgot.
- Before turning in your test, double-check your answers. This is the critical last step in the test-taking process. Pressure and anxiety associated with test taking can cause the test-taker students to overlook details, misread instructions, unintentionally skip questions, or make absentminded mistakes. So, take some time to look over your answers and correct any mindless mistakes you may have made before turning it in. Avoid the temptation to immediately bolt out of class after answering the last test question because you're feeling tired or stressed out. When you think about the amount of time and effort you put into preparing for an exam, it's foolish not to take a little more time at the end of the test to be sure that you avoided any absentminded mistakes that could cost you points that you should have earned.

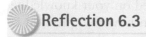**Reflection 6.3**

I'm most likely to experience memory block during exams in the following subjects:

During tests, when I experience memory block, what I usually do is . . .

Strategies for Answering Multiple-Choice Test Questions

You're likely to encounter significant number multiple-choice questions on college tests (particularly in large classes), certification or licensing exams for particular professions (e.g., nursing and teaching), and admissions tests for graduate school (e.g., master's and doctoral degree programs) or professional school (e.g., law school and medical school). Given the ubiquity of multiple-choice tests in college and beyond, the following section of this book contains a comprehensive set of strategies for improving performance on such tests. The following strategies can also be applied to *true–false* questions, which are really essentially multiple-choice questions that have two choice options: (a) true or (b) false.

Read all choices listed and then use a *process-of-elimination* **approach to eliminate answers you know are clearly wrong.** Search for the correct answer by first discarding options that are obviously wrong and continue to do so until you're left with one choice that appears to be the best (truest) option. Keep in mind that the correct answer on a multiple-choice question is often the choice that has the highest probability or likelihood of being true; it doesn't have to be absolutely true—just truer than all the other choices listed.

To be or not to be?
(a) Orange Julius
(b) Julius Erving ("Dr. J.")
(c) Julius Caesar
(d) Caesar Salad
(e) Caesarean Section

A *process-of-elimination* approach is an effective test-taking strategy to use when answering multiple-choice questions.

For a choice to be correct, the *entire statement* **must be true.** If any part of the statement is inaccurate or false, eliminate it because it's an incorrect answer.

When you cannot narrow down your choice to one answer, use *test-wise* **strategies to find clues to the best possible answer.** Your first strategy on any multiple-choice question should be to choose an answer based on your knowledge of the material, not by guessing the correct answer based on how the question is worded. However, if you've relied on your knowledge and used the process-of-elimination strategy to eliminate clearly wrong choices, and you're still left with two or more answers that appear to be correct, then you should turn to being *test-wise*—use the wording or placement of the test question to help you select an answer that's most likely to be correct. Here are three test-wise strategies you can use to make the best choice possible on multiple-choice test questions where more than one choice appears to be correct:

- **Pick the answer that contains qualifying words.** Correct answers are more likely to words that qualify or modify the answer, such as: "usually," "probably," "often," "likely," "sometimes," "perhaps," or "may." Knowledge often doesn't come neatly packaged in the form of absolute or unqualified truths, so choices are more likely to be false if they make broad generalizations or contain absolute words such as "always," "every," "never," "only," "must," and "completely."
- **Pick the longest answer.** True statements often require more words to make them true.
- **Pick a middle answer rather than the first or last answer.** If you've narrowed down the correct answer to either "a" or "c," your best bet may be to go with "c." Similarly, if you've narrowed your choices to "b" or "d," go with "b." Studies show that instructors are more likely to place the correct answer as a middle option rather than as the first or last choice, perhaps because they think the correct answer will be too obvious or stand out if it's placed at the top or bottom of the list.

Check to be sure each answer on your answer sheet aligns with the corresponding test question. Sometimes students skip a test question on a multiple-choice test and forget to skip the corresponding number of that question on the answer form. If this happens, it can throw off all the other answers by one space or line, resulting in a disastrous "domino effect" of wrong answers that can wreak havoc on the student's final test score. To prevent this from happening, look over your test before turning it in and search carefully for questions that you may have skipped and intended to go back to later. Check the alignment of all your answers to be sure there are no blank spaces on your column of answers and that the order of your answers match the order of test questions.

Don't be afraid to change your first answer. A common test-taking myth is that your first answer is always your best answer. Numerous studies on the topic of changing answers on multiple-choice and true–false tests, dating all the way back to 1928, show that most changed test answers go from being incorrect to correct and result in improved test scores. In one study of more than 1,500 students' midterm exams in an introductory psychology course, it was discovered that when students changed answers, 75% of the time they changed from an incorrect to correct answer. This is probably due to the fact that students catch mistakes are caught when they read the question again or they find some information later in the test that causes them to reconsider (and correct) their answer to an earlier test question.

If you have good reason to believe that an answer change should be made, don't be afraid to make it; chances are that it will improve your test score. The only exception to this general rule is when you find yourself changing most of your original answers. This may simply mean that you were not well prepared for the exam and are just doing a lot of guessing and second-guessing.

Reflection 6.4

On multiple-choice exams, do you ever change your first answer to a question?

If you do make changes, what's your usual reason for doing so?

Strategies for Answering Essay Questions

In addition to multiple-choice questions, essay questions are commonly found on college exams. The following strategies may be used to strengthen your performance on essay questions.

Look for "mental action" verbs in the question that point to the type of thinking your instructor expects you to demonstrate in your answer. **Box 6.2** contains a list of thinking verbs that often appear in essay questions and the type of mental action typically called for by each of these verbs.

Box 6.2

Action Verbs Commonly Appearing on Essay-Test Questions and the Type of Thinking They Call For

Analyze—break the topic down into its key parts or essential components.

Compare—identify similarities and differences between key concepts.

Contrast—identify differences between ideas, particularly sharp differences and clashing viewpoints.

Describe—provide details (e.g., who, what, when, and where).

Discuss—analyze (break it into parts) and evaluate the parts (e.g., its strengths and weaknesses).

Document—back up your conclusions and interpretations with supporting evidence.

Explain—provide reasons for; answer the questions, "why?" and "how?"

Illustrate—provide specific instances or concrete examples.

Interpret—draw your own conclusion and explain why you came to that conclusion.

Support—back up your ideas with logical reasoning, persuasive arguments, statistics, or research findings.

Reflection 6.5

Which one of the mental actions listed in **Box 6.2** was most often required on your high school writing assignments?

Which one was least often (or never) required?

Make an outline of your key ideas before you begin writing out your answers. First, do a quick "information dump" by jotting down the main points you plan to make in your essay answer—in outline form. (See **Exhibit 1** for an example.) An outline is effective for several reasons:

- **It ensures that you remember to discuss your most powerful points.** The points listed in your outline can serve as memory-retrieval cues to help you remember the "big picture" before you launch into the smaller details.
- **It earns you points by improving your answer's organizational quality.** One factor that instructors consider when awarding points for an essay is how well that essay is organized. An outline will improve your answer's organization which, in turn, will increase the number of points you're awarded.
- **It helps reduce test anxiety.** By outlining your points ahead of time, you can focus on expressing (writing) those points without the added stress of figuring out *what* you're going to say at the same time you're figuring out *how* to say it.
- **It can earn you points on a question that you don't have time to complete.** If you run out of test time before writing out your full answer to an essay question, an outline shows your instructor what you planned to include in your answer. The outline itself is likely to earn you points because it demonstrates your knowledge of the major points called for by the question.

Exhibit 1

Identical twins
Adoption
Parents/family tree

6/6

1. There are several different studies that scientists conduct, but one study that they conduct is to find out how genetics can influence human behavior in <u>identical twins</u>. Since they are identical, they will most likely end up very similar in behavior because of their identical genetic makeup. Although environment has some impact, genetics are still a huge factor and they will, more likely than not, behave similarly. Another type of study is with <u>parents and their family trees</u>. Looking at a subject's family tree will explain why a certain person is bipolar or depressed. It is most likely caused by a gene in the family tree, even if it was last seen decades ago. Lastly, another study is with adopted children. If an <u>adopted child</u> acts a certain way that is unique to that child, and researchers find the parents' family tree, they will most likely see similar behavior in the parents and siblings as well.

2. The monistic view of the mind-brain relationship is so strongly opposed and criticized because there is a belief or assumption that <u>free will</u> is taken away from people. For example, if a person commits a horrendous crime, it can be argued "monistically" that the chemicals in the brain were the reason, and that a person cannot think for themselves to act otherwise. This view limits responsibility.

No freewill
No afterlife

6/6

Another reason that this view is opposed is because it has been said that <u>there is no afterlife</u>. If the mind and brain are one and the same, and there is <u>NO</u> difference, then once the brain is dead and is no longer functioning, so is the mind. Thus, it cannot continue to live beyond what we know today as life. <u>And</u> this goes against many religions, which is why this reason, in particular, is heavily opposed.

Short Outlines (in Side Margin) Used by a College Sophomore to Earn Maximum Points on Essay Test Questions

Get directly to the point on each question. Avoid elaborate introductions that take up your test time (and your instructor's grading time) but don't earn you any points. An answer that begins with the statement "This is an interesting question that we had a great discussion about in class . . ." is pointless because it doesn't add points to your test score. Timed essay tests often leave you pressed for time, so don't waste time on flowery introductions that contribute nothing to your test grade.

One effective way to get directly to the point on essay questions is to include part of the question in the first sentence of your answer. For example, if the test question asks you to, "Argue for or against capital punishment by explaining how it will or will not reduce the nation's homicide rate." Your first sentence could be, "Capital punishment will not reduce the homicide rate for the following reasons . . ." Thus, your first sentence becomes your thesis statement—it points you directly to the major points you're going to make in your answer and earns you immediate points for your answer.

Answer essay questions in as much detail as possible. Don't assume that your instructor already knows what you're talking about or will be bored by details. Instead, take the approach that you're writing to someone who knows little or nothing about the subject—as if you're an expert teacher explaining it to a beginning student.

> As a general rule, it's better to over-explain than under-explain your answers to essay questions.

Back up your points with evidence—facts, statistics, quotes, or examples. When you're answering essay questions, adopt the mindset of a lawyer: make your case by citing specific supporting evidence (exhibit A, exhibit B, etc.).

Leave space between your answers to each essay question. If you recall something later that you would like to add to your original answer, this space will provide a place to do so.

Proofread your answers for spelling and grammar. Even if your instructors do not explicitly state that grammar and spelling count toward your grade, both are still likely to influence their overall evaluation of your written work. Before turning in your test, taking some time to catch and correct clerical errors will improve your overall test score.

Neatness counts. Many years of research indicate that neatly written essays are scored higher than sloppy ones, even if the content of the answers are essentially the same. These findings aren't surprising when you consider that grading essay answers is a time-consuming, labor-intensive task that requires your instructor to plod through multiple answers written by multiple students with multiple styles of handwriting—ranging from crystal clear to quasi-cryptic. Making your instructor's job a little easier by writing as clearly as possible, and by cleaning up any sloppy markings before turning in your test, is likely to earn you more points on your essay answers.

Post-Test Strategies: What to Do *After* Receiving Test Results

Successful test performance involves both forethought (preparation before the test) and afterthought (reflection after the test). Often, when students get a test back, they just check to see what grade they got and then stuff it in a binder or toss it into the nearest wastebasket. Don't fall prey to this unproductive habit; instead, reflect on your results to: (a) determine where you lost and gained points, and (b) develop strategies for improving your next test performance. STOP and ask yourself questions like the following:

- Were these the results I expected?
- What do the results suggest about the effectiveness of my approach to learning the material?
- How can I use my results as constructive feedback to improve my next test grade?

> *Mistakes should neither be ignored nor neglected; they should be detected and corrected so they don't happen again.*

> "When you make a mistake, there are only three things you should do about it: admit it; learn from it; and don't repeat it."
>
> —Paul "Bear" Bryant, legendary college football coach

If you get a test back with a disappointing grade, don't get bitter, get better. View your mistakes in terms of what they can do for you, not to you. A poor test performance can be turned into a productive learning experience, particularly if it occurs early in the course when you're still learning the rules of the game. A low test does not mean you're incapable of doing better work or are destined to end up with a poor grade in the course. Studies of high-achievers and experts in multiple fields reveal that they hunger for feedback and are more often interested in feedback about what they did *wrong* so they can fix it.

> "A man who has committed a mistake and doesn't correct it is committing another mistake."
>
> —Confucius, ancient Chinese philosopher and educator

Listed below are specific strategies for using test results as feedback to improve your future test performance.

After getting a test back, determine where you *earned* and *lost* points. Identify what went right so you can do it again, and troubleshoot what went wrong so you don't make the same mistake again. On test questions where you lost points, use the strategies summarized in **Box 6.3** to pinpoint the source of the problem.

Reflection 6.6

When you get a test back, do you carefully review the results to see where you gained and lost points?

Do you use this information as feedback to improve your next test performance?

How do you think most students would answer the above two questions?

Reflect on feedback provided by your instructor. Make careful note of any comments the instructor may have written on your exam and keep these comments in mind when you prepare for the next exam. You can seek additional feedback by making an appointment to confer with your instructor during office hours. If you do make an office visit to discuss your test, don't focus on or complain about the

Box 6.3

Strategies for Pinpointing the Source of Lost Points on Exams

On test items where you lost points, try to zero in on the stage of the learning process where the breakdown occurred. You can do so by asking yourself the following questions.

- Did I have the information needed to answer the question correctly? If I didn't, where should it have been acquired in the first place? Was the information presented in class and didn't get into my notes? If yes, consider adopting strategies for improving lecture listening and note-taking. (See the strategies cited on pp. 90–97). If the missing information was contained in assigned reading, check whether you're using effective reading strategies (such as those listed on pp. 98–103).

- Did I have the information, but didn't remember it? Failing to remember information on a test can usually be traced back to the following causes:

  (a) Trying to cram in too much study time just before the exam and not giving the brain enough time to "digest" (consolidate) the information and store it in long-term memory. The solution may be to distribute study time more evenly in advance of the next exam and take advantage of the "part-to-whole"

study method. (See strategies provided on pp. 107–108).

  (b) Not learning the material deeply enough to be able to recall it at test time. This may require using strategies for studying smarter or more strategically. (See study strategies cited on pp. 103–115.)

  (c) Studying and knowing the material well, but experiencing test anxiety that interfered with recalling it at test time. This may require use of strategies for reducing test anxiety (see pp. 135–136). (If problems with text anxiety persist, seek assistance from a professional in the Academic Support Center or Counseling Center.)

- Did I study the material but didn't really understand it? This suggests you may need to self-monitor your comprehension more closely while studying to determine whether you're learning deeply, as opposed to just memorizing. (See the deep learning strategies supplied on pp. 104–106.)

- Did I know the material but lost points due to careless test-taking mistakes? If this happened, the solution may be simply to take some time after completing an exam to check for absentminded errors before turning it in.

---

overall test grade; instead, focus on getting feedback on how you could improve your next future test performance.

Get feedback from professionals in your Learning Center or Academic Support Center. Tutors and other learning support professionals on campus can provide you with constructive feedback about how to improve your test-preparation and test-taking strategies. Ask these professionals to take a look at your tests and seek their advice about how to improve your future test performance.

Seek feedback from classmates. Peers can also be a valuable source of information on how to improve your test results. Consider reviewing your test with trusted classmates, particularly those who did well on the test. Their test answers can provide you with models of the type of work your instructor expects on exams. Ask successful students what they did to be successful, such as how they prepared for the test and what strategies they used during the test.

Teaming up with classmates after exams (and assignments) *early in the term* is especially effective because it enables you to get a better idea of what the instructor will expect of you throughout the remainder of the course. You can use this information as early feedback to diagnose your initial mistakes, improve your next effort, and elevate your overall course grade—while there's still plenty of time left in the term to do so. (See **Box 6.4** for a summary of the most effective forms of feedback to seek for strengthening your academic performance.)

Box 6.4

Seeking Performance-Enhancing Feedback

When asking for feedback from others to improve your academic performance, seek feedback with the following features.

- Specific feedback. Feedback that identifies precisely what needs to be done to improve your performance and how you should go about doing it. For example, after a test, ask for feedback that provides you with more information than just your overall test and course grade. Seek specific information about where you lost points and what specific test-preparation and test-taking strategies you could use to improve your next performance.

- Prompt feedback. After receiving your grade on a test or assignment, *immediately* review the results and seek feedback as soon as possible. Right after getting your test back is the time when you're likely to be most motivated to find out what you got right and wrong; it's also the time when you're most likely to retain the feedback you receive.

- Proactive feedback. Seek feedback *early* in the learning process so that you have plenty of time and opportunity to use the feedback throughout the term to accumulate more points and earn a higher final grade.

AUTHOR'S EXPERIENCE

A study strategy that I developed when I was a college student was to review my previous tests and quizzes in my courses to prepare for my midterm and final exams. I noticed that when my professors gave exams that included material covered up until the middle or end of the term, many of the same questions that were included in previous exams appeared again, often in exactly the same form, or just with a slight twist. Using these earlier, shorter quizzes as practice tests helped prepare for later, larger exams.

—*Michele Campagna*

Test Anxiety: Recognizing and Reducing It

High levels of test anxiety interfere with students' ability to recall information previously studied and increase their risk of making careless concentration-related errors on exams, such as overlooking key words in test questions. When *test anxiety* is experienced, anxious thoughts and feelings (e.g., fear of failure) occupy their mind during exams and take up valuable "mental space" that should be devoted to recalling knowledge and thinking critically. Studies show that students who experience test anxiety are also more likely to use ineffective "surface"-level study practices to prepare for exams that rely on memorization, rather than effective "deep-learning" strategies that enable them to find meaning in what they're learning and making connections between concepts.

Listed below are strategies that can be used to recognize and minimize test anxiety.

Understand what test anxiety is and what it's not. Don't confuse anxiety with stress. Stress is a physical reaction that prepares the body for action by arousing and energizing it; this heightened level of arousal and energy can actually enhance performance (see pp. ____). In fact, being totally stress-free during an exam may mean that you're too laid back and could care less about how well you do. Attaining peak levels of human performance—whether it be athletic or academic—aren't achieved by totally eliminating stress. Instead, research shows that a *moderate* level of stress (neither too high nor too low) during exams and other tests of human performance serves to maximize alertness, concentration, and memory. Thus, the key is keeping stress at a manageable level that capitalizes on its capacity to get you pumped up or psyched out but prevents it from reaching a level where you're stressed or psyched out.

If a student frequently experiences the following physical and psychological symptoms during a test, it probably means that the student's stress level is high enough to be called *test anxiety*.

- Bodily symptoms of nervousness during tests, such as pounding heartbeat, rapid pulse, muscle tension, sweating, or queasy stomach.
- Difficulty concentrating or focusing attention on test questions.
- Experiencing a rush of negative thoughts and feelings, such as fear of failure or self-putdowns (e.g., "I always mess up on exams.")
- Hurrying through the test just to get it over with and get rid of the uncomfortable feelings being experienced.
- "Going blank" during the exam and forgetting much of what was previously studied.
- Suddenly being able to remember information that was forgotten during the exam after turning in the exam and leaving the test situation.

Use effective test-preparation strategies prior to the exam. Test anxiety research indicates that college students who prepare well for exams and use effective study strategies to prepare for exams (such as those discussed in Chapter 5) experience less test anxiety during exams. Studies also show that there's a strong relationship between procrastination and test anxiety—i.e., students who put off studying to the very last minute are more likely to report higher levels of test anxiety. The high level of pretest tension caused by last-minute rushing and cramming for a test often carries over to the test itself, resulting in higher levels of tension during the test. Furthermore, late night cramming deprives the brain of stress-relieving dream (REM) sleep, which leads to higher levels of tension the next day—the day of the test.

Focus on the test in front of you, not the students around you. Don't spend valuable test time looking at how others are doing and wondering if they're doing better than you. If you came to the test well prepared and still find the test difficult, it's likely that other students find it difficult too. If you happen to notice others finishing before you do, don't assume they breezed through the test and are smarter than you. Their faster finish may simply reflect the fact that they didn't know many of the answers and decided to give up and get out (rather than prolong the agony).

Instead of worrying about what you're getting wrong and how many points you're losing, focus on the answers you're getting right and the points you're earning. Thoughts can influence emotions and positive emotions—such as those associated with optimism and a sense of accomplishment—can improve mental performance by enhancing the brain's ability to process, store, and retrieve information. One way to maintain a positive test-taking mindset is to keep in mind that college exams are designed to be more difficult than high school tests. Even without achieving a near-perfect test score, you can still achieve a good test grade.

Keep in mind that tests are not measures of your overall intelligence, personal potential, or self-worth. No single exam can measure your true intellectual capacity or academic talent. In fact, the grade you receive on a test may not even be a good indicator of how much you have learned or your ability to learn.

If you continue to experience test anxiety after trying to overcome it on your own, seek assistance from a professional in your Learning (Academic Support) Center or Counseling Center. Some emotional challenges, like milder forms of personal anxiety and depression, can be managed with self-help strategies (for details, see chapter 13); so, too, can test anxiety. However, if the problem persists after you've done all you can to cope with it on your own, it's time to seek help. This doesn't mean you're academically weak or incompetent; it means you have the emotional intelligence and resourcefulness to realize your limitations and to capitalize on the support networks available to you.

Reflection 6.7

How would you rate your general level of test anxiety during exams? (Circle one.)

high   moderate   low

What types of tests or subjects tend to produce the most test stress or anxiety for you?

Why?

Do you think that the amount of stress you experience during exams is manageable, or do you think it's too high and interferes with your test performance? If it's too high, what step(s) could you take to reduce it to a more manageable level?

Internet-Based Resources

For additional information on test-taking strategies and managing test anxiety, consult the following websites:

Test-Taking Strategies:
https://www.stmarys-ca.edu/tutorial-and-academic-skills-center/additional-resources/test-taking-strategies
http://www.wiu.edu/advising/docs/mastering_test_taking.pdf

Overcoming Test Anxiety:
http://www.studygs.net/tstprp8.htm
http://www.sic.edu/files/uploads/group/34/PDF/TestAnxiety.pdf

Chapter 6 Exercises

6.1 Quote Reflections

Review the sidebar quotes contained in this chapter and select two that were especially meaningful or inspirational to you.

For each quote you selected, provide an explanation why you chose it.

6.2 Strategy Reflections

Review the strategies for *answering essay questions* on pp. 129-131. Select three strategies that you think are most important and intend to put into practice.

6.3 Reality Bite

Bad Feedback: Shocking Midterm Grades

Fred has enjoyed his first weeks on campus. He has met lots of people and really likes being in college. He's also very pleased to discover that, unlike high school, his college schedule doesn't require him to be in class all day long. That's the good news. The bad news is that unlike high school, where his grades were all As and Bs, Fred's first midterm grades are three Cs, one D, and one F. He's stunned and a bit depressed because he thought he was going to do well in college. Because he never received grades this low in high school, he's beginning to think that he's not college material and may flunk out.

Reflection Questions

1. What factors do you think may have caused or contributed to Fred's bad start?

2. What do you recommend Fred do right now to get his grades up and avoid being placed on academic probation?

3. What might Fred do in the future to prevent this midterm setback from happening again?

6.4 Self-Assessment of Test-Taking Strategies

Rate yourself in terms of how frequently you use these test-taking strategies below, using the following scale:

4 = always, 3 = sometimes, 2 = rarely, 1 = never

1. I take tests in the same seat where I usually sit in class and take notes.	4	3	2	1
2. I first answer essay test questions I know well before answering those of which I'm unsure.	4	3	2	1
3. I use a process-of-elimination approach on multiple-choice questions to eliminate clearly wrong choices until I find one that's correct or appears to be the most accurate option.	4	3	2	1
4. I look for key action words that indicate what type of thinking I should display in my answer (e.g., "analyze," "compare").	4	3	2	1
5. On essay questions, I outline or map out the major ideas I'll include in my answer before starting to write out my answer.	4	3	2	1
6. I look for information included on a test that may help me answer difficult questions and that may help me remember information I've forgotten.	4	3	2	1

7. I leave extra space between my answers to essay questions in case I want to come back   4   3   2   1
   and add more information later.

8. After finishing a test, before turning it in, I double-check for errors I may have made   4   3   2   1
   or questions I may have skipped.

Self-Assessment Reflections:

Which of the above strategies do you already use consistently?

Which of the above strategies rated (1) or (2) are you *most* likely and *least* likely to implement? Why?

6.5 Midterm Self-Evaluation

About halfway through an academic term, college students are likely to experience the "midterm crunch"—a wave of major exams and assignments. Midterm a good time to take a close look at your academic progress in all your courses.

Using the form below, list the courses you're taking this term and the grades you're receiving in these courses. If you don't know your current grade in a course, check the syllabus for the instructor's grading scale and estimate your grade based on the scores you've received on your completed tests and assignments. This should give you at least a rough idea where you stand in the course. If you've checked the course syllabus and your results on your completed tests and assignments and are still having difficulty determining your course grade, see your instructor to get an idea of where you stand in class.

	Course No.	Course Title	Grade
1.			
2.			
3.			
4.			
5.			
6.			

Reflections

1. Were these the grades you *expected*? Were they better or worse than you anticipated?

2. Were these the grades you were *hoping* for? Are you pleased or disappointed with them?

3. Do you see any patterns in your performance that point to things you're doing well and things you need to improve?

4. If you had to pinpoint one action you could take right now to improve your lowest course grade, what would it be?

6.6 Calculating Your Midterm Grade Point Average

Use the information below to calculate what your grade-point average (GPA) would be if your current course grades turn out to be your final course grades.

How to Compute Your GPA

Most colleges and universities use a grading scale ranging from 0 to 4 to calculate a student's GPA or quality point average (QPA). Some schools use a grading system that involves only letters (A, B, etc.), whereas others use letters as well as pluses and minuses (A-, B+, etc.). Check your college catalog or student handbook to determine what grading system is used at your campus.

The typical point value (points earned) by different letter grades are listed below.

Grade = Point Value

A	=	4.0
A-	=	3.7
B+	=	3.3
B	=	3.0
B-	=	2.7
C+	=	2.3
C	=	2.0
C-	=	1.7
D+	=	1.3
D	=	1.0
D-	=	.7
F	=	0

Step 1. Calculate the grade points you're earning in each of your courses this term by multiplying the course's number of units (credits) by the point value of the grade you're now earning in the course. For instance, if you have a grade of B in a three-unit course, that course is earning you 9 grade points; if you have a grade of A in a two-unit course, that course is earning you 8 grade points.

Step 2. Calculate your GPA by using the following formula:

$$\text{GRADE POINT AVERAGE (GPA)} = \frac{\text{Total Number of Grade Points for all Courses}}{\text{Divided by Total Number of Course Units}}$$

For example, see the following fictitious courses and course grades:

Course	Units	×	Grade	=	Grade Points
Roots of Rock & Roll	3	×	C (2)	=	6
Daydream Analysis	3	×	A (4)	=	12
Surfing Strategies	1	×	A (4)	=	4
Wilderness Survival	4	×	B (3)	=	12
Fake News	2	×	D (1)	=	2
Love and Romance	3	×	A (4)	=	12
	16				48

$$GPA = \frac{48}{16} = 3.0$$

Reflection Questions

1. What is your GPA at this point in the term?

2. Is this the GPA you expected to attain? If there's a gap between the GPA you expected to achieve and the GPA you now have, what do you think accounts for this discrepancy?

3. Do you think your final GPA at the end of the term will be higher or lower than it is now? Why?

Note: It's very common for college students' first-year GPA to be lower than it was in high school. In one study that compared students' high school GPAs with their GPAs after their first year of college, it was found that:

*   29% of college students had GPAs of 3.75 or higher in high school, but only 17% had GPAs that high at the end of their first year of college.

*   46% of college students had high school GPAs between 3.25 and 3.74, but only 32% had GPAs that high after the first year of college.

CHAPTER 7

Three Key Academic Success and Lifelong Learning Skills

INFORMATION LITERACY, WRITING, AND SPEAKING

Researching, writing, and speaking effectively are flexible skills that can be transferred and applied to all majors and careers. In this chapter, you will acquire strategies to locate and evaluate information, construct papers and reports, and use writing as a tool to learn deeply and think critically. The chapter also includes specific, practical tips for making effective oral presentations, overcoming speech anxiety and becoming a more self-confident public speaker.

Develop skills for accessing and referencing others' ideas through scholarly research, and acquire strategies for effectively communicating your own ideas orally and in writing.

 Reflection 7.1

What would you say is the difference between acquiring factual knowledge and learning a transferable skill?

The Importance of Research and Communication Skills

We're now living in the "information" and "communication" age; more information is being produced, reproduced, and communicated in today's world than at any other time in human history. Since information is now being generated and disseminated at such a rapid rate, "information literacy"—the ability to search for, locate, and evaluate information—has become an essential 21st-century skill. Oral and written communication skills have also become increasingly important for success in the contemporary work world; college graduates with these skills have a clear advantage in today's job market. If you dedicate yourself to improving your speaking, writing, and information literacy, you will improve both your overall academic performance in college and your career performance after college.

"Employers are far more interested in the prospect's ability to think and to think clearly, to write and speak well, and how (s)he works with others than in his [or her] major or the name of the school (s)he went to. Several college investigating teams found that these were the qualities on which all kinds of employers, government and private, base their decisions.

—Lauren Pope, author, *Looking Beyond the Ivy League*

Information Literacy: Research Strategies for Locating and Evaluating Information

As noted in Chapter 2, a key goal of colleges and universities is to empower students to become self-reliant, lifelong learners. One attribute of a self-reliant, lifelong learner is *information literacy*—the ability to locate, evaluate, and use information. When you're information literate, you're a critical consumer of information who knows how to access accurate and relevant information whenever you need it.

Organizing a Research Report

Described below is a systematic set of information literacy strategies that you can use to write research papers and reports in college (and beyond). This stepwise process may also be used for researching and delivering oral presentations.

1. Define Your Research Topic or Question

The first step in the process of writing a college research report is to be sure you're researching a topic that is acceptable to your instructor and is neither: (a) too *narrow*—leaving you with an insufficient amount of information to write about, nor (b) too *broad*—leaving you with too much information to cover. If you have any doubts about your topic's acceptability or scope, before going any further, seek feedback from your instructor or from a professional in your college library.

> College librarians are both information literacy experts and college educators. Be sure to capitalize on the out-of-class, one-on-one educational support they can provide you.

2. Identify Information Resources and Tools You Will Use

Information resources come in two major forms:

- **Print resources**—e.g., card catalogs, published indexes, and guidebooks
- **Online resources**—e.g., online card catalogs, Internet search engines, and electronic databases (Find out what resources your instructor prefers or requires before beginning the information search process.)

Different information search tools are likely to supply you with different source types of information; therefore, it's best to rely on more than one. **Box 7.1** contains a summary of information search terms and tools you can use. As you read through the following list, place a check mark next to those you're familiar with and a plus sign next to those you've used before.

 Reflection 7.2

Look back at the terms listed in **Box 7.1**. What terms were you already familiar with? Which of these tools have you used before?

Box 7.1

Key Information Search Tools and Terms

Search Engine: a computer-run program that allows you to search for information across the entire Internet or at a particular website. For regularly updated summaries of different electronic search engines, how they work, and the type of information they generate, go to: https://researchbuzz.me/

URL (Uniform Resource Locator): An Internet address consisting of letters or numbers that pinpoints the exact location of an information resource (e.g., http://www.thrivingincollege.org/).

Database: a collection of data (information) that's been organized to make it easily accessible and retrievable. A database may include:

a) reference citations—such as author, date, and publication source
b) abstracts—summary of the contents of a scholarly article
c) full-length documents
d) a combination of (a), (b), and (c).

Subscription Database: a database that can only be accessed with a paid subscription. Your college or university library is likely to have subscriptions to many of these databases, so you may be able to access them at no personal cost.

Catalog: a library database containing information about what information sources the library owns and where they're located. Most catalogs are now in electronic form and can be searched by typing in a topic heading, author, or keyword.

Index: an alphabetical listing of topics contained in a database.

Descriptor (a.k.a. Subject Heading): a key word or phrase in the index of a database that describes the subjects or content areas found within it, and enables you to quickly locate sources relevant to your research topic. For example, "emotional disorders" may be a descriptor for a psychology database that leads you to sources of information about anxiety and depression. (Some descriptors or subject headings are accompanied by suggestions for other search words you can use to explore the topic you're researching.)

Keyword: a word used to search multiple databases that matches the search word you've entered with information contained in different databases. (Note: A keyword is very specific, so if information relating to your topic does not exactly match the key word, it isn't likely to be retrieved. For example, if you use the key word "college" and you're also interested in finding information about universities, you may have to use the key word "university" to find sources with that term in their title.

Search Thesaurus: a list of words or phrases with similar meaning that allows you to identify which of these words or phrases can be used as key words, descriptors, or subject headings in the database. This feature enables you to choose the best search terms before beginning the search process.

Wildcard: a symbol, such as an asterisk (*), question mark (?), or exclamation point (!) that can be used to substitute different letters into a search word or phrase, allowing you to conduct an electronic search on all variations of the word represented by the symbol. For example, an asterisk at the end of the key word, *econom**, may be used to search all information sources containing the words "economy," "economical," or "economist."

Citation: a reference to a specific source of information cited in a book, article, or web page that provides information about the source (its author, publication source, and date of publication), which you can use to retrieve the source.

Abstract: a concise summary of the source's content that usually appears at the beginning of an article, which can help you decide quickly whether the source is relevant to your research topic.

For a more extensive glossary of Internet terms, see: Matisse's Glossary of Internet Terms at http://www.matisse.net/files/glossary.html.

After locating a potential information source, the next step is to assess its relevance to your research topic. One simple strategy for determining the relevance of a source is to ask yourself if it will help answer any of the following questions about the topic you're investigating: Who? What? When? Where? Why? or How?

3. Evaluate the Validity and Quality of Your Sources

The primary purpose of searching for and citing sources in your research paper is to provide *documentation*—references that support or confirm your ideas and conclusions. Because sources of information can vary widely in terms of their accuracy or validity, critical thinking must be used to evaluate the quality of information you locate. The ever-growing Internet has made this critical thinking process more important (and more challenging) because much of the information posted on the Web is "self-published" and not subjected to the same quality control measures as information published in professional journals and books—publications that only go public after they've been carefully reviewed, evaluated, and edited by a neutral panel of experts. You can use the following criteria to critically evaluate the quality of information sources.

- **Scholarly:** Does the information appear in a scholarly publication that has been reviewed by a panel or board of impartial experts in the field? Scholarly publications are written in a formal style that include references to other published sources and are "peer reviewed" or "peer refereed," which means that they have been evaluated and approved for publication by other experts in the field. Professional journals are peer reviewed (e.g., *New England Journal of Medicine*), but popular magazines and websites are not.

   Subscription databases available at your college or university library are more likely to contain peer-reviewed sources than free databases available to you on the Internet. However, you can also use websites like "Google Scholar" (scholar.google.com) to find some scholarly sources that may be accessed for free.

> *Wikipedia isn't considered to be a scholarly source, but you can track down scholarly references mentioned on Wikipedia, read them, and cite them in your research report.*

- **Credibility:** Is the source written by an authority or expert in the field (e.g., someone with an advanced educational degree or professional experience relating to the topic)? For example, if your topic relates to an international issue, a highly credible source would be an author who has an advanced degree in international relations or extensive professional experience in international affairs.
- **Objectivity:** Is the author likely to be impartial or unbiased toward the subject? Take into consideration how the professional position or personal background of authors may influence their ideas or their interpretation of evidence. Scholars should be impartial and objective in their pursuit of truth; they should not be in a position to gain fiscally, personally, or politically by reaching a certain conclusion about the topic they're investigating.

   You should be skeptical about the objectivity of information contained in web-based sources with addresses that end with ".com" because these are "com"mercial sites whose primary purpose is to sell products and make money, not educate the public or engage in the objective pursuit of truth. To assess the objectivity of websites, always ask yourself why the site was created, what its objective or purpose is, and who sponsors it.

   Even scientific research may lack objectivity. For instance, if you find an article on climate change written by scientists who work for or with an industry that risks incurring costs or losing revenue by switching to a more ecologically efficient source of energy, it's reasonable to suspect that these researchers have a conflict of interest and may be biased toward reaching a conclusion that will benefit their employer (and themselves). When evaluating an article, check for bias by asking yourself the following questions: (a) Is the author a member of a special interest group or organization that may be affected by or benefit from the article's conclusions? (b) Does the author consider alternative or opposing viewpoints and respond to these viewpoints fairly? (c) Does the author use words that convey rationality and objectivity, or are the ideas (and opinions) expressed in a highly emotional or inflammatory tone? If you think an article may lack complete objectivity, but still contains some good information and strong arguments, you can cite it in your paper, but be sure you demonstrate critical thinking by noting its potential bias.

- **Currency:** Has the source been published or posted recently? In certain fields of study, such as science and technology, recent references may be strongly preferred because new data is generated rapidly in these fields and information can become quickly outdated. In other fields, such as history and philosophy, older references may be viewed as timeless classics, so citing them is perfectly acceptable. Check with your instructor before you begin the search process to be sure if both recent and historical references are equally acceptable, or if either is preferred.

4. Include a Sufficient Number and Variety of Sources

The quality of your research is likely to be judged only on the credibility of your sources, but also on their quantity and variety.

Number of sources: As a general rule, it's better to use as many references as possible because more references supply your report with a broader base of support and a wider range of perspectives. In addition, using multiple sources allows you to demonstrate the higher-level thinking skill of synthesis—the ability to integrate information from multiple sources.

Variety of sources: For some research reports, the variety of references cited may be as important as their sheer quantity. You can intentionally vary and balance your sources by drawing on different types of references, such as:

- Books
- Scholarly journals—written by professionals and research scholars in the field
- Magazine and newspaper articles—written by journalists
- Course readings and class notes
- Interviews and personal experiences.

You can also vary your references by using both (a) *primary* sources—firsthand information or original documents (e.g., research studies or memoirs), and (b) *secondary* sources—publications that build on or respond to primary sources (e.g., textbook chapters or newspaper articles that summarize research findings or analyze previously published information).

Lastly, you can vary your references by blending older, classic sources with more recent, cutting-edge research. Combining the classic with the current can position you to show how certain ideas have changed or evolved over time, while others have withstood the test of time.

5. Use Sources as Stepping Stones to Your Own Ideas and Conclusions

It's your name that appears on the front cover of your research report, so your report should be something more than an accumulation or amalgamation of other peoples' ideas. Simply collecting and compiling the ideas of others will result in a final product that reads more like a high school book report than a college research paper. Look at your sources as raw material that you'll mold and shape into a finished product with your stamp on it. Don't just report or describe the information find; react to it, interpret it, and cite it as evidence to support your own interpretations and conclusions.

6. Cite Your Sources with Integrity

Students with integrity don't cheat on exams and then rationalize that their cheating is acceptable because "others are doing it," nor do they plagiarize others' work and pawn it off as their own. By citing your sources carefully, you demonstrate intellectual honesty by giving credit where credit is due. You credit others whose ideas you've borrowed and you credit yourself for the careful research you've done.

When should sources be cited? Simply put: Reference everything that's included in your paper that was obtained from a source other than yourself. This includes other people's words, ideas, statistics, research findings, and visual work (e.g., diagrams, pictures, or drawings). There's only one exception to this rule: Information that's *common knowledge*—information that most people already know—does not have to be cited. Common knowledge includes information like well-known facts (e.g., the earth is the third planet from the sun) and familiar dates (e.g., the Declaration of Independence was signed in 1776).

The Internet has given us easy access to an extraordinary amount of information, making research much easier; that's the good news. The bad news is that it has also made proper citation more challenging. Determining the true "owner" or original author of posted information isn't always as clear or obvious as it is for published books and articles. If you want to cite information you've found at a website but are unsure of its author, cite the full name of the website, the date of the posted information (if available), and the date you accessed or downloaded it. If you have any doubt about how to cite an online source, print it out and check it out with your instructor or a professional in your college library.

> As a general rule, if you're unsure about whether something needs to be referenced, it's better to reference it and run the risk of unnecessary referencing than to run the risk of plagiarism—a serious violation of academic integrity that can have serious consequences. (See **Box 7.2** on p. 147 for specific details about what constitutes plagiarism and specific ways to avoid it.)

Where and how should a source be cited? A source should be cited in two places: (a) in the *body* of your paper where you used the information, and (b) in the *reference section* at the end of your paper (also known as a "bibliography" or "works cited" section). How sources should be cited depends on the referencing style preferred by the particular academic field in which the paper is written. Your instructor should inform you about the referencing style you should use; if not, seek clarification.

You're likely to be asked to use either of the following two referencing styles in your college research papers:
- *MLA* style—the style adopted by the Modern Language Association—commonly used in the Humanities and Fine Arts

> "When a student violates an academic integrity policy, no one wins, even if the person gets away with it. It isn't right to cheat and it is an insult to everyone who put the effort in and did the work. I learned my lesson and have no intention of ever cheating again."
>
> —First-year college student's reflection on an academic integrity violation

> "Although it may seem like a pain to write a works cited page, it is something that is necessary when writing a research paper. You must acknowledge every single author of whose information you used. The authors spent much time and energy writing their book or article [so] you must give them the credit that they deserve."
>
> —First-year student's reflection on a plagiarism violation

- *APA* style—the style adopted by the American Psychological Association— commonly used in the Social and Natural Sciences

If you go on to take advanced courses in a specialized professional field, you may be asked to use other styles, such as *The Chicago Manual of Style* for papers in history, or the Council of Biology Editors (CBE) style for papers in the biological sciences.

Software programs are now available that automatically format references according to a particular citation style, such as CiteFast (www.citefast.com) and EasyBib (www.easybib.com). If you use these programs, be sure to proofread the results because they can sometimes generate inaccurate or incomplete citations.

 Reflection 7.3

Prior to college, did you write papers that required citation of references? If yes, what referencing style did you use?

Box 7.2

Plagiarism: A Violation of Academic Integrity

What Exactly is Plagiarism?

Plagiarism is a violation of academic integrity that involves intentional or unintentional use of someone else's work without acknowledging it, thus giving the impression it's your own work.

Common Forms of Plagiarism

1. Paying someone, or paying a service, for a paper and turning it in as if you wrote it.
2. Submitting an entire paper, or portion thereof, that was written by someone else.
3. Copying sections of someone else's work and inserting it into your own.
4. Cutting paragraphs from separate sources and pasting them into the body of your own paper.
5. Paraphrasing or rewording someone else's words or ideas without citing that person as a source. (Strategies for paraphrasing without plagiarizing may be found at: https://writing.colostate.edu/guides/page.cfm?pageid=298&guideid=16.)
6. Placing someone else's exact words in the body of your paper and not placing quotation marks around those words.

7. Failing to cite the source of factual information in your paper that's not common knowledge.

Examples of different forms of plagiarism may be found at the following sites:

https://www.bowdoin.edu/dean-of students/judicial-board/academic-honesty-and-plagiarism/examples.html)

https://owl.purdue.edu/owl/research_and_citation/using_research/avoiding_plagiarism/index.html

Final Notes:

- If you include information in your paper and just list its source in your reference (works cited) section, but do not cite the source in the *body* of your paper, this still qualifies as plagiarism.
- Only include sources in your reference section that you actually cited in the body of your paper. Placing sources in your reference section that are not cited in your paper isn't technically a form of plagiarism, but it may viewed as a deceitful attempt to "pad" your reference section and give the reader the impression that you incorporated more sources into your research report than you actually did.

Reflection 7.4

Look back at the different forms of plagiarism described in **Box 7.2**. Were there any that you were surprised to see, or didn't realize were types of plagiarism?

Writing Skills and Strategies

Writing is a versatile academic skill that strengthens academic performance across the curriculum, including general education courses and courses in your major. It's the primary route through which you will communicate your knowledge and the quality of your thinking on college exams and course assignments. It doesn't matter how much knowledge you have in your head, if you can't get that knowledge out of your head and onto paper, you will not be able to demonstrate what you know and get credit for knowing it. Thus, improving your writing will not only enhance your communication skills, it will also elevate your college grades.

In addition, your ability to write clearly, concisely, and persuasively will contribute to your career success after college. When college alumni were asked about the professional skills they needed to succeed in the workplace, more than 90% of them ranked "need to write effectively" as a skill that was of "great importance" to their current work. Employers also report in national surveys that writing is one of the top skills they seek in college graduates. In fact, the letter of application (cover letter) you write to apply for employment positions after college will be the first impression you will make on a potential employer. A well-written letter of application will enable you to get your "foot in the door" and take your first step toward converting your college degree into a professional position.

> "Want one more reason for developing strong writing skills? *Money.* Good writing skills are consistently one of the most sought-after skills by employers."
>
> —Karen Brooks, career development specialist and author of *You Majored in What? Mapping Your Path From Chaos to Career*

Strengthening your writing skills will strengthen your academic performance across the curriculum and your job performance throughout your career.

Writing to Learn

As mentioned in Chapter 1, humans learn most effectively when they're actively engaged in the learning process and reflect on the process after it has taken place. Writing is a powerful tool for promoting engagement in learning and reflection on learning, whether the learning takes place inside or outside the classroom. Research shows that writing promotes learning and thinking, so much so that scholars have coined the term "writing to learn" to capture the idea that writing is not just a communication skill learned in English composition classes, but also a learning strategy that deepens understanding of any academic subject or life experience. Just as you can learn to be a better writer, you can write to be a better learner.

Writing to learn includes practices that differ from the traditional practices of writing essays and term papers in two key ways: (a) they're shorter—requiring less amount of time to complete, and (b) they're written primarily for the benefit of the writer—to stimulate thinking and learning. Writing-to-learn strategies can be applied to a wide range of learning tasks and purposes, such as those listed below. As you read the following list, place a check mark next to any strategy you rarely use or have never used.

Writing to Listen

Writing can improve your ability to listen to and learn from class lectures, class discussions, and study-group sessions. For instance, as soon as a class session ends, you could write a "one-minute paper" (taking no more than a minute to complete) to reflect on the key ideas you heard in class that day—by writing a response to questions such as: "What were the most significant concepts I learned in class today?" "What was the most confusing concept discussed in today's class that I need to clear up with my instructor or a classmate?").

Writing to Read

Just as writing can promote active listening in class, it can promote active reading out of class. Taking notes on *what* you're reading while you're reading implements the learning principle of active involvement more effectively than highlighting because writing a response to what you've read involves more mental and physical energy than highlighting sentences.

Writing to Remember

The physical act of writing creates motor (muscle) memory for the information you're writing, enabling you to better retain and retrieve the information you've written. Writing also improves memory by allowing you to *see* the information you're trying to remember, which lays down a visual memory trace of it in your brain.

> "I would advise you to read with a pen in your hand, and enter in a little book of short hints of what you find that is curious, or that might be useful; for this will be the best method of imprinting such particulars in your memory, where they will be ready.
>
> —Benjamin Franklin, 18th-century inventor, politician, and co-signer of the *Declaration of Independence*

Writing to Organize

Writing summaries, outlines, and ideas on index cards that relate to the same concept are effective ways to organize the information you're trying to learn, which promotes learning by getting those related ideas organized (and connected) in the same place in your brain. These forms of writing also engage the mind in synthesis—a higher-level thinking skill.

Writing to Study

Writing study guides and practice answers to potential test questions are effective ways to prepare for exams, either when studying alone or in a study group. Writing out answers is a particularly effective way to prepare for an essay test because it enables you to practice what you will be expected to do on the test itself—write out answers to essay questions.

Writing to Understand

Paraphrasing or restating what you're trying to learn by writing it down in your own words is an effective way to ensure you're understanding it (not just memorizing it) because it transforms what you're learning into words that are meaningful to you. In addition, the process of writing slows down the process of thinking, making your thinking more deliberate, systematic, and attentive to specific details.

Lastly, writing leaves you with a tangible product of your thinking that you can view, review, and use as feedback to further improve the quality of your thinking. In other words, writing allows you to "think out loud on paper" and hear (as well as see) your thoughts.

> "I write to understand as much as to be understood.
>
> —Elie Wiesel, world-famous American novelist, Nobel Prize winner, and Holocaust survivor

Writing to Create

Writing is not only a *product or a result of* thinking, it's also a *process for* thinking—the act (process) of writing itself stimulates thoughts and generates ideas. One type of writing that can be particularly effective for generating creative ideas is called *free-writing*—writing that involves quickly jotting down free-flowing thoughts on paper—without worrying about spelling and grammar. Freewriting can be used as a warm-up exercise to help you come up with ideas for a research topic, to keep track of ideas generated during group brainstorming sessions, or to record great ideas that suddenly pop into your mind at unexpected times.

Writing to Discuss

Prior to participating in class discussions or small group work, you can gather your thoughts in writing before expressing them orally. This practice ensures that you carefully think through your ideas before sharing them, which, in turn, should improve the quality of ideas you share. Taking a moment to gather your thoughts in writing before delivering them orally will also make you a less anxious, more confident speaker because you know what you're going to say before you start to say it. (Writing down your thoughts prior to a discussion also help you remember all the key points you intend to make during the discussion.)

Writing for Problem Solving

You can use writing while solving problems in math and science to track your thought process. Writing down the thoughts going through your head at each major step in the problem-solving process makes you more aware of how you're thinking while you're thinking. This type of mental self-awareness (referred to as metacognition) has been found to improve thinking and problem-solving. Tracking your thoughts in writing while successfully solving a problem leaves you with a record of the train of thought you used to solve the problem. You can review that record later and ride that train of thought again to solve future problems of the same type or that require a similar thought process.

 Reflection 7.5

Which of the above-listed types of writing have you not tried?

Which one of these untried types of writing do you think would benefit you the most and would you be willing to try? Why?

Writing Papers and Reports

Studies show that only a small percentage of high school students engage in writing assignments that are as lengthy and challenging as those required in college. Most writing assignments before college involved summaries or descriptive reports. College students are expected to complete lengthier writing assignments and engage in more expository (persuasive) writing that requires them to express their point of view and prove their point of view by supporting it with compelling evidence. This is often done in the form of *a term paper*—a research report completed over the course of an academic term that typically accounts for a large part of the student's course grade.

Reflection 7.6

Think about your writing assignments in high school.

a)   What was the longest paper you wrote?

b)   What types of thinking were you usually asked to demonstrate in your writing assignments (e.g., summarize, analyze, criticize)?

Writing a term paper is a multistage process that cannot be completed in one night. Breaking down the writing process into separate stages and completing these stages in advance of the paper's due date is an effective way to strengthen the quality of your final product. These stages include:

- Determining the purpose or goal of the paper
- Generating ideas to write about
- Organizing your ideas into major categories
- Ordering the categories into a logical sequence
- Expressing your ideas in the form of well-written sentences and paragraphs
- Revising your writing after editing and proofreading

©Kendall Hunt Publishing Company

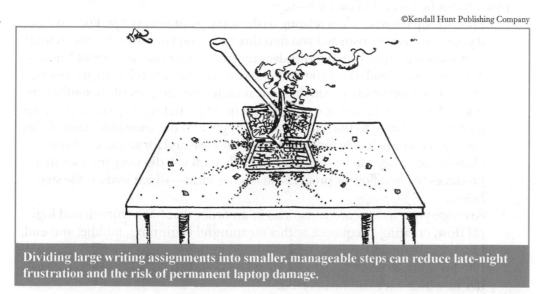

Dividing large writing assignments into smaller, manageable steps can reduce late-night frustration and the risk of permanent laptop damage.

Listed below is a systematic, 10-step process for completing these stages. Using this stepwise process should make your writing of papers more manageable, less stressful, and more successful.

1.   **Determine the purpose and goal of the paper.** The critical first step in the process of writing an effective paper is having a clear understanding of its purpose or goal. This will help you stay on track and moving in the right direction. It also helps you get going in the first place because one of the major causes of writer's block and writer procrastination is uncertainty about the goal or purpose of the writing task.

"Begin with the end in mind.❞
—Stephen Covey, in *The Seven Habits of Highly Effective People*

Before you start to write anything, be sure you know what you're expected to accomplish. Ask yourself the following questions about the writing assignment:
- What is its major objective or intended outcome?
- What type of thinking am I being asked to demonstrate?
- What criteria (standards) will my instructor use to evaluate and grade my performance?

2. **Focus first on generating ideas.** In the initial stages of the writing process, the only thing you should be concerned about is getting ideas you have in your head out of your head and onto paper. Writing scholars refer to this stage of the writing process as *focused freewriting*—writing freely for a certain period on a particular topic just to come up with ideas relating to the topic—without worrying about whether these ideas are expressed in grammatically correct sentences or even complete sentences. Beginning by simply generating ideas serves to jump-start the writing process, creates some initial momentum and helps overcome writer's block. The simple act of writing down your thoughts can, in itself, stimulate additional thoughts. Even if you don't think you have any great ideas, just start by writing down *any* ideas; these ideas can trigger other ideas, some of which may turn out to be great ideas. (Production of new ideas can also be stimulated by just changing your writing environment or format, such as shifting to a different room, or shifting from writing ideas in pen or pencil to typing them on a keyboard.)

3. **Categorize your ideas.** After you have generated ideas, the next step is to sort them out and figure out how they can be pieced together. This organizational process can be tackled in two sub-steps.
- First, group together ideas relating to the same point or concept. For instance, if your topic is terrorism and you find three ideas on your list referring to what motivates terrorists, group those ideas together under the category of "motivational causes." Similarly, if you find ideas on your list that relate to preventing or deterring terrorism, group those ideas under the category of "potential solutions." Consider recording separate ideas on sticky notes and place sticky notes containing relating to the same general category on the same index card. Index cards can come in handy for organizing your ideas and for sequencing your ideas because they can be repositioned easily until you discover an order that produces the best flow or progression of your ideas—which leads to the step below.
- Arrange your index-card categories in an order that has a smooth and logical flow, creating a sequence with a meaningful beginning, middle, and end. Once all the index cards have been placed in this sequence, you have an outline for your paper that includes all major points to be covered and the order in which they will be covered.

> "A writer is not so much someone who has something to say as he is someone who has found a process that will bring about new things he would not have thought of if he had not started to say [write] them."
>
> —*William Stafford, American author and recipient of the National Book Award for Poetry*

AUTHOR'S EXPERIENCE

When I wrote this chapter, I started by writing down ideas on separate pieces of paper. Second, I took pieces of paper relating to different general categories (e.g., information literacy and writing) and put them in separate piles. Third, I took the piles of general categories and broke them into smaller piles of sub-categories (e.g., piles relating to different aspects of information literacy sources and different stages of the writing process). Fourth, I arranged the piles in an order or sequence that seemed to flow logically from start to finish.

I was doing this sorting and ordering while sitting at a table in a Chicago airport. A gentleman at a nearby table caught my eye and said: "I see you're organizing all your receipts." I said: "Actually, I'm organizing all my ideas."

—*Joe Cuseo*

Another effective way to organize and sequence ideas for paper is by arranging them in a drawing or diagram. When ideas are laid out in a visual-spatial format, the product is referred to as a "concept map" or "graphic organizer." **Figure 7.1** illustrates a concept map that organizes major ideas related to higher-level thinking—a topic covered in Chapter 8. This particular type of concept map is known as a "clock map" because its main ideas are organized like the numbers of a clock, beginning at the top (12) and moving sequentially in a clockwise direction. Concept maps can be created in any pattern that works best for the material you're trying to organize and sequence. (For a variety of concept-mapping formats and apps, see: www.graphic.org/concept.html)

FIGURE 7.1: Concept Map Used to Organize and Sequence Major Ideas Relating to Higher-Level Thinking

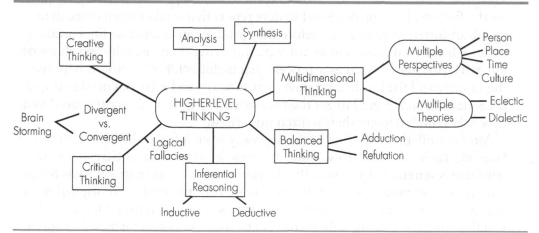

©Kendall Hunt Publishing Company

4. **Write a first draft of your paper that converts your main ideas into a logical sequence of paragraphs.** The previous steps in the writing process are often referred to as *prewriting* because they take place *before* you starting writing full sentences and complete paragraphs. The actual writing process begins with the paper's *first draft*, in which the ideas that have been generated and organized are converted into the sentences and paragraphs. Listed below are strategies for writing a first draft.
    * Use the first section of the paper to create a meaningful introduction, overview, or preview of the major points you will make in the remainder (body) of the paper. Your opening paragraph is critical because it shapes the reader's first impression and sets the stage for what will follow. It should include a *thesis statement*—a short summary (one to three sentences) of the key point you intend to make or the central question you will attempt to answer in the body of your paper. In short, when you construct a thesis statement, you're saying: "My point is . . ." This statement is the compass that guides your thinking and the reader's thinking throughout the paper, keeping both the writer and reader on the same page and moving in the same direction toward the same destination (your conclusion).
    * Place ideas relating to separate points in separate paragraphs. A paragraph should consist of a chain of sentences linked to the same thought or idea. When you shift to a new idea, shift to a new paragraph.
    * Whenever possible, start new paragraphs with a *topic sentence* that introduces the new idea you're about to make. Topic sentences help create a sense of continuity within your paper, connecting successive paragraphs with one another.

- Use the final paragraph (or two) of your paper to "tie it all together," drive home your key points, and finish strong.
- After all your paragraphs have been written, your paper should have three clearly identifiable parts:
  - (a) *introduction*—an opening section that includes your thesis statement;
  - (b) *body*—the middle section ("meat" or "heart" of your paper) that supplies different arguments and sources of evidence supporting your thesis statement; and
  - (c) *conclusion*—a closing section that summarizes the key arguments and evidence cited in the body of your paper and connects them back to your thesis statement to prove your point.

5. **Write more than one draft.** Don't expect to write a perfect draft of your paper on the first try. Even professional writers report that it takes them more than one draft (often three or four) before they produce an acceptable final product. Although the final version of award-winning writers may seem impeccably written, what precedes it is a messy process that includes lots of revisions between the first try and the finished product. Just as actors and actresses need multiple takes (take 2, take 3, etc.) to get their spoken lines right, so do writers need multiple takes (drafts) to get their written lines right.

> "I'm not a writer; I'm a rewriter."
>
> —*James Thurber, award-winning American journalist and author*

After completing your first draft, step away from it for a while and return to it later and review it with a fresh mind and new set of eyes. In particular, review your thesis statement to be sure that it still serves as an accurate compass for the direction your paper has taken. It's okay to go back to tweak your original thesis statement so that it better reflects and captures your conclusion. However, if you find yourself making radical changes to your thesis statement, this suggests you may strayed too far from it and need to replace it with one that aligns more directly with your conclusion.

Reflection 7.7

For papers you have written in the past, did you write more than one draft before submitting them?

If no, why not?

6. **Critically review your own written work as if you were another reader or editor, rather its author.** It's noteworthy that the term "revision" literally means to re-vision (view again). At this stage in the process, you re-view your writing as if the words were written by someone else and your role now is now that of a critic and editor. If you find words and sentences that aren't clearly capturing what you intended to say, now's the time to tweak or rephrase them.

When critiquing and editing your paper, keep in mind the criteria (judgment standards) your instructor will use when reading and grading your paper. If your instructor has shared these criteria with the class, have them in front of you and use them as guidelines to evaluate and improve your work. It's likely that your paper will be evaluated with respect to the following criteria, so keep them in mind during your review process.

- **Documentation.** Are your key points and conclusions supported by evidence? For example:
  - a) direct quotes from authoritative sources

    b) specific examples

    c) statistical data

    d) scientific research findings

    e) firsthand experiences.

- **Overall Organization.** An overview of your paper should reveal that it has three clearly identifiable parts: a beginning (introduction), a middle (body), and an end (conclusion). Ask yourself if these three parts unite to form a connected whole. Also, check to be sure there's *continuity* between paragraphs within your paper: Does your train of thought stay on track and moving in the right direction from start to finish? If you find yourself getting off track at certain points in your paper, eliminate that information or rewrite it in a way that re-routes your thoughts back onto the main track (your thesis).

- **Sentence Structure.** Refine and fine tune your sentences. Keep an eye out for *sentence fragments*—"sentences" without a noun or a verb—and *run-on sentences*—two or more sentences that are not separated by a period or conjunction (e.g., "and" or "but").

    Check for sentences that are too long—those that can go on and on without any punctuation and leave readers without enough time to pause and take a breath. You can tighten up or break up these long-winded sentences by: (a) punctuating them with a comma to give the reader a short pause, (b) punctuating them with a semicolon that provides a longer pause than a comma (but not as long as a period), or (c) dividing them into two shorter sentences (separated by a period).

    Also, check for *choppy sentences* that "chop up" what you've written into such short segments that it disrupts the natural reading rhythm. If you find choppy sentences, combine them into a longer sentence, and, if necessary, punctuate them with a comma or semicolon instead of a period. A good strategy for determining whether your sentences flow smoothly is to read them aloud. Note the places where you naturally tend to pause and where you tend to keep going. Your natural pauses may serve as cues for places where your sentences need punctuation, and your natural runs may indicate sentences that are flowing smoothly and should be left alone.

- **Word Selection.** Are certain words or terms showing up so frequently in your paper that they sound repetitious? If so, remove the redundancy and infuse variety by substituting words that have the same or similar meaning. This substitution process can be made easier by using a thesaurus, which may be conveniently available on your computer's word processing program or by doing a quick "google search" for a synonym.

7. **Seek feedback on your paper from a trusted peer or writing professional.** You should be the first and final reader of your paper reader, but you don't have to be the only one. No matter how honest or objective we may try to be about our own writing, we may still be blind to its weaknesses. We all have a tendency to see what we hope or want to see in our work, especially after we've put a great deal of time, effort, and energy into the process of creating it.

    Whether you're already a good writer or still developing your writing skills, the quality of your written work can be improved by seeking and receiving feedback from others. Even professional writers share their drafts with other writers to obtain feedback. Similarly, you could seek feedback at any stage of the writing process—whether it be for help with getting a better understanding of the purpose or goal of the writing assignment, brainstorming ideas for a topic, writing a first draft, or reviewing your final draft.

A tutor in the Writing or Learning Center would be a good candidate to ask for a second opinion on your paper. Another option would be to pair up with a trusted writing partner to exchange and assess each other's papers by using the same criteria your instructor will use to evaluate and grade your work. Studies show that when students at all levels of writing ability receive feedback from others prior to submitting a paper, the quality of their writing improves, as does their grade on the writing assignment. Getting help with your writing isn't cheating or plagiarizing--as long as you're the one who does the re-writing in response to the feedback you receive.

8. **In your final draft, be sure that your conclusion and introduction are connected or aligned.** Your conclusion should flash back to your initial thesis statement and show how you've addressed it. By connecting your introduction and conclusion, you provide a pair of meaningful bookends to your paper, anchoring it at its two most pivotal points—beginning and end. By doing so, you capitalize on the power of two key impressions—the *first* impression and *last* impression.

9. **Carefully proofread your paper for clerical and technical mistakes before submitting it.** Proofreading may be defined as a micro form of editing in which you focus attention on minute mechanics related to referencing, grammar, punctuation, and spelling. It represents the critical last step in the editorial process that involves detection and correction of small, technical errors which were likely overlooked at earlier stages of the writing process when you were focusing attention on your paper's content and structure.

Don't forget that when you are proofreading for spelling errors, your computer's spell-checker will not catch words that seem to be correctly spelled, but are actually misspelled in the context you're using them. For instance, a spell-checker would not detect any of the four "correctly" spelled words that are really misspelled in the context of the following sentence: "*Where* your high-*heal* shoes when we *meat* for the executive *bored* meeting." A career counselor once reported that a student forgot to proofread her job application before submitting it. Her roommate read her application and laughingly noticed that she mistakenly applied for a job in "pubic service" instead of "public service."

> *Careful proofreading is the crucial last step in the process of writing a high-quality paper. Forgetting to take this simple but essential step, and losing points for minor mistakes on a product that you spent so much time working on, would be like circling the bases after hitting a home run and forgetting to touch home plate.*

10. **After your paper is graded and returned to you, carefully review your instructor's written comments.** Use these comments as constructive feedback to improve your performance on future assignments. If the written feedback you receive still leaves you unclear about what to do to improve your work, make an appointment to discuss the paper with your instructor. Not only will this supply you with the opportunity to receive personalized one-on-one feedback about your writing, your office visit sends a clear message to the instructor that you're a student who is serious about learning and achieving academic excellence.

Public Speaking: Making Oral Presentations and Delivering Speeches

The Importance of Oral Communication

In addition to writing, speaking is the second major channel through which you will communicate and demonstrate your knowledge in college, whether it be by making formal oral presentations, participating in small-group discussions, or raising your hand to contribute ideas in class. When graduating seniors at Harvard University were asked about specific strategies they would recommend to first-year students to overcome shyness and develop social self-confidence, their most frequent recommendation was for first-year students to take classes in which they were expected to speak up.

Developing your ability to speak in a clear, concise, and confident manner will not only strengthen your academic performance in college, it will enhance your career performance after college. In fact, the oral communication skills you display during a job interview will likely play a pivotal role in your being hired for your first position after college graduation. Research repeatedly shows that employers place a high value on oral communication skills and rank them at the very top of characteristics they seek in prospective employees. Speaking skills will also increase your prospects for career advancement by strengthening your professional presentations and performance at group meetings.

> "As you move up through your career path, you're judged on your ability to articulate a point of view.
>
> *—Donald Keogh, former president of the Coca-Cola Company*

 Reflection 7.8

How many times have you made an oral presentation or delivered a speech?

Does your college require a course in speech or public speaking? If yes, when do you plan to take it? If no, would you consider taking an elective course in public speaking? (Why?)

(To assess your verbal skills, complete Exercise 7.6 at the end of this chapter.)

Strategies for Making Effective Oral Presentations

Listed below are strategies for delivering oral presentations and speeches. Because both speaking and writing are forms of verbal communication, you will find that many of the strategies suggested here for improving oral reports are like those for improving written reports. Thus, you can "double dip" and use the following oral presentation strategies to strengthen your written presentations (or vice versa).

First, decide on the purpose or goal of your presentation. An oral presentation usually falls into either of the following two categories, depending on its purpose or objective:

1. *Informative* presentations—provide members of the audience with information that increases their knowledge or supplies them with practical information to help them complete tasks.
2. *Persuasive* (expository) presentations—attempt to persuade (convince) members of the audience to buy into a particular idea or course of action.

The first step to delivering an effective presentation is clarifying what you intend your presentation to accomplish and then keeping that end goal in mind when deciding on what to include in your presentation. When making decisions about whether to include (or exclude) a particular idea or piece of information in your presentation, ask yourself: Will it contribute to the ultimate purpose or goal of my presentation?

In college, most oral presentations will likely fall into the persuasive category, which means that you will research information, draw conclusions about your research, and document your conclusions with evidence. Similar to writing research papers, persuasive oral presentations require you to think critically, cite sources, and demonstrate academic integrity.

Select a topic that matters to you and you're really passionate about. If you have the freedom to choose the topic for your presentation, seize this opportunity to present on a subject that you are enthused about and find especially interesting. Your interest and enthusiasm is likely to show through during the delivery of your presentation, which, in turn, is likely to increase your audience's attention, your self-confidence as a presenter, and the overall quality of your presentation.

Create an outline or bulleted list of the major (general) points you're going to make. First, get your major points down on PowerPoint slides or index cards; second, arrange them in an order that provides the smoothest sequence or flow of your ideas.

Use your slides or index cards as retrieval cues ("cue cards") to remember each of the major points you will make during the presentation. Beneath each major point on your slide or index card, list 3-5 sub-points or specific ideas you intend to make in relation to that general point. Research shows that humans can only keep about four points or bits of information in mind (in their working or short-term memory) at a time.

Rehearse and revise. Just as you should write several drafts of a paper before turning it in, an oral presentation should be rehearsed and revised before it's delivered. Rehearsal will help ensure that your presentation isn't interrupted by long pauses, stops and starts, and distracting "fillers" (e.g., "uh," "umm," "like," "you know,"). Rehearsal will also help reduce your level of speech anxiety. Studies show that fear of public speaking is often really fear of failure—fear of being negatively evaluated by the audience. If your oral presentation is well prepared and well rehearsed, your fear of failure will decrease, along with your level of speech anxiety.

When rehearsing your presentation, pay special attention to the following parts:

- **Introduction.** This part of your speech should be particularly well-rehearsed because it can create a positive first impression of your presentation and a sense of positive anticipation about what's to come next. Like a well written report, the introduction to your oral report should include a thesis statement—a statement about *why* you're speaking about this topic and what you intend to accomplish by the end of your presentation. It should also include a "hook" (e.g., a powerful visual image) that captures the audience's initial interest in, or excitement about, the topic's importance and value.
- **Transition statements.** These are phrases that signal you're moving from one major idea to another (e.g., "Now let's turn to . . ."). These statements serve to highlight the key parts of your presentation and how they're connected.

- **Conclusion.** This is your chance to finish strong and create a powerful last impression that drives home your presentation's most important points. Your conclusion should include a statement that refers back to, and reinforces, your original thesis statement, thereby connecting your ending with your beginning.

> "First, I tell 'em what I'm gonna tell 'em; then I tell 'em; then I tell 'em what I told 'em.
>
> —*Anonymous country preacher's formula for successful sermons*

Lastly, when you rehearse your presentation, keep track of the total time it takes to complete it. Be sure it falls within the time range set by your instructor and is neither too short nor too long.

Before officially delivering your presentation, do a trial run of it in front of a live audience. Ask a friend or group of friends to listen to your presentation and give you some feedback. This trial run can serve as "dress rehearsal," giving you the opportunity to practice your presentation not as a stand-alone soliloquy but in front of a live audience—which is what you'll be doing when you deliver your actual presentation.

Another way to get useful feedback on your presentation prior to its delivery is to have someone video-record it. This will enable you to step outside of yourself and observe your presentation as if you were a member of the audience. Such an "out-of-body experience" enables you to get outside yourself and see yourself as others would see you. This can be especially useful for increasing your self-awareness of the non-verbal communication (body language) habits you engage in while speaking.

As you might expect, when you first see how you look and hear how you sound, you're likely to be quite surprised or even shocked. This is a normal reaction; the initial shock will soon fade and you'll feel more comfortable viewing, reviewing, and improving your presentation.

Reflection 7.9

Have you ever received feedback on the quality of your speaking skills from a teacher, a peer, or by observing yourself on video?

If you have, what did you learn about your speaking habits and how to improve them?

If you haven't, would you be willing to seek feedback from others on your oral presentation skills, or view a video-recording of yourself delivering an oral presentation?

Observe presentations made by others and learn from them. Note the things that effective speakers do when delivering oral presentations and use them as clues to improve the quality of your own presentations.

When delivering your presentation, maximize eye contact with the audience. During your talk, it's perfectly fine to occasionally glance at your index cards and slides and use them as cue cards to help you recall the points you want to make; however, most of your time should be spent looking at your audience. Oral presentations can be deadly boring when the speaker's "presentation" involves looking at and reading slides off a screen, rather than looking at and speaking to the audience. (See **Box 7.3** for a summary of top tips for using, not abusing, PowerPoint.)

Effective oral presentations should not be written out word-by-word and read verbatim, nor should they be entirely impromptu (improvised) presentations delivered off the top of your head. Instead, they should be *extemporaneous*, meaning that they fall somewhere in between "winging it" and memorizing it word-for-word. Extemporaneous speaking involves advanced preparation and the use of notes or slides as memory-retrieval cues, but allows you some freedom to ad lib or improvise. If you happen to forget the exact words you planned to use, you can freely substitute different words to make the same point—without stumbling or stressing out—and without your audience ever noticing that you made any changes or substitutions. The key to extemporaneous speaking is to rehearse and remember all your major points, not the exact words you will use to discuss each and every point. This will ensure that your presentation comes across as natural and authentic, rather than mechanical or robotic.

Box 7.3

Tips for Using (Not Abusing) PowerPoint

- Use the titles of slides as general headings or categories for your major ideas.
- List only 3-5 points (ideas) on each slide.
- List information on your slides as bulleted points, not complete sentences. The more words included on your slides, the more time your audience will spend reading the slides instead of listening to you. You can help keep the focus on *you* by showing only one point on your slide at a time. This will prevent the audience from reading ahead and direct their attention on one point—the point that you're currently discussing.

The points on your PowerPoint slides do not constitute your entire presentation. They are just memories cues and slide holders for ideas relating to those points that you will elaborate on during your presentation.

" A presentation is about explaining things to people that go above and beyond what they get in the slides. If it weren't, they might just as well get your slides and read them in the comfort of their own office, home, boat, or bathroom."

—Jesper Johansson, senior security strategist for Microsoft, in "Death by PowerPoint"

- Use a font size of at least 18 points to ensure that people in the back of the room can read what's printed on each slide.
- Don't use elaborate coloring merely for decorative purposes because it can be a source of distraction; instead, use color for educational purposes—as a visual aid to emphasize and organize your points. For example, a dark or bold blue heading may be used to highlight the title of the slide (representing your major point) and a lighter shade of blue may be used for the bulleted sub-points beneath it.
- Incorporate visual images into your presentation. Don't hesitate to use pictures, graphs, cartoons, or other visual illustrations that relate to and reinforce your major points. (As discussed in chapter 5, this practice allows information to be stored in the brain as two different memory traces—one verbal and one visual—which increases the likelihood the point you're making will be retained by the audience.)

The true "power" of PowerPoint may not be its ability to project printed words, but to project visual images that illustrate or illuminate your spoken words.

- If you include words or images on a slide that are not your own, demonstrate academic integrity by noting their source at the bottom of the slide.
- Before going public with your slides, proofread them with the same care as you would a written paper.

Managing Speech Anxiety

If you're anxious about making stand-and-deliver speeches, you're certainly not alone. It's such a common fear, it could almost be considered "normal." National surveys show that fear of public speaking affects people of all ages, including adolescents and young adults. A significant number of college students also experience *classroom communication apprehension*—anxiety about speaking specifically in classroom settings.

Keep in mind that it's natural to experience at least some stress in any situation where your performance is being observed or evaluated. This isn't necessarily a bad thing because stress that's kept at a moderate level can actually increase energy, concentration, and memory. However, when stress reaches the level of fear or anxiety, it can leave a person unwilling or unable to stand up in front of a group ("stage fright") or speak up in class, that person may be experiencing speech anxiety. Listed below are strategies for managing speech anxiety and keeping it at a moderate and productive level.

Just prior to your speech, take some time to intentionally relax yourself. For example, take deep breaths, or use any other stress-management strategy that works well for you. (See Chapter 13, **pp.** ____, for an assortment of stress-management strategies.)

Avoid consuming caffeine or other "energy drinks" prior to delivering your speech. These substances will elevate your level of physiological arousal during your presentation, which, in turn, can elevate your level of psychological arousal (anxiety).

Approach your speech with a positive mindset. Simply stated, positive thinking triggers positive emotions. Here are some strategies for putting yourself in a positive frame of mind:

- Adopt the mindset that your speech is nothing more than a formal conversation with a group of friends. To help get you into this conversational mode, make eye contact with small sections of the audience while delivering your speech. When you shift to a new idea or section of your speech, shift your focus of attention to a different section of the audience. This strategy will help relax you by making the audience seem smaller; it will also ensure you make periodic eye contact with different sections of the audience.
- Expect to give a good speech, but not a perfect speech. Don't put extra pressure on yourself by thinking that you're going to deliver a presentation like a silver-tongued TV reporter delivering the nightly news (who is actually reading it off a teleprompter). A few verbal mistakes are common during speeches and often go unnoticed by the audience. You can still receive an excellent grade on an oral presentation without delivering a flawless performance.
- Keep in mind that the audience to whom you are speaking is not made up of expert speakers. Most of them have no more public speaking experience than do you, nor are they experienced critics. These are your peers and they know that standing up in front of class and delivering a formal speech isn't an easy thing to do. They're likely to be very accepting of any mistakes you make, as they hope you would be for them when it's their turn to stand and deliver.

When delivering your speech, focus on the *message* (your ideas), not the *messenger* (yourself). By consciously keeping your attention on the ideas you are communicating, you will focus less attention on yourself and become less self-conscious and less anxious about the impression you're making on the audience or the audience's impression (evaluation) of you.

Like any fear, fear of public speaking tends to subside after getting your "feet wet" after doing it for the first time. The anticipation of a stressful experience is often worse than the experience itself. Feelings of anxiety experienced before delivering a speech are often replaced by feelings of accomplishment, pride, and self-confidence after the speech is delivered.

"I was really nervous during the entire thing, but I felt so relieved and proud afterwards.

—*First-year college student commenting on her first public speech*

AUTHOR'S EXPERIENCE

My college required that I take a course in public speaking by the end of my sophomore year. Since I had never before delivered a formal speech, I was extremely nervous about standing up and making a presentation in front of a large group of people so I postponed taking the course as long as I possibly could. Finally, as a second-semester sophomore, I delivered my first oral presentation. When it was done, I felt like I just got a huge gorilla off my back.

After giving that first speech, I noticed that I was more confident about asking questions in my classes, speaking up during group discussions, and expressing myself in situations where a large number of people were present. Eventually, I became a college professor and spent my entire career speaking in front of people. I now make presentations on college campuses across the United States and in other countries.

Every now and then I think about that first speech I gave as a college sophomore and realize that it was a turning point in my life. It gave me the opportunity to overcome my speech anxiety and gave me the self-confidence to succeed in my eventual career. It also gave me the confidence and courage to deliver moving and memorable eulogies at my father's and mother's funerals.

—*Joe Cuseo*

 Reflection 7.10

Are you planning to take a course in public speaking?

If yes, why? If no, why not?

Internet–Based Resources

For additional information on research, writing, and oral communication skills, see the following websites:

Information Literacy (Information Search) Strategies:
https://www.wesleyan.edu/libr/infoforyou/infolitdefined.html#
https://www.pcc.edu/library/services/faculty-services/information-literacy-teaching-materials/information-literacy-in-context/

Writing Strategies:
www.enhancemywriting.com
http://writingcenter.fas.harvard.edu/pages/strategies-essay-writing

Academic Integrity and Character:
https://integrity.mit.edu/

Public Speaking Skills:
www.public-speaking.org/public-speaking-articles.htm
https://www.hamilton.edu/oralcommunication/tips-for-effective-delivery

Chapter 7 Exercises

7.1 Quote Reflections

Review the sidebar quotes contained in this chapter and select two that were especially meaningful or inspirational to you.

For each of the quotes you selected, provide an explanation why you chose it.

7.2 Strategy Reflections

Review the strategies for *writing to learn* on pp. 149-150. Select three strategies that you think are the most important and intend to put into practice.

7.3 Reality Bite

Crime and Punishment: Plagiarism and Its Consequences

An article once appeared in an Ohio newspaper, titled "Plagiarism Persists in Classrooms," in which an English professor is quoted as saying: "Technology has made it easier to plagiarize because students can download papers and exchange information and papers through their computers. But technology has also made it easier to catch students who plagiarize." This professor works at a college which subscribes to a website that matches the content of students' papers with content from books and online sources. Many professors now require students to submit their papers through this website. If students are caught plagiarizing, for a first offense, they typically receive an F for the assignment or the course. A second offense can result in dismissal or expulsion from the college, which has already happened to a few students.

Reflection and Discussion Questions

1. What do you think are the primary motives or reasons why students plagiarize from the web?

2. In your opinion, what would be a fair or just penalty for students who are found guilty of a first plagiarism violation? What do you think would be fair penalty for a second violation?

3. How might web-based plagiarism be minimized or prevented from happening in the first place?

7.4 Internet Research

Go to *www.itools.com/search*. This website allows you to conveniently access multiple search engines, web directories, and newsgroups. Type in the name of a subject or topic you'd like to research and select three of the multiple search engines listed at this site.

1. What differences did you find in the type of information generated by the three search engines?

2. Did any of these search engines locate better or more comprehensive information than the others?

3. Would you return to this website again to help you with future research?

7.5 Is It or Is It Not Plagiarism?

The following four incidents were brought to a college judicial-review board to determine if a student had committed plagiarism and, if so, what the penalty should be. After reading each case, respond to the questions listed below it.

CASE 1. A student turned in an essay that included substantial material copied from a published source. The student admitted that he didn't cite the source properly, but argued that it was because he misunderstood the directions for the assignment, not because he was attempting to steal someone else's ideas.

Is this plagiarism?

How severe is it? (Rate it on a scale from 1 = low to 5 = high)

What should the consequence or penalty be?

How could this accusation of plagiarism been avoided?

CASE 2. A student turned in a paper that was identical to a paper submitted by another student for a different course.

Is this plagiarism?

How severe is it? (Rate it on a scale from 1 = low to 5 = high)

What should the consequence or penalty be?

CASE 3. A student submitted a paper he wrote in a previous course as an extra-credit paper for a course.

Is this plagiarism?

How severe is it? (Rate it on a scale from 1 = low to 5 = high)

What should the consequence or penalty be?

CASE 4. A student submitted a paper in an art history class that contained some ideas from art critics she read about and whose ideas she agreed with. The student didn't cite the critics as sources, but claimed it wasn't plagiarism because their ideas were merely their own subjective judgments or opinions, not facts or findings; furthermore, they were opinions she agreed with.

Is this plagiarism?

How severe is it? (Rate it on a scale from 1 = low to 5 = high)

What should the consequence or penalty be?

How could this accusation of plagiarism been avoided?

Look back at these four cases. Which do you think represents the *most* and *least* severe violation of academic integrity? Why?

7.6 Assessing Your Linguistic Intelligence

1. Review the Communication section of your AchieveWORKS Personality self-assessment and reflect on the strengths, challenges, and recommendations offered.

2. What does your report say about your communication abilities?

3. What personal strengths does the report point to? What areas does it suggest may need further development?

7.7 Preparing an Oral Presentation on Student Success

1. Scan this textbook and identify a chapter topic or chapter section that's most interesting to you or matters most to you.

2. Create an *introduction* for an oral presentation on this topic that:

    a) Provides an overview or sneak preview of what will be covered in your presentation

    b) Creates a favorable first impression of your presentation that you think would grab the attention of your audience (your classmates)

    c) Demonstrates the topic's relevance or importance for your audience.

3. Create a *conclusion* to your presentation that:

    a) Relates back to your introduction

    b) Highlights your most important point(s)

    c) Leaves a memorable last impression.

CHAPTER 8

Higher-Level Thinking

MOVING BEYOND BASIC KNOWLEDGE TO CRITICAL AND CREATIVE THINKING

Chapter Purpose & Preview

National surveys of college professors consistently show that their number one educational goal is developing students' critical thinking skills. In this chapter you will learn what critical thinking actually is, how it relates to creative thinking and other forms of higher-level thinking, and how to demonstrate different forms of higher-level thinking on your college exams and assignments. You will also learn how to use higher-level thinking skills to draw valid conclusions as well as make sound judgments and personal decisions.

Learning Goal

Understand what constitutes critical thinking and other higher-level thinking skills and develop strategies for applying these skills in college and beyond.

Ignite Your Thinking

 Reflection 8.1

To me, critical thinking is . . .

What Is Higher-Level Thinking?

Contestants on TV quiz shows like *Jeopardy* demonstrate their knowledge of facts by responding to such questions as: "Who?", "What?", "When?", and "Where?" If game show contestants were asked to respond to questions such as: "Why?", "How?", or "What if?", they would be asked to engage in higher-level thinking (a.k.a. higher-order thinking). This is a more advanced level of thinking than that used to acquire factual knowledge. It involves reflecting on the knowledge you have acquired and taking it to a higher level—for example, evaluating its validity, integrating it with other ideas, or using it to create new ideas. As its name implies, higher-level thinking involves raising the bar and jacking up your thinking to a level that goes beyond merely remembering, reproducing, or regurgitating factual information.

National surveys repeatedly show that the number one educational goal of college professors is to help students think at a higher or more advanced level. In one national survey of college professors who taught freshman- through senior-level courses in various academic fields, more than 95% of them reported that the most important goal of a college education is to develop students' ability to think

> "To me, thinking at a higher level means to think and analyze something beyond the obvious and find the deeper meaning.
>
> —*First-year college student*

165

critically. Similarly, college professors teaching introductory courses for freshmen and sophomores report that the primary educational purpose of their courses is to develop students' critical thinking skills. Simply stated, professors are more concerned with teaching you *how* to think than teaching you *what* to think or what facts to memorize.

Compared with high school, college courses focus less on acquiring information and more on thinking about issues, concepts, and principles. Memorizing information may get you a grade of "C," demonstrating comprehension of that information may get you a "B," and going beyond comprehension to demonstrate higher-level thinking is likely to earn you an "A." This is not to say that knowledge and comprehension are unimportant; they provide the stepping stones needed to climb to higher levels of thinking—as illustrated in **Figure 8.1**.

©Rafael Ramirez/Shutterstock.com

"The Thinker"—one of the most recognized sculptures in the world—created by August Rodin, 19th-century French sculptor

FIGURE 8.1: The Relationship between Knowledge, Comprehension, and Higher-Level Thinking

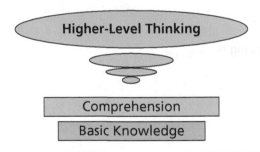

©Kendall Hunt Publishing Company

College professors expect students to do more than just retain or reproduce information; they want students to demonstrate higher levels of thinking with respect to knowledge they acquire (e.g., analyze it, evaluate it, apply it, or integrate it with other concepts).

Benefits of Higher-Level Thinking

In addition to promoting academic excellence in college, other major benefits of developing higher-level thinking skills include the following:

1. **Higher-level thinking is a durable skill that lasts a lifetime.** Studies show that memory for factual information fades quickly with the passage of time. However, higher-level thinking is a *skill* (like learning to ride a bike) that's retained on a long-term basis and can be used throughout life.

2. **Higher-level thinking is essential for success in today's "information age"**—a time when new information is being generated at faster rates than at any other time in human history. Most employees in the 21st century workforce will no longer work with their hands; they will work with their heads. Repetitive work tasks are being increasingly performed by robots and are being replaced by jobs that require the ability to think and solve problems. National surveys repeatedly show that today's employers are looking for college graduates with higher-level thinking skills, including the ability to think critically and solve problems.

3. **Higher-level thinking skills are vital for citizens in a democratic nation.** Authoritarian political systems, such as dictatorships and fascist regimes, suppress critical thought and demand submissive obedience to authority. In contrast, citizens in a democratic nation can control their political destiny by making wise choices about the leaders they elect. Thus, effective use of higher-level thinking skills, such as critical thinking, is essential for effective civic engagement and the preservation of democracy.

4. **Higher-level thinking provides a safeguard against prejudice, discrimination, and hostility.** Racial, ethnic, and national prejudices are often rooted in narrow, self-centered, and group-centered thinking. Oversimplified, dualistic thinking can lead humans to categorize others into either "in" groups (us) or "out" groups (them). Such simplistic thinking can, in turn, lead to ethnocentrism—the tendency to view one's own racial or ethnic group as the superior "in" group and see other groups as inferior "out" groups. Development of higher-level thinking skills, such as taking multiple perspectives and using balanced thinking, counteracts the type of dualistic, ethnocentric thinking that leads to prejudice, discrimination, and hate crimes.

5. **Higher-level thinking helps preserve mental and physical health.** Mentally active people are less likely to suffer memory loss or experience dementia as they age. Similar to how physical activity exercises muscles in the body, thinking exercises the brain. It stimulates neurophysiological activity among brain cells, invigorates them, and reduces the likelihood they will deteriorate with age.

©Kendall Hunt Publishing Company

Contrary to common belief, problem solving and other forms of higher-level thinking will not "fry" your brain; it actually stimulates and exercises the brain, reducing the risk of Alzheimer's disease and other forms of late-life dementia.

Defining and Describing the Major Forms of Higher-Level Thinking

All educators agree that "critical thinking" is an essential skill for students to develop, but it's a skill that has been defined in a variety of ways. When your college professors ask you to "think critically," they're usually asking you to engage in the higher forms of thinking listed in **Box 8.1**. As you read the descriptions of these forms of thinking, note whether you've heard of it before.

Box 8.1

Seven Major Forms of Higher-Level Thinking

1. Analysis (Analytical Thinking). Breaking down information into its essential elements or parts.
2. Synthesis (Integrative Thinking). Connecting separate pieces of information to form a more complete and coherent product or pattern.
3. Application (Applied Thinking). Using knowledge for practical purposes to solve problems and resolve issues.

4. Multidimensional Thinking. Thinking about ourselves and the world around us from multiple angles or perspectives.
5. Balanced Thinking. Carefully considering reasons for and against a particular position or viewpoint.
6. Creative Thinking. Generating ideas that are unique, original, or innovative.
7. Evaluation. Critically judging the soundness of arguments and evidence used to reach conclusions. (This form of higher-level thinking is the one most commonly referred to as "critical thinking.")

> "In college . . . you will be expected to get inside what you are learning to apply it, make comparisons and connections, draw implications, and use ideas."
>
> —*Robert Shoenberg, in* Why Do I Have to Take This Course?

Reflection 8.2

Look back at the seven forms of higher-level thinking described in **Box 8.1**. Which of these forms of thinking have you previously used on exams or assignments?

Analysis (Analytical Thinking)

> "In physics, you have to be analytical and break it [the problem] down into its parts."
>
> —*Physics student*

The higher-level thinking process of analysis is similar to the physical process of peeling an onion. When you analyze something, you take it apart, peeling it away to find its key elements or core components. For example, if you were to analyze a chapter in this book, you would do more than cover its content; you would try to uncover or discover the key ideas embedded within the content, detect its central points, and distinguish them from background information and incidental details. In an art course, analytical thinking would be used to identify elements of a painting or sculpture (e.g., its structure, texture, tone, and form). In the natural and social sciences, analysis would be used to examine the underlying reasons or causes for natural (physical) phenomena and social events—referred to as "causal analysis." For instance, a causal analysis of the September 11 terrorist attack on the United States would involve identifying the key factors that led to the attack or the underlying reasons why the attack took place.

Reflection 8.3

A TV commercial for a particular brand of liquor (which shall remain nameless) once showed a young man getting out of his car in front of a house where a party is taking place. After getting out of his car, he takes out a knife, slashes his tires, and goes inside to join the party. Using the higher-level thinking skill of analysis, what would you say were the underlying or embedded messages in this commercial?

Synthesis (Integrative Thinking)

Synthesis is a higher-level thinking skill that's basically the opposite of analysis. Instead of breaking down or taking apart ideas, synthesis involves piecing together separate ideas to form an integrated whole—like piecing together parts of a puzzle. Connecting ideas learned in different courses is a form of synthesis, such as integrating ethical concepts learned in a philosophy course with marketing concepts learned in a business course to construct a set of ethical guidelines for marketing and advertising products.

Although synthesis and analysis are seemingly opposite thought processes, they actually complement one another. Analysis enables you to disassemble information into its key parts; synthesis allows you to reassemble those key parts into a whole. For instance, when writing this book, the authors analyzed published material in many fields (e.g., psychology, history, philosophy, and biology) to detect pieces of information in these fields that were most relevant to promoting the success of college students. These pieces of information were then synthesized or reassembled into a whole—the textbook you're now reading.

> "Integration of learning is the ability to connect information from disparate contexts and perspectives . . . to connect one field of study with another, the past with the present, one part with the whole—and vice versa.
> —*Wabash National Study of Liberal Arts Education*

> *Synthesis is not just a summary of ideas produced by someone else; it's a thought process that integrates isolated pieces of information to generate a comprehensive product of your own.*

Application (Applied Thinking)

When you learn something deeply, you transform information into knowledge. If you then take that knowledge and transform it into practice, you're engaging in a higher-level thinking process known as *application*. This is a powerful form of higher-level thinking that allows you to take knowledge, transfer it to real-life situations, and put it to practical use. For instance, students would be engaging in application if they take knowledge acquired in an accounting course to help them manage their personal finances, or if they take knowledge acquired about social and emotional intelligence in chapter 9 of this book to improve their interpersonal relationships.

Always be on the lookout for ways to act on the knowledge you acquire and be ready to apply it to better yourself and the world around you. When you use knowledge to improve the quality of your life or the life of others, you're not only engaging in application, you're also exhibiting an admirable character trait known as *wisdom*.

> "As gold which he cannot spend will make no man rich, so knowledge which he cannot apply will make no man wise.
> —Dr. Samuel Johnson, famous English literary figure and original author of the *Dictionary of the English Language* (1747)

Multidimensional Thinking

When you view yourself and the world around you from different perspectives or vantage points, you're engaging in *multidimensional thinking*. Multidimensional thinkers are able to think from the following four key perspectives and see how each of them influences, and is influenced by, the issue they're examining.

1. **Perspective of Person (Self):** How does this issue affect individuals on a personal basis?
2. **Perspective of Place:** What impact does this issue have on people living in different regions of the country or nations of the world?
3. **Perspective of Time:** How will future generations of people be affected by this issue?
4. **Perspective of Culture:** How is this issue likely to be interpreted or experienced by groups of people with different social customs and traditions? (the perspective of culture)

Understanding complex issues requires understanding how they are embedded in and influenced by multiple elements that make up a larger, interconnected system. For example, global warming (climate change) is an issue that involves the gradual thickening and trapping of heat in the earth's atmosphere, due to a buildup of gases generated by humans burning fossil fuels for industrial purposes. The consensus among today's scientists is that this buildup of human-made pollution is causing temperatures to rise (and sometimes fall) around the world, resulting in more extreme weather conditions and more frequent natural disasters—such as droughts, wildfires, hurricanes, and dust storms. As depicted in **Box 8.2**, understanding and addressing the issue of climate change requires understanding interrelationships among the perspectives of person, place, time, and culture.

Box 8.2

Understanding Climate Change from Four Key Perspectives

Person

Addressing the issue of climate change involves humans at a personal level because individual efforts to conserve energy in their homes and their willingness to purchase energy-efficient products.

Place

Climate change is an international phenomenon that extends beyond the boundaries of any one country; it affects all countries and its solution requires the concerted effort of different nations around the world to reduce their level of carbon emissions.

Time

If the current trend toward increased global warming isn't addressed soon, it could seriously threaten the lives of future generations of humans.

Culture

Industries in technologically and industrially advanced cultures are primarily responsible for contributing to the problem of climate change. However, the adverse effects of climate change are likely to be worse for less technologically advanced cultures because they lack the resources to respond to it. Industrially advanced cultures will need to use their advanced resources and technology to devise alternative methods for generating energy in ways that reduce the risk of global warming for all cultures.

 Reflection 8.4

Think of a current national or international issue (other than climate change) whose solution requires multiple perspective-taking or multidimensional thinking.

Balanced Thinking

When you seek out and carefully consider arguments *for* and *against* a particular position, you're engaging in balanced thinking. If you gather supporting evidence or arguments for a position, you're engage in a mental process called *adduction*—when you adduce, you identify reasons *for* a position. In contrast, *refutation* is the process of finding sources of evidence or arguments that fail to support a position; when you refute, you provide reasons *against* a particular position.

The goal of a balanced thinker is not to stack up evidence for one position or the other but to be an impartial judge who weighs both supporting and opposing evidence on both sides of an issue, striving to reach a reasoned conclusion that is neither biased nor one-sided. When you consider the strengths and weaknesses of opposing arguments at the same time, it reduces the likelihood that you'll fall prey to an overly simplistic form of thinking that's typical of many first-year students—*dualistic* thinking—thinking that "truth" comes in the form of clear-cut, black-or-white answers or solutions, with one position or theory being "right" and all others being "wrong."

Don't be surprised or frustrated if you find scholars disagreeing about what positions and theories are more accurate or account for most of the "truth" in their field. Such disagreement represents a constructive thought process known as *dialectic* or *dialogic* thinking (deriving from the root "dialogue" or "conversation"). It's a productive form of intellectual dialogue that acknowledges different sides of a complex issue and results in a more balanced, integrated understanding of it. In a study of leaders who excel in the field of business, it was discovered that one of their distinguishing qualities was their capacity for "integrative thinking"—the ability to hold opposing or conflicting ideas in their head and use that tension to create a new and superior idea—much like how humans use their opposable thumbs to excel at manual tasks.

The first step to take when solving problems or seeking the truth is not to immediately and boldly jump in and take an either-or (for-or-against) position. Instead, take a cautious and balanced approach in which you (a) carefully and equally examine arguments for and against each position, (b) acknowledge the strengths and weaknesses of both positions, and (c) seek to integrate the strongest points of each position.

Lastly, balanced thinking involves more than just totaling the number of arguments for and against a position; it also involves *weighing* the strength of each argument. Arguments can vary in terms of their degree of importance or level of support. When weighing an argument, ask yourself, "What is the quality and quantity of evidence supporting it?" Consider whether the evidence is:

1. Definitive—so strong or compelling that a definite conclusion should be reached
2. Suggestive—strong enough to suggest that a tentative or possible conclusion may be reached
3. Inconclusive—too weak to reach any conclusion.

When making class presentations and writing papers or reports, be mindful of how much weight should be assigned to different arguments and explain how their weight has been factored into your conclusion.

In some cases, after reviewing both supporting and contradictory evidence for different positions, balanced thinking may lead you to suspend judgment and withhold drawing a conclusion that favors one position over another. A balanced thinker may occasionally conclude that the evidence doesn't strongly favor a particular

"The test of a first-rate intelligence is the ability to hold two opposed ideas in mind at the same time and still retain the ability to function.
—*F. Scott Fitzgerald, regarded as one of the greatest American writers of the 20th century*

"[Successful] business leaders have the capacity to hold two diametrically opposing ideas in their heads. And then, without panicking or settling for one alternative or the other, they're able to produce a synthesis that is superior to either opposing idea.
—*Roger Martin, Dean of the Rotman School of Management, University of Toronto*

"Listening well is as important to critical thinking as contributing brilliantly.
—Stephen Brookfield, in *Developing Critical Thinkers*

position, or additional information is needed before a final judgment or firm conclusion can be drawn. These aren't wishy-washy answers; they are legitimate conclusions to reach after all the evidence has been carefully considered and weighed. In fact, it's better to be undecided based on an informed and balanced viewpoint than to be decided based on an uninformed or biased viewpoint.

If you find that the more you learn, the more complicated things seem to be, that's good news. It means you're moving from simplistic to complex thinking that is becoming more nuanced and balanced.

Reflection 8.5

Consider the following positions:

1. Course requirements should be eliminated; college students should be allowed to choose the classes they want to take for their degree.

2. Course grades should be eliminated; college students should take classes on a pass–fail basis.

Using balanced thinking, identify one argument *for* and *against* each of these two positions.

Critical Thinking (Evaluation)

When you *evaluate* or *judge* the quality of an argument or work product, you are engaging in a form of higher-level thinking known as *critical thinking*. This thinking skill is highly valued by professors teaching all subjects in the college curriculum and is expected of students at all stages of the college experience. Thus, by developing your critical thinking skills as a first-year student, you will improve your academic performance across the curriculum and throughout your time in college.

Many students misinterpret critical thinking to mean "being critical"—criticizing something or somebody in a negative way. Although critical thinking does involve making critical judgments, those judgments can be either positive or negative—similar to how a film critic can give a good (thumbs up) or bad (thumbs down) review of a movie. Whether the judgment is positive or negative (or some combination thereof), critical thinking involves backing up the judgment with specific, well-informed reasons and evidence to support it. Failure to do so makes it an unfounded criticism—a criticism that lacks a solid foundation or basis of support.

You can start developing higher-level critical thinking skills by using the following criteria as standards for evaluating an idea or argument:

1. **Validity (Truthfulness):** Is it logically sound or evidence-based?
2. **Morality (Ethics):** Is it fair or just?
3. **Beauty (Aesthetics):** Does it have artistic merit or value?
4. **Practicality (Usefulness):** Can it be used for beneficial purposes?
5. **Priority (How it Ranks in Terms of Importance or Effectiveness):** Is it better than other ideas or courses of action?

Critical Thinking and Inferential Reasoning

When making arguments and drawing conclusions, we use a mental process called *inferential reasoning*. We start with a premise (a statement or observation) and use it to infer (step to) a conclusion. Inferential reasoning is used to reach conclusions through use of (a) logic or (b) empirical (observable) evidence.

1. **Logic.** Reaching a conclusion by showing that it logically follows from, or is logically consistent with, an established premise. In other words, if statement "A" is true, it can be concluded that statement "B" must be true.

   For example:
   Statement A. The constitution guarantees all American citizens the right to vote. (Premise)
   Statement B. Women and people of color are American citizens, therefore, they should have the right to vote. (Conclusion)

2. **Empirical (observable) evidence.** Reaching a conclusion by showing that it is supported with statistical data or research findings. In other words, based on evidence "A," it can be concluded that "B" is true.

   For example:
   Statement A. Statistics show that a much higher percentage of people who smoke experience cancer and heart disease than non-smokers. (Premise)
   Statement B. Based on statistical evidence, smoking is a major health risk. (Conclusion)

Logical reasoning and empirical evidence are different routes through which conclusions are reached (inferred), but these two routes can be combined to make a stronger case for the same conclusion. For instance, those who argue that the legal drinking age should be lowered to 18 have used the following forms of logical reasoning and empirical evidence to support their position:

1. **Logical reasoning:** 18-year-olds in the United States are considered to be legal adults with respect to such rights and responsibilities as voting, serving on juries, joining the military, and being held responsible for committing crimes; therefore, 18-year-olds should have the right to drink.
2. **Empirical evidence:** In other countries where drinking is allowed at age 18, statistics show that they have fewer binge-drinking and drunk-driving problems than the United States.

Reflection 8.6

Can you think of arguments *against* lowering the drinking age to 18 that are based on logical reasoning and/or empirical evidence?

Inferential reasoning based on logic and empirical evidence is the primary thought processes that humans use to reach conclusions about themselves and the world around them. You will also use this form of thinking to make arguments and reach conclusions in your college courses because you will often be required to take positions and support them with sound reasoning and solid evidence.

Logical Fallacies: Inferential Reasoning Errors

Errors can be made in the process of inferential reasoning; these errors are commonly referred to as *logical fallacies*. Listed below is a summary of the major types of logical fallacies. Be mindful of these slips in reasoning and when evaluating your own thinking and the thinking of others. As you read through the following inferential reasoning errors, note in the margin whether you have ever witnessed it or committed it.

- **Non sequitur.** Drawing a conclusion that does not necessarily follow from or connect with the premise—the initial statement or observation. ("Non sequitur" derives from Latin, which literally means, "it does not follow.") Example: There was a bloody glove found at the murder scene and it doesn't fit the defendant, therefore the defendant must be innocent.

- **Selective Perception.** Seeing only examples and instances that support one's position while overlooking or ignoring those that contradict it. Example: Believers of astrology who only notice people whose personalities happen to fit their astrological sign, but overlook those who do not.

- **Dogmatism.** Stubbornly clinging to a personal point of view that's unsupported by evidence while remaining closed-minded (nonreceptive) to other viewpoints that are better supported by evidence. Example: Arguing that adopting a national health system is a form of socialism which cannot or will not work in a capitalistic economy, while ignoring the fact that there are other nations in the world that have both a national health care system and a capitalistic economy.

- **Double Standard.** Using two sets of critical thinking standards—a higher standard for judging the ideas of others and a lower standard for judging one's own ideas. Example: Looking for the flaws in others' arguments and challenging their opinions, but not applying the same critical thinking process to our own arguments and opinions.

- **Wishful Thinking.** Thinking that something is true, not based on logic or evidence, but because it's the way we *want* it to be. Example: A teenage girl who believes she will not become pregnant, despite that fact that she and her boyfriend are having sex regularly without any form of contraception.

- **Hasty Generalization (a.k.a. "Cherry-Picking").** Reaching a general conclusion by picking out a limited number of examples or cases to support it. Example: Concluding that members of a racial or ethnic group are all "that way" based on just a few instances.

- **Jumping to a Conclusion.** Immediately leaping to a conclusion without taking time to consider other reasons or explanations. Example: A shy person immediately concludes that someone doesn't like her because that person didn't make eye contact with her, without considering the possibility that the other person's lack of eye contact may be the result of his being distracted or shy as well.

- **False Cause and Effect (a.k.a. Correlational Error).** Concluding that if two things co-occur at about the same time or in close sequence, one must *cause* the other. Example: Concluding that schizophrenia is caused by drug use because schizophrenics are more likely to use drugs than non-schizophrenics, but failing to consider that schizophrenia is a mentally illness whose victims is not caused by using drugs, but the result of using drugs to help them cope with their symptoms.

- **False Analogy (a.k.a. False Equivalency).** Concluding that because two things are alike in one respect, they must be alike in another respect. This is the classic "comparing apples with oranges" error—both alike in that they are fruits but they're unlike in other ways. Example: People who argue that government is a form of business, therefore it should be run like a business or run by businessmen. Although it's true that government and business are societal institutions that have some similarities (e.g., budgets and payrolls), they are also different: the primary purpose of government is to serve and safeguard citizens; the primary purpose of business is to serve customers and create profit.

- **Glittering Generality.** Making a positive, general statement that is not backed up by specific details or evidence. Example: A letter of recommendation that describes the recommended person as "very intelligent" and having a "great personality," but provides little or no evidence to support of these claims.

- **Straw Man Argument.** Distorting or misrepresenting an opposing argument or position and then attacking it. Example: Criticizing a politician's bill as an attempt to abolish Americans' second amendment right to bear arms (own guns) when, in fact, the bill only calls for a ban on high-powered military assault weapons.

- **Ad Hominem Argument.** Attacking the person, not the person's argument. (Literally translated, ad hominem means "to the man.") Example: Discounting a young person's argument by saying: "you're too young and inexperienced to know what you're talking about," or discounting an older person's argument by stating: "you're too old-school to understand this issue."

- **Red Herring.** Bringing up an irrelevant point that draws attention away from the real issue being discussed or debated. (The term "red herring" derives from an old practice of dragging a herring—a strong-smelling fish—across a trail to distract the scent of pursuing dogs.) Example: People who responded to criticism of former President Richard Nixon's involvement in the Watergate scandal by arguing, "He was a good president who accomplished many great things while he was in office." (Nixon's effectiveness as a president is an irrelevant point or red herring; the real issue under discussion is Nixon's behavior in the Watergate scandal.)

- **Smoke Screen.** Intentionally disguising or camouflaging the truth by providing confusing or misleading explanations. Example: A politician opposes putting limits on prescription drug prices by arguing that it interferes with America's system of free enterprise when the reason for this position is that he or she is receiving campaign funds from drug manufacturing companies.

- **Slippery Slope.** Using fear tactics to argue that not accepting a position will result in a "domino effect"—one bad thing happening after another—like a series of falling dominoes. Example: Arguing that "if America does not intervene militarily in Vietnam to stop communism, it will spread to other countries and, eventually, to America."

- **Rhetorical Deception.** Using slick fast-talk or deceptive language to conclude that something is true without providing reasons or evidence. Example: Using glib expressions like, "*Clearly* this is . . .", "It's *obvious* that . . .", or "Any *reasonable* person can see . . ." without explaining why it's so "clear", "obvious", or "reasonable."

- **Circular Reasoning (a.k.a. "Begging the Question").** Drawing a conclusion by circling back to the premise and restating it—in other words, saying something is true because it is true. Example: Concluding that "stem cell research is unethical because it's morally wrong."

- **Appealing to Authority or Prestige.** Concluding that if an authority figure or celebrity says it's true, it must be true. Example: Believing that Product X should be bought simply because a famous actor or athlete endorses it. Or, concluding that a course of action should be taken simply because the president says it should be taken.

- **Appealing to Tradition or Familiarity.** Concluding that if something has been considered to be true for a long time, or has always been done in a certain way, it must be true or be the best way to do it. Example: "Throughout history, marriage has been a relationship between a man and a woman; therefore, gay marriage should be illegal."

- **Appealing to Popularity or to the Majority (a.k.a. Jumping on the Bandwagon).** Concluding that if an idea is popular or held by the majority of people, it must be true. Example: "So many people believe in psychics, it must be true; they can't all be wrong."
- **Appealing to Emotion.** Concluding that something is true based on how passionately or emotionally it's stated rather than on the quality of reasoning behind the statement. Example: "He must be telling the truth because he denied the allegation so intensely and forcefully."

> "Political talk shows have become shouting matches designed to push emotional hot buttons and drive us further apart. We desperately need to exchange ideas with one another rationally and courteously."
>
> —*David Boren, President, University of Oklahoma, and longest-serving chairman of the U.S. Senate Intelligence Committee*

⚛ Reflection 8.7

Glance back at the reasoning errors just discussed. Identify two that you have witnessed or experienced. What were the situations in which these errors took place? Why do you think they took place?

(Check the results of your AchieveWORKS Learning and Productivity Report and your Personality assessment report and review the personalized strategies suggested to you for becoming a more successful learner. Have you tried these strategies or plan to try them? If not, analyze your reasons. Can you identify any logical fallacies in your reasoning?)

> "Too often we enjoy the comfort of opinion without the discomfort of thought."
>
> —*John F. Kennedy, 35th U.S. president*

AUTHOR'S EXPERIENCE

When I teach classes and give workshops, I often challenge students and participants to debate me on political issues. I ask them to identify their political party affiliation for a debate topic, or their position on a social issue for which there are different political viewpoints. The ground rules are as follows: They choose the topic for debate; they can only use facts to support their argument, rebuttal, or both; and they must respond in a rational manner, without letting emotions drive their answers.

When I conduct this exercise, I usually discover that the topics people feel most strongly about are often those they haven't critically evaluated. For instance, people say they are Democrat, Republican, independent, and so on, and argue from these positions; however, few of them have taken the time to critically examine whether their stated political affiliation is actually consistent with their personal viewpoints. They almost always answer "no" to the following questions: "Have you read the core document (e.g., party platform) that outlines the party stance?" and "Have you engaged in self-examination of your party affiliation through reasoned discussions with others who say they have the same or different political affiliations?"

—*Aaron Thompson*

> "All thinking begins with wonder."
>
> —*Socrates, classic Greek (Athenian) philosopher and founding father of Western philosophy*

Creative Thinking

When you generate something new or different—an original idea, strategy, or work product—you're engaging in creative thinking. Creative thinking leads you to ask the question: "Why not?" (e.g., "Why not do it a different way?").

The process of creative thinking may be viewed as an extended or more advanced form of synthesis. Similar to synthesis, creative thinking involves connecting different ideas, but they're connected or combined in a way that results in something that's unique or distinctively different. For instance, the musical genre of hard rock was created by combining elements of blues and rock and roll, and folk rock was born when Bob Dylan combined musical elements of acoustic blues and amplified rock. In the film, "Flash of Genius" (based on a true story), Robert Kearns combined preexisting mechanical parts to create the intermittent windshield wiper.

Keep in mind that creative thinking is not restricted to the arts; it occurs in all subject areas—even in fields that seek precise and definitive answers. In math, creative thinking is used when new approaches or strategies are used to arrive at a correct solution to a problem. In science, creativity takes place when a scientist first uses imaginative thinking to create a hypothesis or logical hunch ("What might happen if . . . ?") and then tests this hypothesis by conducting an experiment to confirm whether the hypothesis is true.

It could be said that thinking critically involves looking "inside the box" to evaluate the quality of its content. Thinking creatively involves looking "outside the box" to imagine new packages with different content. Creative and critical thinking are two of the most important forms of higher-level thinking and they often work together in a reciprocal and complementary fashion. Creative thinking is used to ask new questions and generate new ideas; critical thinking is used to evaluate or critique new ideas that are generated. If our evaluation (critique) of what's been created reveals that it lacks quality, we shift back to creative thinking to generate something new and improved. For an idea to be truly creative, it must not be just different or unusual, it must also be effective or significant.

The starting point for the complementary processes of creative and critical thinking can also be reversed, whereby we start by using critical thinking to evaluate an established idea or approach. If our evaluation indicates that this idea or approach should be improved, we turn to creative thinking to come up with a new idea or different approach, and then we turn back to critical thinking to evaluate the quality of the new idea we created.

Brainstorming is a problem-solving process that illustrates how creative and critical thinking work hand-in-hand. The steps involved in the process of brainstorming are summarized in **Box 8.3**. This process can be engaged in alone or with others.

> "The blues are the roots. Everything else are the fruits."
>
> —Willie Dixon, blues songwriter; commenting on how virtually all forms of contemporary American music contain elements of blues music, which originated among African American slaves

> "Imagination should give wings to our thoughts, but imagination must be checked and documented by the factual results of the experiment."
>
> —Louis Pasteur, French microbiologist, chemist, and founder of pasteurization (a method for preventing milk and wine from going sour)

> "Creativity isn't 'crazytivity'."
>
> —Edward De Bono, internationally known authority on creative thinking

Box 8.3

The Process of Brainstorming

Key Steps:

1. Generate as many possible ideas as you can and jot them down as soon as they come to mind. At this stage, just let your imagination run wild; don't be concerned about whether the idea you generate is impractical, unrealistic, or outrageous. Studies show that initial concerns about whether ideas will work often blocks our ability to create ideas that have the potential to work.

2. Review the ideas you generated and use them as a springboard to trigger additional ideas.

3. After you run out of ideas, reflect on and critically evaluate the ones listed and eliminate those that you think are least effective or useful.

4. From the remaining list of ideas, choose the best idea or best combination of ideas.

Note that the first two steps in the brainstorming process involve *divergent thinking*—a form of creative thinking in which you go off in different directions to generate diverse ideas. In contrast, the last two steps in the process involve *convergent thinking*—a form of critical thinking in which you converge (focus in) and narrow down the ideas you've generated, evaluating each of them for their effectiveness.

As this 4-step process suggests, creativity doesn't just happen suddenly or effortlessly (the so-called "stroke of genius"); instead, it takes sustained mental effort and thoughtful review. Although creative thinking may occasionally involve spontaneous or intuitive leaps, it typically involves careful reflection and evaluation to determine if any of those leaps actually land us on an innovative and effective idea.

AUTHOR'S EXPERIENCE

I was once working with a friend to come up with ideas for a grant proposal. We started out by sitting at his kitchen table, exchanging ideas while sipping coffee; then we both got up and began to pace back and forth, walking all around the room and bouncing different ideas off each other. Whenever one of us came up with an idea, the other would jot it down (whoever was pacing closer to the kitchen table at the moment).

After we ran out of ideas, we shifted gears, slowed down, and sat down at the table together to critique the ideas we generated during our "binge-thinking" episode. After some debate, we finally settled on an idea that we judged to be the best of all the ideas we generated, and we used this idea for the grant—which, fortunately, was awarded to us.

Although I wasn't fully aware of it at the time, the stimulating thought process my friend and I were engaging in was called brainstorming: first we engaged in creative thinking—a fast-paced, idea-production stage; then followed it with critical thinking—a slower-paced, idea-evaluation stage.

—*Joe Cuseo*

> "Creativity is allowing oneself to make mistakes; art is knowing which ones to keep."
> — Scott Adams, creator of the Dilbert comic strip and author of *The Dilbert Principle*

Creative thinking and critical thinking go hand-in hand. We use the former to generate new ideas and the latter to evaluate the quality of the new ideas we generate.

Strategies for Stimulating Creative Thinking

In addition to brainstorming, creative thinking can be stimulated by adopting the following attitudes and practices.

- **Be flexible.** Think about ideas and objects in alternative and unconventional ways. The power of flexible and unconventional thinking was well illustrated in the movie *Apollo 13*, a true story about astronauts whose lives were saved by the creative use of duct tape as an air filter. Flexible thinking was also used by Johannes Gutenberg, the inventor of the printing press, who made his groundbreaking discovery while watching a machine being used to press (crush) grapes at a wine harvest. He thought that the same type of machine could be used for a different purpose—to press letters onto paper.

- **Be experimental.** Play with ideas; try them out to see whether they'll work or work better than the status quo. Studies show that creative people are mental risk-takers who experiment with different ideas and techniques. When we cling rigidly to what's conventional or traditional, we're clinging to the comfort or security, familiarity, and predictability; this often blocks originality, ingenuity, and openness to change. Tom Kelley, cofounder of the famous IDEO design firm in Palo Alto, California, has found that innovative thinking emerges from an exploratory mindset that's "open to new insights every day." So, be exploratory! Step beyond the comfort zone of the familiar, traditional, and conventional.

- **Get mobile.** Stand up and move around while you're thinking. Research shows that taking a walk (inside or outside) stimulates the production of creative ideas. Even just by standing up, the human brain gets approximately 10% more oxygen than it does when sitting down. Because oxygen provides fuel for the brain, our ability to think creatively is enhanced when we're up on our feet and moving around.

- **Get it down.** Creative ideas can suddenly come to mind at the most unexpected times—a process that creativity researchers refer to as *incubation*. Similar to how incubated eggs can hatch at any time, so too can our thoughts hatch and give birth to original ideas. However, just as suddenly as these innovative ideas slip into our mind, they can just as quickly slip out of our mind as soon as we start thinking about or doing something else. You can prevent this mental slippage from happening by having the right equipment on hand to record your creative ideas before you forget them. Carry a pen and a small notepad, a packet of sticky notes, or a portable electronic recording device at all times to immediately record original ideas the instant you have them.

- **Get diverse.** Seek ideas from a variety of social and informational sources. Bouncing ideas off different people and getting feedback from them about your ideas is a good way to generate mental energy, synergy (multiplication of ideas), and serendipity (accidental discoveries). Studies show that creative people venture beyond the boundaries of their area of training or specialization. They have wide-ranging interests and a broad knowledge base, which they draw upon and combine to generate new ideas. Be on the lookout to combine the knowledge you acquire from different subjects and different people, and use it to build bridges to new ideas.

> "I make progress by having people around who are smarter than I am—and listening to them. And I assume that everyone is smarter about something than I am.
> —*Henry Kaiser, successful industrialist, known as the father of American shipbuilding*

- **Take a break.** If you're having trouble discovering a solution to a problem, stop working on it for a while and come back to it later. Creative solutions often come to mind after you take your mind off the problem you're trying to solve. When you work intensely on a problem or challenging task for a sustained period of time, your attention can get rigidly riveted on just one approach to its solution. By taking your mind off the problem and returning to it later, you allow your attention to shift to a different feature or aspect of the problem. This new focus point puts you in a position to view it from a different angle or vantage point, enabling you to see a solution that you may not have seen before. Taking a break from the problem and coming back to it later also allows the problem to incubate in your mind at a lower level of consciousness (and at a lower level of stress), which can give birth to a sudden solution.

> "Eureka! (literally translated: "I have found it!")
> —*Attributed to Archimedes, ancient Greek mathematician and inventor when he suddenly discovered (while sitting in a bathtub) how to measure the purity of gold*

- **Reorganize the problem.** When you're stuck on a problem, try rearranging its parts or pieces. Reorganization can transform the problem into a different pattern and enable you to suddenly see a solution that you previously overlooked—similar to how changing the order of letters in a word jumble can help you find the hidden word. You can use the same strategy to change the wording of any problem you're working on, or you can record ideas on different index cards and arrange them in different sequences. Sticky notes (a.k.a. post-it notes) are ideal for this purpose. You can post them on almost anything, remove them from where they were stuck (without a mess), and rearrange them in any sequence or pattern you'd like.

> "Creativity consists largely of re-arranging what we know in order to find out what we do not know.
> —*George Keller, prolific American architect and originator of the Union Station design for elevated train stations*

    If you're having trouble solving a problem that involves a sequence of steps (e.g., a math problem), try reversing the sequence and start working from the end or the middle. The new sequence enables you to come at the problem from a different direction and may provide an alternative path to its solution.

- **Be persistent.** Creativity takes time, dedication, and hard work. Studies of creative people indicate that innovative insights typically don't occur effortlessly, but emerge from sustained effort and ongoing commitment. In a survey of more than 140 creativity researchers, the personal attribute they rated number one in importance for creative achievement was perseverance and resilience.

> "Genius is 1% inspiration and 99% perspiration.
> —*Thomas Edison, scientist and creator of more than 1,000 inventions, including the light bulb, phonograph, and motion picture camera*

Reflection 8.8

Do you consider yourself to be a creative thinker? (Why or why not?)

What could you do to enhance your ability to think creatively?

Using Higher-Level Thinking Skills to Improve Academic Performance in College

Thus far, this chapter has focused primarily on helping you get a clear idea of what higher-level thinking is and what its major benefits are. What follows are strategies for developing habits of higher-level thinking that you can apply to improve your performance in college (and beyond).

Connect ideas you acquire in class with related ideas found in your assigned reading. When you discover information in your reading that relates to something you've learned in class (or vice versa), make a note of it in the margin of your text-book or your class notebook. By integrating knowledge from these major sources, you're engaging in the higher-level thinking skill of synthesis. You can then use the information you synthesized on exams and assignments to improve your course grades.

When listening to lectures and completing reading assignments, pay attention not only to the content being covered but also the thought process used by the professors and authors. Ask yourself what forms of higher-level thinking they are using. The more observant you are about the type of higher-level thinking skills that scholars are modeling for you, the more likely you are to emulate those thinking skills and demonstrate them on your exams and assignments.

Pause periodically to think about how you are thinking. When you're working on academic tasks, be mindful of the type of thinking you're engaging in (e.g., analysis, synthesis, or evaluation). Thinking about and becoming more aware of how you're thinking is a mental process called *metacognition*. It's a process that has been found to strengthen higher-level thinking and problem-solving.

A simple but powerful way to develop higher-level thinking skills is by asking yourself questions that prompt you to reflect on your thinking. Because thinking often involves silent self-talk, if you can get in the habit of asking yourself questions that call for higher-level thinking, you can begin training your mind to think at a higher level. You can then routinely apply these questions to the material you're learning in college to demonstrate higher levels of thinking on your exams and assignments, and earn higher grades in your courses.

Box 8.4 contains key questions you can use of yourself to trigger different forms of higher-level thinking. The questions are constructed as incomplete sentences so you can fill in the blank with any topic or concept you may be studying in any course you may be taking. Research indicates that when students get in the habit of using question stems such as these, they get in the habit of engaging in and demonstrating the higher levels of thinking called for by these questions. As you read the questions in the following box, think about how these questions may be applied to material you're learning in courses this term.

> "If you do not ask the right questions, you do not get the right answers."
>
> —*Edward Hodnett, British poet*

Box 8.4

Questions You Can Ask Yourself to Develop Multiple Forms of Higher-Level Thinking

1. ANALYSIS (ANALYTICAL THINKING)—breaking down information into its essential elements or parts.
   * What are the main ideas contained in _____?
   * What are the key issues raised by _____?
   * What hidden assumptions or values are embedded within _____?
   * What are the reasons behind _____?
   * What are the underlying causes of ____?
   * How are the ideas contained in _____similar to or different than ____?
   * How might this ____ be broken down into component parts and addressed in a systematic, step-by-step fashion?
   * What additional information do I need to understand or complete this ____?

2. SYNTHESIS—integrating separate pieces of information into a more complete, coherent product or pattern.
   * In what way(s) is this idea related to ____?
   * How could these different _____ be grouped together into a more general class or category?
   * How can this idea be joined or connected with _____ to create a more comprehensive answer or solution?
   * How might these separate _____ be reorganized or rearranged to get a more complete understanding of the "big picture?"

3. APPLICATION (APPLIED THINKING)—using knowledge for practical purposes to solve problems and resolve issues.
   * What purpose or function could ____ serve?
   * What are the practical implications or consequences of _____?
   * How can ____ be used to improve or strengthen_____?
   * How might this theory or principle be applied to _____?
   * How could _____serve to prevent or eliminate ____?

4. BALANCED THINKING—carefully considering reasons for and against a particular position or viewpoint.
   * What are the strengths (advantages) and weaknesses (disadvantages) of _____?
   * What evidence supports and contradicts _____?
   * What are the arguments for and against _____?
   * What are the major costs and benefits of ____?
   * What are the potential risks and rewards of ____?

5. MULTIDIMENSIONAL THINKING—thinking about ourselves and the world around us from multiple angles or perspectives.
   * What viewpoints need to be considered to get a complete understanding of _____?
   * What factors or variables combine to influence ____?
   * What aspects of personal development should be considered when _____?
   * How would people from different cultural backgrounds interpret or react to _____?
   * What dimensions of the self (personal development) would be affected by ____?
   * What dimensions of the world (global development) would be influenced by ____?

6. CREATIVE THINKING—generating ideas that are unique, original, or innovative.
   * What would happen if _____?
   * What could be invented to _____?
   * What might be a different method for _____?
   * What changes could be made to improve _____?
   * What would be a novel approach to _____?
   * What strategies have not yet been tried for solving the problem of ___?
   * What are alternative ways of looking at _____?

7. EVALUATION—critically judging the soundness of arguments and evidence used to reach conclusions.
   * What examples support the argument that _____?
   * What research evidence is there for _____?
   * What statistical data document or back up this _____?
   * What assumptions are being made to reach the conclusion that ____?
   * If ____ is true, would it follow that ____ is also true?
   * If people believe in _____, then actions or practices consistent with this belief would be ____?
   * What criteria (standards) are being used to judge the validity of ____?

continued...

* What criteria are being used to judge the ethicality or morality of ____?
* What criteria are being used to evaluate the aesthetic value (beauty) of ____?

Save these higher-level thinking questions and keep them in mind when completing different academic tasks required in your courses (e.g., preparing for exams, writing papers or reports, and participating in class discussions or study group sessions). Try to get in the habit of periodically stepping back to reflect on your thinking and think about the type of thinking you're engaging in (analysis, synthesis, application, etc.). You could even keep a "thinking log" or "thinking journal" to become more self-aware of the thinking strategies you're using and developing. This strategy will not only help you acquire higher-level thinking skills for use in college, it will also help you use these skills during job interviews and in letters of application for career positions or admission to graduate or professional schools.

 Reflection 8.9

Look back at the higher-level thinking questions listed in Box 8.4. Identify one question listed under each of the seven forms of thinking that could be asked about a concept or issue being discussed in a course you're taking this term.

Internet-Based Resources

For additional information on the topics discussed in this chapter, see the following websites:

Higher-Level Thinking Skills:
http://burtonslifelearning.pbworks.com/f/BloomDigitalTaxonomy2001.pdf

Critical Thinking:
http://www.criticalthinking.org/pages/college-and-university-students/799

Creative Thinking:
https://courses.lumenlearning.com/suny-collegesuccess-lumen1/chapter/creative-thinking-skills/

Thinking Errors:
https://www.psychologytoday.com/us/blog/what-mentally-strong-people-dont-do/201501/10-thinking-errors-will-crush-your-mental-strength
www.factcheck.org (site for evaluating the validity or factual accuracy of statements made by politicians in TV ads, debates, speeches, interviews, and news releases)

Chapter 8 Exercises

8.1 Quote Reflections

Review the sidebar quotes contained in this chapter and select two that were especially meaningful or inspirational to you.

For each of the quotes you selected, provide an explanation of why you chose it.

8.2 Strategy Reflections

Review the strategies for *stimulating creative thinking* on pp. 178-179. Select three strategies you think would be most useful and intend to put into practice.

8.3 Reality Bite

Trick or Treat: "Confusing" Test or "Challenging" Test?

In Professor Plato's philosophy course, students just had their first exam returned to them and they're going over it in class. Some students are angry because they feel the professor included "trick questions" on the test to intentionally confuse them. Professor Plato responds by saying that his test questions were not designed to trick or confuse them but to "challenge them to think."

Reflection and Discussion Questions

1. What do you think led some students to conclude that some of Professor Plato's test questions were intentionally designed to trick or confuse them?

2. When Professor Plato said that his test was designed to "challenge students to think," what type of test questions do you think he was referring to?

3. On future tests, what might the students do to reduce the likelihood that they'll feel tricked or fooled again?

4. On future tests, what might Professor Plato do to reduce the likelihood that his students will complain about being asked "trick questions"?

8.4 Faculty Interview

Make an appointment to visit a faculty member teaching a course you're taking this term, or a faculty member in a field of study that you're thinking about pursuing as a college major. During your visit, ask the following questions:

1. In your field of study, what key questions do scholars ask?

2. What methods do scholars use to investigate and discover answers to the questions they ask?

3. How do scholars in your field demonstrate critical and creative thinking?

4. What types of thinking skills does it take for students to succeed and excel in your field?

8.5 Self-Assessing Personal Qualities Associated with Higher-Level Thinking

Higher-level thinking is not just a thought process, it's also a personal attribute. Listed below are four key characteristics of higher-level thinkers, accompanied by specific behaviors relating to each of these characteristics. As you read the behaviors listed under each characteristic, place a checkmark (✓) next to any behavior you think you already possess and an asterisk (*) next to any behavior you think you need to acquire or develop.

1. Tolerant and Accepting

    ____ I don't tune out ideas that conflict with my own.

    ____ I try to find common ground with others who hold viewpoints that differ from my own.

    ____ I keep my emotions under control when someone criticizes my viewpoint.

    ____ I feel comfortable discussing controversial issues.

2. Inquisitive and Open Minded

    ____ I'm eager to continue learning new things from different people and different experiences.

    ____ I'm willing to seek out others who hold viewpoints that differ from my own.

    ____ I find differences of opinion and opposing viewpoints to be interesting and stimulating.

    ____ I attempt to understand why people hold different opinions on the same issue.

3. Reflective and Tentative

    ____ I take time to consider all perspectives or sides of an issue before drawing conclusions, making choices, or reaching decisions.

    ____ I give fair consideration to ideas that others often instantly disapprove of or find distasteful.

    ____ I acknowledge the complexity, ambiguity, or uncertainty of certain issues, and am willing to say: "I need to give this more thought" or "I need more information or evidence before I can draw a conclusion."

    ____ I periodically reexamine my own opinions and positions to determine whether they should be maintained or changed.

4. Honest and Courageous

    ____ I'm willing to honestly examine my viewpoints to see if they're biased or prejudiced.

    ____ I'm willing to challenge others' ideas that appear to be based on personal bias or prejudice.

    ____ I'm willing to express a personal viewpoint that may not conform with the majority's viewpoint.

    ____ I'm willing to change my personal opinions or beliefs when they're contradicted by new evidence.

Look back at the list and count the number of checkmarks and asterisks you placed under each of the four general areas:

	Checkmarks	Asterisks
Tolerant and Accepting	_____	_____
Inquisitive and Open Minded	_____	_____
Reflective and Tentative	_____	_____
Honest and Courageous	_____	_____

Reflection Questions

*   Under which attribute did you place (a) the most *checkmarks* and (b) the most *asterisks*? What do you think accounts for the difference?

*   What could you do in college to strengthen your weakest area (the attribute under which you placed the most asterisks)?

8.6 Demonstrating Higher-Level Thinking in Your Courses

Look at the syllabus for three courses you're enrolled in this term and find an assignment or exam that counts the most toward your final course grade. For each of these courses, identify one of the following forms of higher-level thinking you could demonstrate on that assignment or test:

1. Analysis (Analytical Thinking): Breaking down information into its essential elements or parts.

2. Synthesis (Integrative Thinking): Connecting separate pieces of information to form a more complete and coherent product or pattern.

3. Application (Applied Thinking): Using knowledge for the practical purpose of solving a problem or resolving an issue.

4. Multidimensional Thinking: Thinking about yourself or the world around you from different angles or perspectives.

5. Balanced Thinking: Carefully considering reasons for and against a position or viewpoint.

6. Creative Thinking: Generating an idea that is unique, original, or innovative.

7. Evaluation: Critically judging the soundness of arguments and evidence used to arrive at a conclusion.

Course 1 exam or assignment: _____

Form of higher-level thinking I will demonstrate:

How I plan to demonstrate this form of thinking:

Course 2 exam or assignment: _____

Form of higher-level thinking I will demonstrate:

How I plan to demonstrate this form of thinking:

Course 3 exam or assignment: _____

Form of higher-level thinking I will demonstrate:

How I plan to demonstrate this form of thinking:

CHAPTER 9

Social and Emotional Intelligence

RELATING TO OTHERS AND REGULATING EMOTIONS

Chapter Purpose & Preview

Communicating and relating to others are important life skills and essential elements of "social intelligence." Similarly, being aware of, and being able to manage one's own emotions and the emotions of others are key life skills and critical components of "emotional intelligence." This chapter identifies specific ways in which social and emotional intelligence can be exhibited; it also supplies you with interpersonal communication and human relations strategies to promote positive relationships with others and enhance your leadership potential.

Learning Goal

Acquire research-based strategies for strengthening listening and conversational skills, emotional sensitivity, ability to resolve interpersonal conflict, and relate to others in a positive and productive manner.

Ignite Your Thinking

 Reflection 9.1

When you hear the word "intelligence," what characteristics come to mind?

The Importance of Social and Emotional Intelligence

If your answer to the previous question focused on "intellectual" characteristics, your response reflected the traditional definition of intelligence. Human intelligence was once considered to be a general intellectual trait that could be measured by a single intelligence test (IQ). Scholars have since discovered that the singular word "intelligence" is inaccurate and needs to be replaced with the plural "intelligences" to reflect the fact that humans can and do display intelligence in multiple forms that cannot be captured in a single test score. One of these multiple intelligences is *social intelligence* (a.k.a. "interpersonal intelligence")—the ability to communicate and relate effectively to others. It's long been known that social intelligence is essential for effective leadership and more recent research indicates that it's a better predictor of personal and professional success than intellectual ability.

Another recently recognized form of intelligence is *emotional intelligence*—the ability to recognize and manage one's own emotions, emotions of others, and behave in ways that have a positive impact on the emotions of others.

"Relationships are the key to leadership effectiveness ... Leadership is inherently relational.

—*Komives, Lucas, & McMahon,* Exploring Leadership: For College Students Who Want to Make a Difference

187

Similar to research findings on social intelligence, research on emotional intelligence reveals that it's a better predictor of personal and occupational success than intellectual test scores. Research also shows that emotional self-awareness is a key characteristic of effective leaders.

Listening: A Key Element of Social Intelligence

When people answer survey questions that ask them to identify what they like most about their best friend, "good listener" ranks among the top characteristics cited. Effective listening is also a key characteristic of effective problem solvers and ranks among the top skills sought by employers when hiring and promoting employees. Despite the well-documented power of listening, interpersonal communications and human relations experts report that most people spend too much time talking and not enough time listening. Listening well involves use of *active* listening strategies, such as those discussed below.

Active Listening Strategies

Humans can listen to and comprehend words spoken to them at a rate four times faster than the rate at which words can be spoken. Consequently, when we listen to others speak, there's plenty of time for us to slip into *passive listening*—hearing the words, but not really listening to those words—because our mind has wandered off somewhere. *Active listening* is a communication skill that involves: (a) focusing our *full attention* on the speaker's message, as opposed to just waiting for our turn to talk or thinking about what we're going to say next; (b) being an *empathic* listener, who pays close attention not only to the speaker's spoken words but also to what the speaker is communicating nonverbally; and (c) being an *engaged* listener who expresses interest in the speaker, checks for understanding of the speaker's words and feelings, and encourages the speaker to elaborate.

> *By listening actively and empathically to others, and by giving their thoughts and feelings our undivided attention, we send a clear and strong message that we respect them.*

Active listening doesn't happen automatically. It's a skill developed through disciplined effort and deliberate practice that eventually becomes a natural habit. The following practices may be used to develop the disciplined habit of active listening.

- **When listening, monitor your understanding of what's being said.** Good listeners take personal responsibility for following the speaker's message. In contrast, poor listeners put all the responsibility on the speaker to make the message clear and interesting. To check if you're following the speaker's message, particularly if it's a complex or emotionally sensitive message, occasionally paraphrase what you hear the speaker saying in your own words (e.g., "Let me make sure I understand . . ." or "What I hear you saying is . . ."). Such check-in statements ensure that you're following what's being said; they also assure the speaker that you're listening closely to what's being said and taking the message seriously.

- **In addition to checking if you're understanding what the speaker is saying, check if you're understanding what the speaker is** *feeling.* Pay particularly close attention to the speaker's nonverbal messages—such as tone of voice and body language—which often provide clues to the emotions behind the words. For instance, if the person is speaking at a faster rate and at a higher volume than usual, it may indicate that the person is experiencing frustration or anger; in con-

"We have been given two ears and but a single mouth in order that we may hear more and talk less."

—Zeno of Citium, ancient Greek philosopher

trast speaking at an uncharacteristically slower rate and at a lower volume may indicate dejection or depression.

- **Avoid the urge to interrupt the speaker when you think you have something important to say.** Wait until the speaker has paused for a few seconds to be sure that the person completed his or her train of thought.

- **If the speaker pauses and you start to say something at the same time the speaker starts speaking again, let the person continue before expressing your thought.** It's more socially sensitive (and socially intelligent) to listen first and speak second.

- **If your questions are followed by periods of silence, don't become uncomfortable and rush in to ask something else.** Silence may simply mean that the speaker is reflecting and taking time to formulate a thoughtful response.

- **Be sure your listening "body language" sends a message to the speaker that you're interested and non-judgmental.** It's estimated that more than two-thirds of all human communication is nonverbal and this form of communication often sends a stronger and truer message than verbal communication. When a speaker perceives inconsistency between a listener's verbal and nonverbal messages (e.g., one signals interest, the other disinterest), the nonverbal message is more likely to be perceived as the true message. Consequently, body language may be the most powerful way a listener can communicate genuine interest in the speaker's message and convey respect for the speaker. (See **Box 9.1** for effective nonverbal messages to send while listening.)

- **Be an open-minded listener.** Avoid close-mindedness or selective listening—selecting or tuning into only those stations that immediately capture your own interests or reinforce your opinions, and tuning out or turning off everything else. When others express ideas we don't agree with, we still owe them the courtesy of listening to what they have to say, rather than immediately shaking your head, frowning, or interrupting them.

Ignoring or blocking out information and ideas about topics that we don't immediately find interesting or don't support our viewpoint is not only a poor social skill, it's also a poor critical thinking skill because our thinking becomes deeper and more complex when it's challenged by exposure to topics and viewpoints that don't simply match or duplicate our own.

> "Listening well is as important to critical thinking as is contributing brilliantly.
> —Stephen Brookfield, author, *Developing Critical Thinkers*

Box 9.1

Nonverbal Signals Associated with Active Listening

Good listeners listen with good listening body language; they use their whole body to communicate to the speaker they're paying full attention to, and are fully interested in what the speaker is saying. Communication experts have created the acronym "SOFTEN" as a tool for summarizing and remembering the key body-language signals that should be sent while listening. Listed below are the nonverbal signals represented by each letter of the SOFTEN acronym.

S = Smile. Smiling sends signals of acceptance and interest. However, it should be done periodically, not continuously. (A continuous, non-stop smile can come across as inauthentic or artificial.)

Sit Still. Fidgeting or squirming sends the message that you're bored or growing inpatient (and can't wait to get out of there).

O = Open Posture. Avoid closed-posture positions, such as crossing your arms or folding your hands, these nonverbal signals can send a message that you're not open to what the speaker is saying or passing judgment on what's being said.

F = Forward Lean. Leaning *forward* sends the message that you're looking forward to what the speaker is going to say next. In contrast, leaning back can send a signal that you're backing off from (losing interest

continued...

in) what's being said or, worse yet, that you're evaluating (psychoanalyzing) the speaker.

Face the Speaker Directly. Try to line up your shoulders directly or squarely with the speaker's shoulders, as opposed to turning one shoulder toward the speaker and one shoulder away, which may send the message that you want to leave or are giving the speaker the "cold shoulder."

T = Touch. A light touch on the arm or hand occasionally, particularly to reassure a person who's speaking about something they're worried about or seem to be uncomfortable about, can be a good way to communicate warmth and acceptance. However, touch sparingly and make it more like a pat rather than a sustained touch or stroke, which could be interpreted as inappropriate intimacy (or sexual harassment).

E = Eye Contact. Lack of eye contact with the speaker can send the message that you're looking elsewhere to find something more interesting or stimulating to do than listening to what's being said. However, eye contact shouldn't be continuous or relentless because it borders on staring or glaring. Instead, strike a happy medium by making periodic eye contact—occasionally look away and then return your eye contact to the speaker.

N = Nod Your Head. Nodding slowly and periodically while listening sends the signal that you're following what's being said and affirming the person saying it. However, avoid rapid and repeated head nodding—this may send a signal that you want the speaker to hurry up so you can start talking or that you want to end the conversation as soon as possible.

One way to gain greater awareness of your nonverbal communication habits is by asking some people who know you well, and whose judgment you trust, to imitate your body language. This exercise can be very revealing (and sometimes entertaining).

 Reflection 9.2

Are there any effective nonverbal-listening messages cited in **Box 9.1** that you weren't already aware of, or that you think you need to work on? If yes, which one(s)?

Speaking and Conversational Skills

In addition to effective listening skills, social intelligence includes being skilled at speaking and carrying on conversations with others. Listed below are strategies for doing so. Some of these strategies may appear to be obvious or very fundamental, but they're also very powerful. Despite their simplicity, or perhaps because of it, they're often forgotten or overlooked.

Communicate your ideas precisely and concisely. When speaking, your objective should be to get to the point, make your point, get off stage, and give someone else a chance to speak. Nobody appreciates a "stage hog" who dominates the conversation and gobbles up more than his or her fair share of talk time.

Our spoken messages become less time-consuming, less boring, and more to the point when we avoid tangents, unnecessary details, and empty fillers—such as: "like", "kinda like", "I mean", "I'm all", and "you know." Such fillers simply "fill up" time while adding nothing substantive or meaningful to the conversation. Excessive use of fillers can also cause the listener to lose attention to and interest in what we're saying.

> "Be sincere; be brief; be seated."
>
> —Top tip for public speakers offered by Franklin D. Roosevelt, 32nd president of the United States and noted orator

> "It does not require many words to speak the truth."
>
> —Chief Joseph, Leader of the Nez Percé, Native-American Indian tribe

Take time to gather your thoughts mentally before expressing them verbally. It's better to think about what we're going to say *before* saying it than *while* we're saying it. Good conversationalists don't make others listen to their thoughts while they think through them; they give forethought to what they're going to say before speaking, so they're able to speak more economically, minimize their use of fillers, and open more time up for others to speak and be heard.

> "To talk without thinking is to shoot without aiming.
> —An old English proverb

Be comfortable with silent spells during conversations. Silent spots during conversations can sometimes cause us to feel uncomfortable (like standing close to a stranger in an elevator). To relieve the discomfort of silence, it's tempting to rush in and say anything to get the conversation going again. This urge to break the silence may be well intended, but it can result in something being said before or without sufficient forethought. Often, it's better to hold back words and think them through before blurting them out and risk saying something thoughtless.

> "Silence is better than unmeaning words.
> — Pythagoras, Greek philosopher and mathematician

Silent spells during a conversation shouldn't be automatically viewed as a "communication breakdown." Instead, they may indicate that the people involved in the conversation are pausing to think deeply about they hear the other is saying and are comfortable enough with one another to allow these reflective pauses to take place.

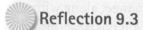

Reflection 9.3

Would you say that you're a good conversationalist?

If yes, what makes you so?

If no, what prevents you from being one?

Interpersonal Relationship Skills (a.k.a. Human Relations Skills)

In addition to communicating effectively with others, interpersonal relationship skills, also referred to as human relations skills, is another key component of social intelligence. These skills involve relating harmoniously with others and building positive relationships with them.

How can you help others view you as approachable and willing to form positive and productive relationships with them? The first steps are knowing (and remembering) who they are and showing interest in them. Listed below are specific strategies for taking these steps.

Learn and remember *names*. When you know someone's name and refer to that person by name, you affirm the person's individuality and uniqueness. You've probably heard people say they have a good memory for faces but not names, which implies that they will never be good at remembering names. The truth is that the ability to remember names is not some kind of natural-born talent or inherited ability. Instead, it's a skill that's developed through intentional effort and effective use of memory-improvement strategies, such as those described below.

> "We should be aware of the magic contained in a name. The name sets that individual apart; it makes him or her unique among all others. Remember that a person's name is to that person the sweetest and most important sound in any language.
> —Dale Carnegie, author of the best-selling book, *How to Win Friends and Influence People,* and founder of The Dale Carnegie Course—a worldwide leadership training program for business professionals

- When you meet someone, pay close attention to that person's name when you first hear it. The crucial initial step to remembering someone's name is to get the name into your brain in the first place. As obvious as this may seem, when we first meet someone, instead of listening actively and carefully for the person's name, we're often more concerned about the first impression we're making on that person after being introduced, or what we're going to say to next after being introduced. Consequently, we *forget* the name because we never did *get* the name into our brain in the first place—because our mind was literally "absent"—somewhere else.

- Strengthen your memory for a person's name by saying the name soon after you first hear it. For instance, if your friend Gertrude has just introduced you to Geraldine, you might say: "Geraldine, how long have you known Gertrude?" When you state a person's name shortly after first hearing it, you prevent memory loss at the time when forgetting is most likely to take place— during the first minutes after the brain takes in new information. There's also another benefit of saying the person's name right after you've heard it: It makes the person feel acknowledged and welcomed.

- Associate the person's name with some other piece of information you've learned or know about the person. For instance, you can associate the person's name with (a) some physical characteristic of the person (e.g., "tall Paul"), (b) the place where you met, or (c) your first topic of conversation. By making a mental connection between the person's name and something else you know about the person, you capitalize on the brain's natural tendency to store (retain) information as part of an interconnected network.

- Keep a name journal that includes the names of people you meet along with some information about them (e.g., where you met, what you talked about, or what their interests are). We write down and make lists of things we want to remember to do or to buy, so why not write down the names of people whose names we want to remember?

> "When I joined the bank, I started keeping a record of the people I met and put them on little cards, and I would indicate on the cards when I met them, and under what circumstances, and sometimes [make] a little notation which would help me remember a conversation."
>
> —David Rockefeller, prominent American banker, philanthropist, and former CEO of the Chase Manhattan Bank

Remembering names is not only a good way to make friends and improve your social life, it's also a professional skill for being successful in any career you choose to pursue.

Refer to people by name when you see them and interact with them. Once you've learned someone's name, be sure to refer that person by name during your interactions. If you happen to see Waldo, saying "Hi, Waldo" will mean a lot more to him than simply saying "Hi" or "Hi there"—which sounds like you've just encountered an unidentifiable object "out there" in public space, or addressing a personal letter as, "to whom it may concern." Continuing to refer to people by name after you've first learned their names strengthens your memory for their names and shows them that you remember who they are (and that they're important to you).

Remember information that people share with you and mention it when you interact with them. Listen closely to what others share with you during conversations, especially to things that seem important to them and they really care about (for one person that may be politics, for another it may be sports, and for another it may be relationships). Remember what seems to matter to the person and bring it up in your future conversations.

Move beyond the routine of asking just the standard, generic questions (e.g., "What's up? What's going on?"). Instead, ask about something you talked about last time (e.g., "How did you make out on that math test last week?"). We tend to remember what's important to us. By remembering what others share with us, we show them that they're important to us.

There's another advantage of showing interest in others and remembering their interests: You're likely to begin hearing them say what a great listener and conversationalist you are. In addition, you're likely to find them becoming more interested in you and listening to what you have to say.

Four keys to relationship building are: (1) referring to people by name; (2) showing interest in people by asking them questions about their interests; (3) remembering what they share with you; and (4) show them you remember what they share with you by bringing it up during your next conversation.

Dating and Romantic Relationships

Romantic relationships traditionally begin through the process of dating. However, college students today take different approaches to dating, ranging from not dating at all to dating with the intent of exploring or cementing long-term relationships. These different approaches to dating and forming romantic relationships are summarized in **Box 9.2**.

Box 9.2

Different Approaches to Dating and Romance among College Students

Postponing Dating. Students who take this approach feel that the demands of college work and college life are too time-consuming to take on the additional social and emotional burden of dating while in college.

It's hard enough to have fun here with all the work you have to do. There's no reason to have the extra drama [of dating] in your life."
—College sophomore

Hooking Up. Students who prefer this approach believe that formal dating is unnecessary; they feel that their social and sexual needs are better met more causally though associations with friends and acquaintances. Instead of going out on a one-on-one date, they prefer to first meet and connect with romantic partners in larger group settings, such as college parties.

Casual Dating. Students using this approach like to date primarily for the purpose of enjoying themselves, rather than getting "tied down" to any one person. These are "casual daters" who prefer to go out on a short series of

Now all a guy has to do to hookup on a Saturday night is to sit on the couch long enough at a party. Eventually a girl will plop herself down beside him . . . he'll make a joke, she'll laugh, their eyes will meet, sparks will fly, and the mission is accomplished. And you want me to tell this guy to call a girl, spend $100 on dinner and hope for a goodnight kiss?"
—College student

dates with one person, then stop and start dating someone else; or, they may date different individuals at the same time. Their primary goal is to meet new people and discover what characteristics they find attractive in others.

Exclusive Dating. Students adopting this approach prefer to date one person for an extended period. Although marriage is not the goal, an exclusive dater takes casual dating one step further: they date for the purpose of getting a better idea about what characteristics they're seeking in a long-term mate or spouse.

Courtship. Students using this approach to dating use it with the intent of finding and continuing a relationship until it culminates in marriage or a long-term commitment.

Reflection 9.4

How would you define *love*? Would you say it's a feeling? An action? Both?

What would you say are the best signs or indicators that two people are "in love"?

What would you say are the most common reasons why people "fall out of love"?

Forms and Stages of Love

Research on romantic relationships reveals that *love* typically is experienced in the following forms and progresses through the following stages.

Stage 1. Passionate Love (Infatuation)

This is the very first stage of romantic love and tends to be characterized by:

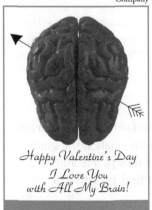

©MarkusManson/Shutterstock.com, compilation ©Kendall Hunt Publishing Company

Happy Valentine's Day I Love You with All My Brain!

Despite expressions like "I love you with all my heart," romantic love takes place in the brain and is accompanied by major changes in the production of brain chemicals.

- **Erotic love**—the relationship involves intense physical arousal and passion; attention is focused primarily on the partner's physical appearance, and physical attraction between the partners is at a peak.
- **Impulsivity**—the partners quickly "fall into" love and are "swept off their feet" (e.g., "love at first sight").
- **Obsession**—the partners can't stop thinking about one another (they're "madly in love").
- **Intense emotions**—a rush of chemicals surges through the body and brain (like a drug-induced state), such as: (a) adrenalin—a bodily hormone that triggers faster heart rate and breathing, and (b) dopamine—a brain chemical that triggers feelings of excitement, euphoria, joy, and general well-being.
- **Idealism**—the partners perceive each other and their relationship as being "perfect." They may say things like: "We're made for each other", "Nobody else has a relationship like ours", and "We'll be together forever." Such idealistic thinking can lead to love being "blind"—a form of denial in which the partners don't "see" (push out of conscious awareness) each other's personal shortcomings or the shortcomings in their relationship (although these shortcomings may be obvious to outside observers).
- **Attachment and Dependency:** The lovers feel insecure without each other and can't bear being separated (e.g., "I can't live without him"). As a result of such attachment and dependency, love at this stage follows the principle: "I love you because I am loved" and "I love you because I need you." It's hard to determine if the person is in love with the other person or is in love with the idea or feeling of being in love.
- **Possessiveness and Jealousy:** The partners feel they have exclusive rights to one another and may quickly become suspicious about the partner's fidelity or be jealous of anyone else who interacts with the partner in a friendly or affectionate manner. These feelings are often unjustified and irrational ("insane jealousy")—for example, the lover suspects the partner is "cheating" when there's no real evidence that cheating is taking place.
- **Love Sickness:** If the partners break up, "love withdrawal" tends to follow the breakup, that is similar to withdrawal from a pleasure-producing drug. Studies show that the most common cause of despair or depression among college students is a romantic breakup.

Stage 2. Mature Love

The partners gradually "fall out" of first-stage (puppy) love and progress or "fall into" a more mature or advanced stage of love that is characterized by the following developments:

- The partners become less selfish and self-centered and more selfless and other-centered. Love is no longer just a noun—an emotion or feeling within the person (e.g., "I'm in love"), but becomes an action verb—a way in which the partners act toward each other and treat one another (e.g., "we love each other"). More emphasis is placed on caring for the partner, rather than being cared for. This more mature stage of love follows two principles:
  1) "I am loved because I love"—rather than "I'm in love because I am loved"
  2) "I need you because I love you"—rather than "I love you because I need you"
- Less of an emotional high is experienced at this stage than at early stages of the relationship. After the passage of time and more experience with the partner, the original "mad rush" of hormones and euphoria-producing brain chemicals gradually levels off—similar to how the effects of a drug level off after being used for an extended period. The intense emotional "ups and downs" of early stage love are now replaced by feelings of emotional serenity (mellowness) and evenness—a less extreme, but more consistently pleasant emotional state characterized by slightly elevated levels of different brain chemicals (endorphins, rather than dopamine). Unlike infatuation or early-stage love, this pleasant emotional state does not decline with time; in fact, it may increase as the relationship continues and matures.
- Physical passion decreases. The "flames of the flesh" don't burn as intensely as in first-stage love, but a romantic afterglow continues. This afterglow is characterized by more emotional intimacy or psychological closeness between the partners and greater self-disclosure, mutual trust, and interpersonal honesty—all of which enhance both the physical and psychological quality of the relationship.
- Interest is now focused on the partner as a whole person, not just on the partner's physical qualities. The partners have a less idealistic, more realistic view of one another, recognizing and accepting both their strengths and weaknesses. They genuinely like each as persons (not just as lovers) and consider their partner to be their "best" or "closest" friend.
- The partners have mutual trust and confidence in each other's commitment; they aren't plagued by feelings of suspicion, distrust, or petty jealousy. Each partner may have interests and close friends outside the relationship without the other becoming jealous.
- The partners have mutual concern for each other's growth and fulfillment. Rather than being envious or competitive, they take joy in the partner's personal successes and accomplishments.
- The relationship contains a balanced blend of independence and interdependence, sometimes referred to as the "paradox (contradiction) of love"—both partners maintain their independence and individuality, and both have their own sense of personal identity and self-worth, but when together, their respective identities become more complete.

"I learned love and I learned you. I learned that, in order to love someone, you must be blind to the physical and the past. You must see their emotional and mental strengths and weaknesses, passions and dislikes, hobbies and pastimes.

—Letter written by a first-year student

"Two become one, yet remain one.

—Erich Fromm, in The Art of Loving

**Reflection 9.5**

Rate your degree of agreement or disagreement with the following statements:

1. "All you need is love."

   Strongly agree   Agree   Not sure   Disagree   Strongly disagree

   Reason for rating:

2. "Love is just a four-letter word."

   Strongly agree   Agree   Not sure   Disagree   Strongly disagree

   Reason for rating:

3. "Love stinks."

   Strongly agree   Agree   Not sure   Disagree   Strongly disagree

   Reason for rating:

Managing Interpersonal Conflict

Disagreement between people is an inevitable aspect of social life. Research shows that even the most happily married couples do not experience continuous marital bliss; they have occasional disagreements and periodic discord. Because interpersonal conflict cannot be completely escaped or eliminated, the best we can do is defuse it, contain it, and prevent it from reaching unmanageable levels. The interpersonal communication and human relations skills already discussed in this chapter can help minimize the severity of disagreements and conflicts. In addition to these general social skills, the following set of specific strategies may be used to handle interpersonal conflicts constructively and compassionately.

Express your point *assertively*—not passively, aggressively, or passive–aggressively. When you're *passive*, you don't stand up for your personal rights; you allow others to take advantage of you by letting them push you around. You say nothing when you should say something. You say "yes" when you want to say "no." You tend to become angry, bitter, or resentful because you keep it all inside.

In contrast, when you're *aggressive*, you stand up for your rights, but at the same time you violate the rights of others with whom you have a conflict by threatening, dominating, humiliating, or bullying them. You use intense, emotionally loaded words to attack the person (e.g., "You spoiled brat" or "You're a self-centered jerk"). You may manage to get what you want but at the other person's expense and at the risk of destroying a relationship or losing a friend. Later, you tend to feel guilty about overreacting or coming on too strong (e.g., "I knew I shouldn't have said that").

When dealing with interpersonal conflict, the goal is reconciliation, not retaliation.

When you're *passive–aggressive*, you're approach to handling conflict is getting back at, or getting even with, the other person by: (a) withholding or taking away something (e.g., not speaking to the person; withdrawing attention and affection), or (b) indirectly hinting that you're angry (e.g., making cynical comments or using sarcastic humor).

When you're *assertive*, you're not aggressive, passive, or passive–aggressive. You handle conflict in a way that protects or restores your rights without violating or stomping on the rights of others. You handle conflict in a direct but even-tempered manner. Rather than yelling, screaming or "getting in the face" of the other person, you speak in a normal volume or tone and you communicate at a normal distance.

Strategies for Resolving Conflicts Assertively

Focus on the *behavior* causing the conflict, not the person. Avoid labeling others as "selfish," "mean," "inconsiderate," etc. If you're upset because your roommate doesn't do his share of cleaning, stay away from aggressive labels such as "slob" or "slacker." Such negative personal labels turn the other person into a verbal punching bag, which is likely to put that person on the defensive and ready to launch a retaliatory counterattack on your personal flaws. Before you know it, you're likely to find yourself in a war of words and mutual character assassinations that end up making the conflict worse.

> "Don't find fault. Find a remedy.
>
> —*Henry Ford, founder of Ford Motor Company and one of the most widely admired people of the 20th century*

Rather than focusing on the person's general character, focus on the specific action or behavior that's causing the problem (e.g., failing to do the dishes or leaving dirty laundry around the room). This lets others know exactly what behavior needs to be changed to resolve the conflict without embarrassing or humiliating them. It's much easier to change a specific behavior than it is to change a general character trait.

Use "I" messages that refer to how the other person's behavior is affecting you. "I" messages don't target the other person; they place the focus on *you*—what you are perceiving and feeling. This sends a message that's less accusatory and threatening. Suppose you receive a course grade that's lower than what you think you earned. You think a mistake was made, so you decide to approach your instructor about it. The conversation shouldn't begin by your saying to the instructor: "*You* made a mistake" or "*You* gave me the wrong grade." These messages are likely to put the professor immediately on the defensive and ready to defend the grade you received. A less threatening way to open the conversation, and one that the instructor is more likely to listen to and consider carefully, would begin with an "I" statement—such as: "I think an error may have been made in my test grade."

"I" messages are less aggressive because they're not aimed at the other person; instead, they focus on the issue and how it's affecting you. For instance, by saying, "I feel angry when . . ." rather than "You make me angry when . . . ," you're honestly conveying how you feel instead of aggressively guilt-tripping the person for making you feel that way.

To maximize the positive impact of "I" messages:

- Be *specific* about what *emotion* you're experiencing. For instance, saying "I feel neglected when you don't write or call" identifies what you're feeling more specifically than saying, "I wish you'd be more considerate." Describing what you feel in specific terms increases the persuasive power of your message and reduces the risk that the other person will misunderstand or discount it.
- Communicate what you want the other person to do in the form of a firm *request* rather than a demand or ultimatum. Saying, "I would like you to . . ." is less likely to put the person on the defensive than saying, "I expect you to . . ." or "I insist that you . . ."

- Be *specific* about what you want the person to *do* to resolve the conflict. Saying, "I would like for you to call me at least once a day" is more specific than saying, "I want you to keep in touch with me."

 Reflection 9.6

You're working on a group project and your teammates aren't carrying their weight. You're getting frustrated and angry because you're doing almost all the work yourself.

Construct an *"I" message* that communicates your concern to your teammates in an assertive, nonthreatening way.

Avoid absolute judgments and overgeneralizations. Compare the following pairs of statements:

   (a) "You're no help at all" versus "You don't help me enough."
   (b) "You never try to understand how I feel" versus "You don't try hard enough to understand how I feel."
   (c) "I always have to clean up" versus "I'm doing more than my fair share of the cleaning."

The first statement in each of the preceding pairs represents an absolute statement that covers all times, situations, and circumstances. Such extreme, blanket criticisms send the message that the person is doing nothing right with respect to the issue or conflict in question. In contrast, the second statement in each of the above pairs phrases the criticism in terms of degree or amount—the person is doing something right at least some of the time, but needs to do more of it right more of the time—which is likely to be less threatening or humiliating (and probably closer to the truth).

Approach the conflict with the attitude that you're going to solve the problem, not win the argument. The goal of resolving a conflict is not to get even or prove you're right. Winning the argument or proving your point, but not persuading the person to change the behavior that's causing the conflict, is like winning a battle and losing the war. Instead, approach conflict resolution with the mindset that both parties can win and will end up with a better relationship in the long run.

Pick a private place and time to resolve the conflict. Avoid airing your grievance with the person while others are present. As the old expression goes, "Don't air your dirty laundry in public." Criticizing someone in the presence of others is akin to a public stoning, and likely to humiliate the person, cause resentment, and result in retaliation not cooperation.

> *Things are better left unsaid until you find the right time and place to say them.*

Decompress emotionally before expressing your concern verbally. A conflict shouldn't be addressed during a fit of anger. Making your point while you're enraged may give you an immediate sense of satisfaction or relief but is less likely to change the other person's attitude or behavior than a calm and reasoned request. Instead of unloading on the person, take the load off yourself—take time to cool down, formulate your arguments, and express them rationally. Responding in a mellow, reflective manner also communicates to the other person that you've given serious consideration to the matter and are not firing away like a "loose cannon."

If things begin to get nasty, call for a time-out or cease-fire and postpone the discussion until both of you cool off. When emotions and adrenaline run high, logic and reason run low, and the anger of both combatants is likely to escalate until it turns into a blow-by-blow volley of verbal punches and counterpunches that may go something like this:

> Person A: "You're way out of control."
> Person B: "I'm not out of control; you're the one who's overreacting."
> Person A: "*I'm* overreacting? You're the one who's acting like a jerk!"
> Person B: "I may be *acting* like a jerk, but you're the *real* jerk!"

Blow-by-blow exchanges such as these are likely to turn up the emotional heat to such a high level that resolving the conflict takes a back seat to winning the fight. Both boxers need to back off, retreat to their respective corners, and try again later when neither is looking to throw a knockout punch.

Give the person a chance to respond. Just because you have a justifiable complaint doesn't mean the other person must forfeit all rights to free speech and self-defense. Avoid jumping the gun and pulling the trigger before hearing the other side of the story and getting all the facts straight. By giving the other person a fair chance to be heard, you increase the likelihood that you'll receive a cooperative response.

After listening to the other person's position, check your understanding by summarizing it in your own words (e.g., "What I hear you saying is . . ."). This is an important step in resolving conflicts because disagreements often stem from a misunderstanding or breakdown in communication. Respectfully hearing the other person's side of the story, and assuring the person that it's been heard, can go a long way toward resolving the conflict.

Acknowledge the person's perspectives and feelings. Once you've heard the person's response, even if you disagree with it, don't dismiss or discount the person's feelings. Avoid saying things like, "That's ridiculous!" or "That's no excuse!" Instead, acknowledge the person's response—for example, by saying: "I can understand what you were thinking" or "I see how you might feel that way." After making this acknowledgement, you can then explain why your complaint or concern is still justified.

End your discussion of the conflict on a warm, constructive note. Finish it by ensuring there are no hard feelings and let the person know that you're optimistic the conflict can be resolved and your relationship strengthened.

If the person makes the change you requested, express your appreciation. Even if your complaint was legitimate and your request justified, the person's effort to accommodate your concern shouldn't be taken for granted. (The worst thing to do is to "rub it in" by saying something like: "That's more like it" or "It's about time!")

Expressing appreciation to the other person for making a change is not only the socially sensitive thing to do, it's also the smart thing to do, because recognizing

"Seek first to understand, then to be understood.
—Stephen Covey, international best-selling author of *Seven Habits of Highly Effective People*

"To keep your marriage brimming with love . . . when you're wrong, admit it; when you're right, shut up.
—*Ogden Nash, American poet*

and reinforcing the person's changed behavior increases the likelihood that the positive change will continue and you will continue to benefit from it.

(Review the Working with Others portion of your AchieveWORKS Personality assessment report to learn more about your strengths and blind spots when it comes to your approach to collaboration.)

Civility

> "The right to do something does not mean that doing it is right."
>
> —William Safire, American author, journalist, and presidential speech writer

At its most basic level, social intelligence involves *civility*—which could be defined as "responsible freedom"—the freedom of people to exercise one's individual rights, but without interfering with the rights of others. Individual freedom shouldn't be confused with egocentrism. The former includes social responsibility and a commitment to the common good; the latter involves thinking only of oneself without concern for the needs or rights of others. Civility respects the rights of others, including their right to hold and express viewpoints that differ from our own—without denying them the opportunity to do so and without derisively dismissing them as being "dumb," "ignorant," or "evil."

> "For some students, college represents their first opportunity to experience what it is like to live in a real community where we assume responsibility for each other."
>
> —David Boren, President of the University of Oklahoma

It's noteworthy that the term "university" derives from the Latin, meaning "the whole," and the term "college" derives from the Latin, meaning "community." Thus, colleges and universities should be places where civility and the principles of community are strongly valued and vigorously practiced, such as those listed in **Box 9.3**.

Box 9.3

Six Principles of Campus Community

A college or university should be:

1. An Educationally Purposeful Community: The campus should be a place where faculty and students share academic goals and work together to strengthen the educational process.

2. An Open Community: The campus should be a place where civility is affirmed—where freedom of expression and differences of opinion are accepted, protected, and promoted.

3. A Just Community: The campus should be a place where the sacredness of each person is honored and where diversity is valued.

4. A Disciplined Community: The campus should be a place where individuals accept their obligations to the group and where well-defined governance procedures guide behavior toward the common good.

5. A Caring Community: The campus should be a place where the well-being of each member is sensitively supported and where service to others is encouraged. (Caring is the glue that makes the first four principles work; it's the key to establishing the campus as a place where personal feelings and freedoms are affirmed.)

6. A Celebrative Community: The campus should be a place where the heritage of the institution is remembered and where rituals affirming its traditions are widely shared.

Civility also involves taking action (not looking way) when the rights or dignity of other community members are being violated. It's been said that in a democratic country, if the rights of any group of citizens are threatened by prejudice and discrimination, the political stability and viability of democracy itself is threatened. The same could be said for a campus community. Students who take an active role in challenging prejudice and discrimination on campus demonstrate both civility and character.

> *Civility and democracy go hand-in-hand; when the former is practiced, the latter is protected.*

"Injustice anywhere is a threat to justice everywhere.

—*Martin Luther King, Jr., civil rights leader and winner of the Nobel Peace Prize*

Emotional Intelligence

Doing college well is a challenging task that will test your emotional strength and your ability to persevere over an extended period of time (to graduation). Research indicates that college students who score higher on tests of emotional intelligence, such as the ability to identify and regulate their emotions and moods, are better able to focus their attention, get absorbed (stay "in the zone") while performing challenging tasks, and persist until they complete those tasks instead of quitting because of frustration or boredom. Research also indicates that experiencing positive emotions, such as optimism and excitement, contributes to academic success. In one study of nearly 4,000 first-year college students, it was found that their level of optimism or hope for success during their first term on campus was a more accurate predictor of their first-year grades than was their SAT score or high school grade point average.

In addition to enhancing academic performance, emotional intelligence strengthens our social interactions by enabling us to relate to others with greater empathy and emotional sensitivity. By engaging in the following practices, we demonstrate emotional intelligence, and in so doing, we enrich the quality of our interpersonal relationships.

"I've learned that people will forget what you said, people will forget what you did, but people will never forget how you made them feel.

—*Maya Angelou, award-winning author and civil rights activist*

Express genuine interest in and concern for others' feelings. Instead of asking the routine questions like, "How are you?" or "How's it goin'?" ask the question, "How are you feeling?" Showing genuine concern for others' feelings increases the likelihood that they will share their feelings with you, and when you validate the feelings they share with you, they feel better about themselves.

Share information about yourself. How often have you witnessed this rapid, ritualistic interchange between two people?

Person A: "Hi, how's it goin'?"
Person B: "Fine, how ya' doin'?"
Person A: "Good. Thanks."

In this exchange, no substantive information is shared by either person and chances are that both persons neither expect nor want to hear about how the other person is truly feeling. These superficial social rituals are understandable and acceptable when people first interact with each other. However, if relationships are to move to a closer, more meaningful level, must move beyond social rituals to mutual sharing of personal experiences.

Building close, authentic relationships is a give-and-take process in which two people progressively share more personal information with one another—an interpersonal process that human relations specialists call the *intimacy spiral*. You can start this reciprocal sharing process by noticing the types of personal information others share with you and then you responding, in turn, by sharing something similar about yourself that's a little more personal or intimate. By relating a similar experience of your own, you demonstrate *empathy*—the ability to identify with and relate to the feelings of others.

Naturally, this mutual sharing should be progress in small doses; you don't want to suddenly blow others away with hot blasts of intimacy and overwhelm them with private details about your personal life. Instead, the sharing process should proceed gradually and sensitively. As you continue to have more contact and conversations with someone who you see as a potential friend, continue to engage in further self-disclosure by disclosing a little more of yourself. If that person asks you, "How's it going?" or "How are you?" take these questions seriously and respond by sharing something meaningful about yourself. Your sharing could include sharing your aspirations, fears, success stories, and challenges. By sharing yourself with others, it shows you trust them, and in turn, they're more likely to trust you.

> "Kind words can be short and easy to speak, but their echoes are truly endless."
>
> —*Mother Teresa of Calcutta, Albanian Catholic nun and winner of the Nobel Peace Prize*

Look for opportunities to provide others with genuine compliments. Keep your eye out for positive behaviors displayed by others and praise them when you see them. Small, simple compliments can often have large, long-term impact on reinforcing positive behaviors in others and developing close relationships with others. Simply stated, people like to be around others who make them feel good about themselves and who provide them with feedback on what they're doing well.

Remember that compliments can be given for many things besides physical appearance (e.g., "you look nice" or "that's a cute outfit"). Compliments about others' actions and inner character are more powerful because they recognize not for how they look, but for *who* they are and *what* they do.

Strive to display positivity and enthusiasm. Not surprisingly, people prefer to be around people who are upbeat and enthusiastic. Studies show that when people interact with others who are in a good mood, it elevates their own mood. As the old adage goes, "Enthusiasm is contagious"—others can "catch" our good mood, and when they do, their own mood improves. In contrast, when we're pessimistic, angry, or "down", we bring others down with us, and we drive down our chances of connecting with them.

 Reflection 9.7

What do you think will be your biggest challenge to staying positive and optimistic while you're in college? What could you do, or what resources could you use, to help you handle this challenge?

Becoming a Leader

Leadership is a process of exerting positive *influence* or *change*. Effective leaders use social and emotional intelligence to promote positive change in: (a) individuals, (b) groups, (c) organizations, (d) communities, or (e) society.

Why Student Leadership Matters

Student leaders are likely to be seen by their peers as more approachable and less threatening than older professionals and authority figures. Because they're at a similar age and stage of development, students more readily relate to and identify with peer leaders.

In addition to having positive impact on their peers, students who become leaders experience positive change in their own social and emotional development, such as improving their interpersonal skills, self-confidence, self-esteem, sense of purpose, and personal identity. It's also been found that when students become involved in peer leadership and peer mentoring, they benefit by experiencing gains in concern for others, altruistic values, character development, and civic engagement.

Peer leaders also provide students with valuable social support at a critical stage of development—when they're in the midst of making the transition to college and an unfamiliar social environment in which they are likely to have considerably more individual freedom, more personal choices, and more decision-making responsibilities than at any other time in their lives. In fact, many peer mentors report that their motive for getting involved in peer mentoring programs was to give first-year students the support they had received from peer mentors when they were first-year students making the transition to college. When people find themselves in unfamiliar, challenging, and stressful situations, they often look to others for cues on how to act. Your peers are watching you. The behavior you model matters, and by modeling positive behavior, you have the potential to be a student leader.

> "I think they're really searching for someone to kind of follow, someone to see as an example, more than we think.
> —Peer leader

AUTHOR'S EXPERIENCE

I was the first in my family to go to college. I didn't know anyone who had done college or knew how to "do college." My parents told me that if I could find a group of peers who seemed to understand the lay of the land, I'd be able to use their knowledge to help myself. So, I spent my first semester looking out for students who made good grades and I joined organizations where motivated students were likely to be found. Making connections with these students also helped me make connections with supportive faculty and staff.

Because I took the initiative to identify successful peers and because of their leadership skills and willingness to share their knowledge with me, instead of feeling like I was a stranger in a strange land, I found myself being part of a positive, socially supportive community.

—*Aaron Thompson*

As a first-year student, you can be a peer leader even though you don't hold a formal leadership position. Leadership development scholars argue that leadership development should begin early in college so that students can practice and refine their leadership skills throughout the remaining years of their college experience. By developing your leadership skills while in college, you will be developing one of the most important skills that today's employers seek in college graduates. Even if you have never thought of yourself as a "leader," you can begin right now to develop and demonstrate leadership skills. Don't let your leadership potential be limited by common misconceptions about what makes a leader, such as the three myths listed below.

> "It's not the absence of leadership potential that inhibits the development of more leaders; it's the persistence of the myth that leadership can't be learned.
> —Kouzes & Posner, The Student Leadership Challenge

Myth #1. Effective leaders are "natural" ("born") leaders. Contrary to popular belief, leadership is not an inherited personality trait or a genetic gift. Leadership doesn't take place automatically and effortlessly; it's a *learned* skill acquired over time through practice and feedback.

Myth #2. Effective leaders are extroverted, bold, forceful, and aggressive. These traits may characterize some famous (or infamous) political and military leaders, but effective leaders are not typically dominant, controlling, or power-driven. Power simply means the ability to influence others. Successful leaders are powerful because they can influence (and motivate) others, not because they can dominate or overpower them. Often, leaders display their leadership skills in subtle, socially sensitive ways. Powerful leaders don't always roar; many of them are "quiet leaders" who influence and empower others with a soft voice, or without doing much talking at all. Instead, they lead primarily by example—by modeling positive behaviors and strategies for others to observe and emulate.

Myth #3. Leadership is exercised by people who hold official leadership positions and have formal leadership titles. Leadership can either be *assigned* or *emergent.* Assigned leaders are those who occupy leadership positions in an organization. People holding such positions have the potential to be leaders but do not actually exhibit leadership until they use their position to exert positive influence on others. Leadership isn't automatically bestowed or guaranteed by a position or title; it's *earned* by the leader's ability to have a positive impact and make productive change happen. People who do not occupy formal leadership positions can still be leaders by positively influencing other people and promoting productive change. Such people are referred to as "emergent leaders" because their positive influence develops over time and emerges from the social and emotional skills and attributes they possess, not from the official title or position they hold.

Positive Outcomes of Peer Leadership

Contrary to how peers are portrayed in the popular media, they can be much more than a source of negative "peer pressure" but a source of positive "peer power," serving as productive collaborators, teammates, and role models. Research repeatedly shows that peer leaders make significant contributions to the educational and personal development of other students.

In short, when all the research on the positive impact of peer leadership is viewed together, it points strongly to the conclusion that student leaders create a "win-win-win" scenario that benefits:

1. Their *peers*—who improve academically and personally from interacting with student leaders.
2. Their *campus*—where peer leaders help build a campus culture characterized by higher levels of student satisfaction and higher rates of college completion.
3. *Themselves*— by contributing to the development of other students, peer leaders simultaneously acquire knowledge and skills that contribute to their own college and career success.

Reflection 9.8

Which one of the above three benefits of peer leadership were you least aware of?

Areas of Student Leadership in College

On college campuses across the country, students are now serving as leaders in multiple roles and positions. You can become a peer leader in any of three key areas or arenas student leadership:

1. **Academic Leadership.** Students who lead study groups, provide peer tutoring, or serve as co-educators in college courses (e.g., first-year seminars). You can provide effective academic leadership in any of these roles without necessarily being intellectually gifted or brilliant, but simply by being as a learning resource for students who may be struggling academically and by modeling effective learning strategies, such as: exhibiting intellectual curiosity, engaging in active note-taking in class, and contributing insightful questions and informed comments during class discussions.
2. **Social and Emotional Leadership.** Students who lead and mentor other students in ways that are more personal than academic, such as: making minority students feel welcome, reaching out to shy or bashful students, being an empathic listener, and supporting students who are experiencing setbacks or crises.
3. **Organizational and Civic Leadership.** Students who lead larger groups of peers, such as leading student clubs, campus organizations, fraternities, sororities, and athletic teams, or organizing community-outreach efforts and political campaigns.

Box 9.4 lists some of the formal positions that student leaders now hold on college campuses. The wide variety of positions that appear on the list is testimony to the diversity and versatility of student leadership. The list is long, but not exhaustive; it's likely that students occupy additional leadership positions on college campuses that do not appear on this list. As you read the leadership positions and descriptions listed in the box below, place a checkmark next to those that seem to best "fit" your personal talents, interests, and values.

Box 9.4

Positions Occupied by Student Leaders at Colleges and Universities

1. Student Ambassadors—work with college admissions offices to represent the college, recruit new students, and facilitate campus visits from prospective students and their families.
2. Peer Orientation-Week Leaders—welcome new students to campus and facilitate their transition to college life.
3. Student Leaders of Campus Clubs & Organizations—provide leadership for student government and student groups who share common interests or goals.
4. Peer Resident Advisors (a.k.a. Community Assistants)—provide advice, support, and guidance to students living in campus residences.
5. Peer Mentors—serve as role models and success coaches for new students.

6. Peer Tutors—provide learning assistance to students on an individual or group basis.
7. Supplemental Instruction (SI) Leaders—provide learning assistance for students enrolled in difficult courses (e.g., courses with high rates of Ds, Fs, or Ws) and lead supplementary group-study sessions scheduled outside of class time.
8. Peer Leaders for Learning Communities—meet regularly to support students who enroll in two or more courses together (a learning community), helping these students connect with one another, their course instructors, and learning-support professionals.
9. Peer Co-Educators/Co-Facilitators for First-Year Seminars—work with instructors in first-year experience courses, serving as a liaison between instructor and students, providing a student

continued...

perspective on course topics, and facilitating student involvement in class and on campus.

10. Peer Academic Advisors—help students schedule classes and register for courses.

11. Peer Counselors—provide students with support on social or emotional issues and mental health.

12. Peer Wellness Counselors—assist students on matters relating to physical health and well-being.

13. Peer Ministers—support students' spiritual development and organize faith-based experiences.

14. Peer Community-Service Leaders—facilitate volunteerism and service to the community by organizing, publicizing, and encouraging student involvement in community-based experiences.

15. Team Captains—provide leadership for teammates participating in intercollegiate or intramural athletic programs.

 Reflection 9.9

Review the checkmarks you placed next to the leadership positions listed in Box 9.4.

Why did you think those positions best matched your personal talents, interests, and values?

Internet-Based Resources

For additional information on leadership relating to social and emotional intelligence, consult the following websites:

Social Intelligence
https://www.socialintelligenceinstitute.org/

Interpersonal Communication Skills
https://www.skillsyouneed.com/ips/what-is-communication.html

Emotional Intelligence
https://www.psychologytoday.com/us/basics/emotional-intelligence

Leadership
https://www.psychologytoday.com/us/basics/leadership

Chapter 9 Exercises

9.1 Quote Reflections

Review the sidebar quotes contained in this chapter and select two that you found to be especially meaningful or inspirational.

For each quote you selected, provide an explanation of why you chose it.

9.2 Strategy Reflection

Review the practices suggested for demonstrating *emotional intelligence* and *enhancing the quality of interpersonal relationships* described on pp. 201-202. Select two you think are most important and intend to put into practice.

9.3 Reality Bite

Caught Between a Rock and a Hard Place: Romantic versus Academic Commitments

Lauren has been dating her boyfriend (Nick) for about two months. She's deeply in love and is convinced that this is the real thing. Lately, Nick has been asking her to skip class to spend more time with him. He tells Lauren: "If you really love me, you would do it for our relationship." Lauren feels that Nick truly loves her and wouldn't do anything to intentionally hurt her or interfere with her goals. So she accommodates Nick's request and begins skipping some classes to spend more time with him. Lauren's grades soon start to slip; at the same time, Nick continues to demand more of her time.

Reflection and Discussion Questions

1. What concerns you most about Lauren's behavior?
2. What concerns you most about Nick's behavior?
3. Would you agree with Lauren's decision to start skipping classes?
4. If you were Lauren's friend, what advice would you give her?
5. If you were Nick's friend, what advice would you give him?
6. What might Lauren do to keep her grades up and still sustain her relationship with Nick?

9.4 Self-Assessment of Interpersonal Relationships

On a scale of 1-5 (1 = low, 5 = high), rate yourself on each of the following characteristics.

_____ I am good at initiating relationships.

_____ I am accessible.

_____ I am approachable.

_____ I am a good listener.

Provide a reason or explanation for each of your ratings that describes: (1) what you're doing well, (2) what you'd like to improve, and (3) what you could do to improve (or what resource you could use to help you improve).

9.5 Identifying Major Ways of Handling Interpersonal Conflict

1. Think of a social situation or interpersonal relationship that's currently creating some conflict or stress in your life. Describe how this conflict could be approached in each of the following ways:

    (a) Passively

    (b) Aggressively

    (c) Passive-aggressively

    (d) Assertively

    (See pp. 32-33 for descriptions of each of these four approaches.)

2. Practice the *assertive* approach by role-playing it with a friend or classmate and consider applying it to the actual relationship that's currently creating conflict or stress for you.

9.6 Leadership Information Interview

Interview someone holding a leadership position, particularly someone you consider to be an effective leader. Possible candidates for this interview include professionals working on or off campus, peer leaders, friends, or family members. During the interview, ask the leader some or all the following questions. (Feel free to add or substitute questions of your own.)

1. What interested you in, or led you to, your current leadership position?
2. What advice would you give to others about how they could best prepare for the leadership position you hold?
3. During a typical day or week, what types of leadership responsibilities or activities consume most of your time?
4. What personal qualities or prior experiences have contributed most to your effectiveness as a leader?
5. What skills, perspectives, or attributes do you see as being critical for success in your particular leadership role?
6. What do you like most about your leadership role?
7. What are the most difficult or frustrating aspects of your leadership position?
8. Are there particular moral issues or ethical challenges that you encounter in your leadership role?
9. Do your leadership responsibilities include interacting with people from diverse ethnic/racial groups and cultural backgrounds?
10. What impact do your leadership responsibilities have on other aspects of your life?
11. How do you continue learning and developing as a leader?
12. To help me gain additional insights into the nature of effective leadership, is there a leader you respect or admire who you would recommend I speak with?

Personal Reflections on the Interview:

a) What impressed you most about this leader?

b) What was the most useful leadership idea or strategy you acquired during the interview?

c) Did you learn anything during the interview that surprised or concerned you about the process of leadership?

d) As a result of conducting the interview, did your interest in or motivation for becoming a leader increase, decrease, or remain the same? Why?

CHAPTER 10

Diversity

LEARNING ABOUT AND FROM HUMAN DIFFERENCES

Today's college students will experience more diversity on their campuses than at any other time in American history. This chapter defines "diversity", identifies its major forms, and documents how experiencing diversity deepens learning, enhances critical and creative thinking, and contributes to career success. The chapter also includes specific strategies for breaking down barriers and biases that often block humans from experiencing the full benefits of diversity and supplies specific strategies for initiating and sustaining rewarding relationships with members of diverse groups.

Learning Goal

Gain greater appreciation of human differences and develop skills for making the most of diversity in college and beyond.

Ignite Your Thinking

 Reflection 10.1

When I hear the word "diversity," the first thought that comes to mind is . . .

What is Diversity?

Literally translated, the word "diversity" derives from the Latin *diversus*, meaning "various" or "variety." Thus, human diversity refers to the variety of differences among people that comprise humanity (the human species). The relationship between humanity and diversity may be likened to the relationship between sunlight and the variety of colors that comprise the visual spectrum. Similar to how sunlight passing through a prism disperses into different colors that comprise the visual spectrum, the human species residing on planet earth is dispersed into different groups that comprise the human spectrum (humanity). **Figure 10.1** illustrates this metaphorical relationship between diversity and humanity.

As depicted in **Figure 10.1**, human diversity manifests itself in a multiplicity of ways, including differences among people in their national origins, cultural backgrounds, physical characteristics, sexual orientations, and sexual identities. Some dimensions of diversity are easily detectable, some are very subtle, and others are invisible.

"We are all brothers and sisters. Each face in the rainbow of color that populates our world is precious and special. Each adds to the rich treasure of humanity.

—*Morris Dees, civil rights leader and co-founder of the Southern Poverty Law Center*

Reflection 10.2

Look at the diversity spectrum in Figure 10.1 and look over the list of groups that make up the spectrum. Do you notice any groups missing from the list that should be added, either because they have distinctive characteristics or because they've been targets of prejudice and discrimination?

FIGURE 10.1: Humanity and Diversity

SPECTRUM
of
DIVERSITY

HUMANITY →

Gender (male/female/transgender/gender transition)
Age (stage of life)
Race (e.g., White, Black, Asian)
Ethnicity (e.g., Native American, Hispanic, Irish, German)
Socioeconomic status (job status/income)
National *citizenship* (citizen of U.S. or another country)
Native (first-learned) *language*
National *origin* (nation of birth)
Geographical *region* (e.g., North or South; urban or rural)
Generation (historical period during which a group was born & raised)
Political ideology (e.g., liberal/conservative)
Religious/spiritual beliefs (e.g., Christian/Buddhist/Muslim)
Family status (e.g., single-parent/two-parent family)
Marital status (single/married)
Parental status (with/without children)
Sexual orientation (heterosexual/homosexual/bisexual)
Physical ability/disability (e.g., able to hear/deaf)
Mental ability/disability (e.g., mentally able/challenged)
Learning ability/disability (e.g., absence/presence of dyslexia)
Mental health/illness (e.g., absence/presence of depression)

– – – – – – = dimension of diversity

*This list represents some of the major dimensions of human diversity; it does not constitute a complete list of all possible forms of human diversity. Also, disagreement exists about certain dimensions of diversity (for example, whether certain groups should be classified as races or ethnic groups).

©Kendall Hunt Publishing Company

> "Ethnic and cultural diversity is an integral, natural, and normal component of educational experiences for all students."
>
> — *National Council for Social Studies*

Diversity is a topic that includes issues relating to equal rights and social justice for minority groups. However, it's not just a political or social justice issue that pertains only to certain groups of people; it's also an *educational* issue—an integral element of the college experience that enhances the learning, development, and career preparation of *all* students. Diversity brings different perspectives and approaches to *what* is learned (the content) and *how* it is learned (the process), which serves to enrich the quality of any learning experience.

Diversity is a human issue that embraces and benefits all people; it's not a code word for "some" people. Although one major goal of diversity is to promote appreciation and equitable treatment of particular groups of people who have experienced and continue to experience prejudice and discrimination, it's also a learning experience that enhances the quality of all students' college education, career preparation, and leadership potential. (For specific details about these benefits of diversity, see pp. 224-225.)

Diversity and Humanity

Diversity represents variations on the same theme: humanity. Thus, diversity and humanity are interdependent, complementary concepts. To understand human diversity is to understand both our differences and our *similarities*. Diversity appreciation includes valuing the unique experiences of different groups of humans as well as the common (universal) experiences shared by all humans. Members of different ethnic and racial groups may have distinctive cultural or physical characteristics, but members of all ethnic and racial groups live in communities, develop interpersonal relationships, have personal needs, and undergo life experiences that shape their individual identity. Humans of all races and cultures also share the same emotions and facially communicate those emotions in similar ways (see **Figure 10.2**).

FIGURE 10.2:

Humans all over the world display similar facial expressions when they experience and express certain emotions. See if you can detect the universal emotions being expressed by the following faces of people from different cultural backgrounds.

Answers: The emotions expressed by the top-three faces (left to right): anger, fear, and sadness.
Bottom-three faces (left to right): disgust, happiness, and surprise.

Anthropologists have also found that all groups of humans in every corner of the world share the following characteristics: storytelling, dance, music, decorating, adorning the body, socialization of children by elders, moral codes of conduct, supernatural beliefs, and mourning the dead. Although different cultural groups may express these experiences in distinctive ways, these are universal experiences shared by all cultural groups.

 Reflection 10.3

In addition to the universal characteristics already mentioned, can you think of any other human characteristic or experience shared by all human groups, no matter what their race or culture may be?

> "We are all the same, and we are all unique."
>
> —*Georgia Dunston, African-American biologist and research specialist in human genetics*

> "We have become not a melting pot but a beautiful mosaic."
>
> —*Jimmy Carter, 39th president of the United States and winner of the Nobel Peace Prize*

You may have heard the question: "We're all human, aren't we?" The answer to this question is "yes and no." Yes, all humans are the same, but not in the same way. A metaphor for making sense of this apparent contradiction is to visualize humanity as a quilt composed of multiple patches representing different cultural groups, which are woven together by a common thread: their shared humanity. (See picture on the right.) The quilt metaphor acknowledges the identity and beauty of all cultures. It differs from the old American "melting pot" metaphor, which viewed cultural differences as something to be melted down and obliterated. It also differs from the old "salad bowl" metaphor that depicted America as a hodgepodge or mishmash of cultures thrown together without any common connection. In contrast, the quilt metaphor suggests that the cultures of different human groups should be recognized, preserved, and valued. Even though these cultures are different, they come together to form a seamless, unified whole. This blending of diversity and unity is captured in the Latin expression *E pluribus unum* ("Out of many, one")—the motto of the United States—which appears on all its currency.

©steven r. hendricks/Shutterstock.com

AUTHOR'S EXPERIENCE

I was 12 years old, living in New York City, when I returned home after school one Friday. My mother asked me if anything interesting happened in class that day. I told her that the teacher went around the room asking students what they had for dinner the night before. At that moment, my mother stopped what she was doing and nervously asked me: "What did you tell the teacher?" I said: "I told her and the rest of the class that I had pasta last night because my family always eats pasta on Thursdays and Sundays." My mother became very agitated and fired the following question back at me in a very annoyed tone: "Why didn't you tell her we had steak or roast beef?" I was stunned and confused because I didn't understand what I'd done wrong or why I should have hidden the fact that we had eaten pasta. Then it dawned on me: My mom was embarrassed about being an Italian-American. She wanted me to conceal our family's ethnic background and make us sound more "American."

As I grew older, I understood why my mother felt the way she did. She was raised in America's "melting pot" generation—a time when different American ethnic groups were expected to melt down and melt away their ethnicity. They were not to celebrate diversity; they were to eliminate it.

—*Joe Cuseo*

When different human groups are appreciated for both their diversity and their commonality, their separate cultural streams merge into a single river, harnessing the collective power of humanity.

Diversity and Individuality

When we talk about diverse groups, it's important to keep in mind that individual differences among members within a particular racial or ethnic group are greater than the average difference between groups. Said in another way, there's more variability (individuality) within the same group than between groups. For instance, the differences that exist among individuals of the same race in terms of their physical characteristics (e.g., height and weight) and psychological characteristics (e.g., temperament and personality) are greater than the average difference between their racial group and other racial groups. Although it's valuable to learn about differences between different groups, the substantial differences among individuals within the same group should neither be overlooked nor underestimated. We shouldn't assume that individuals who share the same racial or ethnic characteristics share similar personal characteristics.

> "I realize that I'm black, but I like to be viewed as a person, and this is everybody's wish.
>
> —*Michael Jordan, Hall of Fame basketball player*

As you encounter diversity in college and beyond, keep the following key distinctions in mind:

- **Humanity.** All humans are members of the *same group*—the human species.
- **Diversity.** All humans are members of *different groups*—for example, different racial and ethnic groups.
- **Individuality.** Each human is a *unique individual* who differs from other members of the same group(s) to which he or she may belong.

> "Every human is, at the same time, like all other humans, like some humans, and like no other human.
>
> —*Clyde Kluckhohn, famous American anthropologist*

AUTHOR'S EXPERIENCE

I am a highly educated, straight, Latina, born and raised in NYC. I am an educator and an administrator. I am also a daughter, a mother, a sister, and a wife. And there are many, many other characteristics that I could add to this list. As I have grown older, I realize more and more that there isn't one characteristic that defines who I am. The diverse characteristics that comprise me make me the unique person that I am.

—*Michele Campagna*

Forms and Varieties of Diversity

Cultural Diversity

Culture is the distinctive pattern of beliefs and values learned by a group of people who share the same social heritage and traditions. In short, culture is the whole way in which a group of people has learned to live. It includes their style of speaking (language), fashion, food, art, and music, as well as their beliefs and values. **Box 10.1** summarizes the key components of culture that are typically shared by members of the same cultural group.

Box 10.1

Key Components of Culture

- Language: How members of the culture communicate through written or spoken words, including their dialect and their distinctive style of nonverbal communication (body language).
- Use of Physical Space: How cultural members arrange themselves with respect to social-spatial distance (e.g., how closely they stand next to each other when having a conversation).
- Use of Time: How the culture conceives of, divides up, and uses time (e.g., the speed or pace at which they conduct business).
- Aesthetics: How cultural members appreciate and express artistic beauty and creativity (e.g., their style of visual art, culinary art, music, theater, literature, and dance).
- Family: The culture's attitudes and habits with respect to family interactions (e.g., its customary styles of parenting children and caring for the elderly).
- Economics: How the culture meets its members' material needs, and the customary ways in which

wealth is acquired and distributed (e.g., its overall level of wealth and the wealth gap between its very wealthy and very poor members).

- Gender Roles: The culture's expectations for "appropriate" male and female behavior (e.g., how men and women are expected to dress and whether women can hold the same occupational positions as men).
- Politics: How decision-making power is exercised in the culture (e.g., democratically or autocratically).
- Science and Technology: The culture's attitude toward, and use of, science and technology (e.g., the degree to which the culture is technologically "advanced").
- Philosophy: The culture's ideas and views about wisdom, goodness, truth, and social values (e.g., whether its members place greater value on individual competition or collective collaboration).
- Spirituality and Religion: Cultural beliefs about the existence of a supreme being and an afterlife (e.g., its members' predominant faith and belief systems about the supernatural).

Reflection 10.4

Look back at the components of culture cited in **Box 10.1**. Add another component that you think may be an important characteristic of a culture and explain why you chose it.

Culture serves to bind its members into a supportive, tight-knit community. Unfortunately, however, culture can not only bind us, it can also blind us from seeing things from different cultural perspectives. Because culture shapes thought and perception, people from the same ethnic (cultural) group run the risk of becoming *ethnocentric*—centered so much on their own culture that they end up perceiving the world only through their own cultural lens and fail to consider or appreciate other cultural viewpoints.

Optical illusions are a good example of how strongly our cultural perspective can influence (and distort) our perceptions. Compare the lengths of the two lines in **Figure 10.3**.

FIGURE 10.3:
Optical Illusion

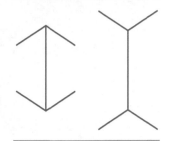

If you perceive the line on the right to be longer than the one on the left, it's because your perception has been shaped by your cultural background. People from Western cultures (e.g., Americans and Europeans) perceive the line on the right to be longer. However, both lines are actually equal in length. (If you don't believe it, take out a ruler and measure them.) Interestingly, this optical illusion is experienced only by people in Western cultures whose living spaces and architectural structures consist primarily of rectangular-shaped building and angled corners. The illusion is not experienced by people from non-Western cultures whose living spaces and architectural structures are predominantly circular—e.g., huts or igloos (see the photo below).

©Kendall Hunt Publishing Company

People whose cultural experiences involve living and working in circular structures are not deceived by the optical illusion depicted in Figure 10.3.

©James Michael Doresey/Shutterstock.com

The optical illusion depicted in Figure 10.3 is just one of several illusions experienced by people in some cultures but not others. These cross-cultural differences in susceptibility to optical illusions illustrate how strongly our cultural experiences can influence and sometimes misinform our perception of reality. People think they're seeing things objectively (as they are), but they're actually seeing things subjectively (from the perspective shaped by their particular cultural background).

If our cultural experiences can shape our perception of the physical world, they can certainly shape our perception of the social world. Research in social psychology reveals that the more exposure people have to something (or somebody), not only does it become more familiar, it also tends comes to be perceived more positively and judged more favorably. This phenomenon is so prevalent and powerful that social psychologists have come to call to it the "familiarity principle"—what is familiar is perceived as better or more likeable. One consequence of the familiarity principle is that our familiar cultural experiences can bias us toward viewing our culture as being better or more "normal" and acceptable than others. By remaining open to the viewpoints of people from other cultures who perceive the world from vantage points different than our own, we uncover our cultural blind spots, expand our range of perception, and put ourselves in a position to view the world with greater objectivity and cultural sensitivity.

AUTHOR'S EXPERIENCE

I was once watching a basketball game between the Los Angeles Lakers and Los Angeles Clippers. During the game, a short scuffle broke out between two members of the opposing teams: the Lakers' Pau Gasol—who is from Spain, and the Clippers' Chris Paul—who is African American. After the scuffle ended, Gasol tried to show Paul there were no hard feelings by patting him on the head. Instead of interpreting Gasol's head pat as a peace-making gesture, Paul took it as a putdown and returned the favor by slapping (rather than patting) Gasol in the head.

This head patting–head slapping misunderstanding stemmed from a basic difference in nonverbal communication between two players from different cultures. Patting someone on the head in European cultures is a friendly gesture; European soccer players often do it to an opposing player to express no ill will after a foul or collision. However, this same nonverbal message meant something very different to Chris Paul—an African American raised in urban America.

—Joe Cuseo

Ethnic Diversity

An *ethnic group* refers to a group of people who share the same culture. Thus, a "culture" is *what* an ethnic group has in common (e.g., common language and traditions) and "ethnic group" refers to the *people* who share the same cultural characteristics—which have been acquired (learned) through shared social experiences. Members of different ethnic groups may still be members of the same racial group—a group of people whose shared physical characteristics that have been *inherited*. For instance, white Americans constitute the same racial group, but are members of different ethnic groups (e.g., French, German, Irish). Similarly, Asian Americans constitute the same racial group, but are members of different ethnic groups (e.g., Japanese, Chinese, Korean).

European Americans are still the majority ethnic group in the United States; they account for more than 50 percent of the American population. Native Americans, African Americans, Hispanic Americans, and Asian Americans are *minority* ethnic groups because each of these groups represents less than 50 percent of the American population.

 Reflection 10.5

Are you a member of, or do you identify with, any ethnic group(s)? If yes, what would you say are the key cultural characteristics or values shared by your ethnic group(s)?

Racial Diversity

A *racial group (race)* is a group of people who share distinctive physical traits—most notably, skin color. The variation in skin color we now see among humans is largely due to biological adaptations that have evolved over thousands of years, beginning when humans first began to migrate to different climatic regions of the world. Currently, the most widely accepted explanation for racial differences in skin color is the "Out of Africa" theory. Genetic studies and fossil evidence indicate that all *Homo sapiens* inhabited

Africa 150,000-250,000 years ago; over the course of time, some of them migrated from Africa to other parts of the world. Those who lived and reproduced in hotter regions of the world nearer the equator (e.g., Africa and South America) developed darker skin color, which helped them adapt and survive by providing them with better protection from the potentially damaging effects of intense sunlight. In contrast, lighter skin tones emerged over time among humans inhabiting colder climates farther from the equator (e.g., Central and Northern Europe). Their lighter skin color contributed to their survival by enabling them to absorb greater amounts of vitamin D from the less direct and intense sunlight available to them in their region of the world.

Currently, the US Census Bureau categorizes humans into five racial categories:

- **White:** people whose lineage may be traced to the original humans inhabiting Europe, the Middle East, or North Africa.
- **Black or African American:** people whose lineage may be traced to the original humans inhabiting Africa.
- **American Indian or Alaska Native:** people whose lineage may be traced to the original humans inhabiting North and South America (including Central America), and who continue to maintain their tribal affiliation or attachment.
- **Asian:** people whose lineage may be traced to the original humans inhabiting the Far East, Southeast Asia, or the Indian subcontinent, including Cambodia, China, India, Japan, Korea, Malaysia, Pakistan, the Philippine Islands, Thailand, and Vietnam.
- **Native Hawaiian or Other Pacific Islander:** people whose lineage may be traced to the original humans inhabiting Hawaii, Guam, Samoa, and other Pacific Islands.

It's important to keep in mind that racial categories merely represent classifications that human societies have decided to construct—in other words, race is a socially constructed concept. No identifiable set of genes distinguishes one race from another; in fact, there continues to be disagreement among scholars about what groups of people constitute a human race or whether distinctive races actually exist. No blood test or any other type of biological test on a person will immediately and accurately indicate the person's race. Humans have simply created social categories called "races" based on certain external differences in peoples' outer physical appearance. Although skin color was used as the primary basis for creating these categories, "racial" groups could have just as easily been categorized on the basis of eye color (blue, brown, and green), hair color (brown, black, blonde, or red), or body size (tall, short, or mid-sized).

AUTHOR'S EXPERIENCE

My father stood approximately six feet tall and had straight, light brown hair. His skin color was that of a Western European with a very slight suntan. My mother was from Alabama; she was dark in skin color with high cheekbones and had long curly black hair. In fact, if you didn't know that my father was of African American descent, you would not have thought he was black.

All my life, I've thought of myself as African American and all people who know me think of me as being African American. I've lived more than half of a century with that as my racial identity. Several years ago, I carefully reviewed records of births and deaths in my family history and discovered that I had less than 50% African lineage. Biologically, I can no longer call myself Black; socially and emotionally, I still am. Clearly, my "race" has been socially constructed, not biologically determined.

—*Aaron Thompson*

Although the color of humans' external layer of skin may be dissimilar, all members of the human species are remarkably similar at an internal biological level. More than 98% of the genes found in humans are exactly the same, regardless of what their particular racial category may be. This large amount of genetic overlap among us accounts for the fact that we humans are clearly distinguishable from members of all other animal species. The tremendous amount of genetic overlap among humans also explains why the internal body parts of all humans look the same and no matter what the color of our outer layer of skin, when it's cut, we all bleed in the same color.

Differences between human races in their external appearance are superficial and easily detectable; commonalities across races in their internal biological make-up are less obvious and more meaningful.

AUTHOR'S EXPERIENCE

I was sitting in a coffee shop in the Chicago O'Hare airport while proofreading my first draft of this chapter. I looked up from my work for a moment and saw what appeared to be a white girl about 18 years of age. As I lowered my head to return to work, I did a double-take and looked at her again because something about her seemed different or unusual. When I looked more closely at her the second time, I noticed that although she had white skin, the features of her face and hair appeared to be those of an African American. After a couple of seconds of puzzlement, I figured it out: she was an *albino* African American. That satisfied my curiosity for the moment, but then I began to wonder: Would it still be accurate to say she was "black" even though her skin was not black? Would her hair and facial features be sufficient for her to be considered or classified as black? If yes, then what would be the "race" of someone who had black skin tone, but did not have the typical hair and facial features characteristic of black people? Is skin color the defining feature of being African American or are other features equally important?

I was unable to answer these questions, but found it amusing that all of these thoughts were crossing my mind while I was working on a chapter dealing with diversity. On the plane ride home, I thought again about that albino African American girl and realized that she was a perfect example of how classifying people into "races" isn't based on objective, scientific evidence, but on subjective, socially constructed categories.

—*Joe Cuseo*

Attempting to categorize people into distinct racial groups is more difficult today than at any other time in history because humans of different racial groups are increasingly forming interracial families. By 2050, the number of Americans who identify themselves as being of two or more races is projected to more than triple, growing to 26.7 million.

 Reflection 10.6

What race(s) do you consider yourself to be? Would you say you identify strongly with your racial identity, or do you rarely think about it? How do you think other students would answer these questions?

The Growing Ethnic and Racial Diversity in America

Racial and ethnic minorities now account for almost 37% of the total American population—an all-time high. In 2011, for the first time in history, more than half (50.4%) of all children born in the United States were members of racial and ethnic minority groups. By the middle of the 21st century, minority groups are projected to comprise 57% of the American population and more than 60% of our nation's children.

The growing diversity in America's overall population is matched by growing diversity in its colleges and universities. In 1960, whites made up almost 95% of the total college population; in 2010, that percentage had decreased to 61.5%. Between 1976 and 2010, the percentage of ethnic minority students in higher education increased from 17% to 40%.

The rising diversity on American campuses is particularly noteworthy when viewed in light of the historical treatment of racial and ethnic minority groups in the United States. In the early 19th century, education was not a right, but a privilege available only to those who could afford to attend private schools. That privilege was experienced largely by Protestants of European descent. Later, white immigrants from other cultural backgrounds began migrating to the United States and public education then became mandatory—with the goal that schools would acculturate or "Americanize" these new immigrants and obliterate their former cultural identities. In many states, Americans of color were left out of the educational process altogether or were educated in separate, racially segregated schools with inferior educational facilities. It was not until a groundbreaking Supreme Court ruling (*Brown v Board of Education*, 1954) that the face of education changed for people of color. On that day, the US Supreme Court ruled that "separate educational facilities are inherently unequal." This decision made it illegal for Kansas and 20 other states to deliver education in segregated classrooms.

Today, a major goal of virtually all American colleges and universities is to ensure that students from diverse backgrounds have the opportunity to enter higher education, benefit from the college experience, and enrich the learning experience of their college classmates.

> "For many students, regardless of racial background, the higher education environment will be the most racially diverse learning environment they have experienced in their lives.
>
> —Beverly Daniel Tatum, former president, Spelman College and author of *Why Are All the Black Kids Sitting Together in the Cafeteria*

Socioeconomic Diversity

In addition to racial and ethnic diversity, human diversity exists among groups of people in terms of their socioeconomic status (SES)—their level of education, level of income, and the occupational prestige of the jobs they hold. Societies are stratified into upper, middle, and lower (working) classes, with groups occupying lower social strata having fewer economic resources and social privileges.

Sharp socioeconomic differences exist across different racial, ethnic, and gender groups. For instance, in 2012, the median income for non-Hispanic white households was $57,009, compared with $39,005 for Hispanics and $33,321 for African Americans. The great housing and mortgage collapse after the turn of the 21st century had its most damaging impact on lower-income, ethnic minorities: between 2005-2009, household wealth fell by 66% for Hispanics and 53% for blacks, versus 16% for whites.

A *privilege* is an unearned advantage. Students coming from wealthier families have advantages that poorer students do not. Families with higher income levels and socioeconomic status are privileged with two major forms of capital: (a) *economic* capital—*what* they have (e.g., homes, health benefits, and discretionary

> "Being born in the elite in the U.S. gives you a constellation of privileges that very few people in the world have ever experienced. Being born poor in the U.S. gives you disadvantages unlike anything in Western Europe, Japan and Canada."
>
> —*David I. Levine, economist and social mobility researcher*

income for travel and other educational experiences for their children), and (b) *social* capital—*who* they know (e.g., contacts with employers, college admissions personnel, and "power players" in the legal and political system). Students from higher-income families acquire these privileges without having to earn them and they will benefit from these privileges throughout life. For instance, families with higher socioeconomic status have greater social capital for getting their children into college and have greater economical capital for preparing them to gain college access (e.g., financial resources to pay for college-admissions test preparation services and to hire independent counselors to help their children get into college or the "best" colleges). Similarly, privileged legacies—advantages handed down without being earned, such as inheriting money or being admitted to a college because a family member previously attended the college, or donated to the college, are not available to less privileged students who lack such social and economic capital.

Socioeconomic differences also affect access to and success in college. Young adults from high-income families are seven times more likely to earn a college degree and hold a prestigious job than young adults from low-income families. Among low-income students who do enroll in college, national surveys reveal that almost one-third of them report that food and housing challenges are interfering with their educational efforts. Twenty-two percent of these students reported that during the previous month, they experienced very low levels of food security—inability to access sufficient amounts of nutritious foods (to the point of being hungry), and over 60% of students who experienced food insecurity also experienced housing insecurity—difficulty paying their rent or utility bills. Fifteen percent of food-insecure students also reported experiencing occasional homelessness.

 Reflection 10.7

Are you the first member of your family to attend college?

Would you be the first member of your family to graduate from college?

How do your answers to the above two questions make you feel?

International Diversity

Adding further to the diversity on college campuses are international students. Since the turn of the century, the number of international students in the United States has grown by 72%. During the 2016-2017 academic year, over a million international students were enrolled on American campuses—more than any other country in the world.

The need for American college students to better understand and appreciate international diversity is highlighted in a study conducted by an anthropologist who went "undercover" and posed as a student in a university residence hall. She found that the biggest complaint international students had about American students was their lack of knowledge about other countries and the misconceptions they held about people from certain nations. Leadership scholars have also noted that because of increasing economic interdependence among nations and the growing number of multinational organizations, future leaders of businesses and organizations need to have a stronger "global leadership mindset"—that is, greater commitment to gaining knowledge about other nations' cultures and stronger intercultural communication skills. For instance, an effective American business leader in today's global economy needs to know that American business culture values risk taking and making quick business decisions, whereas Middle Eastern countries (e.g., Kuwait and Egypt) value a more conservative approach to decision-making that involves taking fewer risks, longer time to deliberate before reaching decisions, and more emphasis on relationship building during the decision-making process.

Gender Diversity

At one point in history, all college students were men. In fact, the term "freshman" literally meant "fresh man" because every new college student was, indeed, a man; no females were enrolled in (or could enroll in) college. Even as late as 1955, only 25% of American college students were female. By 2000, that percentage had jumped to almost 66%. Between 1990 and 2009, the proportion of women enrolling in college increased at a rate almost three times faster than that of men. Women now earn the majority of bachelor's, master's, and doctoral degrees granted in the United States. Women also hold almost 40% of all management positions in American organizations.

Sexual-Orientation and Gender-Identity Diversity

Humans experience and express their gender and sexuality in diverse ways. *Sexual orientation*—"an inherent or immutable enduring emotional, romantic or sexual attraction to other people," and *gender identity*—a person's innermost concept of self as male, female, a blend of both or neither—are two important dimensions of sexual diversity themselves. An individual's gender identity may be the same or different from the sex assigned at birth, and a person's *gender expression*—the external appearance of one's gender identity as expressed through behavior, clothing, haircut or voice also may or may not conform to behaviors and characteristics typically associated with being either masculine or feminine. There are many terms associated with gender-expression identity and sexual orientation that people often don't talk about because they're uncomfortable with them or are simply unfamiliar with them. **Box 10.2** contains an alphabetical listing of these terms and what they mean.

Box 10.2

Androgynous: A person who has the physical characteristics of both sexes, or who identifies with being both male and female.

Asexual: A person who has no sexual feelings or desires, or who is not sexually attracted to anyone.

Bisexual: A person who is sexually attracted to both men and women.

Cisgender: People whose gender identity matches the sex they were assigned at birth (as opposed to transgender).

Coming out (a.k.a. Coming out of the of the closet): Accepting and revealing one's sexual orientation or gender identity.

Gay: People who are attracted to members of their same gender.

Gender dysphoria: A condition in which a person experiences discomfort or distress because of a mismatch between their biological sex and gender identity.

Gender-fluid: People who do not identify themselves as one set or fixed gender identity.

Gender identity: A sense of one's own personal gender; it can align with the person's sex assigned at birth or differ from it.

continued...

Genderqueer (a.k.a. Non-binary): A range of gender identities that are not exclusively masculine or feminine, such as having two or more gender identities, moving between gender identities, or gender identity.

Heterosexism: Prejudice or discrimination against homosexuals based on the belief that heterosexuality is the only normal sexual orientation.

Heterosexual: A person who is sexually attracted to members of the opposite sex.

Homophobia: Negative attitudes and feelings (e.g., discomfort or fear) toward people who are attracted to members of their own sex.

Intersex: Individuals born with bodily variations in sexual characteristics that are not typical of a male or female (e.g., variations in sex chromosomes, genitals, or hormones).

Lesbian: A female who is sexually attracted to other females.

LGBTQ: An acronym for lesbian, gay, bisexual, transgender, and/or queer or questioning.

Outing: Disclosing an LGBTQ person's sexual orientation or gender identity without that person's consent.

Pansexual (a.k.a. Omnisexual): a person who can be romantically or sexually attracted to people of any gender or sexual orientation.

Sexual Orientation: A person's pattern of romantic or sexual attraction to other people, whether they be of the opposite sex or gender, the same sex or gender, or both sexes and more than one gender.

Transgender (a.k.a. Trans): people whose gender identity differs from the sex they were assigned at birth.

Transphobia: Negative attitudes and feelings (e.g., fear discomfort, or hostility) toward people who are transgender.

College campuses across the country are increasing their support for **LGBTQ** (**L**esbian, **G**ay, **B**isexual, **T**ransgender and **Q**ueer or **Q**uestioning) students by creating centers and services whose purpose is to promote their acceptance by the college community. These campus support services play an important role in combating homophobia and related forms of sexual prejudice on campus, while promoting awareness and tolerance of all forms of sexual orientation and identity. By accepting individuals who span the full spectrum of sexual diversity, we acknowledge and appreciate the reality that heterosexuality is just one form of human sexual expression. Our growing acknowledgement of sexual diversity is reflected in the Supreme Court's historic decision to legalize same-sex marriage nationwide.

Reflection 10.8

What forms of diversity do you see represented on campus?

When you first arrived on campus, did you find certain groups that you: (a) didn't expect to see, (b) didn't expect to see in such large numbers, or (c) didn't expect to be open about their group membership?

Generational Diversity

Human diversity also exists with respect to the historical time period during which different groups of people grow up. The term "generation" refers to a cohort (group) of individuals born during the same historical period, whose attitudes, values, and habits have been shaped by events that took place in the world during their formative years of development. People growing up in different generations tend to develop different attitudes and beliefs because of the different historical events they experienced during their upbringing.

Box 10.3 contains a brief summary of different generations that have been identified, the key historical events they experienced, and the personal characteristics commonly associated with each generational group.

Box 10.3

Generational Diversity: A Snapshot Summary

- The Traditional Generation (a.k.a. "Silent Generation") (born 1922–1945). This generation was influenced by events such as the Great Depression and World Wars I and II. Characteristics associated with people growing up at this time include loyalty, patriotism, respect for authority, and conservatism.
- The Baby Boomer Generation (born 1946–1964). This generation was influenced by events such as the Vietnam War, Watergate, and the civil rights movement. Characteristics associated with people growing up at this time include idealism, emphasis on self-fulfillment, and concern for social justice and equal rights.
- Generation X (born 1965–1980). This generation was influenced by Sesame Street, the creation of MTV, AIDS, and soaring divorce rates. They were the first "latchkey children"—youngsters who used their own key to let themselves into their home after school because their mothers (or single mothers) were working outside the home. Characteristics associated with people growing up at this time include self-reliance, resourcefulness, and the ability to adapt to change.
- Generation Y (a.k.a. "Millennials") (born 1981–2002). This generation was influenced by the September 11,

2001, terrorist attack on the United States, the shooting of students at Columbine High School, and the collapse of the Enron Corporation. Characteristics associated with people growing up at this time include a preference for working and socializing in groups, familiarity with technology, and willingness to engage in volunteer service in their community (which is why they're sometimes referred to as the "civic generation"). Millennials also represent the most ethnically diverse generation, are more open to experiencing diversity than previous generations, and are more likely to view diversity positively.

> You guys [in the media] have to get used to it. This is a new day and age, and for my generation that's a very common word. It's like saying 'bro.' That's how we address our friends. That's how we talk."
>
> —*Matt Barnes, millennial, biracial professional basketball player, explaining to reporters after being fined for using the word "niggas" in a tweet to some of his African American teammates*

- Generation Z (a.k.a. "The iGeneration") (born 1994–present). This generation includes the latter half of Generation Y. They grew up with wars being fought in Afghanistan and Iraq, international terrorism, global recession, and climate change. As a result of these

continued...

experiences, they tend to have less trust in political systems and industrial corporations than previous generations. During their formative years, the Internet was in place, so they are very comfortable with technology and rely heavily on Google, YouTube, Twitter, Snapchat, and HouseParty. They have come to expect that their needs will be met immediately through technology and aren't threatened by the lack of privacy associated with social networking. For these reasons, they're also referred to as the "digital generation."

 Reflection 10.9

Look back at the characteristics associated with your generation. Which of these characteristics do you think accurately reflect your personal characteristics and those of your closest friends? Which do not?

The Benefits of Experiencing Diversity

National surveys show that by the end of their first year in college, almost two-thirds of students report having "stronger" or "much stronger" knowledge of people from different races and cultures than they did before entering college. Most first-year students also report becoming more open to experiencing diverse cultures, viewpoints, and values than they had been previously. The diversity on college campuses today represents an unprecedented educational opportunity. After college, students may never again be members of a community that includes so many people from such a wide variety of backgrounds. Now is the time to reap the benefits of the diversity that surrounds you.

Experiencing and appreciating diversity is not just a socially sensitive or "politically correct" thing to do, it's also an educationally effective thing to do. Diversity will enrich the quality of your education and the education of the diverse students with whom you interact. Below is a summary of the key advantages of experiencing diversity. Keep these benefits in mind and use them to motivate yourself to capitalize on the power of diversity.

Diversity Increases Self-Awareness and Self-Knowledge

Interacting with people from diverse backgrounds enables us to compare and contrast our life experiences with others whose experiences differ sharply from our own. Seeing how our life experiences differ from others serves to deepen our understanding of ourselves and how we got to be who we are; it helps us step outside ourselves and gain a *comparative perspective*—a reference point that enables us to see more clearly how our particular cultural background has shaped our personal development and identity.

> *The more we learn about people different than ourselves, the more we learn about ourselves.*

A comparative perspective also allows us to gain insight into how our cultural background may have advantaged or disadvantaged us. For instance, learning about cross-cultural differences in access to higher education can raise our awareness of the more limited educational opportunities there are for people in other countries.

> "I am very happy with the diversity here, but it also frightens me. I have never been in a situation where I have met people who are Jewish, Muslim, atheist, born-again, and many more."
>
> —First-year student (quoted in Erickson, Peters, & Strommer, *Teaching First-Year College Students*)

> "Empirical evidence shows that the actual effects on student development of emphasizing diversity and of student participation in diversity activities are overwhelmingly positive."
>
> —Alexander Astin, *What Matters in College*

> "It is difficult to see the picture when you are inside the frame."
>
> —An old saying (author unknown)

By gaining this cross-cultural knowledge, we gain greater appreciation of how advantaged we are in America—where college is available to everyone—regardless of race, gender, age, social class, or level of academic performance prior to college.

Diversity Deepens Learning

Research consistently shows that students learn more from students who are different than themselves than they do from students who are similar to themselves. Learning about different cultures and interacting with people from diverse cultural groups supplies the brain with more varied routes or pathways through which to connect (learn) new ideas. Experiencing diversity also "stretches" the brain beyond its normal "comfort zone" by pushing it to compare, contrast, and connect something unfamiliar to something it already knows. This added expenditure of mental energy results in the brain forming deeper and more durable neurological connections. Simply stated: We learn more deeply from diversity than we do from similarity or familiarity. In contrast, when we restrict the diversity of people with whom we interact (out of habit or prejudice), we limit the breadth and depth of our learning.

Diversity Promotes Higher–Level Thinking

Studies show that college students who have more exposure to diversity—such as enrolling in multicultural courses, participating in diversity programs on campus, and interacting with peers of different races and ethnicities—experience greater gains in:

* thinking *complexity*—the ability to think about all parts of an issue and from multiple perspectives
* *reflective* thinking—the ability to think deeply about personal and global issues
* *critical* thinking—the ability to evaluate the validity of one's own reasoning and the reasoning of others

These mental benefits of experiencing diversity stems from the fact that exposure to perspectives different than our own creates *cognitive dissonance*—a state of cognitive (mental) disequilibrium or imbalance. This tension "forces" our minds to deal with different perspectives simultaneously, resulting in thinking that is less simplistic, more nuanced, and more complex.

Diversity Stimulates Creative Thinking

In addition to promoting critical thinking, research reveals that diversity enhances creativity. When ideas are exchanged among people from diverse cultures, a "cross-stimulation" effect is generated in which ideas exchanged by people from different cultural backgrounds stimulate creation of additional ideas, which can "cross-fertilize" and give birth to new ideas and solutions for tackling old problems. Research also indicates that when people seek out alternative viewpoints and diverse perspectives, it increases their openness to pursuing different goal options and their willingness to try different goal-achievement strategies.

In contrast, when diverse cultural perspectives are dismissed or devalued, the variety of lenses through which we can view issues and problems is reduced. This restricts our ability to engage in divergent thinking (thinking that takes off in different directions), which, in turn, restricts our capacity to think creatively. By limiting our interactions to groups of people like us, our ideas are less likely

"What I look for in musicians is generosity. There is so much to learn from each other and about each other's culture. Great creativity begins with tolerance.

—Yo-Yo Ma, French-born, Chinese-American virtuoso cellist, composer, and winner of multiple Grammy Awards

to diverge; instead, they're more likely to converge and merge into one cultural channel—the cultural perspective of the same group of people doing the thinking. Thus, segregation not only separates people socially, it also segregates their ideas and suppresses their collective creativity. This is well illustrated in the book and movie *Hidden Figures*, which documents how a group of bright, talented African American female mathematicians—initially segregated from their white male coworkers at NASA—were eventually integrated into the work team and made crucial, creative contributions to the successful launching of America's first astronaut.

> Drawing on the ideas of others from diverse backgrounds and bouncing our ideas off them stimulates divergent (out-of-the-box) thinking, generates synergy (multiplication of ideas), and creates serendipity (unexpected discoveries of innovative ideas).

Diversity Enhances Career Preparation and Career Success

Whatever line of work today's college graduates decide to pursue, they're likely to find themselves working with employers, co-workers, customers, and clients from diverse cultural backgrounds. America's workforce is now more diverse than at any time in history and will grow ever more diverse throughout the 21st century. By 2050, the proportion of American workers from minority ethnic and racial groups will jump to 55%.

National surveys show that policymakers, business leaders, and employers seek college graduates who are more than just "aware" or "tolerant" of diversity. They want graduates who have actual *experience* with diversity and can collaborate with diverse co-workers, clients, and customers.

In addition to the growing domestic diversity within the United States, the current "global economy" requires skills relating to international diversity. The work world today if characterized by economic interdependence across nations, international trading, multinational corporations, international travel, and instantaneous worldwide communication (due to ongoing advances in electronic technology). Even smaller companies and corporations are becoming more international in nature. As a result, employers in all sectors of the economy are seeking job candidates with the following skills and attributes: sensitivity to human differences, ability to understand and relate to people from different cultural backgrounds, international and intercultural knowledge, and ability to communicate in a second language.

The growth in both domestic and international diversity has made *intercultural competence* an essential 21st century skill. Intercultural competence may be defined as the ability to appreciate and learn from human differences and to interact effectively with people from diverse cultural backgrounds. It includes knowledge of cultures and cultural practices (one's own and others), complex cognitive skills for decision making in intercultural contexts, social skills to function effectively in diverse groups and such personal attributes flexibility and openness to new ideas.

Reflection 10.10

What intercultural skills do you think you already possess? What additional intercultural skills do you think you need to develop to maximize your career readiness?

Stereotyping: A Barrier to Diversity

The word "stereotype" derives from two roots: *stereo*—to look at in a fixed way, and *type*— to categorize or group together (as in the word "typical"). Thus, to stereotype is to view individuals of the same type (group) in the same (fixed) way. Stereotyping overlooks or disregards individuality; instead, all individuals sharing the same group characteristic (e.g., race or gender) are viewed as having similar personal characteristics—as reflected in comments like: "You know how they are; they're all alike."

Stereotypes involve *bias*, meaning "slant." This bias or slant can tilt toward the positive or the negative, and be conscious or unconscious—referred to as *implicit bias*. Positive bias results in favorable stereotypes (e.g., "Asians are great in science and math"); negative bias leads to unfavorable stereotypes (e.g., "Asians are nerds who do nothing but study"). Although most people would reject such blatant stereotypes, humans can (and do) hold overgeneralized beliefs about members of certain groups. When these overgeneralizations are negative, they malign a group's reputation, rob its members of their individuality, and can damage their self-esteem or self- confidence—as is illustrated in the following story.

AUTHOR'S EXPERIENCE

When I was six years old, a six-year-old girl from a different racial group told me that people of my race could not swim. Because I couldn't swim at that time and she could, I assumed she was correct. I asked a boy (a member of the same racial group as the girl) whether her statement was true. He responded emphatically: "Yes, it's definitely true!" Since I grew up in an area where few other African Americans were around to counteract this belief about my racial group, I continued to buy into this stereotype until I finally took swimming lessons as an adult. After many lessons, I am now a lousy swimmer because I didn't even attempt to swim until I was an adult. Moral of this story: Group stereotypes can limit the personal confidence and performance potential of members of the stereotyped group.

—*Aaron Thompson*

Gender stereotypes continue to impair women's potential to pursue leadership opportunities. Although significantly more women today hold management positions, they hold a very small percentage of high-level leadership positions in America's top (Fortune 500) companies, and compared to other countries, American women hold fewer political leadership positions in our nation's legislature. A key factor contributing to the high-level leadership position gap between men and women is the long-held gender stereotype that "women take care and men take charge." Women continue to be responsible for the majority of childcare responsibilities, and when working women take time off from their careers to bear and care for children, their lost work time is often held against them when they are evaluated for promotion to high-level leadership positions.

The adverse effects of gender stereotyping on women's career advancement is compounded further by a phenomenon known as *homosocial reproduction*—the tendency for organizations to replace departing members with candidates whose characteristics are similar to the departing members or similar to the characteristics of the person hiring the departing members' replacements. In elite organizations, males dominate high-level leadership positions, so when it's time to hire or advance another member, their tendency (sometimes unconscious) is to select another male.

Even when female leaders manage to rise to high-level leadership positions, they often encounter a double standard: They're likely to be expected to display traditional, masculine-like leadership traits while still remaining "feminine." For

instance, being assertive and task-oriented are considered positive leadership qualities in men, but if women display these traits, they may be viewed as being unfemi-
nine and lacking warmth. Such gender bias not only limits leadership opportunities
for women, it also limits the diversity of the pool of leadership candidates an organization can choose from, which, in turn, can limit an organization's overall
effectiveness.

 Reflection 10.11

1. Have you ever been stereotyped based on your appearance or group membership? If so,
   what was the stereotype and how did it make you feel?

2. Do you think there are certain groups on your campus that may be especially vulnerable
   to stereotyping? If yes, what are these groups and what type of stereotypes do you think
   they encounter?

Neither males nor females should let gender stereotypes limit their career options.

Prejudice

If members of a stereotyped group are judged and evaluated in a negative way, the result is *prejudice*. Typically, prejudice involves *stigmatizing*—ascribing inferior or unfavorable traits to people who belong to the same group. The word "prejudice" means to "pre-judge." Thus, prejudice may be defined as a negative stereotype about a group of people that's formed before the facts are known.

A person who holds a group prejudice typically avoids contact with members of the stigmatized group. This avoidance leaves little or no opportunity for the prejudiced person to have positive experiences with members of the stigmatized group that could contradict or disprove the prejudice. The result is a vicious cycle whereby the prejudiced person continues to avoid contact with members of the stigmatized group, which, in turn, continues to maintain and reinforce the prejudice.

Another way in which prejudice remains intact after it's formed is through a psychological process known as *selective perception*—the tendency for biased (prejudiced) people to see what they *expect* to see and fail to see what contradicts their bias. Have you ever noticed how fans rooting for their favorite sports team tend to focus on and "see" the referees' calls that go against their own team, but don't seem to react (or even notice) the calls that go against the opposing team? This is a classic example of selective perception. In effect, selective perception takes the adage, "seeing is believing" and turns it into "believing is seeing." It leads prejudiced people to continue "seeing" things that are consistent with their prejudicial belief while remaining "blind" to things that refute or contradict it.

Making matters worse, selective perception is often accompanied by *selective memory*—the tendency for prejudiced people to remember information that supports their prejudicial belief and forget information that contradicts it. The two prejudice-preserving processes of selective perception and selective memory work together, and often *unconsciously*. As a result, people may not even be aware that they are using these processes and that their use of them is holding their prejudice in place and preventing it from being challenged or changed.

> "See that man over there? Yes. Well, I hate him. But you don't know him. That's why I hate him.
> —Gordon Allport, influential social psychologist and author of *The Nature of Prejudice*

> "We see what is behind our eyes.
> —*Chinese proverb*

Reflection 10.12

Have you ever witnessed selective perception or selective memory—people seeing or recalling what they believe to be true (due to bias) rather than what's actually true?

If yes, what bias was involved and how was selective perception or selective memory used to support the bias?

Discrimination

The term "discriminate" means to "divide" or "separate." In contrast to prejudice, which is a belief, attitude, or opinion, discrimination is an *action*. Technically, discrimination can be either negative or positive—for example, a discriminating eater may be careful about eating only healthy foods. However, the term is most often associated with a harmful act that results in a prejudiced person engaging in unfair or unjust action toward another person or group. For instance, the action of firing or not hiring people based on their race, gender, or sexual orientation is an act of discrimination. Thus, discrimination could be described as prejudice put into action.

Box 10.4 contains a summary of biases, prejudicial beliefs, and discriminatory behaviors that have plagued humankind and interfered with acceptance and appreciation of human diversity. As you read through the list, place a checkmark next to any form of prejudice that you, a family member, or a friend has experienced.

Box 10.4

Barriers to Diversity Acceptance and Appreciation: Biases, Prejudices, and Discriminatory Behaviors

- **Ethnocentrism:** viewing one's own culture or ethnic group as "normal" or "superior" while viewing other cultures as "deficient" or "inferior."
  Example: Viewing another culture as "abnormal" or "uncivilized" because its members eat animals that our culture views unacceptable to eat, although we eat animals their culture views unacceptable to eat.

- **Stereotyping:** viewing all (or virtually all) members of the same group in the same way—as having the same personal qualities or characteristics.
  Example: "If you're Italian, you must be in the Mafia, or have a family member who is."

- **Prejudice:** negative pre-judgment about another group of people.
  Example: Women can't be effective leaders because they're too emotional.

- **Discrimination:** unequal and unfair treatment of a person or group of people that puts prejudice into action.
  Example: Paying women less than men for performing the same job, even though they have the same level of education and job qualifications.

- **Segregation:** intentional decision made by a group to separate itself (socially or physically) from another group.
  Example: "White flight"—white people moving out of neighborhoods when people of color move in.

- **Racism:** belief that one's racial group is superior to another group and expressing that belief in attitude (prejudice) or action (discrimination).
  Example: Confiscating land from American Indians based on the unfounded belief that they are "uncivilized" or "savages."

- **Institutional Racism:** racial discrimination rooted in organizational policies and practices that disadvantage certain racial groups.
  Example: Race-based discrimination that denies or restricts mortgage lending, bank loans, and housing opportunities to members of certain racial groups.

- **Racial Profiling:** investigating or arresting someone solely based on the person's race, ethnicity, or national origin, without sufficient evidence of criminal behavior.
  Example: Police making a traffic stop or conducting a personal search based solely on an individual's racial features.

- **Slavery:** forced labor in which people are viewed as property, held against their will, and deprived of the right to receive wages.
  Example: The legal enslavement of blacks in the United States until 1865.

- **"Jim Crow" Laws:** formal and informal laws created by whites to segregate blacks after the abolition of slavery.
  Example: laws in certain parts of the US that required blacks to use separate bathrooms and be educated in separate schools.

- **Colorism:** a form of racism that is biased against darker-skinned people of color.
  Example: Darker-skinned Mexican Americans are more likely to be singled out and targeted with "go back to Mexico" chants than lighter-skinned Mexican Americans.

- **Apartheid:** an institutionalized system of "legal racism" supported by a nation's government. (Apartheid derives from a word in the Afrikaan language, meaning "apartness.")
  Example: South Africa's nationalized system of racial segregation and discrimination that was in place from 1948 to 1994.

> Never, never, and never again shall it be that this beautiful land will again experience the oppression of one by another."
>
> —Nelson Mandela, anti-apartheid revolutionary, first black president of South Africa after Apartheid, and winner of the Nobel Peace Prize

- **Hate Crimes:** criminal action motivated solely by prejudice toward the crime victim.
  Example: Acts of vandalism or assault that explicitly target members of a particular ethnic group or persons of a particular sexual orientation.

- **Hate Groups:** organizations whose primary purpose is to promote prejudice, discrimination, or aggression toward certain groups of people based on their ethnicity, race, religion, etc.

continued...

Example: The Ku Klux Klan—an American hate group that harbors and perpetrates prejudice against all non-white races.

- Genocide: mass murdering of a particular ethnic or racial group.
Example: The Holocaust, in which millions of Jews were systematically murdered during Germany's Nazi regime. Other examples include the mass murdering of Cambodians under the Khmer Rouge regime, the mass murdering of Bosnian Muslims in the former country of Yugoslavia, and the systematic slaughter of the Tutsi minority by the Hutu majority in Rwanda.

- Classism: prejudice or discrimination based on social class, particularly toward people of lower socioeconomic status.
Example: Acknowledging the contributions made by politicians and wealthy industrialists to America, while ignoring the contributions of poor immigrants, farmers, slaves, and pioneer women.

- Religious Intolerance: denying the fundamental human right of people to hold religious beliefs, or to hold religious beliefs different from one's own.
Example: An atheist who forces non-religious (secular) beliefs on others, or a member of a religious group who believes that other groups holding different religious beliefs are infidels or "sinners."

> "Rivers, ponds, lakes and streams— they all have different names, but they all contain water. Just as religions do— they all contain truths."
>
> —Muhammad Ali, three-time world heavyweight boxing champion, member of the International Boxing Hall of Fame, and recipient of the Spirit of America Award as the most recognized American in the world

- Anti-Semitism: prejudice or discrimination toward Jews and other people who practice the religion of Judaism.
Example: Disliking or discriminating against Jews because they're the ones who "killed Christ."

- Xenophobia: fear or hatred of foreigners, outsiders, or strangers.
Example: Believing (without evidence) that certain immigrant groups should be banned from entering the country because they'll undermine the nation's economy and increase its crime rate.

- Nativism: a political policy of preserving or advancing the interests of native inhabitants against those of immigrants, including opposition to immigration based on fears that immigrants (particularly those of certain nations) will distort or displace the nation's existing cultural norms and values. (Note: People who

hold this political position, however, do not view it as a form of prejudice, but as a form of patriotism.) Example: The Chinese Exclusion Act—a federal law passed in 1882 that banned all Chinese immigrants from entering the United States, based on the belief that Chinese workers were hurting the American economy. It was the first law implemented in America that prohibited all members of a specific ethnic or national group from entering the country.

- Regional Bias: prejudice or discrimination based on the geographical region in which an individual is born and raised.
Example: A northerner who thinks that all southerners are racists.

- Nationalism: extreme identification with one's own nation, to the point of overlooking any of its flaws and neglecting the needs of other nations or the common needs of all nations.
Example: "Blind patriotism"—failing to see the shortcomings of one's own nation and viewing anyone who questions or criticizes one's own nation as being disloyal or "unpatriotic." (As in the slogan, "America: right or wrong" or "America: love it or leave it!") Note: *Jingoism* is an extreme form of nationalism characterized by an aggressive foreign policy that advocates for use of threat and military force (rather than peaceful relations and negotiation) to preserve or advance the interests of one's own nation, often without regard for the needs and interests of other nations.

> "Above all nations is humanity."
>
> —Motto of the University of Hawaii

- Terrorism: intentional acts of violence committed against civilians that are motivated by political or religious prejudice.
Example: The September 11, 2001 attacks on the United States.

- Sexism: prejudice or discrimination based on sex or gender.
Example: Believing that women should not pursue careers in fields traditionally occupied by men (e.g., engineering or politics) because they lack the innate qualities or natural skills to succeed.

- Heterosexism: belief that heterosexuality is the only acceptable sexual orientation.
Example: Believing gays should not have the same legal rights and career opportunities as heterosexuals.

- Homophobia: extreme fear or hatred of homosexuals.
Example: Creating and contributing to anti-gay

continued...

websites, or "gay bashing" (physical acts of violence toward gays).

- **Ageism:** prejudice or discrimination toward certain age groups, particularly the elderly.
  Example: believing that "old" people are too frail or demented to drive or make important decisions.

- **Ableism:** prejudice or discrimination toward people who are disabled or handicapped (physically, mentally, or emotionally).
  Example: Intentionally avoiding social contact with people in wheelchairs.

Reflection 10.13

As you read through the above list, were there any forms of prejudice that you, a family member, or a friend experienced?

What happened in these instances and why do you think it happened?

Strategies for Overcoming Stereotypes, Prejudice, and Discrimination

People often hold prejudices, stereotypes, or subtle biases without being fully aware that they hold them. The following strategies may be used to remain aware of our unconscious biases and reduce our risk of developing them in the first place.

Consciously avoid preoccupation with physical appearances. Remember the old proverb: "It's what's inside that counts." Judge others not by the familiarity of their outer features, but by the merits of their inner qualities.

> **"Stop judging by mere appearances, and make a right judgment."**
> —Bible, John 7:24

Form impressions of others on a person-to-person basis, not according to their group membership. This may seem like a simple and obvious thing to do, but research shows that humans have a natural tendency to perceive individuals from unfamiliar groups as being more alike than individuals of their own group. We need to remain mindful of this tendency and make a conscious effort to avoid perceiving and treating members of unfamiliar groups in terms of some general (stereotypical) rule of thumb, but as unique individuals.

> **"You can't judge a book by the cover."**
> —1962 hit song by Ellas McDaniel, a.k.a. Bo Diddley (Note: a "bo diddley" is a one-stringed African guitar)

Take a stand against prejudice and discrimination by constructively disagreeing with others who make stereotypical statements and prejudicial remarks. By saying nothing, you may avoid conflict, but silence can send the message that you tacitly agree with the person making a prejudicial remark. Studies show that when members of the same group observe one of its own members making a prejudicial comment about a member of another group, prejudice increases among other members of the prejudiced member's group—probably due to peer pressure and group conformity. However, if the group member's prejudicial remark is challenged by a member of his or her own group, particularly a member who is liked and respected by other group members, it reduces the prejudice of the person making the remark as well any similar prejudice held by other members of the group. Thus, by taking a leadership role and challenging a peer who makes prejudicial comments, you're not only likely to reduce the prejudice of the person making the comments, but also the prejudice of others who may have heard the prejudicial remark.

> **"In the end, we will remember not the words of our enemies, but the silence of our friends."**
> —Martin Luther King, civil rights leader and winner of the Nobel Peace Prize

> *By actively opposing prejudice on campus, you demonstrate leadership qualities and personal character, and you send a clear message to other members of the campus community that valuing diversity is not just the "politically correct" thing to do, but the morally right thing to do.*

Reflection 10.14

Would you say your campus climate or culture supports and facilitates intercultural interaction among students from different racial and cultural backgrounds? Is there anything you could do to try to improve your campus climate so that it's more supportive of, or conducive to, intercultural interaction?

(Review your results from our AchieveWORKS Personality assessment report. How might the recommendations you received about your interpersonal skills enable you to become more adept at connecting with people from cultural backgrounds that are different from your own?)

Strategies for Increasing Personal Contact and Interpersonal Interaction with Members of Diverse Groups

Research shows that humans display a strong tendency to associate and develop relationships with others with whom they share similar backgrounds, beliefs, and interests. Scholars refer to this phenomenon as the "self-similarity principle." To experience diversity and its benefits, we need to resist falling prey to the self-similarity principle by stepping out of our comfort zone and seeking opportunities to interact with others whose physical and cultural characteristics differ from our own. Distancing ourselves from diversity ensures we'll never experience it and benefit from it. The following practices increase your access to and interaction with members of diverse groups.

Place yourself in situations and locations on campus where you're most likely to encounter and experience diversity. Research in social psychology confirms what we'd expect: People who regularly find themselves in the same place at the same time are more likely to communicate and form relationships with one another. Research also shows that if regular contact takes place between members of different racial or ethnic groups, stereotyping is sharply reduced and intercultural friendships are more likely to form. You can create these conditions by making an intentional attempt to position yourself near diverse students in class, the library, or student café, and by teaming up with them for group discussions, study groups, and group projects. Also, consider spending time at the multicultural center on campus or become a member of a campus club or organization whose purpose is to promote diversity awareness, interaction, and appreciation (e.g., multicultural or international club). Putting yourself in these social contexts will enable you to make regular contact with members of unfamiliar cultural groups, and by taking the initiative to visit with them on "their turf," you send a clear message that you value them and are ready to learn with and from them.

Reflection 10.15

Your comfort level seeking out diversity is likely to depend on how much prior experience you've had with diverse groups. Rate the amount of diversity you have experienced in the following settings:

1. The high school you attended	high	moderate	low
2. The college or university you now attend	high	moderate	low
3. The neighborhood in which you grew up	high	moderate	low
4. Places where you have been employed	high	moderate	low

Which one of these settings had the *most* and *least* diversity? What do you think accounted for, or contributed to, this discrepancy?

Take advantage of social media to "chat" virtually with students from diverse groups. Electronic communication can be a convenient and comfortable way to initiate contact with members of groups with whom you've had little prior experience. Interacting *online* can also serve to "break the ice" and lead to future interaction *in person*.

Engage in co-curricular diversity programs. Studies indicate that student participation in co-curricular experiences relating to diversity improves critical thinking and reduces unconscious prejudice. Review your student handbook to identify co-curricular programs, student activities, student clubs, and campus organizations that emphasize diversity awareness and intercultural interaction. If your campus sponsors multicultural or cross-cultural retreats, strongly consider participating in them. A retreat setting provides an intimate and comfortable off-campus environment in which personal interaction with diverse students can take place without the distractions of familiar friends and regular routines.

Seek out the views and opinions of classmates from diverse backgrounds. Group discussions among students of different cultures can reduce prejudice and promote intercultural appreciation, but only if each member's cultural identity and perspective is sought out and valued by members of the discussion group.

During group discussions in class, you can demonstrate leadership by seeking out the views and opinions of classmates from diverse backgrounds and ensuring their ideas are heard. After class discussions have ended, you can also ask students from different backgrounds if there were points made or positions taken in class that they would strongly question or challenge but didn't get the chance or opportunity to do so.

In classes where there's little or no student diversity, encourage your classmates to approach course topics and issues from diverse perspectives. For instance, you might ask: "If there were international students here, what might they be adding to our discussion?" Or, you could ask: "If members of certain minority groups were here, would they be offering a different viewpoint?"

Be a community builder who identifies similarities and recurring themes that unite the ideas and experiences of students from diverse backgrounds. Look for the common denominators—themes of unity that co-exist with or cut across. As you discuss issues relating to diversity, look to discover and discuss commonalities that traverse or transcend group differences, and use these commonalities to create a sense of community among members of diverse groups. For instance, individuals from different ethnic and racial groups are likely to have shared experiences as citizens of the same country, persons of the same gender, or members of the same generation.

When discussions of diversity focus exclusively on intergroup differences without also attending to intergroup commonalities, it can heighten divisiveness between groups and cause members of minority groups to feel further isolated or alienated. To minimize this risk, dig below the surface of group differences and unearth common ground on which all groups stand. One way to do so is by calling students' attention to the universal experiences shared by all human groups. For instance, before immediately launching into a discussion of diversity, first discuss the common elements of all cultures (see **Box 10.1**, p. 214), or common components of the human self and development (described in Chapter 2, pp, 42-43). Taking time to raise awareness of what different groups have in common can help defuse feelings of divisiveness and supply a solid foundation on which open and honest discussions of group differences can be built.

If you are given the opportunity to form your own discussion groups and group-project teams, join or create groups of students from diverse backgrounds. You can gain greater exposure to diverse perspectives by intentionally joining or forming learning groups with students that differ in terms of their members' gender, age, race, or ethnicity. Including diversity in your discussion groups not only creates social variety, it also enhances the quality of the group's discussion by allowing members to gain access to and learn from multiple perspectives. For instance, if a group is composed of members who are diverse with respect to age, older students will bring a broad range of practical life experiences to the group discussion that younger students can draw on and learn from, while younger students will bring a more contemporary and idealistic perspective that can enrich the intergenerational group discussion.

Intentionally incorporating gender diversity into your group discussions can expose group members to different learning approaches and ways of understanding issues exhibited by males and females. Studies show that males are more likely to be "separate knowers"—they tend to "detach" themselves from the concept or issue being discussed so they can analyze it. In contrast, females are more likely to be "connected knowers"—they tend to relate personally to concepts and connect them with their own experiences and the experiences of others. For example, when interpreting a poem, males are more likely to ask: "What techniques can I use to analyze it?" In contrast, females are more likely to ask: "What is the poet trying to say to me?" Both learning approaches are valuable, and you can capitalize on the benefits of both approaches by forming gender-diverse discussion groups.

It's also been found that during group discussions females are more likely to work collaboratively, sharing their ideas with others and collecting ideas from others. In contrast, males are more likely to adopt a competitive approach and debate the ideas of others. Consistent with these results are studies of females in leadership positions, which reveal that women are more likely to adopt a democratic or participative style of leadership than men.

Form and facilitate collaborative learning teams composed of students from diverse backgrounds. A learning *team* is much more than a discussion group. A discussion group simply discusses (tosses around) ideas. A learning team moves beyond discussion to *collaboration*—its members "co-labor" (work together) to reach the same goal. Research from kindergarten to college indicates that when students' academic performance and interpersonal skills are strengthened when they work collaboratively in teams. Also, when individuals from different racial groups work in teams toward the same goal, racial prejudice decreases and interracial friendships increase. These positive developments may be explained, in part, by the fact that when members of diverse groups join together on the same team, nobody belongs to an "out" group ("them"); instead, everybody belongs to the same "in" group ("us").

The physical environment or location where teamwork takes place can also influence the nature and quality of the team's work. Teammates are more likely to interact openly and work collaboratively if their work takes place in a friendly, informal environment that's conducive to relationship building. If possible, have your team come together in a living room or a lounge area. Compared with a sterile classroom, these environments supply a warmer atmosphere that's more conducive to collaboration.

After engaging in group work, take time to reflect on the experience. The final step in any learning process, whether it be learning from a professor or learning from a group discussion, is to step back from what's taken place and thoughtfully review it. Deep learning requires not only effortful action but also thoughtful reflection. You can reflect on and learn from learning experiences that take place in diverse groups by asking yourself (and your group) the following questions:

- What major similarities in viewpoints did all group members share? (What common themes emerged?)
- What major differences of opinion were expressed by diverse members of the group? (What were the variations on the themes?)
- Were there particular topics or issues raised that provoked intense discussion or passionate reaction from certain members of the group?
- Did the group discussion cause individuals to change their mind about an idea or position they originally held?

 Reflection 10.16

Do you think you will you have opportunities to form diverse discussion groups or learning teams? If yes, what types of diversity would you seek to include?

Internet-Based Resources

For additional information related to the ideas discussed in this chapter, consult the following websites:

Cross-cultural communication:
http://www.pbs.org/ampu/crosscult.html
Understanding Privilege:
https://msw.usc.edu/mswusc-blog/
diversity-workshop-guide-to-discussing-identity-power-and-privilege/
Combating stereotypes, prejudice, and discrimination:
www.tolerance.org
www.splcenter.org/
LGBTQ Acceptance and Support:
"It Gets Better Project," at www.itgetsbetter.org
Preservation of human rights worldwide:
www.amnesty.org/en/discrimination

Chapter 10 Exercises

10.1 Quote Reflections

Review the sidebar quotes contained in this chapter and select two that you found to be especially meaningful or inspirational.

For each quote you selected, provide an explanation of why you chose it.

10.2 Strategy Reflections

Review the practices suggested for *increasing personal contact and interpersonal interaction with members of diverse groups* on pp. 233–236. Select two that you think are most important and intend to put into practice.

10.3 Reality Bite

Hate Crime: A Racially Motivated Murder

Jasper County, Texas, has a population of approximately 31,000 people. In this county, 80% of the people are white, 18% are black, and 2% are of other races. The county's poverty rate is considerably higher than the national average, as its average household income. In 1998, the mayor, the president of the Chamber of Commerce, and two councilmen were black. From the outside, Jasper appeared to be a town with racial harmony, and its black and white leaders were quick to state that there was no racial tension in Jasper.

However, one evening in Jasper, James Byrd Jr.—a 49-year-old African American man—was walking home along a road and was offered a ride by three white males. Rather than taking Byrd home, Lawrence Brewer (age 31), John King (age 23), and Shawn Berry (age 23)—three men linked to white-supremacist groups—took Byrd to an isolated area and began beating him. They then dropped his pants to his ankles, painted his face black, chained Byrd to their truck, and dragged him for approximately three miles. The truck was driven in a zigzag fashion to inflict maximum pain on the victim. Byrd was decapitated after his body collided with a culvert in a ditch alongside the road. His skin, arms, genitalia, and other body parts were strewn along the road, and his torso was found dumped in front of a black cemetery. Medical examiners testified that Byrd was alive for much of the dragging incident.

When the three assailants were brought to trial, their bodies were covered with racist tattoos. As a result of the murder, Byrd's family created the James Byrd Foundation for Racial Healing. A wrought iron fence that separated black and white graves for more than 150 years in Jasper Cemetery was removed in a special unity service. Members of the racist Ku Klux Klan have since visited the gravesite of Byrd several times, leaving racist stickers and other marks that angered the Jasper community and Byrd's family.

Reflection Questions

1. What factors do you think were responsible for this incident?

2. Could this incident have been prevented? If yes, how? If no, why not?

3. How likely do you think an incident like this could take place in your hometown or in the community near your campus?

4. If this event happened to take place in your hometown, how do you think members of the community would react?

10.4 Reality Bite

Hate Crime: Homophobic Murder

In October 1998, Matthew Shepard—a 21-year-old University of Wyoming freshman— was fatally beaten a few hours after attending a planning of a Gay Awareness Week meeting on campus. Following the meeting, Matthew went to local bar where he met two individuals, Aaron James McKinney and Russell Henderson, who pretended to be gay and lured Matthew to their truck, where McKinney said: "Guess what, we're not gay. You're going to get jacked. It's Gay Awareness Week!" McKinney and Henderson began beating Shepard inside the truck and drove him to an isolated place in the countryside. They tied him to a fence and pistol whipped him with a handgun. The assailants then stole Shepard's wallet and shoes, tied him to a fence, and left him to die. Matthew Shepard died five days after the attack. An autopsy revealed that he had been hit in the head 18 times. He also sustained bruises on the back of his hands while trying to protect himself as well as bruises around his groin—indicating that he'd been kicked numerous times. After the incident, one of the assailants explained his actions to his girlfriend, by saying: "Well you know how I feel about gays."

Russell Henderson pleaded guilty and was sentenced to life in prison. McKinney was about to begin trial to determine whether he should be put to death, but Matthew Shepard's parents persuaded the prosecution not to pursue the death penalty and allow him to be sentenced to life in prison instead.

In October 2018—20 years after his slaying—a service and celebration of Matthew Shepard's life was conducted and attended by more than 2,000 people; many others watched online. The service was led by Gene Robinson—the first openly gay bishop of the Episcopal Church. For Shepard's family and friends, the 2018 service was their first opportunity to publicly celebrate Matthew's life because at the time of his 1998 slaying, anti-gay protesters disrupted his funeral service by confronting and screaming at the funeral-goers. The hostility at the first service was so intense, that Matthew's father was advised to wear a bulletproof vest under his suit.

Questions for Reflection and Discussion

1. Why or how do you think the attackers developed such an intense hatred of gay men?

2. What, if anything, could have been done to prevent the attackers' hatred toward gays from developing in the first place?

3. Do you think the attackers could ever be successfully rehabilitated, educated, or treated for their homophobia?

4. Would you say that homophobia and hatred of gays is currently decreasing or increasing? Why?

10.5 Gaining Awareness of Your Group Identities

An individual is likely to be a member of multiple groups at the same time and membership in these overlapping groups is likely to have a combined effect on that individual's development and personal identity. In the adjacent figure, consider the shaded center circle to be yourself and the six non-shaded circles to be six different groups of which you are a member. You can use the diversity spectrum on p. 210 to identify different group memberships that apply to you.

Fill in the non-shaded circles with the names of groups to which you belong that have had the most influence on your personal development and identity. Don't feel compelled to fill in all six circles; more important than filling in all the circles is identifying those groups to which you belong that have most influenced your life.

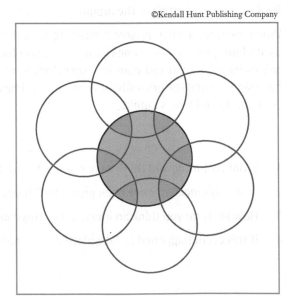

©Kendall Hunt Publishing Company

Self-Assessment Questions:

1. Which one of your groups has had the *greatest influence* on your development or identity? Why?

2. Have you ever felt *limited* or *disadvantaged* by being a member of any group(s) to which you belong? Why?

3. Have you experienced *advantages* or *privileges* as a result of being a member of any group(s) to which you belong? Why?

10.6 Intercultural Interview

1. Find a person on campus from a cultural group with which you've had little previous contact. Ask that person for an interview, and during the interview, ask the following questions.

   - What does "diversity" mean to you?

   - What prior experiences have affected your current viewpoints or attitudes about diversity?

   - What would you say have been the major influences and turning points in your life?

   - Who would are your role models, heroes, or sources of inspiration?

   - What societal or national contributions made by your cultural group are you most proud of and think should be acknowledged?

   - What is something that you hope will never again be said about your cultural group?

2. Answer the above questions as If you were the interviewee instead of the interviewer.

10.7 Hidden Bias Test

Go to www.tolerance.org/activity/test-yourself-hidden-bias and take one or more of the hidden bias tests on this website. These tests assess subtle or unconscious biases a person may have with respect to gender, age, ethnic minority groups, religious denominations, sexual orientations, disabilities, and body weight.

After completing the test, answer the following questions:

1. Do you think your results were accurate?

2. Did the results suggest that you had a bias of which you were unaware?

3. If your answer to the previous question was "yes," what do you think may have caused or contributed to this bias?

4. If your closest family member and best friend took the test, how do you think their results would compare with yours?

CHAPTER 11

Financial Literacy

MANAGING MONEY AND MINIMIZING DEBT

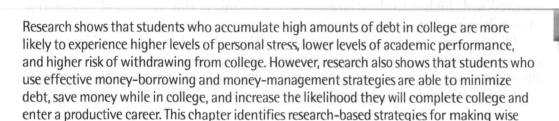

Research shows that students who accumulate high amounts of debt in college are more likely to experience higher levels of personal stress, lower levels of academic performance, and higher risk of withdrawing from college. However, research also shows that students who use effective money-borrowing and money-management strategies are able to minimize debt, save money while in college, and increase the likelihood they will complete college and enter a productive career. This chapter identifies research-based strategies for making wise decisions about student loans and managing debt, tracking personal income and expenses, and striking a healthy balance between working for grades and working for pay.

Chapter Purpose & Preview

Gain greater fiscal self-awareness and knowledge of effective strategies for managing money, financing your college education, and planning your financial future.

Learning Goal

Ignite Your Thinking

 Reflection 11.1

When it comes to managing money or financial planning, would you rate yourself as: good, adequate, or poor?

What would be one thing about your money-management or financial planning skills that you think needs the most improvement?

For many students, starting college marks the start of greater personal independence and greater responsibilities for financial self-management and fiscal planning. College students' ability to manage money is growing in importance for a number of reasons. One reason is that the rising cost of a college education has resulted in students working more hours while in college and trying to save enough money to pay for college. The higher cost of a college education also requires more difficult fiscal decisions about what options (or combination of options) to use to meet college expenses. Unfortunately, research indicates that many students today make decisions about financing their college education that are not most the effective way to promote their academic success and make steady progress to graduation.

Another reason why money management is growing in importance for college students is the availability and convenience of credit cards. It's never been easier to access, use, and abuse credit cards. Credit agencies and bureaus now closely monitor college students' credit card payments and routinely report their "credit score" to credit card companies and banks. There is a statistical relationship between using credit cards responsibly and being a responsible employee, so employers are checking a student's credit score and using it as an indicator or predictor of how responsible that student is likely to be as an employee. Thus, using credit irresponsibly while in college can affect a student's ability to land a job after (or during) college. In addition, students' credit scores affect their likelihood of qualifying for car and home loans as well as their ability to rent an apartment.

College graduates today can do everything right while they were in college, such as get good grades, get involved on campus, and get work experience before graduating, but a poor credit history while in college can harm them after college, reducing their opportunities to obtain future credit and their prospects for future employment. Furthermore, accumulating high levels of debt while in college is associated with higher levels of stress, lower academic performance, and greater risk of withdrawing from college.

On the positive side of the ledger, studies show that when college students learn to use effective money-management and financial-planning strategies (such as those discussed in this chapter), they can reduce unnecessary spending, minimize accumulation of debt, and lower their level of stress.

Sources of Income for Financing a College Education

College students' income typically comes from three sources:

- Loans that are to be repaid
- Scholarships or grants that are not repaid
- Salaries earned from part-time or full-time work

The *Free Application for Federal Student Aid (FAFSA)* is the application used by the US Department of Education to determine a student's financial aid eligibility. It asks for personal and family financial information to assess whether the student qualifies for federal, state, and college-sponsored financial aid, including grants, loans, and work-study employment. To make this assessment, the government uses a formula to calculate the student's *estimated family contribution (EFC)*—the amount of money the student's family should be able to contribute to the cost of the student's college education.

No fee is charged to complete the FAFSA application, so if you think you are eligible, or might be eligible for financial aid, you should complete an application. (See the Financial Aid Office on your campus for a copy of the FAFSA form and for help completing it.)

Student Loans

One financial aid option for footing the cost of college are student loans that need to be eventually repaid. Listed below are some of the more well-known, federally-funded student loan programs.

- *The Federal Perkins Loan:* a low-interest loan awarded to exceptionally needy students. Repayment of the loan begins nine months after a student is no longer enrolled in college at least half-time.
- *The Federal Subsidized Stafford Loan:* a loan available to students who are enrolled at least half-time that has a fixed interest rate established each year on July 1. The federal government pays the interest on the loan during the time that the student is enrolled in college. Repayment for this loan begins six months after a student is no longer enrolled at least half-time.

> "Anecdotes about former students struggling with large amounts of student debt and low earnings get a lot of press coverage [yet] we rarely hear about ways in which the student loan system increases opportunities for students."
>
> —Sandy Baum, research professor, George Washington University and a national expert in college education finance

- *The Federal Unsubsidized Stafford Loan:* a loan not based on need that has the same interest rate as the Federal Subsidized Stafford Loan. Students are responsible for paying the interest on this loan while they are enrolled in college.

Keep in mind that federal loans and private loans differ in two important ways:

- *Federal* loans have fixed interest rates that are comparatively low and cannot go higher.
- *Private* loans have variable interest rates that are very high (often more than twice that of federal loans) and can go higher at any time.

Despite the much higher interest rate of private loans, they're the fastest growing type of loans being used by college students—largely because of aggressive and sometimes misleading or unethical advertising on loan-shopping websites. Students sometimes think that they're getting a federal loan only to find out later that they've taken on a more expensive private loan.

Keep in mind that not all loans are created equal. Compared with private loans, federally guaranteed student loans are relatively low-cost and may be paid off slowly after graduation. On the other hand, private lenders of student loans are like credit-card companies; they charge extremely high interest rates (that can go even higher at any time) and the loans must be paid off quickly. Private loans should not be used as a primary loan to help pay for college and they should only be used as a last resort—when no other option is available for covering college expenses.

Also, keep in mind that federal and state regulations require that students receiving financial aid must maintain "satisfactory academic progress." In most cases this means that these students must:

1. Maintain a satisfactory grade point average (e.g., 2.0 or above) for all college courses they have taken, even if they have paid for some of these classes with their own resources.
2. Make satisfactory academic progress (e.g., 12 to 15 units per semester). Their academic progress will be evaluated at least once per year, usually at the end of the spring semester to determine if they have earned at least 67% of their attempted credits.
3. Complete a degree or certificate program within a certain period of time. (Check with your institution's Financial Aid Office for details.)

If you happen to find yourself temporarily short of funds and need just a small loan to stay enrolled, your college may offer an *emergency student loan program*, which provides students with an immediate, interest-free loan to help them cover short-term expenses (e.g., cost of textbooks) or deal with financial emergencies (e.g., accidents or illnesses). Emergency student loans are typically granted within 24–48 hours, sometimes even the same day, and usually need to be repaid within two months.

Scholarships

Typically, scholarships are awarded to students at the time they are admitted to college, but some scholarships may be awarded at a later point in the college experience. Scholarships tend to fall into two general categories:

- *Merit-based scholarships*—awarded on the basis of academic performance or achievement
- *Need-based scholarships*—awarded on the basis of financial need

> "Apply for as much grant aid as possible before borrowing, and then seek lower-interest federal student loans before tapping private ones. There is a lot of student aid that can help make the expense [of college] more manageable.
>
> —*Sandy Baum, senior policy analyst, College Board*

To see if there are merit-based or need-based scholarships that you may still be eligible to receive, check with your Financial Aid Office. Scholarships are also available from organizations other than your college. To find them, just conduct an Internet search using the term "college scholarships." Keep in mind that scholarships are very competitive and deadlines are strictly enforced.

Grants

Grants are considered to be "gift" aid because, unlike loans, they don't have to be repaid. Grants vary in amount, depending on such factors as: (a) the anticipated contribution of the family to the student's education (EFC), (b) the cost of the college or university the student is attending, and (c) the enrollment status of the student (part-time or full-time).

The Federal Pell Grant is the largest grant program; it provides need-based aid to low-income students. If you think you may be eligible, do not hesitate to contact the Financial Aid Office on your campus.

Veterans Benefits

If you are currently a veteran, you may be eligible for GI Bill benefits. The Montgomery GI Bill (MGIB) provides educational benefits for eligible veterans that include (but are not limited to) tuition and fees, housing allowance, and stipends for books or supplies. To receive these benefits, veterans need to maintain certain academic standards. For details, see if your campus has an office for veteran affairs, or consult the following website: http://www.benefits.va.gov/gibill/.

Salary Earnings

If you're relying on salary from off-campus work to pay for college tuition, check to see if the company that employs you offers tuition reimbursement. Also, check with the Student Accounts Office on your campus to see if your college offers tuition-payment plans that allow you to pay tuition on an installment schedule that aligns with the timing of your paychecks. Tuition-payment plans may also be available on your campus that allow you flexibility in terms of (a) the amount due per payment, (b) deadline for payments, and (c) how remaining debt owed to the institution is dealt with at the end of the term. (Keep in mind that you may not be allowed to register for the following term until tuition for the previous term has been completely paid.)

If possible, try to find work *on campus* rather than off campus. Research shows that students who work on campus are more likely to succeed in college. This is probably due to the fact that these students become more connected to the college and because on-campus employers are more flexible than off-campus employers in allowing them to work around their academic commitments. For instance, on-campus employers will arrange students' work schedule around their class schedule and allow students to reduce their work hours during midterms and finals. Thus, if at all possible, rather than working off campus, seek employment on campus.

Reflection 11.2

Circle any of the following financial resources that you're currently using to help pay for your college education: loans, grants, scholarships, salary earnings, savings, monetary support from parents or other family members, other resources (please identify).

Right now, do you think you have sufficient fiscal resources to complete college? If yes, why? If no, why not?

Developing Financial Self-Awareness

Developing any good habit begins with the critical first step of self-awareness. Developing effective money-management habits starts with self-awareness of your *cash flow*—the amount of money you have coming in and going out. As illustrated in **Figure 11.1**, cash flow is monitored by tracking:

- Income—the amount of money you have coming in versus the amount going out (expenses or expenditures)
- Savings—the amount of money you have earned and not spent (saved) versus the amount you have borrowed and haven't paid back (debt)

Once you're aware of the amount of money you have coming in (and from what sources) and the amount of money you're spending (and on what), you're positioned to develop a plan for managing your cash flow. The bottom line is simple: Ensure that the sum of money you have coming in (income) is equal to or greater than the sum of money going out (expenses). If the amount of money going out exceeds the amount coming in, you're "in the red" or have "negative cash flow."

FIGURE 11.1: The Two-Way Street of Cash Flow

Income ←——→ Expenses

Savings ←——→ Debt

©Kendall Hunt Publishing Company

"Never spend your money before you have it.

—*Thomas Jefferson, third president of the United States and founder of the University of Virginia*

Tracking Cash Flow

You can track your cash flow by using any of the following tools:

- Checking accounts
- Credit cards
- Charge cards
- Debit cards

Checking Accounts

Long before credit cards were created, a checking account was the method most people used to keep track of their money. Many people still use checking accounts in addition to (or instead of) credit cards. A checking account may be obtained from a bank or credit union; its typical costs include a deposit ($20–$25) to open the account, a monthly service fee (e.g., $10), and small fees for checks. Some banks charge customers a service fee based on the number of checks written; this is a good option if you do not plan to write many checks each month. Look for a checking account that doesn't charge you if your balance drops below a certain minimum figure. If you maintain a high enough *balance* (amount of money deposited in your account), the bank may not charge any extra fees; if you're able to maintain an even higher balance, some banks may also pay you interest—known as an interest-bearing checking account.

Along with your checking account, banks usually provide you with an automatic teller machine (ATM) card that you can use to get cash. Look for a checking account that offers free ATM service along with your checking account, rather than one that charges a separate fee for ATM transactions.

A checking account has several advantages:
- You can carry checks and use them instead of cash for some purchases.
- You have access to cash at almost any time through an ATM.
- You can keep a visible track record of your income and expenses in your checking account.
- If you manage a checking account responsibly, it can serve as a good credit reference for future loans and purchases.

To make the most effective use of a checking account, apply the following strategies:
- Whenever you write a check or make an ATM withdrawal, immediately subtract its amount from your *balance* (the amount of money remaining in your account) and determine your new balance.
- Keep a running balance in your checking account. This will ensure you always know exactly how much money you have in your account and your risk of *bouncing* a check—writing a check for an amount that exceeds the total amount you have in your account. (If you bounce a check, you'll probably have to pay a charge to the bank and possibly to the business that attempted to cash your bounced check.)
- Double-check the balance in your checking account after each monthly statement you receive from the bank. Be sure to include the service charges your bank makes to your account; these charges will appear on your monthly statement. Reviewing your checking account on a regular basis will enable you to catch errors that you or the bank may have made. (Banks can and do occasionally make mistakes.) Also, track your monthly statements to ensure the charges that appear on your account were not the result of identity theft. (For more information on identity theft, see **Box 11.1**, p. 249.)

Credit Cards

A credit card is basically a tool for getting money loaned to you by the company issuing the card, which must be paid back to the company on a monthly basis. You can pay the whole bill or a portion of the bill each month—as long as some minimum payment is made. However, for any remaining (unpaid) portion of your monthly bill, you are charged a high interest rate—which can be as much as 30%. Consequently, if you decide to use a credit card, be sure you're able to pay off your whole bill (loan) each month.

Also, pay attention to its *annual percentage rate (APR)*—the interest rate you must pay for previously unpaid monthly balances. This rate can vary from one credit card company to the next. Credit card companies also vary in terms of their annual service fee. You'll find that companies charging higher interest rates also charge lower annual fees, and vice versa. As a general rule, if you expect to pay the full balance every month, you're probably better off choosing a credit card that doesn't charge you an annual service fee. On the other hand, if you think you'll need more time to make the full monthly payments, you're probably better off with a credit card company that offers a low interest rate.

Credit card companies also differ from one another in terms of whether they allow a *grace period*—a period of time after you receive your monthly statement to pay back the company without paying additional interest fees. Some companies will allow you a grace period of a full month, while others may allow you any grace (forgiveness) period and begin charging interest immediately after they don't receive payment on the bill's due date.

Credit cards also differ in terms of their *credit limit* (also known as a "credit line" or "line of credit")—the maximum amount of money the credit card company will make available to you. If you're a new customer, most companies will set a credit limit beyond which no additional credit will be granted.

If used responsibly, a credit card has the following benefits:

- Because the credit card company sends you a monthly statement with an itemized list of all your card-related purchases, a credit-card account can be an effective and convenient way to track your spending habits. The itemized list of purchases included in your monthly statement supplies you with a "paper trail" of *what* you spent each month and *when* you spent it.
- A credit card allows you to make purchases online, which can save you time and money that would otherwise be spent traveling to and from stores.
- A credit card gives you access to cash whenever and wherever you need it. Any bank or ATM that displays your credit card's symbol will advance you cash up to a certain limit (usually for a small transaction fee). However, keep in mind that some credit card companies charge a higher interest rate for cash *advances* than credit card *purchases*.
- A credit card enables you to establish a personal credit record. If you use a credit card responsibly, you can establish a good credit history that can be used later in life for big ticket purchases—such as a car or home. A history of responsible credit-card use shows others from whom you wish to seek credit (or borrow money) that you will pay it back. However, don't buy into the common belief that the *only* way you can establish a good credit history is by using a credit card. It's not your only option; you can also establish a good credit history by responsible use of a checking account and by always paying your bills on time.

The advantages of a credit card are only gained only if the card is used strategically. If not, its advantages are quickly and greatly outweighed by its disadvantages. Listed below are some strategies for using a credit card in ways that maximize its advantages and minimize its potential disadvantages.

Do not use a credit card to obtain a long-term loan. The credit provided by a credit card should be seen simply as a short-term loan that must be paid back at the end of every month. Don't use credit cards for long-term credit or a long-term loan because their interest rates are outrageously high. Paying such an exorbitantly high rate of interest for a loan is an ineffective (and irresponsible) money-management practice.

Limit yourself to one credit card. Having more than one credit card means having more accounts to keep track of and more opportunities to accumulate debt. You don't need additional credit cards from department stores, gas stations, or any other profit-making business because they duplicate what your personal credit card already does (plus these other cards often charge very high interest rates for late payments).

Make sure you know the specific terms of the credit card agreement. Credit card companies vary in terms of what they charge you for not paying your full bill on time and what restrictions they will impose on your use of the card if you accumulate debt. Be sure to read the fine print on your contract; if you have any doubts or questions, contact a representative of the credit card company.

Pay off your credit-card balance each month *in full* and *on time*. If you pay the full amount of your bill each month, this means you're using your credit card effectively to obtain an interest-free, short-term (one-month) loan. It means that you're just paying the *principal*—the total amount of money borrowed and nothing more. However, if your payment is late and you end up paying *interest*, then you end up paying more for the items you purchased than their actual ticket price. For instance, if you have an unpaid balance of $500 on your monthly credit bill for merchandise purchased the previous month and you're charged the typical 18% credit card interest rate for late payment, you end up paying $590: $500 (merchandise) + $90 (18% interest to the credit card company).

Credit card companies make their profit by the interest they collect from cardholders who don't pay back their credit on time. Just as procrastinating about completing schoolwork is a poor time-management habit that can hurt students' grades, procrastinating about paying credit card bills is a poor money-management habit that can hurt students' pocketbook by forcing them to pay high interest rates.

Don't allow credit card companies to make profit at your expense. Pay your total balance on time and avoid paying exorbitantly high interest rates. If you cannot pay the total amount owed at the end of the month, don't just make the minimum monthly payment, pay as much as you possibly can. If you only make the minimum credit-card payment each month, you will gradually accumulate a huge amount of credit-card debt.

> *If you keep making charges on your credit card while you have an unpaid balance (debt), you no longer have a grace period to pay back your charges; instead, interest is charged immediately on all your purchases.*

 Reflection 11.3

If you have a credit card, do you pay off the entire balance each month? If you don't:

a) What's your average unpaid balance per month?

b) What changes could you make in your money-management habits that would enable you to pay off your entire balance each month?

Do you have more than one credit card? Why?

Charge Cards

A charge card works similar to a credit card in that you're given a short-term loan for one month; the only difference is that you must pay your bill in full at the end of each month and you cannot carry over any debt from one month to the next. Compared to a credit card, the major disadvantage of a charge card is that it has less flexibility—no matter what your expenses may be for a particular month, you must still pay up or lose your ability to obtain credit for the following month. However, the key advantage of charge card is that if you're someone who consistently has trouble paying your monthly credit-card bill on time, it will prevent you from accumulating debt.

Debit Cards

A debit card looks almost identical to a credit card (e.g., it has a *MasterCard* or *Visa* logo), but it works differently. When you use a debit card, money is immediately taken out of (subtracted from) your checking account. Like a check or ATM withdrawal, any purchase you make with a debit card is immediately subtracted from your balance. Thus, rather than borrowing money, you can only use money that's already in your account. At the end of the month, unlike a credit card, you don't receive a bill; instead, you get a statement with information about checks you deposited and cashed as well as your debit card transactions. If you attempt to purchase something with a debit card that costs more than the amount of money you have in your account, your card will not allow you to do so. Similar to a bounced check, a debit card will not permit you to pay out any money that's not in your account.

Like a credit card, a major advantage of a debit card is that it provides you with the convenience of plastic; however, unlike a credit card, it will not allow you to spend beyond your means and accumulate debt. For this reason, many financial advisors recommend to abusers of credit cards that they use a debit card instead of a credit card.

Box 11.1

Minimizing Risk of Identity Theft

Another key element of effective money management is being strategic about reducing the risk of financial loss due to identity theft. Identity thieves steal your personal information to make transactions or purchases in your name. This can damage your credit status and cost you time and money to restore your financial credibility. Listed below are key strategies for reducing your risk of identity theft.

- Don't share information about your personal identity over the phone, especially your social security or credit card number, with anyone you don't know or trust.
- Don't share identity information over the phone with anyone who claims to be an Internal Revenue Service (IRS) agent and threatens you with arrest or deportation, or who requests personal information for the purpose of sending you a refund. The IRS will contact you in writing if it needs anything.
- Don't respond to e-mails from anyone claiming to be from the IRS. This is always a scam because the IRS doesn't initiate contact with taxpayers by e-mail or social media to request personal or financial information. (The only legitimate communication you will receive from the IRS is through postal mail.)
- Don't click on links or open e-mail attachments from anyone unfamiliar to you. Scam artists create fake websites and send "phishing" e-mails that use the names of trustworthy electronic sources (e.g., an Internet service provider) to get personal information

from you, such as usernames, passwords, and credit card details.
- Don't enter your credit card or bank account information on any websites.
- Install firewalls and virus detection software on your computer to protect yourself from being a victim of "cybercrime."
- When using your laptop in public, shield your screen from "shoulder surfers."
- Don't carry your Social Security (SSN) card in your wallet or write it on your checks or emails. Only give out your SSN to people you know and trust.
- Conceal your personal identification number (PIN). Don't supply it to anyone and don't keep it in your wallet.
- Shred documents containing personal information you no longer need. (Some identity thieves are "dumpster divers" who go through garbage to get personal information.)
- Compare your receipts with your account statements and credit card statements to be sure there are no transactions you didn't authorize. If you have an online account, you can check your account at any time. It's a good idea to check your account regularly (e.g., on a weekly basis).
- If you believe you've been victimized by identity theft, contact your local police department and alert one of the following credit reporting companies:
  Equifax: 1-888-766-0008
  Experian: 1-888-397-3742
  TransUnion: 1-800-680-7289

Developing a Plan for Managing Money and Minimizing Debt

The ultimate goal of money management is to save money and steer clear of debt. Here are some strategies for accomplishing both of these goals.

Prepare a personal budget. A budget is simply a plan for coordinating income and expenses in a way that ensures you're left with sufficient money to cover your expenses. A budget enables you to be your own accountant and keep an accurate account of your expenses. Personal expenses for college students typically fall into three categories:

1. **Basic needs or essential necessities**—these are "fixed" expenses because you can't live without them—such as, expenditures for food, housing, tuition, textbooks, phone, transportation to and from school, and health-related costs
2. **Incidentals or extras**—these are "flexible" expenses that are optional or discretionary—you choose whether or not to purchase them. These expenditures include:
    * money spent on entertainment, enjoyment, or pleasure (e.g., music, movies, and vacations)
    * money spent on promoting personal status or self-image (e.g., buying the latest gadgets, brand name products, fashionable clothes, jewelry, and other personal accessories)
3. **Emergency expenses**—unforeseen or unexpected expenditures (e.g., money spent to cover unanticipated car repairs or medical services)

> **Reflection 11.4**
>
> What are your most expensive incidentals (optional purchases)?
>
> What could you do to reduce some of these expenses?

Similar to managing time effectively, the first step to managing money effectively is identifying your priorities. First, determine your most important expenses—the indispensable necessities you can't live without and separate them from incidentals—dispensable luxuries you can live without or that can be purchased at a later time. People often confuse *essentials* (things they really *need* or must have) with *desirables* (stuff they just *want* or like to have). For instance, some people will see a piece of merchandise on sale that's desirable to purchase because it's such a great deal and immediately buy it, even though it's not an essential purchase—they don't really need it or don't need it at that time.

> *Remaining aware of the distinction between essentials that need to be purchased and incidentals that are desirable (but not essential) to purchase is an important first step toward money management.*

It's clearly logical that postponing short-term material satisfaction contributes to long-term financial success. Unfortunately, however, research shows that humans are often more motivated by short-term rewards that provide immediate gratification. One simple reason why so many people pile up so much debt is because the short-term satisfaction of an immediate purchase trumps the delayed gratification of long-term saving.

We need to offset *impulsive* spending on what we want with *reflective* thinking about what we need. The truth is that humans spend money for a host of psychological reasons (conscious or subconscious) that has nothing to do with meeting their basic needs. For instance, research reveals that people buy things for themselves to: (a) build up (or restore) their self-esteem or self-image, (b) because they're bored, or (c) because shopping gives them an emotional rush or "high." For others, spending is an addiction: they do it because they're obsessed with shopping and do it compulsively. It was this type of addiction that led to the creation of Debtors Anonymous (DA)—a self-help group for compulsive spenders or "shopaholics" that employs a 12-step recovery program similar to that used by Alcoholics Anonymous (AA).

> "I need to save money and not shop so much and impulse buy.
> —*First-year student*

> What you're willing to sacrifice and save for, and what you're willing to spend on and go into debt for, says a lot about who you are and what you value.

Make all your bills visible and, if possible, pay them as soon as you see (get) them. What's in our sight stays on our mind. If we keep our bills in sight, we're less likely to forget about paying them, or forget to pay them on time. If you have the money needed to pay a bill when you first receive it and see it, pay it then and there, rather than setting it aside and running the risk of forgetting to pay it (or losing it altogether).

You can increase the visibility of your bills and their due dates by posting a financial calendar in full view on which you record all fiscal deadlines related to college (e.g., due dates for tuition payments and financial aid applications). Also, consider setting up an online banking program that will enable you to visually track your transactions and make credit card payments automatically. The advantage of an online account is that it's paperless and you don't have to deal with bills sent to you through postal mail. Its disadvantage, however, is that the bills don't appear in tangible form in your mailbox, thus you don't get a visual reminder to pay them. So, if you set up an online account, be sure to get into the habit of checking it regularly. Otherwise, bills that stay out of your sight may stay out of your mind and not get paid on time.

Live within your means. Simply stated: we shouldn't buy what we can't afford. If we're spending more money than we're taking in, it means we're living *beyond* our means. To begin living *within* our means, we have two options: (a) decrease our expenses (reduce our spending) or (b) increase our income (earn more money).

Most college students work while attending college and work so many hours that it interferes with their academic performance and educational progress. For college students who find themselves in debt, their best option is not to work more hours for more spending money but to reduce spending on nonessentials and begin living within their means.

> "We choose to spend more money than we have today. Choose debt, or choose freedom, it's your choice.
> —Bill Pratt, in *Extra Credit: The 7 Things Every College Student Needs to Know About Credit, Debt & Cash*

AUTHOR'S EXPERIENCE

When I was a 4-year-old boy living in the mountains of Kentucky, it was safe for a young lad to walk the roads and railroad tracks alone. Knowing this, my mother would send me on long walks to the general store to buy a variety of small items we needed for our household. Since we had very little money, she was very aware that money should be spent money only on the most basic necessities. I could only buy items from the general store that my mother strictly ordered me to purchase. In the early 1960s, most of these items cost less than a dollar and many times you could buy multiple items for a dollar. At the store's checkout counter, there were jars with different kinds of candy or gum. Since you could buy two pieces for one cent, I didn't think there would be any harm in rewarding myself for completing my shopping errand with just two pieces of candy. I could even devour the evidence of my disobedience on my slow walk home. When I returned home from the store, my mother—being the protector of the vault and the sergeant-of-arms in our household—would count each item I bought to make sure I had been charged correctly. She never failed to notice if the total was off by a single cent. After discovering that I had spent an extra cent on something unessential, she scolded me and said in no uncertain terms: "Boy, you better learn how to count your money if you're ever going to be successful in life!" Needless to say, I learned the value of living within my means at a very early age.

—Aaron Thompson

 Reflection 11.5

1. Are you working while attending college?

2. If you are:

   a) How many hours per week do you currently work?

   b) Do you think that the number of hours you're working is interfering with your academic performance or educational progress?

   c) Are you working for things you need or for things you want?

Economize. Intelligent consumers use critical thinking skills when making purchases. For example, they don't pay more for brand name products that are exactly the same as less expensive products. Why pay 33% more for Advil or Tylenol when the very same pain-relieving ingredient (ibuprofen or acetaminophen) is found in a less-expense generic brand? People can be thrifty without compromising the quality or effectiveness of the products they use. When we buy a brand name product, what we're often paying for is all the advertising that the company making the product pays the media and celebrities to promote the product and give it a brand (familiar) "name."

> *Advertising increases product familiarity, not product quality. The more money manufacturers pay for advertising to create a well-known brand name, the more money we pay for the product with that name.*

Downsize. Cut down or cut out spending for products you don't need. Avoid conspicuous consumption or exhibitionistic (look-at-me) spending just to keep up with (or show off to) others. We shouldn't allow peer pressure to determine our spending habits; instead, our consumer decisions should reflect our ability to think critically, not our desire to conform socially.

Save money by living with others rather than living alone. You lose some privacy when you share living quarters, but you also save a substantial amount of money. If you can find roommates or housemates with whom you're compatible and whose company you enjoy, living with them will have both fiscal and social benefits.

"It is preoccupation with possessions, more than anything else, that prevents us from living freely and nobly.
—*Bertrand Russell, British philosopher and mathematician*

Give gifts of time instead of money. Spending money on gifts for family, friends, and romantic partners isn't the only way to show love or affection. The point of gift giving isn't to show others that you have money or aren't cheap, but to show that you care. You can demonstrate this by making or doing something nice for those you care about. Compared with store-bought gifts, gifts of time and kindness are not only more economical, they're often more personal and special—as illustrated in the story below.

AUTHOR'S EXPERIENCE

When my wife (Mary) and I were first dating, I was trying to gain weight because I was on the thin side. One day when I came home from school, I found this hand-delivered package in front of my apartment door. I opened it up and there was a homemade loaf of whole-wheat bread made from scratch by Mary. That gift didn't cost her much money, but she took the time to do it and she remembered to do something that was important to me (gaining weight). That gift really touched me; it's a gift I've never forgotten. Since I eventually married her and we're still happily married, I guess I could say that inexpensive loaf of bread was a "gift that kept on giving."

—*Joe Cuseo*

Develop your own money-saving strategies and habits. Doing things on daily basis to save a little money can add up to saving a lot of money in the long run. The following money-saving strategies were shared by students in a first-year experience course. Some of these strategies may work for you as well.

- Don't carry a lot of extra money in your wallet. (It's just like food; if it's easy to get to, you're more likely to eat it up.)
- Shop with a list—get in, get just what you need, and get out before you spend money on anything else.
- Put all your extra change in a jar.
- Put extra cash in a piggy bank that requires you to smash the piggy to get at it.
- Seal your savings in an envelope.
- When you get extra money, get it immediately into the bank (and out of your hands).
- Bring (don't buy) your lunch.
- Take full advantage of your meal plan—you've already paid for it, so don't pay twice for your meals by buying food elsewhere.
- Use e-mail instead of the phone.
- Hide your credit card or put it in the freezer so that you don't use it on impulse.
- Use cash (instead of credit cards) because you can easily set aside a certain amount of it for yourself each week and can clearly see how much of it you have at the start of a week and how much you have left at any point during the week.

"If you would be wealthy, think of saving as well as getting.
—Benjamin Franklin, 18th-century inventor, newspaper writer, and cosigner of the *Declaration of Independence*

Reflection 11.6

Do you use any of the money-saving strategies mentioned on the above list?

Have you found any money-saving strategies of your own that could be added to the above list?

AUTHOR'S EXPERIENCE

There is a large jug in my house that my husband and I use to collect change we receive from our cash purchases. When we shop, we sometimes pay in cash just to get the change in coins to put in our jug. For example, if a bill comes to $3.02, I will pay the cashier $4.00 and deposit the 98 cents into the jug when I get home. Over time, our jug really fills up! By each of us adding a dollar a week to the jar, we can save over $200 a year, which is cash that certainly comes in handy.

—*Michelle Campagna*

When making a purchase, consider not only the initial cost, but also the long-term cost. Short-term thinking leads to poor long-term money management and financial planning. Short-term (e.g., monthly) installment plans that businesses offer to entice you to buy expensive products make the initial purchase of those products appear attractively affordable. However, when you factor in the interest rates you pay on monthly installment plans, plus the length of time (number of months) you're making installment payments, you get a more accurate picture of the product's total cost. Taking this long-range perspective on potential purchases can keep you aware of the reality that a product's sticker price often represents a partial short-term cost; its total long-term cost is the true indicator of its affordability.

Furthermore, the total long-term cost for purchases sometimes involves additional "hidden costs" that that are not included in the product's initial price but must be paid in order for you to continue using the product. For example, the sticker price paid for clothes doesn't include the hidden, long-term costs of having those clothes dry-cleaned. By just taking just a moment to check the inside label on a clothing item, you can save yourself this hidden, long-term cost by purchasing clothes that are machine washable. Similarly, deciding to buy a new car instead of a used car brings with it not only the cost of a higher sticker price, but also the higher hidden costs of licensing and insuring the new car (plus any interest fees that must be paid if the new car was purchased on an installment plan). When you add in these hidden, long-term payments to a new car's total cost, buying a good used car is clearly a much more effective money-management strategy.

Long-Range Fiscal Planning: Financing Your College Education

Thus far, this chapter has focused primarily on short-range and mid-range financial planning strategies. We turn now to long-term strategies for financing your entire college education. Although there's no "one-size-fits-all" method for handling the cost of college, research suggests that the following strategies are usually the most effective.

Go to college full-time and limit part-time work to no more than 15-20 hours a week. Studies show that paying for college by obtaining a student loan and working no more than 15-20 hours per week is a long-range financial strategy that works best for the vast majority of students. Students who use this strategy are more likely to graduate from college, graduate in a more timely manner, and graduate with higher grades than students who go to college full-time and work part-time for more than 15-20 hours per week, or students who work full-time and go to college part-time.

Unfortunately, less than 10% of first-year students use the most effective college-financing strategy, which is to borrow money in the form of a student loan, attend college full-time, and work part time for 20 or fewer hours a week. Instead, almost 50% of first-year students choose a strategy that research indicates is the *least* likely to be associated with college success: borrowing nothing and trying to work as much as 30 hours a week. Students who use this strategy earn poorer grades because they underestimate the amount of time that college students need to spend on academic work outside of class. As a result, some of these students switch from being a full-time to a part-time student, which delays their time to graduation and increases their risk of not graduating at all.

Students who decide to finance their college education by working full-time and attending college part-time believe it will be less expensive in the long run because they can avoid or minimize student loans. However, research indicates that when students use this strategy, it lengthens their time to college completion and increases their risk of not even completing college. Studies also show that students who are most likely to default on their loan are students who take out the smallest loan amount; these students try to work full-time while attending college to minimize their loans, but end up dropping out before earning a degree that would enable them to pay back their loans. Even if these full-time working students manage to complete a college degree, it takes them longer to do so, which costs them more money in the long run because the hourly pay that students earn from the part-time jobs they hold while attending college is less than half what they would earn in full-time positions after college graduation. Thus, the longer it takes students to graduate from college, the longer they must wait to enter higher-paying, full-time positions that require a college degree. This delays their opportunity to "cash in" on the monetary benefits of a college diploma.

> *The bottom line: Going to college full-time and working part-time for no more than 15-20 hours per week is the best way to balance earning grades with earning money.*

You may have heard the expression: "Time is money." One way to interpret this expression is that the more money we spend, the more time we need to spend making money. College students who spend more time earning money to pay for material things that they want but don't need, end up spending less time studying, complete fewer classes, and earn lower grades. You can avoid this negative cycle by viewing academic work as work that "pays" you in terms of earned credits and higher grades. By putting in more academic time to earn more course credits and graduate in less time, you're paid back by earning a college degree sooner and earning sooner the full-time salary of a college graduate—which will pay you about twice as much per hour than part-time work done without a college degree (plus additional "fringe benefits" such as health insurance and paid vacation time). Furthermore, the time you put into earning higher college grades will likely earn you a higher starting salary in your first full-time position after college. Research shows that for students graduating with the same major, those with higher grades earn higher starting salaries.

"People don't realize how much work it is to stay in college. It's its own job in itself, plus if you've got another job you go to, too. I mean, it's just a lot.
—First-generation college student

"If a man empties his purse into his head, no one can take it away from him. An investment in knowledge always pays the best interest."
—*Benjamin Franklin, 18th-century scientist, inventor, and a founding father of the United States*

Reflection 11.7

Do you need to work part-time to meet your college expenses?

If you answered "yes" to the above question, are you working more than 15 hours per week?

If you answered "yes" to the above question, are you working these many hours because you *have* to, or because you *want* to?

If you need loans to finance your college education, rely on federally-funded student loans and avoid credit-card loans. Studies show that two out of three college students have at least one credit card and nearly one-half of students with credit cards have an average balance of more than $2,000 per month. A debt level this high is likely to force many students into working more than 15 hours a week to pay it off. (As the saying goes, "I owe, I owe, so off to work I go.") To pay off their credit card debt, students often end up taking fewer courses per term so they can work more hours, which results in taking longer to complete a college degree and to start earning the salary of a college graduate.

Instead of paying almost 20% interest to credit card companies for their monthly debt, these students would be better off obtaining a student loan with a much lower interest rate that they don't have to begin paying back until six months after graduation—when they will be college graduates making more money in full-time positions. Despite this clear advantage of student loans compared to credit card loans, studies show that only about 25% of college students with credit cards take out student loans.

> *Student loans are provided by the American government with the intention of helping its citizens become better educated. In contrast, for-profit businesses (such as credit card companies) lend students money with the intention of helping themselves make money—from the high rates of interest they collect from students who fail to pay off their debt in full at the end of each month.*

Keep in mind that not all debt is bad. Debt can be good if it represents an investment in something that will *appreciate*—gain in value over time and eventually turn into profit for the investor. Purchasing a college education on credit is a good investment because it's an investment in your future that appreciates in the form of higher income and benefits accumulated over the course of your life. One study estimates that, on average, the fiscal benefits of a college degree are equivalent to an investment that returns 15.2% per year—which is more than twice the average return from stock market investments and more than five times the average returns on investments in bonds, gold, or home ownership.

The long-term fiscal rewards reaped from a college degree clearly offset and outweigh the debt initially taken on by investing in a college education. In contrast, purchasing a new car is a poor long-term investment because that investment begins to *depreciate* or lose monetary value immediately after it's purchased. The instant you drive that new car off the dealer's lot, you become the proud owner of a used car that's worth much less than what you just paid for and will continue to lose monetary value over time.

> " Unlike a car that depreciates in value each year that you drive it, an investment in education yields monetary, social, and intellectual profit. A car is more tangible in the short term, but an investment in education (even if it means borrowing money) gives you more bang for the buck in the long run."
>
> —Eric Tyson, financial counselor and national best-selling author of *Personal Finance for Dummies*

Box 11.2

Financial Literacy: Understanding the Language of Money Management

As you can tell from the number of financial terms used in this chapter, there's an entire language that must be learned to be *financially literate*. As you read the financial terms listed below, place a checkmark next to any term you didn't know.

Account. A formal business arrangement in which a bank provides financial services to a customer (e.g., checking account or savings account).

Annual Fee. Yearly fee paid a credit-card holder pays to a company to cover the cost of maintaining an account.

Annual Percentage Rate (APR). Interest rate that must be paid when monthly credit card balances aren't paid in full.

Balance. Amount of money in a person's account, or the amount of unpaid debt the person owes.

Bounced Check. A check written for a greater amount of money than the amount contained in a personal checking account, which often requires the account holder to pay a charge to the bank and possibly to the business that attempted to cash the bounced check.

Budget. A plan for balancing income and expenses to ensure that sufficient money is available to cover personal expenses.

Cash Flow. Amount of money flowing in (income) and flowing out (expenses); "negative cash flow" occurs when the amount of money going out exceeds the amount coming in.

Credit. Money obtained with the understanding that it will be paid back.

Credit History. Record of how timely and completely a person has paid off credit in the past.

Credit Line (a.k.a. Credit Limit). The maximum amount of money (credit) made available to a borrower.

Credit Score. Measure used by credit card companies to determine if someone applying for a credit card is "credit worthy" (likely to repay). An applicant with a low credit score may be denied credit.

Debt. Amount of money owed.

Default. Failure to meet a financial obligation (e.g., a student who fails to repay a college loan "defaults" on that loan).

Emergency Student Loan. An immediate, interest-free loan provided by a college or university to help financially strapped students cover short-term expenses (e.g., cost of textbooks) or deal with financial emergencies (e.g., accidents and illnesses). Emergency student loans are typically granted within 24–48 hours (sometimes even the same day) and usually need to be repaid within two months.

Deferred Student Payment Plan. A plan that allows student borrowers to temporarily defer or postpone loan payments for an acceptable reason (e.g., to pursue an internship or do volunteer work after college).

Estimated Family Contribution (EFC). Amount of money the government determines a family can contribute to the educational costs of a family member who wants to enroll in college.

Fixed Interest Rate. A loan with an interest rate that remains the same for the entire term of the loan.

Free Application for Federal Student Aid (FAFSA). Free application that asks a student for personal and family financial information to determine eligibility for federal, state, and college-sponsored financial aid, including grants, loans, and work-study employment.

Grace Period. Amount of time given to a credit-card holder to pay back the company without paying added interest fees.

Grant. Financial aid received that doesn't have to be repaid.

Gross Income. Income generated before taxes and other expenses are deducted.

Identity Theft. A crime committed by stealing stealing another person's identity information, assuming that person's identity, and using that stolen identity to make financial transactions.

Insurance Premium. Amount of money paid in regular installments to an insurance company to remain insured.

Interest. Amount of money paid to a customer for deposited money (as in a bank account) or paid by a customer for borrowed money (e.g., interest on a loan). Interest is usually calculated as a percentage of the total amount of money deposited or borrowed.

Interest-Bearing Account. A bank account that earns interest if the customer keeps a minimum amount of money in the bank.

continued...

Loan Consolidation. Consolidating (combining) separate smaller student loans into a single larger loan to make the process of tracking and repaying the loan easier. Loan consolidation typically requires the borrower to pay slightly more interest.

Loan Premium. The amount of money loaned without interest.

Merit-Based Scholarship. Money awarded to a student on the basis of performance or achievement, which does not have to be repaid.

Need-Based Scholarship. Money awarded to a student on the basis of financial need, which does not have to be repaid.

Net Income. Money earned after all expenses and taxes have been paid.

Principal. Total amount of money borrowed or deposited, not counting interest.

Variable Interest Rate. An interest rate on a loan that can vary (go up or down) over the term of the loan.

Work Study. A program funded by the federal government that enables college students to earn money while working on campus.

Yield. Amount of revenue gained that exceeds the amount invested or paid. (For example, amount of revenue gained by college graduates through higher lifetime salaries and benefits that exceeds the amount of money invested in a college education.)

 Reflection 11.8

Which terms in **Box 11.2** were you not familiar with?

Which of these unfamiliar terms apply to your current financial decisions or money management plans?

Internet-Based Resources

For additional information on fiscal literacy, money management, and financial planning, see the following websites.

Fiscal Literacy and Money Management:
www.360financialliteracy.org
www.cashcourse.org

Financial Aid and Federal Funding Sources for a College Education:
https://studentloans.gov/myDirectLoan/index.action

Student Loan Management Strategies:
https://studentloans.citizensone.com/ERL?WT.mc_id=Merkle-GoogleSEM-_-Group4-8_Y_NB_General

Chapter 11 Exercises

11.1 Quote Reflections

Review the sidebar quotes contained in this chapter and select two that you found to be especially meaningful or inspirational.

For each quote you selected, provide an explanation why you chose it.

11.2 Strategy Reflections

Review the practices suggested for *developing a plan for managing money and minimizing debt* on pp. 250–254. Select three that you think are most important and intend to put into practice.

11.3 Reality Bite

Problems Paying for College

A college student once posted the following message on the Internet:

"I went to college for one semester, failed some of my classes, and ended with $900 in student loans. Now I can't even get financial aid or a loan because of some stupid thing that says if you fail a certain amount of classes you can't get aid or a loan. And now since I couldn't go to college this semester they want me to pay for my loans already, and I don't even have a job."

Any suggestions?

Reflection and Discussion Questions

1. What would you suggest this student do right away and in the future?

2. What should the student have done to prevent this from happening in the first place?

3. Do you know of any students who are in a similar predicament or soon could be? What would you recommend they do?

11.4 Connecting Financial and Career Goals

1. Using the AchieveWORKS Careers Summary, review your saved careers and the potential earnings associated with your career interest(s).

2. For the career(s) that interest you:

    a) Are the earnings what you expected?

    b) Would you be satisfied with these salaries? If not, would this information cause you to reconsider your career interests? What other related careers might allow you to earn the salary you desire?

11.5 Self-Assessment of Financial Attitudes and Habits

Answer the following questions about yourself as accurately and honestly as possible.

	Agree	Disagree
1. I pay my rent or mortgage on time each month.	_____	_____
2. I avoid maxing out or going over the limit on my credit cards.	_____	_____
3. I balance my checking account each month.	_____	_____
4. I set aside money each month for savings.	_____	_____
5. I pay my phone and utility bills on time each month.	_____	_____
6. I pay my credit card bills in full each month to avoid interest charges.	_____	_____
7. I believe it's important to buy the things I want when I want them.	_____	_____
8. Borrowing money to pay for college is a smart thing to do.	_____	_____
9. I have a monthly or weekly budget that I follow faithfully.	_____	_____
10. The thing I enjoy most about making money is spending money.	_____	_____
11. I limit myself to one credit card.	_____	_____
12. Getting a degree will get me a good job and a good income.	_____	_____

Give yourself one point for each item you marked "agree"—except for items 7, 9, and 10—for these items, give yourself a point if you marked "disagree."

A perfect score on this short survey would be 12.

Reflection Questions

1. What was your total score?

2. Which items lowered your score?

3. Do you detect any pattern across the items that lowered your score?

4. What's one thing you could do to improve your score on this test?

11.6 Financial Self-Awareness: Monitoring Money and Tracking Cash Flow

Step 1. Use the "Financial Self-Awareness" worksheet below to *estimate* your income and expenses per month, and enter them in column 2.

Step 2. Track your *actual* income and expenses for a month and enter them in column 3. To do this accurately, save your cash receipts, bills paid, and credit card or checking account records for one month.

Step 3. After a month of tracking your cash flow, answer the following questions.

a) Were your estimates generally accurate?

b) Where were there the largest discrepancies between your estimated cost and actual cost?

c) Comparing your bottom-line total for monthly expenses with your monthly income. Are you satisfied with your monthly cash flow?

d) What changes could you make to create more positive cash flow (to increase your income or savings and reduce your expenses or debt)?

e) How likely is it that you will make the changes you mentioned in the previous question?

	Estimate	Actual
Income Sources		
Parents/Family		
Work/Job		
Grants/Scholarships		
Loans		
Savings		
Other:		
TOTAL INCOME		
Essentials (*Fixed* Expenses)		
Living Expenses:		
Food/Groceries		
Rent/Room and Board		
Utilities (gas/electric)		
Clothing		
Laundry/Dry Cleaning		
Phone		
Computer		
Household Items (dishes, etc.)		
Medical Insurance Expenses		
Debt Payments (loans/credit cards)		
Other:		
School Expenses:		
Tuition		
Books		
Supplies (print cartridges, etc.)		
Special Fees (lab fees, etc.)		
Other:		
Transportation:		
Public Transportation (bus fees, etc.)		
Car Insurance		
Car Maintenance		
Fuel (gas)		
Car Payments		
Other:		
Incidentals (*Variable* Expenses)		
Entertainment:		
Movies/Concerts		
DVDs/CDs		
Restaurants (eating out)		
Other:		

	Estimate	Actual
Personal Appearance/Accessories:		
Hairstyling/Coloring		
Cosmetics/Manicures		
Fashionable Clothes		
Jewelry		
Other:		
Hobbies:		
Travel (trips home, vacations)		
Gifts		
Other:		
TOTAL EXPENSES		

Physical Wellness

MAINTAINING BODILY HEALTH AND ATTAINING PEAK PERFORMANCE

Achieving peak levels of performance, including academic performance, cannot be attained until physical wellness is maintained, which involves being mindful of what we put into our body (healthy food), what we keep out of it (unhealthy substances), how we move it (regular exercise), and how well we restore and rejuvenate it (quality sleep). This chapter identifies strategies for attaining optimal physical wellness by (a) maintaining a balanced, performance-enhancing diet, (b) getting high-quality sleep, (c) exercising for total fitness, and (d) avoiding risky behaviors that undermine personal health, threaten physical safety, and impair human performance.

Chapter Purpose & Preview

Acquire strategies for enhancing physical wellness to promote peak personal performance during the first year of college, throughout the college experience, and in life beyond college.

Learning Goal

Ignite Your Thinking

 Reflection 12.1

What would you say are the three most important things that students should do to preserve their health and promote peak performance?

1.

2.

3.

What is Wellness?

Wellness may be defined as a high-quality state of health in which risk of illness is minimized and the quality of personal performance is maximized. During any major life transition, such as the transition to college, unhealthy habits add to a person's level of transitional stress. In contrast, engaging in healthy habits reduces stress at all stages of life—especially during stages of transition.

There is still some debate among scholars about the key components of total wellness. However, the following dimensions of holistic (whole person) development are commonly cited as key elements of the "wellness wheel."

"Wellness is an integrated method of functioning, which is oriented toward maximizing the potential of the individual.

—H. Joseph Dunn, originator of the term, "wellness"

263

1. *Physical* Wellness: adopting a healthy lifestyle (e.g., balanced diet and regular exercise) and avoiding health-threatening habits (e.g., smoking and drug abuse).
2. *Intellectual* Wellness: openness to new ideas, learning from new experiences, and willingness to continue learning throughout life.
3. *Emotional* Wellness: awareness of personal feelings, effectively expressing feelings, and handling stress constructively.
4. *Social* Wellness: interacting harmoniously with others and maintaining healthy relationships with family, friends, and romantic partners.
5. *Occupational (Vocational)* Wellness: finding personal fulfillment in a job or career and having positive, productive experiences with employers and coworkers.
6. *Environmental* Wellness: preserving the ecological health of the planet that humans depend on to maintain their own health (i.e., the quality of the earth's air, land, and water).
7. *Spiritual* Wellness: finding meaning, purpose, and peace in life.

Physical Wellness

The physical component of wellness is the primary focus of this chapter. It could be said that physical health is a precondition or prerequisite that enables all other elements of wellness can be experienced. It's hard to grow intellectually and emotionally if you're not well physically, and it's hard to become wealthy and wise without first being healthy. Wellness starts with, but goes beyond, maintaining physical health to attain a higher quality of life that includes increased vitality (energy and vigor), longevity (longer life span), and life satisfaction (personal happiness).

Promoting physical wellness involves more than reacting to and treating illness or disease after it occurs. It includes engaging in health-promoting behaviors that proactively prevent illness from happening in the first place. Wellness puts into practice two classic proverbs: "Prevention is the best medicine" and "An ounce of prevention is worth a pound of cure."

As depicted in **Figure 12.1**, there are three key points along a timeline for preventing illness, preserving health, and promoting peak performance; they range from reactive (after illness) to proactive (before illness).

> Buono salute é la veraricche-
> zza" ("Good health is true
> wealth.")
> —*Italian proverb*

> Health is a state of complete
> well-being, and not merely
> the absence of disease or
> infirmity."
> —*World Health Organization*

FIGURE 12.1: Key Timeline for Preventing Illness, Preserving Health, and Promoting Peak Performance

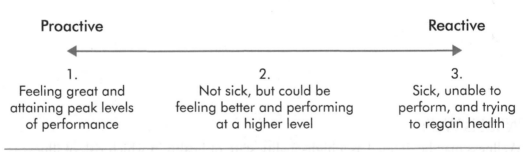

Proactive		Reactive
1.	2.	3.
Feeling great and attaining peak levels of performance	Not sick, but could be feeling better and performing at a higher level	Sick, unable to perform, and trying to regain health

©Kendall Hunt Publishing Company

**Reflection 12.2**

If you could single out one thing about your physical health right now that you'd like to improve or learn more about, what would it be?

A healthy physical lifestyle includes three key elements:

1. Supplying our body with effective fuel (nutrition) to generate energy
2. Resting our body (sleep) so it can recover and replenish the energy it has expended
3. Avoiding risky behaviors that can threaten our bodily health and safety

Reflection 12.3

Have your eating habits changed since you've begun college? If yes, in what way(s)?

Nutrition Management Strategies

In addition to eating for taste and convenience, we should "eat to win" by intentionally consuming foods that promote optimal health and peak performance. Unfortunately, national surveys reveal that less than 40% of college students report having a healthy diet; additional studies confirm these survey findings, indicating that college students' diets include too much fat and too little fruits and vegetables. To maintain wellness and maximize performance in college, students need to eat in a more thoughtful, nutritionally conscious way. The following nutrition-management strategies can be used as guidelines for eating in a way that preserves health and promotes peak performance.

Follow a dietary plan that supplies nutritional variety and balance. Doing just a little advanced planning about the foods we're going to eat can prevent us from falling into the mindless habit of just grabbing what's available, quick, and convenient—such as "fast food" and pre-packaged or processed food—which are the least healthy eating options.

Because different foods contain different types of nutrients (carbohydrates, protein, and fat) and in different amounts, no single food group can supply all the nutrients we need. Thus, consuming a balanced blend of different food groups is the best way to ensure that the human body functions at maximum capacity. Figure **12.2** depicts the American Dietetic Association's *MyPlate* chart, an updated version of what was formerly called the "Food Guide Pyramid." To find the daily amount of food from each of the major food groups that should be consumed for your age and gender, see either of the following websites: *www.ChooseMyPlate* or https://www.cnpp.usda.gov/2015-2020-dietary-guidelines-americans. You can use the guidelines supplied at these sites to develop and follow a personal nutritional plan that ensures you consume each of these key food groups on a consistent basis.

"Tell me what you eat and I'll tell you what you are.
—*Anthelme Brillat-Savarin, French gastronomist*

"If we are what we eat, then I'm cheap, fast, and easy.
—*Steven Wright, award-winning comedian*

FIGURE 12.2: MyPlate

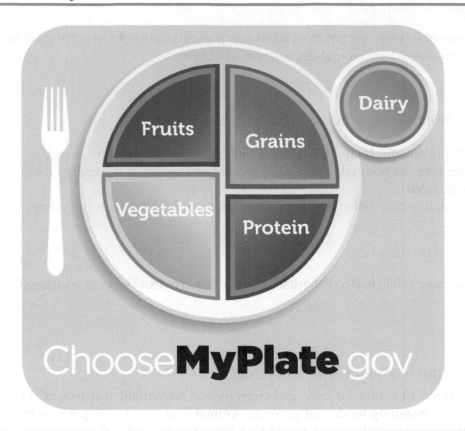

Source: USDA

Another effective nutrition-management strategy is to "eat the rainbow"—consume a variety of colorful fruits and vegetables. This is a simple but surefire way to get an ample number of vitamins, minerals, and disease-fighting nutrients. The external color of fruits and vegetables provides clues to the specific nutrients found within them. Fruits and vegetables that are:

- Orange and Yellow (e.g., carrots, squash, melons) contain high amounts of vitamins A and C as well as nutrients that prevent cataracts and other types of eye disease
- Green (e.g., spinach, broccoli, avocado) contain high levels of vitamins B, E, and K, as well as anti-cancer agents
- Red (e.g., tomatoes, strawberries, cherries) contain an antioxidant that reduces the risk of cancer and heart disease
- Purple and Blue (e.g., grapes, eggplant, red cabbage) contain abundant amounts of vitamins C and K as well as antioxidants that reduce the risk of cancer and cardiovascular disease
- Brown and White (e.g., cauliflower, mushrooms, bananas) contain chemicals that attack viruses and bacteria, reducing the risk of infectious diseases

Reflection 12.4

Do you regularly eat fruits and vegetables that fall into each of the above five color categories? What are your weakest categories? To strengthen your weakest color category, what could you eat that you would be willing to eat?

Maintain self-awareness of your eating habits. In addition to planning our diet, effective nutrition management requires conscious awareness of what's in the foods we consume. We can monitor our eating habits by simply taking a little time to read the labels on food products to determine what healthy nutrients (vitamins and minerals) and unhealthy ingredients (fats, sugar, and sodium) they contain. Keeping a nutritional log or journal of what we eat in a typical week can be an effective way to gain awareness of the nutrients and caloric content of foods we typically consume. (You can use the following website to evaluate the nutrient labels on packaged food products: https://www.foodandwaterwatch.org/about/live-healthy/consumer-labels?gclid=CjwKCAiAwojkBRBbEiwAeRcJZPpbBtnT9jso86tWG MgblUejZuQgdE3w5CzPTvufYAuNzQACrc3VAxoC2sUQAvD_BwE)

Minimize consumption of foods that have low (or zero) nutritional value and increase risk for heart disease and cancer. Fried and fatty foods such as pizza, hamburgers, French fries, donuts, butter, and margarine not only contain lots of calories, they also increase risk of heart disease because they contain substantial amounts of saturated fats and trans fats—"bad" fats that tend to stick to blood vessel walls and block normal blood flow. These types of fats also increase the risk of certain forms of cancer, such as breast and bowel cancer.

Saturated fats should comprise less than one-tenth of the total number of calories we consume. Even if we exercise regularly and are physically active, we still must be conscious of the food we put into our body. Well-conditioned athletes still can be at risk for heart disease and cancer if they consume too much food containing high amounts of saturated fat.

Reduce consumption of high-fat dairy products (e.g., cheese, butter, margarine, cream, and whole milk). High-fat dairy products are high in saturated fat and sodium, both of which increase the risk of heart disease. The calcium contained in dairy products is good for you, but you're better off getting that calcium from low-fat dairy products, such as low-fat milk, yogurt, and cottage cheese.

Minimize consumption of animal meat, particularly red meat such as hamburger and steak. Meat typically contains a large amount of saturated fat, which poses a major risk for heart disease. Many people believe they must consume a substantial amount of meat because the body needs protein. It's true that meat provides large amounts of protein, but protein should make up only 15% of our daily calories. Americans tend to consume about twice as much protein as the body needs. Consequently, most people can (and should) decrease the amount of protein they get from meat and increase the amount they get from sources that are low in saturated fat, such as plants (e.g., beans and peas), nuts (e.g., walnuts and almonds), and low-fat dairy products (e.g., low-fat milk and yogurt).

The health risk associated with meat consumption can be minimized by eating lean meat that's less fatty and by removing fatty skin from the meat we eat (e.g., the outer layer of skin from chicken and turkey). Meat's unhealthy effects can also be reduced by not frying it, because the oils used in the frying process increase the concentration of saturated fat contained in the meat. Instead of frying the meat we eat, it's healthier to roast, grill, bake, or broil it.

Manage body weight by minimizing or eliminating junk-food snacks. Replace sugary and salty snacks with healthier munchies, such as fruits, nuts, seeds, and raw vegetables. Many healthier snacks are just as sweet, crispy, and crunchy as junk-food snacks. Natural fruits, for example, provide sweetness with more nutrients and fewer calories than processed sweets, such as candy bars and blended coffee drinks. (Unfortunately, advertisers spend millions of dollars convincing consumers that processed sweets are the only ones that are "indescribably delicious.") Also, from an economic standpoint, nutritious snacks represent a better financial investment because you get a bigger bang for your buck—more nutrients (and less empty calories) for your snacking dollar.

Weight can also be controlled by downsizing or downright abstaining from downing sodas, which typically contain plenty of sugar and no nutrients. Drinking juices is a much healthier alternative, but not to excess, because they also contain a significant number of calories.

 Reflection 12.5

What type of junk food (if any) do you currently eat? Why?

If you eat junk food, do you think you could down on the amount you consume, or cut out junk food altogether? Why?

Don't pack most the calories you consume during the day into one or two large meals. Most nutritionists recommend that we should eat large meals less often and small meals more often. No research evidence or dietary rule supports the American habit of eating three times a day as the best nutritional practice. Six smaller meals or healthy snacks per day may be a more effective way to fuel the body than three full-sized meals. When our ancient ancestors foraged for food, it's unlikely they consumed large meals; they probably ate in smaller portions, which provided them with a steady stream of energy throughout the day.

Ideally, the meal eaten closest to bedtime should be our lightest meal containing the fewest calories because it will be followed by an extended period of sleep, during which time the body will be inactive and not in need of fuel. Consuming lots of calories in the evening and then lying down and sleeping soon thereafter means those evening calories don't get burned as physical energy but are stored as body fat. Remember that calories are measures of the amount of energy contained in food. (One calorie may be described as one unit or degree of energy.) If we consume a unit of energy and don't use it, we don't lose it; instead, we save it or store it—as fat.

Don't skip or skimp on breakfast. As the origin of the word "breakfast" suggests, a good breakfast provides energy that enables us to "break our nighttime fast" and fuel the body with energy for the upcoming day. The first meal of the day should be the one during which we consume most of our daily calories because we need energy for the next 16 hours of awake time and activity. Unfortunately, Americans tend to do it backward by skipping or skimping on breakfast and piling on calories at dinner—a time when the day has wound down and they'll soon be lying down to go to sleep.

Reduce consumption of processed foods. Processed foods were originally natural foods, but synthetic ingredients have been added to them so they can be preserved, packaged, jarred, canned, or bottled and sold later to the public in bulk quantities. Additives are also contained in processed foods to preserve their shelf life, which have no nutritional value and possibly unhealthy effects on the body.

Salt and sugar are often added to processed foods just to increase their taste appeal (and sales appeal), but which also increase weight gain and elevate blood pressure, respectively. Why do humans often find sweeter and saltier processed foods tastier than natural foods? One theory is that processed foods haven't been around as long as unprocessed "natural" foods that have been available for millions of years and were the only foods available to and consumed by our ancient ancestors. Because processed foods provided humans with a historical break from the "old" natural foods they consumed (and adapted to) over the course of millions of years, human taste buds may find these "newer" processed foods to be more stimulating and flavorful. So, ironically, humans may have developed or evolved a taste preference for the very foods that have the lowest nutritional value and the highest number of calories. The unfortunate consequence of this double whammy is that the foods most likely to stimulate our taste buds are the ones also most likely to inflate our fat cells. As a rule, the food that was good for our ancient ancestors and ensured the survival of our species is good for us now. These foods supply the most nutrition and the best protection against our two leading killers: heart disease and cancer. The following natural (non-processed) foods have been available to, and consumed by, humans for thousands of years and should appear regularly in our diet.

- **Fruit.** Fresh fruit has multiple healthy nutrients, including substantial amounts of vitamins (especially A and C) and minerals. Many fruits also contain fiber, which helps to purify the bloodstream, lower the bad type of cholesterol that causes heart disease, and rid the body of toxins found in the intestine. Other fruits, such as berries, are rich in antioxidants—substances that lower the risk of cancer by attacking oxidants (toxins) in the body that damage genetic DNA and weaken the immune system. (Blueberries are thought to contain the most antioxidants, followed by blackberries, raspberries, and strawberries.) Keep in mind that fresh fruit is superior to canned fruit, which has been processed and artificially preserved. Also, to manage weight, fresh fruit is superior to dried fruit, which contains more calories.
- **Vegetables.** The natural oils in certain vegetables (e.g., olive, corn, avocado, and soy) are rich sources of unsaturated fat. Unsaturated fats, also known as essential fatty acids, are "good" fats because they remain in liquid form in the body so they don't coagulate in the bloodstream and congregate as solid fat along the walls of our blood vessels. Unsaturated fats also help wash away and flush out bad fats from the bloodstream. In addition to containing good (unsaturated) fats, many vegetables—such as raw carrots and green beans—also contain fiber that reduces the risk of heart disease and certain forms of cancer. (Like fruit, vegetables that are fresh or frozen are superior to those that are canned and processed.)

 Reflection 12.6

Do you eat fresh fruit and vegetables daily? Why or why not?

- **Grains.** Natural grains contain complex carbohydrates, which the body uses to generate steady, sustained energy. These carbohydrates are called "complex" because their molecular structure is harder for the body to digest and break down into blood sugar. Their more complex molecular structure slows the digestion process, causing them to be absorbed into the bloodstream more gradually and allows them to deliver energy to the body more evenly over an extended period (similar to a coated pill or time-released capsule). Thus, grains are an excellent source of food for producing the steady, long-term energy necessary for athletic activities that require endurance and stamina. Grains are also high in fiber, which helps fight heart disease and certain forms of cancer. Lastly, many complex carbohydrates contain an amino acid that helps manufacture serotonin—a brain chemical associated with relaxation and feelings of emotional serenity.

  Whole-wheat bread and pasta, whole-grain cereals, oatmeal, and bran are good sources of healthy grains. Be sure to look for the term *whole* in the product's name (e.g., "whole-wheat bread" or "whole-grain cereal"). The word "whole" indicates that the grain is natural and not processed. For example, whole-wheat bread is made from a natural grain, but wheat bread and white bread have been processed.

- **Fish.** In addition to being high in protein, the natural oils found in fish are rich in unsaturated fat, which flush out and wash away cholesterol-forming fat from the bloodstream. Thus, a diet high in unsaturated fats (and low in saturated fats) reduces the risk for cardiovascular ailments, such as high blood pressure, heart attacks, and strokes. This explains why fish-eating Eskimos have a significantly lower rate of cardiovascular disease.

- **Legumes.** The word "legumes" derives from the Latin root "legumend," meaning "to gather." This food group includes plants and seeds, such as beans (black, red, and navy), lentils, Brussels sprouts, peas, and peanuts. Such foods are great sources of fiber, protein, iron, and B vitamins; plus, they're naturally cholesterol-free and low in saturated fat. The natural oil found in legumes contains unsaturated fats—good fats that reduce buildup of bad cholesterol in the bloodstream. It's interesting to note that in developing countries, which are less affluent than the United States, people eat mainly legumes, grains, fruits, and vegetables. Despite having less income and poorer medical care, people living in many of these underdeveloped countries have significantly lower rates of heart disease and diet-related cancers than people living (and eating) in the United States.

Drink plenty of water. Most people do not consume the recommended amount of water (seven 8-ounce glasses per day). Simply stated, the human body needs to be hydrated. Similar to how a car uses motor oil and transmission fluid, the body uses water to drive nutrients (fuel) to their proper destinations and drive waste products out of the system. Water also improves the human nervous system's ability to conduct electrochemical signals, which improves the brain's ability to process information. In addition to these internal benefits, water has a cosmetic benefit—it improves the appearance of our skin. Given the multiple health benefits of water, we should drink water only when we feel thirsty, but regularly throughout the day.

Don't forget to hydrate. Even mild dehydration can drain our physical energy and create feelings of fatigue. Men should drink about 15.5 cups of fluids per day and women about 11.5 cups.

Women should make a conscious effort to consume more calcium. Females should take in at least 1,200 mg of calcium per day to reduce their risk of osteoporosis (thinning of bones and loss of bone mass or density), which, in turn, reduces their risk of experiencing bone fractures and curvature of the upper spine. Although osteoporosis can happen in men as well as women, it's much more likely to afflict females. It's estimated that one of three women over the age of 40 will develop osteoporosis.

In Western cultures, there is considerable pressure on females to remain thin. This societal pressure often causes women to avoid high-calcium dairy products because these high-calcium products are also high in calories, thus women end up consuming less calcium than their body needs. However, women can still minimize their consumption of high-calorie dairy products and still get plenty of calcium by consuming low-fat, low-calorie dairy products (e.g., cottage cheese and low-fat yogurt). Other low-calorie foods that contain sizable amounts of calcium include certain fish (e.g., salmon), vegetables (e.g., broccoli), and fruit (e.g., oranges). In addition, women can ensure they're getting sufficient amounts of calcium by taking a daily calcium supplement.

Reflection 12.7

Is there any disease or illness that tends to run in your family?

Can you reduce your risk of experiencing it through your diet? If yes, how?

Exercise and Fitness

Physical wellness not only involves fueling the body with balanced nutrition but also using that fuel to move the body. As previously mentioned, consuming natural (unprocessed) foods is better for our health because those foods were consumed by our ancient ancestors and were instrumental to ensuring the survival of the human species. Similarly, exercise is another "natural" health-promoting activity that's deeply rooted in human history and has been instrumental to the survival of our species. Our ancient ancestors did not have the luxury of motorized vehicles to get them from point A to point B, nor could they stroll up leisurely to grocery stores and purchase food or have food served to them while sitting in restaurants. Instead, they had to roam and rummage for fruit, nuts, and vegetables, or chase down animals for meat to eat. Exercise was naturally built into their daily routine. This may explain why exercise is the most effective "medicine" available to humans for preventing disease and preserving lifelong health.

The benefits of physical exercise for preserving human health and the longevity of human life are extraordinary. The extensive bodily benefits of exercise are described below. (Its multiple mental benefits are discussed in the next chapter.)

> "If exercise could be packaged into a pill, it would be the single most widely prescribed and beneficial medicine in the nation.
>
> —Robert N. Butler, former director of the National Institute of Aging

Physical Benefits of Exercise

Exercise promotes cardiovascular health. Simply stated, exercise makes the heart stronger. Because the heart is a muscle, like any other muscle in the body, its size and strength are increased though exercise. A bigger and stronger heart pumps more blood per beat, reducing the risk for heart disease and stroke (loss of oxygen to the brain) by increasing circulation of oxygen-carrying blood throughout the body and by increasing the body's ability to dissolve blood clots.

Exercise further reduces risk of cardiovascular disease by: (a) decreasing blood levels of triglycerides (clot-forming fats), (b) increasing blood levels of "good" cholesterol (high-density lipoproteins), and (c) preventing "bad" cholesterol (low-density lipoproteins) from sticking to and clogging up blood vessels.

Exercise stimulates the immune system. Exercise enables us to better fight off infectious diseases (e.g., colds and the flu) because it:

- Reduces stress—which normally weakens the immune system
- Increases blood flow throughout the body—which increases circulation of antibodies that flush germs out of our system
- Increases body temperature—which helps kill germs similar to what a low-grade fever does to kill germs when we have a cold or flu

Exercise strengthens muscles and bones. Exercise helps prevent muscle strain and pain; for example, exercise that strengthens our abdominal muscles reduces our risk of developing lower back pain. Exercise also maintains bone density and reduces the risk of osteoporosis (brittle bones that bend and break easily). It's noteworthy that our bone density before age 20 affects our bone density throughout life. Thus, by engaging in regular exercise early in life, we minimize risk of bone deterioration throughout life.

 Reflection 12.8

Have your exercise habits changed (for better or worse) since you've begun college? If yes, why?

Exercise promotes weight loss and weight management. In a study of 188 countries, the highest proportion of overweight and obese people was found to live in the United States, and our obesity rates are rising. America's overweight issue is not only due to its citizens' consuming higher numbers of calories, but also to lower levels of physical exertion. Americans are now playing double jeopardy with their health by eating more and moving less.

The reduced level of physical activity among people today can be attributed, in part, to the emergence of modern technological conveniences that make it easier for us to go about our daily business without exerting ourselves in the slightest. Unlike decades past, TVs now come with remote controls so we don't have to move an inch to change channels, change volume, or turn them on and off. Kids today now have access to all sorts of video games that they can play "virtually" without having to run, jump, walk, or even get off their derriere.

The best antidote to overcoming the increasing inactivity built into modern-day life is to offset it with an exercise plan that includes regular physical activity. As a weight-control strategy, exercise is more effective than dieting in one key respect: It raises the body's rate of metabolism—the rate at which consumed calories are burned as energy rather than stored as fat. In contrast, dieting lowers the body's rate of metabolism and the rate at which calories are burned. Studies show that after two or three weeks of low-calorie dieting without exercising, the body "thinks" it's starving and compensates by saving more calories as fat so that the saved fat can be used as a source of future energy. In contrast, exercise speeds up basal metabolism—the body's rate of metabolism while resting. Thus, exercise does double-duty to burn body fat: it burns fat while we're exercising by using calories to

> "I'm less active now than before college because I'm having trouble learning how to manage my time."
>
> —First-year student

> "Video games have displaced a major activity in the lives of teenage boys, but that activity isn't reading; it's playing outdoors. That may be one reason why boys today are four times more likely to be obese compared with boys a generation ago."
>
> —Leonard Sax, psychologist, physician, and author of *Boys Adrift*

fuel the physical activity we're engaging in, and it burns calories when we're resting after exercising—by speeding up our body's basal (resting) rate of metabolism.

Strategies for Maximizing the Physical Benefits of Exercise

Different types of exercise benefit the body in different ways. However, there are general guidelines that can be followed to maximize the impact of any exercise routine or fitness program. These guidelines are provided below.

Before exercising, warm up; after exercising, cool down. Start with a 10-minute warm up of low-intensity movements that are similar to the movements you will use once you begin exercising. This warm-up activity increases circulation of blood to the muscles that will be exercised, which, in turn, will reduce muscle soreness and risk of muscle pulls.

Finish your exercise routine with a 10-minute cool down that involves stretching the muscles used during the exercise; stretch these muscles until they burn a little bit, then release them. This cooling down routine after exercise improves circulation to the exercised muscles, enabling them to return more gradually to a tension-free state, which minimizes the risk of muscle tightness, cramps, pulls, and tears.

Engage in cross-training for total body fitness. A balanced, well-rounded fitness program includes cross-training—a combination of different exercises to achieve total-body fitness. Combining different exercise benefits the body by increasing:

- Endurance and weight control (e.g., running, cycling, or swimming);
- Muscle strength and tone (e.g., weight training, push-ups, or sit-ups); and
- Flexibility (e.g., yoga, Pilates, or tai chi).

Cross-training also involves rotating exercise across different muscle groups (e.g., upper body muscles one day, lower body muscles the next day). This gives each set of muscles extra time to rest, repair, and recover before being exercised again.

Include *interval training* as part of your exercise plan. Interval training involves alternating high-intensity physical activities with low-intensity activities or short rest periods (e.g., alternating between running and walking). Research indicates that switching back-and-forth between higher- and lower-intensity exercises effectively strengthens the heart muscle and increases its oxygen-carrying capacity; it also burns calories faster and enables us to exercise longer and more vigorously.

Exercise according to a schedule that allows you to build up strength and stamina gradually. Fitness is attained and wellness is maintained through physical training, not physical straining. One simple strategy that can be used to ensure that you're training rather than straining your body is to see if you can talk while exercising. If you cannot continue speaking without stopping to catch your breath, this may indicate you're overdoing it and need to drop it down a notch to a less strenuous level. After continuing at this lower level for a while, try again at a higher level and try to talk while you exercise. If you can do both, you're ready to continue at that level for some time. By using this strategy, you can gradually increase the intensity, frequency, or duration of your exercise routine to an optimal level that maximizes its benefits and minimizes post-exercise discomfort and recovery time.

AUTHOR'S EXPERIENCE

I had a habit of exercising too strenuously—to the point where my body felt sore for days after I worked out. I eventually discovered a way to avoid overdoing it. I began listening to music through headphones while exercising to see if I could sing along without having to stop and catch my breath. If I could, I knew I wasn't overextending myself. This strategy helped me manage my exercise intensity level and minimize post-exercise soreness. (Plus, I gained more confidence as a vocalist—my singing sounded a lot better to me when hearing it while my ears were covered with headphones!)

—*Joe Cuseo*

Take advantage of exercise and fitness resources on your campus. The tuition you're paying for college pays for use of the campus gym or recreation center, so take advantage of it. If exercise groups or clubs meet on campus, join them; they can serve as a motivational support group that converts exercise from a solitary endeavor into an interactive experience. (It's also a good way to meet people.) In addition, consider taking physical education courses that may be offered on your campus. They count toward your college degree and typically carry one unit of credit so that they can be easily added to your course schedule.

Take advantage of natural opportunities for physical activity that present themselves during the day. Exercise can take place in places other than gyms or fitness centers and at times other than scheduled workout times. As you go about your daily routines, look for opportunities to build in some physical activity. If you can walk or ride a bike to class, do that instead of driving a car or riding a bus. If you can climb some stairs instead of taking an elevator, take the path of more resistance—the one that requires more physical exertion.

 Reflection 12.9

Do you have a regular exercise routine?

If yes, what do you do and how often do you do it? If no, why not?

What more could you do to improve your:

a) Endurance?

b) Strength?

c) Flexibility?

Rest and Sleep

In addition to eating well and exercising regularly, getting high-quality sleep is another key component of wellness. The quantity and quality of our sleep plays a pivotal role in preserving our health and enhancing our performance. Sleep researchers agree that in today's information-loaded, multi-tasking world, humans are not getting the quantity and quality of sleep they need to perform at their highest levels. College students in particular tend to have poorer sleep habits and experience more sleep problems than people in general. Because they're in an environment that provides them with many opportunities for late-night socializing, requires heavier academic workloads than high school and more late-night (or all-night) study sessions, college students often develop irregular sleep schedules and are more likely to experience sleep deprivation. It's estimated that 60% of college students get an insufficient amount of sleep—a rate twice that of the general population.

How much sleep do we need and should we get? The answer lies in our genes and varies from person to person. On average, adults need 7 to 8 hours of sleep each day and teenagers need slightly more—about 9 hours. Research shows that college students get an average of less than 7 hours of sleep per night, which means they're not getting the amount of sleep they need to perform at optimal levels.

Attempting to train ourselves to sleep less is attempting to do something that our body is not genetically "hard-wired" to do. When we deprive our body of the amount of sleep it's genetically designed to receive, it accumulates "sleep debt," which, like financial debt, must be paid back. If our sleep debt isn't repaid, it catches up with us and we pay for it with lower energy, lower mood, poorer health, and impaired mental and physical performance. For example, studies show that sleep deprivation impairs one's ability to drive a car in ways similar to alcohol intoxication. Studies also show that sleep-deprived college students exhibit poorer academic performance than students who get sufficient sleep.

> "Sleep deprivation is a major epidemic in our society. Americans spend so much time and energy chasing the American dream that they don't have much time left for actual dreaming.
>
> —William Dement, pioneering sleep researcher and founder of the American Sleep Disorders Association

> "I'm not getting enough sleep. I've been getting roughly 6–7 hours of sleep on weekdays. In high school, I would get 8–9 hours of sleep.
>
> —First-year student

> "First of all, you should probably know that your body will not function without sleep. I learned that the hard way.
>
> —Words written by a first-year student in a letter of advice to incoming college students

✳ Reflection 12.10

How many hours of sleep per night do you need to perform at your highest level, both mentally and physically?

Do you typically get this amount of sleep each night? If not, why not?

How do you think most students would answer the above two questions?

The Value and Purposes of Sleep

Resting and reenergizing the body are the most obvious purposes of sleep. Other benefits of sleep are less well known but are equally important, including the three key benefits below.

Sleep restores and preserves the power of our immune system. Studies show that when humans lose sleep, it lowers their production of disease-fighting antibodies, rendering them more susceptible to illness, such as common colds and flu.

Sleep helps humans cope with daily stress. Sleep research shows that when we're experiencing stress, we spend more time in the rapid eye movement (REM) stage of sleep, which is the stage when most dreaming takes place. This suggests that dreaming is our brain's natural way of coping with stress. When we lose dream sleep, emotional problems—such as anxiety and depression—worsen. Researchers suspect that the biochemical changes that take place in the brain during dream sleep help restore imbalances in brain chemistry that are triggered by anxiety or depression experienced during the day. Thus, getting high-quality sleep (especially high-quality dream sleep) helps us maintain emotional stability and keeps us in a positive frame of mind. Indeed, surveys reveal that people who report sleeping well also report feeling happier.

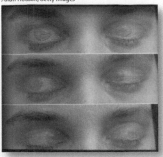
Allan Hobson/Getty Images

Studies show that dreaming during the REM stage of sleep helps us cope with stress and retain memories.

Sleep helps the brain form and retain memories. When we're sleeping, the brain isn't bombarded with sensory input from the outside world. Thus, while sleeping, our brain is free to expend more of its energy (metabolism) on processing and storing information taken in during the day. If we get less sleep than we need (especially REM-stage sleep), our ability to learn and retain information is impaired. Studies show that loss of dream sleep at night results in poorer memory for information learned during the day. For instance, teenagers who get less than adequate amounts of sleep have more difficulty retaining information they learn in school. Studies also show that increasing sleep time from six or fewer hours per night to eight hours can increase memory by as much as 25%. Additional research indicates that when students study before going to bed and stop studying when they begin to feel drowsy (rather than trying to continue studying and losing sleep), they display superior memory for the material that was studied.

Strategies for Improving Sleep Quality

Because sleep has powerful benefits for both the body and mind, if we can improve the quality of our sleep, we can improve our physical and mental wellness. Listed below are specific strategies for improving the quality of your sleep, which, in turn, should improve your overall health and performance.

Gain greater awareness of your sleep habits by keeping a sleep log or journal. Tracking your sleep experiences in a journal may enable you to discover patterns in the things you do (or don't do) before going to bed on nights you sleep well and nights when you sleep poorly. If you discover a pattern, you can use this information to get into a pre-bedtime routine that gets you a good night's sleep on a more consistent basis.

Try to get into a regular sleep schedule by going to bed and getting up at about the same time every day. The human body functions best when it gets into a rhythm of set cycles. If you can get your body on a regular sleep cycle, you can establish a biological rhythm that makes it easier for you to fall asleep, stay asleep, and wake up naturally according to your own "internal alarm clock."

Getting on a regular sleep schedule is particularly important for students to do at times during the academic term when they need to perform at peak levels, such as midterms and finals. Sleep research shows that to be at their physical and mental best for upcoming exams, students should get on a regular schedule of going to sleep and waking up at about the same time at least one week before major exams are to be taken. Unfortunately, for many college students, the opposite happens. Midterms and finals are the times during the term when their regular sleep cycles are likely to be disrupted by the need to stay up later to cram for exams, get up earlier to squeeze in extra study time, or pull all-nighters and not sleep at all. Make every effort to avoid this sleep-disruptive pattern of cramming by getting into a regular, more productive sleep schedule near midterms and finals. (This could be done by avoiding last-minute, late-night cramming through use of the "distributed practice" and "part-to-whole" study methods described in chapter 5, pp. 107-108.)

Attempt to get into a relaxing pre-bedtime ritual. Taking a hot bath or shower, consuming a hot (non-caffeinated) beverage, or listening to relaxing music are activities that can get us into a worry-free state before sleep and help us fall asleep sooner. Also, making a list of things that need to be done the next day before going to bed may help us relax and fall asleep because we know that we're all set and ready to handle the tasks we need to do the following day.

Because sleep helps the brain retain what it takes in just before falling asleep, a light review of class notes or reading highlights just before bedtime might be another good pre-bedtime practice. Many years of research indicates that the best thing to do to remember information other than studying it some more is to "sleep on it." Sleep gives the brain time to process and store studied information without having to deal with external stimulation or outside distractions.

Try using a sleep app. You can download apps to your phone or tablet that are designed to help you relax, fall asleep, and stay asleep by playing soothing sounds and melodies which drown out external sounds and ease you into a restful state. Some apps also monitor and evaluate your sleep cycles and will wake you at a time in the morning when you're least likely to be groggy. (Best of all, many of these apps can be downloaded for free.)

> "People don't realize how much work it is to stay in college. It's its own job in itself, plus if you've got another job you go to, too. I mean, it's just a lot.
> —First-generation college student

Reflection 12.11

Just before going to bed at night, what do you typically do? Do you think this helps or hinders the quality of your sleep?

Avoid intense mental activity just before going to bed. Light school work or list-making may serve as a relaxing pre-sleep ritual, but intense reading, writing, or complex thinking before bedtime can induce a heightened state of mental arousal that interferes with your ability to wind down and fall asleep.

Avoid intense physical exercise before bedtime. Vigorous physical activity elevates muscle tension and increases oxygen flow to the brain, both of which can hinder your ability to fall asleep. If you like to exercise in the evening, do it at least three hours before bedtime.

Avoid consumption of sleep-interfering foods, beverages, or drugs in the late afternoon or evening. In particular, avoid the following sleep-disruptive substances near bedtime:

- **Caffeine.** It's a stimulant drug; for most people, it stimulates the nervous system and keeps them awake.
- **Nicotine.** It's another stimulant that's likely to reduce the depth and quality of sleep. (Note: Smoking hookah through a water pipe delivers the same amount of nicotine as a cigarette.)
- **Alcohol.** It's a depressant (sedative) substance that induces drowsiness in larger doses; however, in smaller doses, it can have a stimulating effect. Furthermore, when alcohol induces sleep, it interferes with the quality of sleep by reducing the amount of time spent in dream-stage sleep. (Marijuana does the same.)
- **High-fat foods.** Eating just before bedtime (or during the night) increases digestive activity in the stomach. This "internal noise" can interfere with the depth and quality of sleep. In particular, high-fat foods such as peanuts, beans, fruits, raw vegetables, and high-fat snacks should be avoided before bedtime because these foods require the stomach to engage in more digestive effort and activity.

> *Alcohol and marijuana are substances that make us feel sleepy but that doesn't mean they enhance sleep quality. In fact, they typically reduce the quality of sleep by interfering with dream-stage sleep.*

Keep the temperature in the room where you sleep no higher than 70 degrees Fahrenheit. Warm temperatures often make us feel sleepy, but they usually don't help us stay asleep or sleep deeply. This is why people have more trouble sleeping on hot summer evenings. High-quality, uninterrupted sleep is more likely to take place at cooler room temperatures that don't exceed 70 degrees.

Keep your electronic devices turned off in the room where you're sleeping. The screens on cell phones, computers, and tablets can make it harder to fall asleep and stay asleep because they emit a certain form of light that suppresses the brain's production of melatonin—a neurochemical that promotes sleep. Sleep researchers recommend that we stop using electronic devices at least 30 minutes before going to bed.

Wellness is built on a balanced foundation of nutrition, exercise, and rest.

Adjusting Academic Work Tasks to Your Biological Rhythms

When planning your daily work schedule, be mindful of your "biological rhythms"—your natural peak periods and down times. Studies show that humans differ in terms of when they naturally prefer to fall asleep and wake up; some are "early birds" who prefer to go to sleep early at night and wake up early in the morning; others are "night owls" who prefer to stay up late at night and get up late in the morning. As a result of these differences in sleep patterns, individuals differ with respect to the time during the day when they experience their highest and lowest levels of energy. Naturally, early birds are more likely to be "morning people" whose peak energy period takes place before noon; night owls are likely to be more productive in the late afternoon and evening. Most people, whether they're night owls or early birds, tend to experience a "post-lunch dip" in energy in the early afternoon.

Listed below are a few key strategies for adjusting your work schedule and tasks in ways that align with your daily biological rhythms.

- When creating daily to-do lists, tackle your highest priority and most urgent tasks at times during the day when you tend to work at peak effectiveness.
- When scheduling courses, be mindful of your natural peak and down times. Try to arrange your schedule in such a way that you're sitting in your most challenging courses at times of the day when your body and mind are most ready to rise to those challenges.
- Schedule out-of-class academic work so that you tackle tasks requiring the most intense thinking (e.g., technical writing or complex problem-solving) at times of the day when you tend to be most productive; schedule lighter work (e.g., light reading or routine tasks) at times when your energy level tends to be lower.

(Exercise 12.6 at the end of this chapter can help you identify your peak performance times.)

Alcohol Use among College Students

Research indicates that first-year college students drink more than they did in high school and have higher rates of alcohol abuse than high school students and students at more advanced stages of the college experience. Beginning college students think that most of their college peers drink and report that the number-one reason why they choose to drink is to "fit in" and feel socially accepted. However, research shows college students overestimate how many of their peers drink and how much drinking they actually do. This overestimation can lead first-year students to try to conform to what they perceive to be the norm (average), and if they don't, they won't be "normal."

Whatever the legal age for drinking may be, the reality is that first-year college students are confronted with the following choices:

1. To drink or not to drink.
2. To drink responsibly or irresponsibly.

If you choose to drink, it should be *your* choice, not a choice imposed on you by social pressure or peer conformity. If you decide to drink, listed below are some quick tips for drinking safely and responsibly. These are offered to you as recommended health-promoting practices, not as pious platitudes or preachy warnings.

- **Don't feel pressured to drink to an excessive degree.** Remember that college students overestimate how many of their peers drink and how much they drink. So, you shouldn't feel "uncool," unusual, or abnormal if you prefer to drink only occasionally and in moderation, rather than consistently or to the point of inebriation.
- **Don't drink with the intention of getting intoxicated; set a limit about how much you will drink.** Use alcohol as a beverage, not as a mind-altering substance.
- **Eat well before drinking and snack while drinking.** This helps lower the peak level of alcohol in the bloodstream.
- **Drink slowly.** Sip, don't gulp; avoid "shot-gunning" or "chug-a-lugging" drinks.
- **Spread out drinking over time so that drinks are consumed intermittently, not consecutively.** If you're having more than one drink during the course of an evening, space them out across time. This gives your body time to metabolize the alcohol consumed and keeps the percentage of alcohol in your bloodstream at lower, more manageable levels.

- **Monitor your physical and mental state while drinking.** Don't continue to drink after you've reached a state of moderate relaxation or a mild loss of inhibition. Drinking to the point of borderline intoxication or a drunken state will not improve one's physical health or social life. Slurring speech, nodding out, or vomiting in the restroom isn't likely to make a partying student the life of the party.

> *Alcohol can be costly, in terms of both dollars and calories. Limiting the amount of alcohol consumed is not only an effective way to preserve health and safety, it's also a good money- and weight-management strategy.*

Alcohol Abuse

Alcohol is a legal substance (at least for people who have reached the legal drinking age), and unlike most other mind-altering substances, it's ingested as a beverage, rather than being injected, smoked, or snorted. That being said, alcohol is still a *drug*, particularly when consumed in large quantities (doses). In moderate amounts, alcohol could be described as a relaxing beverage; however, in larger doses, it's a mind-altering substance with a mind-altering ingredient: ethyl alcohol (see **Figure 12.3**). The average percentage ("dose") of ethyl alcohol in beer is about 4% to 6%; in wine, it's 12% to 14%; and in "hard liquor" (distilled spirits), such as vodka, whiskey, gin, and rum, it's 40%.

Also, like any other mind-altering drug, alcohol has the potential to be addictive; approximately 7% to 8% of people who drink experience alcohol dependency (alcoholism). Alcohol dependency has genetic roots, so if there is a history of alcohol abuse in a person's family, that person should be especially cautious about his or her drinking habits.

Although alcohol dependency is the most talked about form of alcohol abuse, the number one alcohol and drug abuse problem on college campuses is *binge drinking*—episodes during which large amounts of alcohol (4-5 or more drinks) are consumed in a short period of time, resulting in an acute state of intoxication—more commonly referred to as a "drunken state."

Although binge drinking isn't necessarily a form of alcohol dependency, it's still a form of alcohol *abuse* because it has direct, negative effects on the physical or mental well-being of the drinker. Research indicates that whenever a person drinks to the point of drunkenness, it reduces the size and effectiveness of the part of the brain involved with memory formation. This finding has led alcohol-abuse researchers to a simple but disturbing conclusion: Each time a person gets drunk, the dumber that person gets.

Binge drinking also reduces students' inhibitions about engaging in risk-taking behavior, which puts them at greater risk for accidents and injuries. When drinkers consume a substantial amount of alcohol in a short period of time, they become much less cautious about doing things they normally would be hesitant or reluctant to do. This chemically induced sense of self-confidence (colloquially referred to as "liquid courage") overrides logical thinking and rational decision-making and increases the likelihood that the drinker will engage in irrational, risk-taking behavior—such as fighting or destroying property. Binge drinkers are also more willing to risk unprotected sex—increasing their risk of pregnancy and contracting sexually transmitted infections (STIs), and are more likely to engage in reckless driving—increasing their risk of serious injury or death. It's noteworthy that the legal age for consuming alcohol was once lowered to 18 years,

FIGURE 12.3: Ethyl Alcohol: The Mind-Altering Ingredient Contained in Alcohol

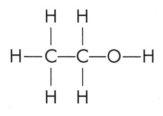

©Kendall Hunt Publishing Company

> "If you drink, don't park. Accidents cause people."
> —Steven Wright, American comedian

but it was raised back to 21 because the number of drunk-driving accidents and deaths among teenage drinkers increased dramatically after the legal age for drinking was lowered. Traffic accidents still account for more deaths of Americans between the ages of 15 and 24 than any other cause.

Arguably, no other chemical substance has the capacity to lower a person's inhibitions as dramatically as alcohol. It's been said that binge drinking can lower inhibitions so much that it deludes drinkers into thinking they're "invincible, immortal, and infertile." The dramatic loss of inhibition that takes place during binge-drinking episodes stems biologically from the fact that alcohol is a depressant drug that depresses (slows down) the upper, front part of the brain (the "human brain") which is responsible for rational thinking and controlling or inhibiting the lower, middle part of the brain (the "animal brain")—which is responsible for basic animal drives, such as sex and aggression. When the upper (rational) brain is slowed down by alcohol, the animal brain is freed from the signals that normally restrain or inhibit it, thus allowing basic drives to be released and expressed (see **Figure 12.4**). This is the underlying biochemical reason why binge drinking increases the drinker's risk of engaging in aggressive and sexually aggressive behavior, such as sexual harassment, sexual abuse, and relationship violence.

FIGURE 12.4: How Alcohol Works in the Brain to Decrease Personal Inhibitions and Increase Risk-taking Behavior

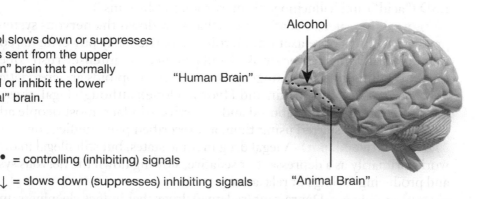

Alcohol slows down or suppresses signals sent from the upper "human" brain that normally control or inhibit the lower "animal" brain.

•••••• = controlling (inhibiting) signals

↓ = slows down (suppresses) inhibiting signals

©Kendall Hunt Publishing Company

 Reflection 12.12

Do you drink alcohol?

If yes, why? If no, why not?

How do you think most students on your campus would answer these questions?

Use and Abuse of Illegal Drugs

In the United States, alcohol is a substance that citizens can use legally once they reach a certain age. Other chemical substances cannot be used legally at any age. Although the college years are often a time for exploring and experimenting with different ideas, feelings, and experiences, experimenting with illegal drugs can be risky business. Unlike legal drugs, which must pass through rigorous testing by the Federal Drug Administration before being approved for public consumption, similar safeguards are not in place for the production, packaging, and distribution of illegal drugs. We don't know if or what substances have been "cut" (mixed into) an illegal drug during its production process. Thus, consuming an illegal drug is not only a criminal risk, it's also a health risk because it involves consumption of an *unregulated* and potentially unhealthy substance. For these reasons, the best rule to follow about using illegal drugs is this: When in doubt, keep it out. Don't put anything into your body that's totally unregulated, possibly adulterated, and potentially unpredictable.

Listed below are the major types of illegal drugs in circulation, accompanied by a short description of their primary physical and psychological effects.

- **Cocaine (coke, crack).** A stimulant that's typically snorted or smoked, which produces a strong "rush" (intense feeling of euphoria)
- **Amphetamine (speed, meth).** A strong stimulant that increases energy and general arousal; it's usually taken in pill form but may also be smoked or injected
- **Ecstasy (X).** A stimulant typically taken in pill form that speeds up the nervous system and reduces social inhibitions
- **Hallucinogens (psychedelics).** Drugs that alter or distort perception—e.g., LSD ("acid") and hallucinogenic mushrooms ("shrooms")
- **Narcotics (Opioids).** Sedative drugs that slow down the nervous system and produce feelings of relaxation. Heroin is a particularly powerful narcotic that's typically injected or smoked and produces an intense "rush" of euphoria. Also falling into this category of narcotics or opioids are *prescription pain medications* (e.g., OxyContin and Hydrocodone); although legal, these drugs have the potential to be abused and addictive—in fact, most people addicted to opioids today started using them as prescribed pain medication.
- **Marijuana (weed, pot).** A legal drug in some states, but still illegal in others; it works primarily as a depressant or sedative, slowing down the nervous system and producing feelings of relaxation.
- **Date Rape Drugs.** Depressant (sedative) drugs that induce sleepiness, memory loss, and possible loss of consciousness, thus rendering the drinker vulnerable to rape or other forms of sexual assault. These drugs are typically colorless, tasteless, and odorless; thus, they can be easily mixed into a drink without the drinker noticing it. Common date-rape drugs include Rohypnol ("roofies") and GHB ("liquid E").

Reflection 12.13

What illegal drugs (if any) have you seen students use in high school or college?

Have you witnessed use of any illegal drugs that do not appear on the above list?

Motives (Reasons) for Drug Use

People use drugs for a variety of reasons, the most common of which are listed below. Increasing awareness of the motives behind drug use can help reduce one's tendency to do drugs for unconscious or subconscious reasons.

- **Social Pressure.** To "fit in" or feel socially accepted (e.g., drinking alcohol because everyone else seems to be doing it)
- **Recreational (Party) Use.** For fun, stimulation, or pleasure (e.g., smoking marijuana at parties to relax, loosen inhibitions, and have a "good time")
- **Experimental Use.** Doing drugs out of curiosity—to test out their effects (e.g., experimenting with LSD to see what it's like to have a psychedelic or hallucinogenic experience)
- **Therapeutic Use.** Using prescription or over-the-counter drugs for medical purposes (e.g., taking Prozac for depression, Adderall to treat attention deficit disorder, or Fentanyl to treat pain)
- **Performance Enhancement.** To improve physical or mental performance (e.g., taking steroids to improve athletic performance or stimulants to stay awake and study longer for exams)
- **Escapism.** To escape a personal problem or an unpleasant emotional state (e.g., taking Ecstasy to escape depression or boredom)
- **Addiction.** Because of physical or psychological dependence (e.g., habitually using cocaine or prescription drugs because stopping use of them triggers uncomfortable withdrawal symptoms)

"For fun." "To party." "To fit in." "To become more talkative, outgoing, and flirtatious." "To try anything once." "To become numb." "To forget problems." "Being bored."

—Responses of freshmen and sophomores to the question, "Why do college students take drugs?"

Reflection 12.14

What motives for drug use listed above would you say are the most common reasons for drug use by students?

Do you think students' common motivations (reasons) for using drugs could be satisfied by substituting alternative drug-free experiences? If yes, what might those alternative experiences be?

Sexually Transmitted Infections (STIs)

STIs represent a group of contagious infections spread through sexual intercourse that can threaten a person's health and well-being. More than 25 types of STIs have been identified and virtually all of them are effectively treated if detected early. However, if ignored, some STIs can progress to the point where they result in serious infection and possible infertility.

Common early symptoms of STI are experiencing pain during or after urination, or unusual discharge from the penis or vagina. Sometimes, however, symptoms can be subtle and undetectable. If there's any doubt, it's best to play it safe and get it checked. If you discover that you have a STI, immediately inform anyone you've had sex with so that he or she can receive early treatment before the disease progresses. This is not just the polite thing to do; it's the right (ethical) thing to do.

Latex condoms provide the best protection against STIs. Also, having sex with fewer partners reduces the risk of contracting an STI. Obviously, not engaging in sexual intercourse is the most foolproof way to eliminate the risk of an STI (and unwanted pregnancy). When making decisions about sexual intercourse, college students have three basic options: Do it recklessly and run a high risk of contracting an STI, do it safely and minimize risk of an STI, or don't do it at all. Students who choose abstinence shouldn't be perceived as being cold or prudish. It just means they prefer not to have sexual intercourse at this time or stage of their life.

Campus Safety

College campuses are generally safe places; crimes are not more likely to take place on campuses than in other places. However, crimes can and do occur on campus, and one aspect of maintaining wellness for college students is avoiding behavior that puts them at risk of experiencing crime, particularly crime that threatens their personal safety and physical well-being. Listed below are some top tips for doing so.

- After dark, don't walk alone; use a buddy system.
- Check if your campus has an escort service at night; if it does, take advantage of it.
- If you're walking alone, don't get so absorbed in texting or listening to iTunes that you tune out or block out what's going on around you.
- If you're carrying valuable electronics, keep them concealed.
- Call ahead for campus shuttles and escort services to reduce the amount of time you wait for a ride.
- Have your keys out and ready to use when entering your building or your car, and double-check to be sure the door locks behind you.
- Be aware of the location of emergency phones in campus buildings.
- Know the phone number and location of the office for campus safety.
- Include emergency numbers in your cell phone.

You can also take advantage of mobile apps to enhance safety. For instance, "Circle of 6" (www.circleof6app.com) is a free mobile map that allows you to choose a network of six friends whom you can contact with emergency text messages, such as: "Call me immediately," "Come and get me," or "I need help getting home safely." When you text a message, your GPS location is included. This app won the national "Apps Against Abuse Challenge" sponsored by the White House. "ArcAngel" (https://www.patrocinium.com/arcangelapp/) is another mobile safety app that notifies you within seconds of an emergency or if you're near danger (e.g., a crime scene, fire, or flood). It also provides ongoing status reports throughout the emergency and recommends evacuation routes as needed. If you need help, you can click a button that informs local authorities, campus security teams, and family members of your exact location.

Take advantage of these new safety technologies to reduce your risk of being victimized by crime, both on or off campus.

Internet-Based Resources

For additional information on promoting physical wellness, consult the following Web sites.

Nutrition: www.eatright.org
Physical Activities and *Fitness:*
http://www.ncppa.org/resources-reports

Sleep:
https://www.sleephealth.org/
www.sleepfoundation.org

Alcohol and Drugs:
https://www.responsibility.org/
https://www.drugabuse.gov/

Chapter 12 Exercises

12.1 Quote Reflections

Review the sidebar quotes contained in this chapter and select two that you found to be especially meaningful or inspirational.

For each quote you selected, provide an explanation why you chose it.

12.2 Strategy Reflections

Review the strategies suggested for *improving the quality of sleep* on pp. 276-278. Select three you think are most important and intend to put into practice.

12.3 Reality Bite

Drinking to Death: College Partying Gone Wild

It's estimated that at least 50 college students nationwide die each year as a result of drinking incidents on or near campus. During a single month in the fall, three college students died as a result of binge drinking at college parties. The first incident involved an 18-year-old freshman at a private university who collapsed after drinking a mixture of beer and rum, fell into a coma at his fraternity house, and died three days later. He had a blood-alcohol level of more than .40, which would be equivalent to gulping down about 20 shots in one hour. The second incident involved a student from a public university in the South who died of alcohol poisoning (overdose). The third student died at another public university in the Northeast after an evening of partying and heavy drinking; he accidentally fell off a building in the middle of the night and fell through the roof of a greenhouse. Some colleges in the Northeast now have student volunteers roaming the campus on cold winter nights to make sure that no students freeze to death after passing out from an intense episode of binge drinking.

More recently, a student at a university on the East Coast guzzled an excessive amount of vodka and beer at a fraternity hazing party, staggered around repeatedly during the night, and eventually fell (head first) down a flight of stairs. He died of a fractured skull and damaged spleen.

Listed below are strategies that have been suggested or enacted by politicians and university officials to reduce the problem of dangerous binge drinking:

1. A state governor announced he was going to launch a series of radio ads designed to discourage underage drinking.

2. A senator filed a bill to toughen penalties for those who violate underage drinking laws, such as producing and using fake identification cards.

3. A group of city council members considered stiffening penalties for liquor stores that deliver directly to fraternity houses.

4. A university banned the drinking of hard liquor at college parties.

5. Six states enacted laws that make fraternity hazing a criminal offense.

Reflection and Discussion Questions

1. Rank the above strategies in terms of how effective you think they'd be for reducing the problem of binge drinking (1 = the most effective strategy to 3 = the least effective).

2. Comparing your highest ranked and lowest ranked choices, why do you think:

   (a) your highest-ranked choice would be most effective?

   (b) your lowest-ranked choice would be least effective?

3. What additional strategies would you suggest that might effectively reduce the number of dangerous binge-drinking episodes?

12.4 Wellness Self-Assessment

For each aspect of wellness listed below, rate yourself in terms of how close you are to doing what you should be doing.

	Nowhere Close to What I Should Be Doing		Not Bad but Should Be Better		Right Where I Should Be
	1	2	3	4	5
Nutrition	1	2	3	4	5
Exercise	1	2	3	4	5
Sleep	1	2	3	4	5
Alcohol and Drugs	1	2	3	4	5

For each area in which there's a gap between where you are and where you should be, identify the best action step you could take right now to reduce or eliminate this gap.

Do you think the ratings of most college students would be like yours? Why?

12.5 Nutritional Self-Assessment and Self-Improvement

1. Go to: *www.ChooseMyPlate.gov*.

2. For each of the five food groups listed at this site, use the grid below to record in the first column the amount you *should* consume on a daily basis. In the second column, estimate the amount you *do* consume on a daily basis.

Basic Food Type	Amount Recommended	Amount Consumed
Fruits		
Vegetables		
Grains		
Protein Foods		
Dairy		

3. For any food group that you're consuming in less than the recommended amount, use the website to find foods that would enable you to meet the recommended daily amount. Make note of these foods, and answer the following questions about each of them:

   (a) How likely is it that you will add these food items to your regular diet?

   Very Likely   Possibly   Very Unlikely

   (b) For those food items you identified as "very unlikely," why would is it very unlikely that you would add these items to your regular diet?

12.6 Biological Rhythms

Refer to the results of your AchieveWORKS Learning and Productivity report, under the Environmental Preferences section. What do the results suggest about times during the day when you're at your best and when it would be best to schedule your most challenging academic work?

How could you set up a study schedule that enables you to make effective use of your most productive time while still allowing time for your other responsibilities?

CHAPTER 13

Psychological Wellness

PRESERVING AND PROMOTING MENTAL HEALTH

Physical and mental health represent the "twin towers" of personal wellness; this chapter focuses on the latter tower—psychological well-being. Academic achievement in college and the ability to persist to college completion depend on students' ability to maintain their mental health and cope effectively with psychological stressors, particularly anxiety, depression, unhealthy relationships, and substance abuse. This chapter supplies specific strategies for preserving self-esteem, coping with college stressors, maintaining mental health, and attaining optimal psychological wellness.

Chapter Purpose & Preview

Acquire knowledge of strategies and resources for strengthening self-esteem, maintaining stress at moderate, performance-enhancing levels, and coping with anxiety, depression, unhealthy social relationships, eating disorders, and substance abuse.

Learning Goal

Ignite Your Thinking

 Reflection 13.1

How would you rate your overall sense of self-esteem?

In what situations or circumstances would you say your self-esteem tends to be *highest* and *lowest*? Why?

"I think there should be a mental health and wellness course that is mandatory for the first semester of all incoming students.

—*College student responding to a national survey on mental health*

Mental Health and Self-Esteem

Self-esteem refers to our sense of self-worth; it's a value judgment about ourselves that affects how we feel about ourselves. If that value judgment is positive, it contributes positively to our mental health; if it's negative, it detracts from it. Self-esteem can vary across time and circumstances, even if we have a generally positive sense of self-esteem, there are likely to be certain times and situations when we don't feel good about ourselves. It's at these times that we need to intentionally restore our self-esteem and preserve our mental health. Here are some strategies for doing so.

Strategies for Improving and Preserving Self-Esteem

Be mindful of negative self-talk. Research shows that how we think affects how we feel, and if we think positive thoughts about ourselves, we're more likely to reduce stress and strengthen our self-esteem. Thinking often involves talking silently to ourselves silently and our inner voice can sometimes speak self-critical words. If we hear these words repeatedly, they can lower our self-esteem, often without our full conscious awareness. By remaining self-aware of the critic within us, we can combat these negative verbal messages through *thought stopping* (e.g., responding to the negative self-talking by saying: "shut up!") and *thought substitution* (e.g., replacing negative self-statements like: "I'm an idiot" with positive self-talk such as: "I'm not understanding this right now, but by keeping at, I soon will.") Psychologists refer to such positive self-statements as affirmations, and research indicates that when people practice making affirmations (for example, writing down as many different positive things they can think about themselves in a minute), it decreases negative self-talk and increases self-esteem.

Avoid comparing yourself to others; focus on your own special gifts and talents. A healthy sense of self-esteem involves a realistic, appreciative view of the self that doesn't depend on external forms of self-validation, such as wealth or social status. In the words of a renowned humanistic psychologist, healthy self-esteem is built on "unconditional positive regard"—the belief that all human beings are to be valued (positively regarded) for who they are, not by what they have or haven't done, accomplished, or accumulated relative to others.

Comparisons can lead to negative self-talk, particularly when they involve comparisons with talented or successful people in the media who may have achieved fame and fortune. We need to remind ourselves that these rich and famous people, or other successful people, may be good at what they do, but do not have the talent or skill to do what we do well. Research shows that talent and intelligence come in multiple forms and a key to maintaining a healthy sense of self-esteem is not losing sight of our distinctive strengths, particularly at times when we're down or experiencing self-doubt.

If you're having trouble identifying your special talents or personal strengths, ask your closest friend to point them out to you. It's sometimes easier to see the positive qualities of others than our own because we cannot step outside ourselves to see our strengths as others do. Therefore, it's important to accept and reflect on the compliments we receive, rather than deflect or disregard them as being insincere or unwarranted. Compliments are often genuine and well-deserved and should be viewed as indicators of our personal strengths and self-worth. Don't confuse valuing yourself with arrogance or conceit. Actually, when we value ourselves, we're less likely to be boastful or egotistical because we don't have to build up our self-value (self-esteem) by bragging or boasting to others.

When making mistakes, view them as specific and temporary setbacks, not as generalized and permanent failures. Unsuccessful experiences in life are inevitable and often beyond our control; how we react to them is variable and within our control. We should avoid reacting to setbacks with negative, emotionally-charged self-talk that makes permanent, generalized statements about ourselves (e.g., "I always screw up"); instead we should respond rationally with positive self-talk (e.g., "I'm not going to let this one get me down; I'm going to rebound and get it right next time"). Reacting to setbacks as *temporary* (not permanent) and *specific* (not generalized) increases our sense of self-efficacy and self-esteem.

As can be seen in **Figure 13.1**, information passes through the emotional center of the brain (lower, shaded area) before reaching the center responsible for rational thinking and future planning (upper area). As a result, when we encounter setbacks, our initial (and subconscious) tendency is to react emotionally and defensively. To counteract this tendency, we need to slow down, calm down, and make a conscious attempt to respond rationally—using positive self-talk to think logically about how we can overcome setbacks, learn from them, and prevent them from

> "Everybody is a genius. But if you judge a fish by its ability to climb a tree, it will live its whole life believing that it is stupid."
> —*Albert Einstein*

> "When written in Chinese, the word 'crisis' is composed of two characters. One represents danger, and the other represents opportunity."
> —*John F. Kennedy, 35th president of the United States*

damaging our self-esteem. Responding in this way, prevents us from becoming resentful and getting bitter, and enables us to be resilient and get better.

FIGURE 13.1: How Information is Processed in the Brain

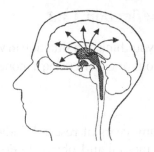

Information entering the human brain is first processed emotionally at a subconscious level (lower shaded area) before it reaches higher conscious areas of the brain responsible for rational thinking. Thus, we need to respond to emotional setbacks with rational, positive self-talk.

©Kendall Hunt Publishing Company

Set realistic "get better" goals rather than idealistic "be perfect" goals. Setting idealistic goals for ourselves and then beating ourselves up for failing to reach them is a perfect recipe for creating low self-esteem. We need to set personal goals that are challenging and meaningful, but also realistic and attainable. By so doing, we're more likely to reach our goals and more likely to feel better about ourselves. As mentioned in Chapter 3, studies show that when people set get-better goals (instead of be-perfect goals), they pursue these goals with greater interest, intensity, and joy. This is probably due to the fact that get-better goals give us a sense of progress and keep us focused on how far we've come. In contrast, perfection (be-good) goals focus on how far we still have to go.

Associate with others who strengthen, rather than sabotage, your sense of self-worth. Being around "toxic people" who are boastful, cynical, and critical of others (including you) is very likely to have a negative effect on how you feel about yourself. Regardless of what these people may be able to do for you in terms of advancing your career, income, or love life, it's not worth the price of damaged self-esteem. Dump them and spend time with people who are optimistic, accepting of others, and appreciate you for who you are.

Emotional Disorders

In a recent national survey of over 8 million people, it was discovered that the emotional well-being of young adults (18-25 years of age) was poorer than all other age groups and the previous generation of young adults.

Depression and anxiety are the two most common emotions that adversely effect on mental health of human beings in general and college students in particular. Discussed below are the key signs (symptoms) of anxiety and depression, accompanied by top strategies for coping with each of these emotions.

Stress and Anxiety

College students report higher levels of stress than they experienced in high school. But what exactly is *stress*? Biologically, it's an emotion that's rooted in the "fight-or-flight" response—an automatic physical reaction wired into the human body that contributed to the survival of our ancient ancestors by helping them fight or flee from life-threatening predators. The word "stress" itself derives from a Latin root, meaning "to draw tight." As its root meaning suggests, stress isn't necessarily bad; in the right amount, it can be productive. For instance, a tightened bow delivers a more powerful arrow shot, and a tightened muscle generates more strength and speed. In fact, physiologists and psychologists draw a distinction between good (productive) stress—referred to as "eustress" and bad (unproductive) stress—referred to as "distress."

Reflection 13.2

Can you think of a situation in which you performed better because you were slightly nervous or experiencing a moderate amount of stress?

Many years of research indicate that a *moderate* or intermediate level of stress improves mental and physical performance (see **Figure 13.2**). When stress is moderate and manageable, it generates energy, increases motivation, and sharpens attention. We need to remind ourselves that not all stress is bad; it can work either for us or against us, depending on its level of intensity and how long it continues. We shouldn't expect to eliminate stress entirely, nor should we want to; instead, our goal should be to contain it and maintain it at a level where it's productive rather than destructive.

FIGURE 13.2: Relationship between Stress and Performance

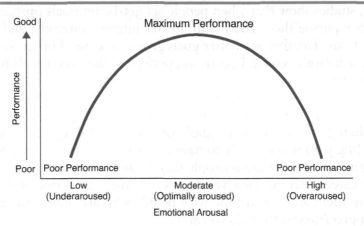

Moderate challenge that produces moderate stress typically promotes maximum (peak) performance.

Source: Williams, Landers, & Boutcher (1993)

When stress is overly intense and chronic (ongoing), it becomes distress, or what's more commonly called *anxiety*. Anxiety experienced over an extended period jeopardizes physical health by suppressing the immune system and leaves the body more vulnerable to flu, colds, and other infectious diseases. Studies show, for example, that the immune system of college students who report higher levels of stress during midterms and finals produces fewer antibodies, rendering them more susceptible to physical illness.

Studies also show that anxiety interferes with the brain's ability to (a) store and retrieve memories and (b) engage in higher-level thinking. For instance, students experiencing higher levels of academic anxiety are more likely to use "surface" approaches to learning that rely on memorization rather than "deep learning" strategies, such as reflecting on and finding meaning in what they're learning.

Below is a list of signs or symptoms of anxiety. If you experience these symptoms for more than a week or experience them repeatedly during or around the time of exams and other performance-evaluation situations, seek help from a counseling professional, either on or off campus.

Symptoms (Signs) of Anxiety

- Jitteriness or shaking—especially the hands
- Accelerated heart rate or heart palpitations (irregular heartbeat)
- Sweating—especially sweaty (clammy) palms
- Dry mouth. Caused by decreased production of saliva (which is why nervous speakers may experience "cotton mouth" and repeatedly sip water)
- Muscle tension. Tightness in the chest, upper shoulders or neck (hence, the expression "uptight"), or a feeling of tightness (lump) in the throat—which accounts for the term "choking" under pressure
- Body aches. Caused by heightened muscle tension, which can lead to tension headaches, backaches, or chest pain; in some cases, chest tension can be so intense that the anxious person feels as if he or she is having a heart attack, but in reality, it's an anxiety attack (a.k.a. panic attack)
- Weakness and fatigue. Caused by a sustained state of muscle tension that leaves the anxious person feeling physically exhausted
- Cold, pale hands and feet. As captured in the expressions "white knuckles" and "cold feet"
- Feeling faint or dizzy. Due to blood vessels constricting, which reduces oxygen flow to the brain
- Stomach cramps, indigestion, or queasiness. Caused by increased secretion of stomach acid (as reflected in the expression, "having butterflies in the stomach")
- Elimination problems (e.g., constipation or diarrhea)
- Difficulty sleeping. Having trouble falling asleep, staying asleep, or experiencing interrupted (fitful) sleep
- Increased susceptibility to colds, flu, and other infections. Due to suppression of the body's immune system and lower production of antibodies.

When anxiety escalates to a serious level, it's referred to as an anxiety disorder. An anxiety disorder can be experienced in different types or forms. The five major types of anxiety disorders are summarized in **Box 13.1**.

Box 13.1

Major Types of Anxiety Disorders

Generalized Anxiety Disorder (GAD): chronic anxiety (a steady state of excessive worry and tension), which can take place without the person experiencing anything to be anxious about.

Obsessive-Compulsive Disorder (OCD): recurrent, unwanted thoughts (obsessions) and/or repetitive behaviors (compulsions—for example, repeated hand washing, counting, checking, or cleaning). Anxiety is experienced when these rituals are not performed; however, performing them only provides temporary tension relief.

Panic Disorder: unexpected and repeated episodes of intense fear accompanied by physical symptoms that typically include chest pain, heart palpitations, shortness of breath, dizziness, or abdominal discomfort.

Social Anxiety Disorder (a.k.a. Social Phobia): overwhelming anxiety and excessive self-consciousness in everyday social situations, which may be limited to just one type of situation (e.g., fear of speaking in formal or informal situations, or eating or drinking in front of others). In its most severe form, the person experiences anxiety almost anytime they are around other people.

Posttraumatic Stress Disorder (PTSD): an anxiety disorder that takes place after someone has had a traumatic experience—an emotionally intense, extremely dangerous, or life-threatening event, such as military combat, violent personal assault, sexual assault, or natural disaster. After such events, it's normal for a person to experience anxiety for several weeks or months. However, if intense feelings of anxiety do not gradually

continued...

subside with time, or if they intensify over time, that person may be experiencing PTSD.

Specific symptoms of PTSD include the following:
- Constantly feeling tense or "on edge"
- Easily startled
- Difficulty concentrating
- Difficulty sleeping
- Emotional numbness
- Sudden outbursts of anger
- Memory loss for the traumatic experience or for events around the time of the experience
- Avoiding places, events, or objects that are reminders of the traumatic experience

- "Flashbacks"—reliving the traumatic experience along with feelings of fright and physical arousal (e.g., heart palpitation and sweating). Flashbacks can happen suddenly and spontaneously, or they may be triggered by sights, sounds, and dreams that remind the person of the traumatic experience.

Anyone experiencing any of the above symptoms for three or more months after experiencing a traumatic event should seek professional help by contacting the Counseling Center on campus or the PTSD Information Line (802-296-6300; e-mail: ncptsd@va.gov).

 Reflection 13.3

How would you rate your level of anxiety in the following situations?

1. Taking tests or exams   high   moderate   low

2. Interacting in social situations   high   moderate   low

3. Making decisions about the future   high   moderate   low

If you rated your level of anxiety as "high" in any of the above situations, what could you do or who might you see to help you help you reduce it to a more manageable level?

Stress-Management Strategies

Anxiety that is intense and chronic requires help from a professional therapist. Milder forms of stress may not require professional assistance and may be self-managed by using the following stress-management strategies.

Exercise. Counselors and psychotherapists often recommend exercise for people experiencing milder forms of anxiety. Exercise lowers stress by increasing the brain's production of serotonin—a mellowing neurochemical (brain chemical) that reduces feelings of tension.

Journaling. Writing about our feelings in a personal journal helps us identify and express the emotions we're experiencing (a form of emotional intelligence). It can also serve as a cathartic outlet for coping with stress.

AUTHOR'S EXPERIENCE

I'm the kind of person who carries the worries of the day with me to bed at night, which really affects my sleep. I'm also the type of person who juggles many balls during the day, which also adds to my stress level. By chance, I discovered a great strategy for managing my stress while I was conducting a conflict-resolution workshop about 15 years ago. During the workshop, I asked the participants to write down in a journal all the stressors they encountered during the day for 30 consecutive days. Then I told them we would come together as a group at the end of the 30 days to identify our stressors.

After the workshop, I decided to do this for myself on a regular basis. Each night before going to bed, I wrote down the categories or sources of stress that I experienced during the day. After 30 days, I recognized patterns in what triggered my stress and was able devise strategies for reducing or avoiding my stressors. I also noticed that over time, my level of anxiety decreased and the quality of my sleep increased. I still use this strategy whenever I'm feeling stressed or not sleeping well.

—*Aaron Thompson*

Substitute positive thoughts for negative (anxious) thoughts. The part of the human brain involved in thinking (the cortex) has multiple connections with the part of the brain responsible for emotions (the limbic system). Thus, the brain is wired in such a way that our thoughts can influence our emotions. Thus, by changing how we think, we can change how we feel, including whether we feel stressed or anxious. Changing negative, anxiety-producing thoughts to positive, relaxing thoughts, can lower the level of stress or tension we're experiencing. For instance, during an exam, if you see other students turning in their tests early, you may have negative thoughts like, "They must all be smarter me." You could block that anxiety-producing thought by substituting a more positive thought, such as: "They're getting up and getting out because they're giving up." Or, "They're rushing out without taking the time to carefully review their test before turning it in."

One of the keys to substituting positive thoughts for negative thoughts is to focusing our thinking on what we want to happen, not on what we're afraid might happen. For instance, you can reduce your level of test anxiety by not focusing on (and worrying about) how many points you might be losing during an exam, but by focusing on how many points you're earning.

> "There are thousands of causes for stress, and one antidote to stress is self-expression. That's what happens to me every day. My thoughts get off my chest, down my sleeves, and onto my pad.
>
> —*Garson Kanin, American write actor, and film director*

⊛ Reflection 13.4

If you sometimes experience negative (anxiety-producing) thoughts, what are they about? What positive thoughts could you substitute for these negative thoughts?

Depression

Along with anxiety, depression is another major emotional problem that afflicts a significant number of people, including college students. As its name implies, depression involves an emotional state that has been "depressed" (lowered or pushed down). It is an emotional condition characterized by feelings of sadness, accompanied by loss of interest, hope, and energy. Students who experience depression in college tend to exhibit lower levels of academic performance and have a higher risk of withdrawing from college, even if they are highly motivated and academically well-prepared.

In contrast to anxiety—which typically involves worrying about something that's currently happening or is about to happen, depression more often stems something that has already happened—particularly a *loss*, such as a lost relationship (e.g., broken romance or death of a family member) or a lost opportunity (e.g., losing a job or not getting into a desired school). It's natural and normal for someone to feel dejected after losses such as these. However, if this dejection continues for an extended period of time and reaches such a level of intensity that the person is so overcome with sadness and lacks the interest or energy to complete daily tasks related to work or school, the person may be experiencing what psychologists call *major depression (a.k.a. clinical depression)*—a serious emotional disorder for which professional help should be sought. For instance, after loss of a loved one, it's natural or normal to experience grief. However, if this feeling of sadness continues for an extended period that goes well beyond the time of the loss and continues to impair the grieving person's ability to function, the person may no longer be experiencing grief, but major depression.

Reflection 13.5

Have you ever been concerned about someone who you thought might be experiencing serious depression? If yes:

(a) What specific behaviors did the person exhibit that caused you to be concerned?

(b) What would you have recommended that person do?

Listed below is a summary of the key signs or symptoms of major depression. If you find yourself experiencing these symptoms for two or more weeks, seek help from a professional.

Symptoms (Signs) of Major Depression

- Feeling very low, down, dejected, sad, or blue
- Low self-esteem; feeling worthless or guilty (e.g., thinking "I'm a failure" or "I'm a loser")
- Loss of energy
- Speaking much more slowly and softly than normal
- Stooped posture (e.g., hung head or drawn face)
- Less animation and slower bodily movements
- Decreased sense of humor
- Difficulty finding pleasure, joy, or fun in anything
- Lack of concentration and increased forgetfulness
- Loss of motivation and interest in things previously found to be interesting or important (e.g., loss of interest in school, sharp drop in rate of class attendance, or suddenly failing to turn in class assignments)
- Social withdrawal
- Neglect of physical appearance
- Changes in eating patterns (e.g., eating much more or much less than usual)
- Changes in sleeping patterns (e.g., sleeping much more or less than usual)

- Pessimistic feelings about the future (e.g., expecting failure or bad things to happen; feeling helpless or hopeless)
- Suicidal thoughts (e.g., "I can't take it anymore," "People would be better off without me," or "I don't deserve to live")
  Note: Suicidal thoughts occur at alarmingly high rates among college students. In one national study of more than 26,000 students at 70 campuses, it was found that 15% of the students surveyed reported that they "seriously considered" suicide and 5% reported that they actually attempted suicide. Only half of the students who had suicidal thoughts sought counseling or treatment. From 2008 and 2017, suicides among young adults between the ages of 18-25 increased by more than 50% and the rate at which this age group experienced suicidal thoughts increased by over 66%.

If you think you may be experiencing depression, seek professional help. If you are concerned about someone else being seriously depressed, express your concern in a supportive, non-threatening way (e.g., "You don't seem like yourself today" or "You seem kind of down, are you okay?). If your concern is confirmed, encourage that person to connect with a counseling psychologist or psychotherapist.

Bipolar Disorder (a.k.a. Manic Depression)

This is a distinctive type of depressive disorder that involves radical mood swings from emotional lows (major depression) to extreme emotional highs (mania)—a condition that includes three or more of the following symptoms:

- Exaggerated sense of well-being and self-confidence (euphoria)
- Being abnormally upbeat, jumpy, or wired
- Increased activity, energy, or agitation
- Decreased need for sleep
- Unusual talkativeness
- Racing thoughts
- Distractibility
- Poor decision-making—for example, going on buying sprees, taking sexual risks, or making foolish investments

People experiencing mania may enjoy the feeling of euphoria and boundless energy. However, these feelings are always followed by an emotional crash that leaves them depressed, fatigued, and sometimes with social, financial, or legal problems caused by the poor decisions made during the manic episode.

Although bipolar disorder can occur at any age, it's typically first experienced during the late teens and 20s and is most often a lifelong condition that requires mood-stabilizing medication and counseling or psychotherapy.

Major forms of depression are often rooted in genetic factors that trigger chemical imbalances in the brain and typically require psychiatric medication. Anyone diagnosed with a serious form of depression should take prescribed medication as directed. Sometimes, students who have been taking psychiatric medication prior to college stop taking medication once they begin college. This is not a good mental health practice because this sudden stoppage can result in withdrawal effects from the medication and symptoms returning or worsening. This is illustrated by the following student experience:

After coming to the decision that I was, in fact, bipolar, I went off my medication. That was a big mistake. For about 4 months, I was fine, but then I graduated from high

"It is extremely difficult for students to come out and talk about mental health problems and they may not want to tell you this is why they are falling behind, missing class, seeming disengaged, etc. Please be sensitive and understand mental health problems are 'real' problems. Encourage them to find help."

—*College student responding to a national survey on mental health*

school to attend _____ State University. The stress of a new school, new friends, and new intense party environment altogether caused a manic episode. When I went home after my first week of school, I watched the movie, "Sylvia." It was about Sylvia Path's life and her struggle with mental illness. Sadly, in the end, she kills herself. That really opened my eyes to my problem. I recognized myself in Sylvia's episodes. I finally realized I was indeed bipolar and I did not want to end up like Sylvia. The next day I saw my psychiatrist and got back on my medication.

—Personal story shared by a college sophomore

Strategies for Coping with Milder Forms of Depression

Depressive disorders can vary in intensity from severe to mild. For milder forms of depression, the coping practices described below may be used as self-help strategies. These strategies can be used alone or in conjunction with help from a professional.

Make a conscious effort to focus on your strengths and accomplishments. One way to drive away the blues is by keeping track of the positive developments in our lives. We can do this by keeping a "positive events journal" in which we note the good things that happen to us, things we're grateful for, and accomplishments we've achieved. Positive journal entries leave us with an uplifting visible record that can be viewed and reviewed anytime we're feeling down.

Continue to get things done. At times when we're feeling despondent, staying busy and accomplishing things can boost our mood by providing us with a sense of achievement. Helping others less fortunate than ourselves can be a particularly effective mood elevator because it gets us outside ourselves, increases our sense of self-worth, and helps us realize that our issues are often much more manageable than the challenges facing others.

> "The best way to cheer yourself up is to try to cheer somebody else up."
>
> —Samuel Clemens, a.k.a. Mark Twain, writer, lecturer, and humorist

Make a determined effort to continue engaging in activities that are fun and enjoyable. When we're down, we are less likely to do the things that usually bring us up because we're too down to do them. Naturally, this brings us down further. To break this cycle, when we're emotionally low we should intentionally try harder to continue doing the things that bring us joy, such as socializing with close friends and engaging in our favorite recreational activities. (Interestingly, the root of the word "recreation" means to re-create or create again, suggesting that recreational activity can restore, revive, and renew us—both physically and emotionally.)

When we engage in upbeat behavior, our mind (mood) is likely to follow suit. You may have heard of the expression, "Put on a happy face." Smiling is a behavior that can actually elevate mood because it produces changes in facial muscles, which, in turn, increase the brain's production of mood-elevating chemicals. In contrast, frowning activates a different set of facial muscles that tend to interfere with production of these mood-elevating brain chemicals.

> "We don't laugh because we're happy; we're happy because we laugh."
>
> —William James, influential philosopher and psychologist who taught the first psychology course in the United States

Intentionally seek out humor and opportunities to laugh. Laughter can brighten a dark mood by increasing endorphins—brain chemicals that improve mood and promote a feeling of well-being. Furthermore, humor enhances memory, which can help counteract with lapses of memory that sometimes accompany depression.

Exercise! The mental health benefits of exercise are numerous; they're summarized below in **Box 13.2**.

Box 13.2

Mental Health Benefits of Exercise

In addition to benefitting the body, exercise benefits the mind. The powerful effects of physical exercise on psychological health and mental performance are summarized below.

Exercise elevates mood. Exercise stimulates release of: (a) serotonin—a mellowing brain chemical that reduces feelings of tension, anxiety and depression, and (b) endorphins—morphine-like brain chemicals that produce a natural high. It is for these reasons that psychotherapists often prescribe exercise for patients experiencing mild cases of anxiety and depression. Studies also show that people who exercise regularly report feeling happier.

> "It is exercise alone that supports the spirits, and keeps the mind in vigor."
>
> —*Marcus Cicero, ancient Roman orator and philosopher*

Exercise improves self-esteem. Exercise enhances feelings of self-worth by providing us with a feeling of accomplishment and improving our physical self-image (e.g., weight control, muscle tone, and skin tone).

Exercise deepens and enriches the quality of sleep. Sleep research indicates that exercising at least three hours before bedtime helps us fall asleep, stay asleep, and sleep more deeply. In fact, exercise is often included in treatment programs for people suffering from insomnia.

Exercise increases mental energy and improves mental performance. Have you noticed how red your face gets after engaging in strenuous physical activity? This rosy complexion is the result of physical activity pumping larger amounts of blood into your head region along with more oxygen into your brain. In fact, exercise increases blood flow to all parts of the body, but because the brain uses more oxygen than any other organ of the body, it's the organ that benefits most from exercise. Moreover, aerobic exercise (exercise that increases respiratory rate and circulates oxygen throughout the body) has been found to (a) enlarge the brain's frontal lobe—the part of the brain responsible for higher-level thinking, and (b) increase production of brain chemicals that enable neurological connections to form between brain cells. As noted in Chapter 5, these are the connections that provide the biological basis of learning and memory. One well-designed study of more than 250 college students discovered that students who regularly engaged in vigorous physical activity had higher grade point averages (GPAs).

> "To keep the body in good health is a duty, otherwise we shall not be able to keep our mind strong and clear."
>
> —*Buddha, founder of Buddhism*

Exercise is also a physiological stimulant whose stimulating effects is similar to that produced by popular energy drinks (e.g., Red Bull, Full Throttle, and Monster). However, they key difference is that exercise delivers its stimulating effects without sugar, caffeine, and the negative side effects they produce—such as increased nervousness, higher blood pressure, followed by a sharp drop in energy ("crash") and mood after the energy drink's stimulating effects wear off.

A final note on emotional disorders: Anxiety and depression can sometimes by managed through personal effort and use of effective coping strategies, particularly if these emotions are experienced in mild forms and for short periods of time. However, more serious and long-lasting episodes of anxiety and depression often have genetic roots and are beyond the person's ability to control through self-management or self-help strategies. Thus, anyone experiencing these more serious and chronic emotional challenges should not feel embarrassed about, or reluctant to, seek professional help.

Reflection 13.6

If you thought you were experiencing anxiety or depression, would you feel comfortable seeking help from a professional? If yes, why? If no, why not? How do you think most students would answer these questions?

Unhealthy Relationships

A relationship is unhealthy if it threatens a person's physical or psychological well-being. Whether the threat is emotional, psychological, physical, or sexual, it's a threat that shouldn't be tolerated. Behaviors that qualify as threatening include, but are not limited to, degrading language, dominating or dictating a partner's actions, and physical or sexual assault.

Victims and offenders of relationship abuse are often unwilling to admit, or are in complete denial about, the abuse that's taking place. Even when victims are aware of it, they often don't seek help because they're embarrassed or fear retaliation from their abusive partner. Anyone involved in a relationship in which he or she is repeatedly disrespected, excessively controlled, or concerned about personal safety should acknowledge it and take immediate steps to do something about it. Not taking early action increases the risk that the abusive relationship will escalate in intensity or become violent.

Unfortunately, the prevalence of abusive relationships among college students is surprisingly high. A survey conducted by the National Institutes of Health revealed that 44.7% of college students experienced partner or non-partner violence; 72.8% were women and 27.2% were men. Relationship abuse has been found to occur among college students of all races, ethnicities, and socioeconomic groups, including gay and bisexual students. College students who are involved in (or think they may be involved in) an abusive relationship should seek immediate help by consulting a counseling professional, either on or off campus.

Listed below are descriptions of different forms of unhealthy relationships, followed by strategies for escaping or avoiding them. Note that the examples cited are not just physical or sexual in nature; they include emotional and psychological abuse, which can be just as harmful.

Abusive Relationships

An abusive relationship may be defined as one in which a partner is abused physically, verbally, or emotionally. Abusers are often dependent on their partner for their sense of self-worth and fear the partner will abandon them, so they attempt to prevent this from happening by over-controlling their partner. Abusers may also feel powerless or weak in other areas of their life and attempt to bolster their self-esteem or self-efficacy by exerting power over their partner.

Signs of an Abusive Relationship:

- The abuser is possessive and tries to dominate or control all aspects of the partner's life (e.g., discourages the partner from having contact with friends or family members).
- The abuser frequently yells, shouts, intimidates, or physically threatens the partner.
- The abuser constantly puts down the partner and attempts to damage the partner's self-esteem.
- The abuser displays intense and irrational jealousy (e.g., accuses the partner of infidelity without evidence).
- The abuser demands affection or sex, even when the partner is uninterested or unwilling.
- The abuser often appears charming to others in public settings but is abusive toward the partner in private.
- The abused partner behaves differently (typically more reserved or inhibited) in the partner's presence.
- The abused partner fears the abuser.

Strategies for Avoiding or Escaping Abusive Relationships:

- Don't rationalize or make excuses for the abuser's behavior (e.g., he was drinking or she was under stress).
- Minimize relationship isolation by maintaining social ties with friends outside of the relationship.
- Get an objective, "third party" perspective by asking close friends for their views on the relationship. Love can often be "blind," so it's possible to be involved in a romantic relationship and be blind to (in denial about) the abuse that's taking place.
- Speak with a professional counselor on campus to help view the relationship more objectively.

Sexual Assault a.k.a. Sexual Violence

Sexual assault refers to nonconsensual (unwanted or unwilling) sexual contact forced on another person without that person's consent. One form of sexual assault is rape, defined legally as forced sexual penetration (intercourse) imposed through physical force, by threat of bodily harm, or when the victim is incapable of giving consent due to alcohol or drug intoxication. Rape typically falls into two major categories:

(1) **Stranger Rape**—a total stranger forces sexual intercourse on the victim.
(2) **Acquaintance Rape or Date Rape**—the victim knows, or is dating, the person who forces unwanted sexual intercourse.

It's estimated that 85% to 90% of reported rapes on college campuses are committed by someone with whom the victim is acquainted and 50% of these acquaintance rapes take place on a date. Alcohol is frequently associated with acquaintance rapes because it lowers the rapist's inhibitions and reduces the victim's ability to determine if it's a potentially dangerous situation. Because the partners are familiar with each other, the victim may feel that what happened was not really rape. However, acquaintance rape *is* rape and it's still a crime because it involves nonconsensual sex.

Suggested Strategies for Preventing Rape:

- If you drink, or go to places where others drink, remain aware of the possibility of date-rape drugs being dropped into your drink. To guard against this risk, don't let others give you drinks and hold onto your drink at all times (for example, don't leave it, go to the restroom, and come back to drink it again).
- When you attend parties, go with a friend so you can keep an eye out for one another.
- Clearly and assertively communicate what your sexual limits are. Use "I messages" to firmly resist unwanted sexual advances by focusing specifically on the person's actions or behavior (e.g., "I'm not comfortable with you touching me that way").
- Carry mace or pepper spray and be prepared to use it if necessary.
- Take a self-defense class. Research shows that taking a course on avoiding or resisting sexual assault reduces the course taker's risk of rape by almost 50%.

Assumptions that Should not be Made:

- Don't assume that someone wants to have sex just because that person is very friendly or flirtatious, dressed in a particular way, or drinking alcohol.

- If someone says "no," take it as a firm no. Don't interpret it to mean that the person is really saying "yes."
- Don't assume you're the one who has to "take charge" and initiate a sexual relationship.
- Don't interpret rejection of your sexual advances as a personal insult or a blow to your self-image; take it to mean that the other person is not ready or willing to have sex.

Sexual Harassment

In college settings, sexual harassment includes any unwanted or unwelcome sexual behavior initiated by another student or an employee of the college that interferes with a student's education. Sexual harassment can take the following forms:

(1) Physical—initiating contact with another person by touching, grabbing, pinching, or brushing up against the person's body.
(2) Verbal—making sexual comments about someone's body or clothes; telling graphic sexual jokes to the person; spreading sexual rumors about a person's sexual activity or orientation; requesting sexual favors in exchange for a better grade, job, or promotion.
(3) Nonverbal—staring or glaring at another person's body; making erotic or suggestive gestures toward the person; sending obscene messages or unsolicited pornographic material to the person.

Recommendations for Dealing with Sexual Harassment:

- Make your objections clear and firm. Tell the harasser directly that you're offended by the unwanted behavior and that you know it constitutes sexual harassment.
- Become aware of the sexual harassment policy on campus. (The school's policy is likely to be found in the *Student Handbook* or may be obtained from the Office of Human Resources.)
- Keep a written record of any harassment. Record the date, place, and specific details about the harassing behavior.
- If you are unsure about whether you're experiencing sexual harassment, or what to do about it, contact the Counseling Center or Office of Human Resources.

Note: Sexual harassment is a form of *peer harassment*—a broader category of harassment that includes taunting, bullying (in person or online), and harassing other students based on their race or sexual orientation. These behaviors violate a federal law that guarantees the right of all students to experience a learning environment that's conducive to learning. If you experience any of these forms of harassment, don't tolerate them silently; instead, report them immediately to school authorities.

 Reflection 13.7

Have you ever known or witnessed someone who was involved in an abusive relationship? (If yes, was the person aware that the relationship was abusive?)

Did the person deal with it effectively? (If yes, what did the person do?)

Eating Disorders

Although some students may experience the "freshman 15"—a 15-pound weight gain during the first year of college, others may experience eating disorders associated with weight loss and loss of control of their eating habits. These disorders are being discussed in a chapter on mental health because the unhealthy eating behavior is typically accompanied by, or triggered by, emotional issues (e.g., depression and anxiety) that often require psychotherapy. Listed below are descriptions of the major eating disorders experienced by college students. These disorders are more common among females, largely because Western cultures place more emphasis (and pressure) on females to be thinner and trimmer. Studies show that approximately one of every three college females report worrying about their weight, body image, or eating habits.

Box 13.3 contains a summary of the key symptoms (signs) of the major disorders experienced by college students.

Box 13.3

Major Eating Disorders

Anorexia Nervosa

Students experiencing this disorder are dangerously thin yet see themselves as overweight and have an intense fear of gaining weight. They are obsessed about controlling or losing weight, eat infrequently, and when they do eat, consume extremely small portions. They may also use a variety of methods to lose weight, such as exercising compulsively and taking diet pills, laxatives, diuretics, or enemas. Anorexics are typically in denial about their condition. Even if their weight drops to the point where they may look like "walking skeletons" to others, they fail to see themselves as being dangerously underweight.

> " I had a friend who took pride in her ability to lose 30 lbs. in one summer by not eating and working out excessively. I know girls that find pleasure in getting ill so that they throw up, can't eat, and lose weight."
>
> —Comments written in a first-year college student's journal

Bulimia Nervosa

This disorder is characterized by repeated episodes of "binge eating"—consuming exorbitant amounts of food (bingeing) within a short period of time. Bulimics lose self-control during their binges, and after bingeing, they attempt to purge themselves of the calories they just consumed (and their guilt about consuming them) by

using methods such as: self-induced vomiting, ingesting laxatives or diuretics, taking enemas, or fasting. If a person engages in this binge-purge pattern at least twice a week and continues for three or more months, that person would be diagnosed as a bulimic.

Like anorexics, bulimics are not happy with how their bodies look, fear gaining weight, and are driven by an intense desire to lose weight. However, unlike anorexics, bulimics are harder to identify because their binges and purges typically take place secretly and their body weight looks about normal for their age and height.

Binge-Eating Disorder

Similar to bulimics, binge eaters engage in repeated, out-of-control eating episodes during which they consume large amounts of food. However, unlike bulimics, binge eaters don't purge after their binging episodes. To be diagnosed with binge-eating disorder, the person must exhibit at least three of the following symptoms, two or more times per week, for several months:

1. Eating at an extremely rapid rate.
2. Eating until becoming uncomfortably full.
3. Eating large amounts of food when not physically hungry.
4. Eating alone because of embarrassment about being seen by others.
5. Feeling guilty, disgusted, or depressed after overeating.

College students exhibiting symptoms of any of the above eating disorders should seek professional assistance immediately because the earlier an eating disorder is detected (diagnosed) and treated, the better the prognosis (the greater the likelihood of a quicker and more complete recovery).

Substance Abuse and Chemical Dependency

Using alcohol or recreational drugs can worsen symptoms of anxiety and depression and can interfere with the therapeutic effect of medication prescribed for these emotional disorders. Sometimes, people attempt to cope with depression or anxiety by using recreational drugs, which can lead to dependency on these drugs. Any drug has the potential to be addictive, especially if it's injected intravenously (directly into a vein) or smoked (inhaled through the lungs). These drug-delivery routes are particularly dangerous because they deliver the drug to the brain faster and heighten the drug's peak effect (its highest level of impact). When a drug has a fast and high-peak effect ("rush"), it's soon followed by a sharp and sudden drop ("crash") (see **Figure 13.3**). This peak-to-valley experience results in the drug generating an immediate positive impact on mood (e.g., euphoria) followed soon thereafter by an opposite, negative effect on mood (e.g., dysphoria). To eliminate this state of dysphoria, the drug is used again, which over time can lead to drug dependency (addiction).

FIGURE 13.3: **Drugs Smoked Produce a Higher, More Rapid Peak Effect and Create a Greater Risk for Addiction**

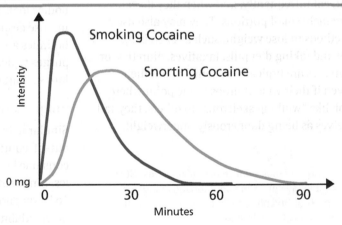

©Kendall Hunt Publishing Company

Listed below are the most common signs that a person's drug use (including alcohol) is moving in the direction of *dependency* (*addiction*):

- Steadily increasing the amount (dose) of the drug and/or using it more consistently
- Difficulty cutting back—for example, being unable to reduce the frequency of drug use or to use the drug in smaller amounts)
- Difficulty controlling or limiting the amount taken after starting
- Keeping a steady supply of the drug on hand
- Spending more money on the drug than can be afforded
- Using the drug alone
- Hiding or hoarding the drug
- Lying about drug use to family and friends

- Reacting angrily or defensively when questioned about use of the drug
- Rationalizing drug abuse (e.g., "I'm just partying. It's a normal part of the college experience.")
- Being "in denial" about abusing the drug (e.g., "I don't have a problem")
- Using the drug matters more to the user than putting a stop to the personal and interpersonal problems being caused by its use.

Overcoming drug dependency or other psychological problems (e.g., eating disorders) can be challenging because the person experiencing them is often in *denial*—doesn't "see" the problem because they've pushed it out of conscious awareness. People in denial are not simply lying; they're using a defense mechanism unconsciously to protect their self-image or self-esteem. Thus, an important first step in helping ourselves or helping others overcome drug abuse and other mental health issues is overcoming denial.

Reflection 13.8

Have you ever known anyone who was in denial about substance abuse or a mental health issue?

Did the person eventually overcome denial and deal effectively with the issue? If yes, how?

Internet-Based Resources

For additional information on promoting psychological wellness and mental health, consult the following Web sites.

Mental Health:
https://www.bestcolleges.com/resources/top-5-mental-health-problems-facing-college-students/
http://www.ulifeline.org/

Abusive Relationships:
http://www.byui.edu/counseling-center/self-help/abusive-relationships

Eating Disorders
https://www.nationaleatingdisorders.org/warning-signs-and-symptoms

Substance Abuse
https://www.addictioncenter.com/college/

Chapter 13 Exercises

13.1 Quote Reflections

Review the sidebar quotes contained in this chapter and select two that you found to be especially meaningful or inspirational.

For each quote you selected, provide an explanation why you chose it.

13.2 Strategy Reflections

Review the strategies recommended for *coping* with *mild depression* on pp. 296-298. Select two you think are most important and intend to put into practice.

13.3 Reality Bite

College Anxiety

Leo was really looking forward to college but didn't anticipate the amount of stress that has come along with it during his first term. In high school, teachers always reminded him when things were due and he hardly had any homework. In college, his workload seems overwhelming and his instructors expect him to keep track of all the work he's supposed to get done and when to get it done by. His stress has been mounting and has reached a point where he's beginning to feel his heart racing and tightness in the back of his neck. These feelings intensify when he's in class, so he has begun skipping class.

Discussion Questions

1. How realistic do you think this case is? Why?

2. What would you recommend Leo do to decease his level of anxiety and increase the likelihood that he will weather his first-term stress storm and succeed in college?

13.4 College Stress: Identifying Sources and Solutions

Read through the following list of potential college stressors and rate them in terms of how much stress each one is currently causing you—on a scale of 1 to 5 (1 = lowest, 5 = highest).

Potential Stressors	Stress Rating				
	1	2	3	4	5
Tests and exams	1	2	3	4	5
Assignments	1	2	3	4	5
Class workload	1	2	3	4	5
Pace of courses	1	2	3	4	5
Performing up to expectations	1	2	3	4	5
Handling personal freedom	1	2	3	4	5
Time pressure (e.g., not enough time)	1	2	3	4	5
Organizational pressure (e.g., misplacing things)	1	2	3	4	5
Living independently	1	2	3	4	5
The future	1	2	3	4	5
Decisions about a major or career	1	2	3	4	5

Moral and ethical decisions	1	2	3	4	5
Finding meaning in life	1	2	3	4	5
Emotional issues	1	2	3	4	5
Physical health	1	2	3	4	5
Social life	1	2	3	4	5
Intimate relationships	1	2	3	4	5
Sexuality	1	2	3	4	5
Family responsibilities	1	2	3	4	5
Family conflicts	1	2	3	4	5
Family pressure	1	2	3	4	5
Peer pressure	1	2	3	4	5
Loneliness or isolation	1	2	3	4	5
Roommate conflicts	1	2	3	4	5
Conflict with professors	1	2	3	4	5
Campus policies or procedures	1	2	3	4	5
Transportation	1	2	3	4	5
Technology	1	2	3	4	5
Safety	1	2	3	4	5

On the following form, jot down your three highest-rated stressors along with: (a) a coping strategy you could use on your own to deal with that source of stress and (b) a campus resource you could consult to help you deal with that source of stress.

Stressor #1:_____

Personal coping strategy:

Campus resource:

Stressor #2:_____

Personal coping strategy:

Campus resource:

Stressor #3: _____

Personal coping strategy:

Campus resource:

13.5 Relationships Self-Assessment

Refer to the "Working with Others" section of your AchieveWORKS Personality assessment and identify the relationship strengths and challenges identified in your report.

13.6 Relationship Reflections

Identify a relationship you currently have with someone that is having a positive effect on your mental health and ability to succeed in college. How is this relationship helping you?

Identify a relationship that may be having a negative effect on your mental health and ability to succeed in college. How is this relationship affecting you and what might you do to improve it or escape it?

CHAPTER 14

Educational Planning and Decision-Making

MAKING WISE CHOICES ABOUT YOUR COLLEGE COURSES, COLLEGE MAJOR, AND ACADEMIC PATHWAY

Chapter Purpose & Preview

Achieving your educational goals requires making strategic choices about your college courses and your college major. Having an educational plan in mind (and in hand) early in your college experience will enable you to explore your academic options and make a well-informed decision about your college major. Your major field of study should reflect who you are—your personal strengths, talents, interests, and values. This chapter will supply you with strategies for deepening awareness of your personal attributes, educational options, and educational goals, and help you design a strategic plan to reach those goals.

Learning Goal

Acquire knowledge and strategies for making wise decisions about college courses and for determining an educational pathway that closely aligns with your personal interests, talents, values, and goals.

Ignite Your Thinking

Reflection 14.1

At this point in your college experience, are you decided or undecided about a major?

1. If you're undecided, what subjects are you considering as possibilities?

2. If you think you're decided about a major:

   a) What's your choice?

   b) What led you to this choice?

   c) How sure are you about this choice? (Circle one.)

   absolutely sure   fairly sure   not too sure   likely to change

To Be or Not to Be Decided: What Research Shows about Students' Choice of a College Major

When people hear that a student is going to college, the student is often immediately asked: "What's your major?" (Even before the student has stepped foot on campus). You probably saw this question on your college application form and you likely heard it again during your first few days on campus.

Family members are also likely to ask the student the same question, particularly if they're paying for, or helping to pay for, the cost of the student's college education. They want to be sure that their investment will pay off and often think that if their student is decided on a major, it means that he or she is on course and moving in the direction of a financially secure career.

However, despite the push for (and pressure on) students to make a quick and firm decision about a college major, research shows that:

- Fewer than 10% of new college students feel they know a great deal about the field in which they intend to major
- As students proceed through the first year of college, they grow more uncertain about the major they chose when they entered college
- More than one-third of new students change their mind about their major during their first year of college
- Only one in three college seniors are majoring in the same field they thought they were going to major in when they started college.

These findings demonstrate that many first-year students are uncertain about what they will major in, and don't reach a final decision about their major *before* starting college; instead, they reach that decision *during* their college experience.

Thus, being undecided about a major isn't something that first-year students should feel anxious or embarrassed about; it doesn't mean they're aimless or clueless. It may just mean that they're open-minded and do not want to limit their options prematurely. In fact, studies show that new students are often undecided for very good reasons. Some are undecided because they have multiple interests, which is a healthy form of indecision that suggests they are well-rounded and have a wide range of intellectual curiosities. Students may also be undecided because they're reflective, deliberate decision-makers who prefer to explore and weigh their options carefully before making a firm and final commitment. In a national study of students who were undecided about a major at the start of college, 43% of them had certain majors in mind but were not quite ready to commit to one of them.

Reaching a decision about a major can be stressful, especially if you're unsure what your options are and where to begin. Although making this decision can feel like a daunting task, it's less overwhelming if you take time to confer with an academic advisor to explore your college's degree programs and identify an academic pathway fits well with your interests and talents.

To be at least somewhat uncertain about one's educational goals at the start of the college experience is quite natural because you haven't yet experienced many of the subjects in which you could major. In fact, one purpose of the general education (liberal arts) curriculum is to expose students to different fields of study and equip them with the critical thinking skills needed to make a wise choice about their major.

The college curriculum includes fields of study that most students have never experienced before, and almost all of these fields represent possible choices for a college major. The variety of courses you're exposed to in college will not only help you become more aware of the range of academic disciplines and subject areas available to you as potential majors, it will also help you become more aware of yourself. As you gain experience with the college curriculum, you gain greater self-insight into your academic interests, strengths, and weaknesses. You can use this self-knowledge to identify an academic field that best capitalizes on your intellectual curiosities, personal interests, and special talents.

It's true that some students can take too long to choose a major or procrastinate about making this important decision. However, it's also true that some students make this decision too quickly, making a premature choice that lacks self-reflection and careful consideration of different options. Judging from the large number of students who end up changing their college major, it's probably safe to say that more students should take some time to explore their options, examine themselves, and make a well-informed first choice.

If are currently feeling pressure or being pressured to make an early decision about a major, we encourage you to respectfully resist that pressure until you've gained more self-knowledge and more experience with the college curriculum and co-curriculum. As a first-year student, you can still make steady progress toward your destination (a college degree) by taking general education courses that will count toward a college degree in any major you eventually declare.

If you have already decided on a major, be sure to take a course or two in the field right way to confirm whether it truly aligns with your interests, talents, and values. By taking courses in your major early in your college experience, if you discover that it isn't a good fit, you have time to change your mind without delaying your time to graduation. Changing your major, or postponing your initial choice of a major, only becomes problematic if you take *too long* to make your first choice or to change your mind about your first choice. Prolonged delay in choosing a major or changing a major can lengthen your time to graduation (and increase the cost of a college education) because you may need to complete additional courses for your newly chosen major—particularly if it's in a very different field than your original major. The key to avoiding this scenario is to begin the process of educational planning and decision-making *early* in your college experience—starting in the first term of your first year.

> "I see so many people switch [their] major like 4 or 5 times; they end up having to take loads of summer school just to catch up because they invest time and money in classes for a major that they end up not majoring in anyway.
>
> —*College sophomore*

When students are required to declare a major varies from campus to campus and across different fields of study. Generally, you should reach a firm and final decision about your major during your second (sophomore) year. However, regardless of how much time your campus gives you to declare a major, the process of educational planning and decision-making should start now—during your first term in college.

Reflection 14.2

At your college or university, when are students required to declare a major?

Do you think you will be able to make an informed and confident decision by this time? Why?

When students make late changes in their college major, it lengthens the time it takes to complete a college degree and adds to the cost of a college education.

The Importance of Long-Range Educational Planning: Paving Your Academic Pathway

As a first-term college student, if you haven't yet decided on a major, that's perfectly fine. However, being undecided doesn't mean you can put all thoughts about your major on the back burner and simply drift along until you're forced to decide. It doesn't mean that you have no educational plan; it means that your educational plan is to discover a major. Now is the time to start the major exploration-and-selection process by testing out your interests, narrowing down your choices, and paving your own customized pathway to a college degree.

If you have already chosen a major, it doesn't mean that you don't have to give any more thought to that decision; you still need to engage in the process of confirming that major by testing out whether it's truly compatible with your talents, interests, and values. Take the approach that the major you've chosen is your *first* choice; whether it becomes your *final* choice will depend on how well you perform (and how interested you are) in the first courses you take in the field.

By looking ahead and developing an educational plan, you get a sneak preview and "big picture" overview of your total college experience. In contrast, looking at and scheduling your classes one term at a time—just before each registration period—chops up your college experience into a series of separate snapshots or still frames, leaving you with little sense of continuity, connection, and direction. On pp. 327-336, you will find directions and guidelines for developing an educational plan. This is an opportunity for you to begin steering your educational future in a direction that has meaning and purpose for you. Rather than waiting and passively letting your educational future happen *to* you, advanced planning makes it happen *for* you.

> *"Some people make things happen, while others watch things happen or wonder what has happened."*
> —*Author unknown*

Keep in mind that a long-range educational plan isn't something set in stone. As you gain more educational experience, your specific academic and career interests may change and so may the specifics of your plan. The purpose of an educational plan is not to tie you up or pin you down but to put you on an academic pathway that keeps you on course and moving in the right direction—toward a college degree in a college major that's best for you.

> *"When you have to make a choice and don't make it, that is in itself a choice."*
> —*William James, philosopher and one of the founders of American psychology*

©Kendall Hunt Publishing Company

Educational planning prevents students from taking a passive, avoidance-and-denial approach to their future.

Factors to Consider When Choosing a Major

Self-awareness is the critical first step in the process of making an effective personal decision or choice. You need to know yourself before you know what major is best for you. When choosing a major, self-awareness should include awareness includes knowing your:

- Learning Talents
- Personal Values
- Personal Interests

As illustrated in **Figure 14.1**, these three pillars provide a solid foundation on which to base your choice of a college major.

FIGURE 14.1: Three Key Personal Characteristics to Consider when Choosing a College Major

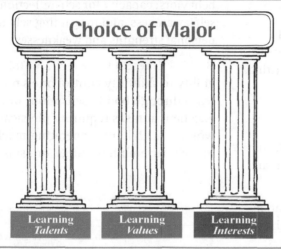

©Kendall Hunt Publishing Company

Research indicates that students who choose majors that are compatible with their talents, interests, and learning preferences are more likely to be academically successful in college and more likely to complete their degree.

Learning Talents: Multiple Intelligences

Among the personal characteristics that should be taken into consideration when choosing a major are your intellectual talents and strengths. Intelligence was once considered to be a single, general trait that could be identified by one intelligence test score. Scholars have since discovered that intelligence doesn't come conveniently wrapped in a one-size-fits-all package. The singular word "intelligence" has been replaced by the plural word "intelligences" to reflect the fact that humans display intelligence (mental ability) in a variety of forms that are not measured by or captured by their score on an IQ or SAT test.

Based on studies of gifted and talented individuals, experts in different professional fields, and research on the human brain, psychologist Howard Gardner has identified the multiple forms of intelligence listed in **Box 14.1**. Keep these forms of intelligence in mind when deciding on a college major because different majors emphasize different intellectual skills. Ideally, you want to major in an academic field that fits well with, and allows you to capitalize on, your strongest mental attributes

> "Exceptional individuals have a special talent for identifying their own strengths and weaknesses."
>
> —Howard Gardner, *Extraordinary Minds*

and talents. This "fit" should enable you to master the concepts and skills required by your major more efficiently and more deeply. Choosing a major that aligns well with your particular form(s) of intelligence should also increase the likelihood that you will experience early success in your major, giving you academic momentum and academic self-confidence to continue your studies and complete your degree.

Box 14.1

Multiple Forms of Intelligence

As you read through the following forms of intelligence, place a checkmark next to the types that you think represent your strongest abilities or talents. (You can possess more than one type.)

Linguistic Intelligence: ability to comprehend language and communicate through language; possessing strong verbal skills for speaking, writing, listening, and/or learning foreign languages.

Logical–Mathematical Intelligence: aptitude for understanding logical patterns and making and following logical arguments; ability to work well with numbers; good at solving mathematical problems and making quantitative calculations.

Spatial Intelligence: aptitude for visualizing relationships among objects arranged in different spatial positions and perceiving or creating visual images; ability to form mental images of three-dimensional objects; capable of detecting fine and subtle details in objects or pictures; proficient at drawing, painting, sculpting, or graphic design; good sense of direction and ability to navigate unfamiliar places.

Musical Intelligence: able to appreciate or create rhythmical and melodic sounds; skilled at playing, composing, or arranging music.

Interpersonal (Social) Intelligence: ability to relate to people and accurately identify their needs, motivations, and emotional states; effective at expressing personal emotions and feelings to others; good interpersonal communication skills; ability to accurately "read" the feelings of others and meet their emotional needs.

Intrapersonal (Self) Intelligence: ability to introspect and understand one's own thoughts, feelings, and behaviors; capacity for self-reflection, emotional self-awareness, and for gaining self-insight into personal strengths and weaknesses.

Bodily–Kinesthetic (Psychomotor) Intelligence: ability to skillfully control one's own body and to learn through bodily sensations or movements; excellent at tasks requiring physical coordination, working with hands, operating machinery, building models, assembling things, or using technology.

> "I used to operate a printing press. In about two weeks I knew how to run it and soon after I could take the machine apart in my head and analyze what each part does, how it functioned, and why it was shaped that way."
>
> —*Response of college sophomore to the questions: "What are you really good at? What comes easily or naturally to you?"*

Naturalist Intelligence: ability to carefully observe and appreciate features of the natural environment; keen awareness of nature and natural surroundings; ability to understand causes and consequences of events occurring in the physical world.

Existential Intelligence: ability to conceptualize phenomena and ponder experiences that go beyond the physical world and physical evidence, including questions relating to the origin, meaning, and purpose of human existence.

**Reflection 14.3**

Look back at the nine forms of intelligence listed in Box 14.1.

Which of these types of intelligence do you think represents your strongest talent(s)?

What college major(s) do you think would best fit or match your strongest talents?

Learning Values

Besides your intellectual talents, another key factor to consider when choosing a major field of study is your *values*—what you believe is important to study or worth studying. For example, if helping others is something that you really value, a major that emphasizes this value may be a good choice for you. Reflecting on and identifying your personal values will help you pursue an academic pathway that makes a meaningful connection between your current education with your future vocation.

**Reflection 14.4**

Think about your learning values. List three values that best capture what is really important or matters most to you.

Are these values consistent with the major you have chosen or are considering?

AUTHOR'S EXPERIENCE

As a college student, my degree was in anthropology and I had visions of travelling the world after graduation, studying different cultural groups and conducting research. As graduation approached, I realized that this lofty goal was not realistic. I was a bit crushed at first, then rebounded and reassessed my "plans" to find an alternative pathway that would allow me to pursue the same interests but in a different way. I knew I had a strong interest in connecting with people across cultures, but I also valued education and helping others. Drawing on these interests and values, I decided to pursue a master's degree in cross-cultural counseling. Also, while completing my degree, I worked as a tutor—an experience that deepened my interest in helping students succeed. Now I am employed as a college administrator and am in charge of academic programs designed to promote student success. Looking back, I now recognize that following my interests and values led me to the personally fulfilling career I have today.

—Michele Campagna

Learning Interests

In addition to your talents and values, a third key personal characteristic to consider when choosing a major are your *interests*—what you like to study or enjoy studying (e.g., topics that intrigue you, capture your curiosity, and hold your attention).

This consideration also includes ways in which you prefer to learn—how you like to *perceive* information (receive or take it in) and *process* information (deal with it after taking it in). For instance, individuals differ in terms of whether they prefer to take in information by reading about it, listening to it, viewing it in diagrammatic form, or physically touching and manipulating it. Individuals may also vary in terms of whether they like to receive information in a structured, orderly format or in a more unstructured format that allows them the freedom to explore, play with, and restructure it in their own way. In addition, individuals may also differ in terms of how they prefer to process (think about) information after it has been received. Some prefer to process it on their own, others prefer to discuss it with someone else; some may like to outline it, others prefer to map it out or draw it.

AUTHOR'S EXPERIENCE

In my family, whenever something has to be assembled or set up (e.g., a ping-pong table or new electronic equipment), I've noticed that my wife, my son, and myself take very different approaches. I like to read the manual's instructions carefully and completely before I even attempt to touch anything. My son prefers to look at the pictures or diagrams in the manual and uses them as models to find the parts; then he begins to assemble those parts. My wife seems to prefer not to look at the manual at all. Instead, she likes to figure things out as she goes along, grabbing different parts from the box, assembling those parts that look like they should fit into each other, and piecing them together as if she were completing a jigsaw puzzle.

—*Joe Cuseo*

Tests have been designed to assess a person's preferred way to learn. (If you're interested in taking one, the Learning Center and Career Center are two places on campus where you may be able to do so.) Probably the most frequently used learning preferences test is the *Myers-Briggs Type Indicator (MBTI)*—a test based on the personality theory of psychologist Carl Jung. It assesses how people vary along a scale (low to high) on each of four sets of opposing traits—illustrated in **Figure 14.2**.

Read through these pairs of opposite traits and place a mark along the line where you think you fall with respect to each set. Place a mark toward the far left or far right if you think you lean strongly toward one end of the scale; place a mark in the middle of the line if you don't think you lean strongly in either direction.

FIGURE 14.2: Traits and Learning Preferences Measured by the Myers-Briggs Type Indicator (MBTI)

Extraversion	*Introversion*
Prefer to focus on the "outer" world of persons, actions, or objects	Prefer to focus on the "inner" world of thoughts and ideas

Sensing	*Intuition*
Prefer interacting with the world directly through concrete, sensory experiences	Prefer dealing with symbolic meanings and imagining possibilities

Thinking	*Feeling*
Prefer to rely on logic and rational thinking when making decisions	Prefer to rely on human needs and feelings when making decisions

Judging	*Perceiving*
Prefer to plan for and control events	Prefer flexibility and spontaneity

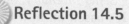

Reflection 14.5

For each of the following traits and learning preferences, rate yourself in terms of how you think you would compare with others.

	Low	Middle	High
Extraversion			
Introversion			
Sensing			
Intuition			
Thinking			
Feeling			
Judging			
Perceiving			

What majors or fields of study do you think would be most compatible with your personality traits and learning preferences?

Research on the MBTI suggests that students may differ in terms of the mental tasks they prefer to perform. For instance, students who score high on the introversion scale of the MBTI are more likely to stay engaged and attentive when performing mental tasks that require repetition and involve little external stimulation. It has also been found that students who score differently on the MBTI prefer different writing styles and writing assignments. These differences are summarized below.

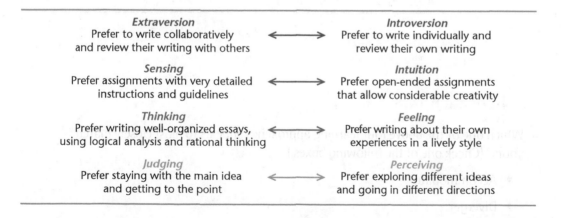

Extraversion
Prefer to write collaboratively and review their writing with others ⟷ *Introversion*
Prefer to write individually and review their own writing

Sensing
Prefer assignments with very detailed instructions and guidelines ⟷ *Intuition*
Prefer open-ended assignments that allow considerable creativity

Thinking
Prefer writing well-organized essays, using logical analysis and rational thinking ⟷ *Feeling*
Prefer writing about their own experiences in a lively style

Judging
Prefer staying with the main idea and getting to the point ⟷ *Perceiving*
Prefer exploring different ideas and going in different directions

Since writing and thinking are interrelated, how your preferred writing style compares with the preferred style of different academic fields may be one factor to consider when choosing a major. Different academic fields emphasize different styles of learning; some place heavy emphasis on structured, tightly focused writing (e.g., science and business), while other fields encourage writing with personal style, flair, and creativity (e.g., English).

Another popular learning preferences test is the *Learning Styles Inventory*, originally developed by David Kolb, a professor of philosophy. It's based on how individuals differ with respect to the following two dimensions of learning:

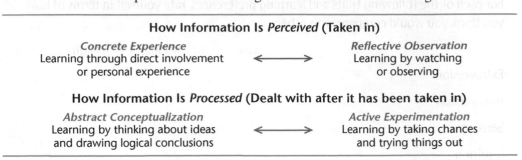

How Information Is *Perceived* (Taken in)

Concrete Experience		*Reflective Observation*
Learning through direct involvement or personal experience	⟷	Learning by watching or observing

How Information Is *Processed* (Dealt with after it has been taken in)

Abstract Conceptualization		*Active Experimentation*
Learning by thinking about ideas and drawing logical conclusions	⟷	Learning by taking chances and trying things out

When these two dimensions are crisscrossed, four sectors (areas) are created, each of which represents a different learning preference—as illustrated in **Figure 14.3**. As you read the characteristics associated with each of the four areas, circle the one you think best reflects your most preferred way of learning.

FIGURE 14.3: Learning Styles Measured by the Learning Styles Inventory (LSI)

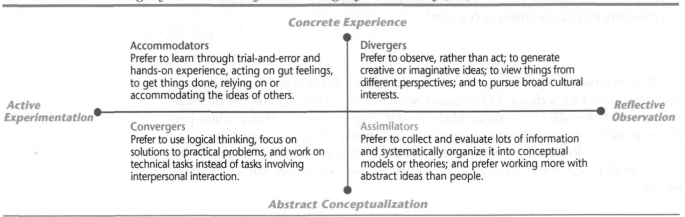

Concrete Experience

Accommodators
Prefer to learn through trial-and-error and hands-on experience, acting on gut feelings, to get things done, relying on or accommodating the ideas of others.

Divergers
Prefer to observe, rather than act; to generate creative or imaginative ideas; to view things from different perspectives; and to pursue broad cultural interests.

Active Experimentation ———————————— **Reflective Observation**

Convergers
Prefer to use logical thinking, focus on solutions to practical problems, and work on technical tasks instead of tasks involving interpersonal interaction.

Assimilators
Prefer to collect and evaluate lots of information and systematically organize it into conceptual models or theories; and prefer working more with abstract ideas than people.

Abstract Conceptualization

 Reflection 14.6

Which one of the above four learning approaches appears to most closely match yours? (Check one of the following boxes.)

- Accommodator

- Diverger

- Converger

- Assimilator

What majors or fields of study appear to be a good match for your approach to learning?

Research indicates that students who display differences in these four learning approaches tend to major in different fields. "Assimilators" are more often found majoring in mathematics and natural sciences (e.g., chemistry and physics), probably because these subjects emphasize reflection and abstract thinking. In contrast, "accommodators" tend to be more commonly found majoring in business, accounting, and law, perhaps because these fields involve taking practical action and making concrete decisions. "Divergers" are more often attracted to majors in the fine arts (e.g., music, art, and drama), humanities (e.g., history and literature), or social sciences (e.g., psychology and political science), likely due to the fact that these subjects accommodate multiple (divergent) viewpoints and perspectives. In contrast, "convergers" are more often found majoring in fields such as accounting, engineering, medicine, and nursing, perhaps because these subjects emphasize focusing in (converging) on specific answers and solutions. This pattern of preferences was also discovered among college instructors when they were asked to classify different academic fields in terms of the learning approaches they emphasized.

Because individuals have different learning preferences and academic fields emphasize different learning approaches, it's important to be mindful of whether your learning preference is compatible with the type of learning emphasized by the field you're considering as a major. If it's a good marriage it could lead to a very satisfying and successful learning experience.

AUTHOR'S EXPERIENCE

I first noticed that students in different academic fields may have different learning styles when I was teaching a psychology course to students majoring in nursing and social work. When we got involved in extended discussions of controversial issues and theories, some students in class seemed to lose interest (and patience) while others really got into it. On the other hand, when I gave lectures that required students to take notes on factual and practical information, some students seemed to lose interest (and attention) while others perked up, listened attentively, and took copious notes.

After one class session that involved quite a bit of student discussion, I thought about the students who were most engaged and those who seemed to drift off or lose interest. I discovered that the students who did most of the talking and were most enthused during the class discussion were the students majoring in social work. Most of the students who appeared disinterested or a bit frustrated were the nursing majors. The more I thought about this, it dawned on me that nursing students were accustomed to gathering factual information and learning specific skills in their major courses. They felt more comfortable with structured class sessions in which they received lots of factual, practical information from the professor. On the other hand, the social work majors were more comfortable with unstructured class discussions because courses in their major often emphasized debating social issues and considering multiple viewpoints.

When I left class that day, I wondered if the differences in learning preferences between the nursing and social work students accounted for why they chose a major whose primary method of teaching matched their preferred method of learning.

—*Joe Cuseo*

Consider visiting the Learning Center or Career Development Center on your campus to take a learning preference test or complete the learning inventory that accompanies this text (**for details, see the inside of the front cover**). Even if the test doesn't help you choose a major, it can help increase awareness of your preferred way(s) of learning. This alone can contribute to your academic success because studies show that college students who have greater self-awareness of their learning preferences and approaches exhibit stronger academic performance.

 Reflection 14.7

In addition to taking formal tests to assess your learning preferences, you can gain awareness of them through some simple self-reflection. Take a moment to think about the ways you prefer to learn by completing the following statements:

I learn best if ...

I learn most from ...

I enjoy learning when ...

Do you see any pattern in your answers that suggest certain majors may be more compatible with your preferred way of learning?

Reflect on learning experiences you've had in the past that you found enjoyable or stimulating. Think about previous classes that piqued your curiosity and in which you did your best work. The subjects of these courses may represent fields of study that match up well with your interests, talents, and preferred learning methods.

At the website *www.mymajors.com*, you can enter information about your academic performance in high school courses. Your inputted information will be analyzed and you'll receive a report on what college majors appear to be a good match for you. You can do the same analysis for the courses you complete in college.

Strategies for Learning about Different Majors

In addition to knowing yourself well, deciding on a major also requires knowing your major well. Listed below are specific strategies you may use to acquire deeper knowledge about a major you have chosen are considering.

Look at introductory textbooks in the field associated with the major. Review the table of contents and read a few pages of the text to get some sense of how information is presented in the field and whether the topics are compatible with your educational interests. You should be able to find introductory textbooks for different fields of study in your college bookstore.

Discuss the major with an academic advisor. To get unbiased feedback about the pros and cons of majoring in a field, speak with an academic advisor who works with students who have different majors. After this meeting, if you're still interested in the major, you can get more specific details by consulting with an advisor who specializes in that major.

Speak with a faculty member in the department. Consider asking the following questions:

- What academic skills or qualities are needed for a student to be successful in your field?
- What are the greatest challenges faced by students majoring in your field?

- What can students do with a major in your field after graduating?
- What types of graduate programs or professional schools would a student in your major be well prepared to enter?

(For additional questions, see exercise **14.4** at the end of the chapter.)

Seek out students majoring in the field and ask them about their experiences. Talk to several students to get different perspectives on what the field is like. You can find these students by visiting campus clubs related to the major (e.g., psychology club or history club). You could also check the class schedule to see when and where classes in the major are meeting. Go to one of these classes, and either before or after class, ask students about the major. The following questions may be good ones to ask:

- What attracted you to your major?
- What types of skills or talents are needed to succeed in your major?
- What would you say are the advantages and disadvantages of majoring in your field?
- Knowing what you know now, would you choose the same major again?

Also, ask students about the quality of teaching and advising in the department offering the major. Studies show that different departments within the same college or university can vary greatly in terms of their instructional effectiveness as well as their educational philosophy and attitude toward students.

Sit in on some classes in the major. If the class you'd like to visit is large, you may be able to just slip into the back row and listen. If the class is small, ask the instructor for permission. During your class visit, focus on how well you respond to the content or ideas being covered, rather than the instructor's personality or teaching style. Remember: you're deciding on whether to major in the subject, not the professor.

Surf the website of the professional organizations associated with the major. These websites often contain useful information for students interested in majoring in the field. To locate the professional website for a major you're considering, ask a faculty member in that field or search the web by simply entering the name of the field followed by the word "association." For example, if you're thinking about becoming an anthropology major, check the website of the American Anthropological Association; or if you're considering history as a major, look at the website of the American Historical Association. These websites also identify various careers that students majoring in the field are qualified to pursue after graduation.

Visit your Career Development Center to inquire about what graduates have gone on to do with the major. Ask if the Center has information about the type of positions that students majoring in the field have entered following graduation, or what graduate programs and professional schools they went on to attend.

Be sure you're aware of all courses required by the major. You can find this information in your college catalog, university bulletin, or campus website. If you're in doubt, seek assistance from an academic advisor. College majors sometimes require courses that students never expect to be required. For example, students considering the field of forensics are often surprised by the number of science courses required by this major. Keep in mind that college majors often require courses in fields outside of the major that are designed to support the major. For instance, psychology majors are often expected to take at least one course in biology, and business majors are often required to take calculus.

If you're interested in majoring in a field, be sure you are fully aware of such outside requirements and are comfortable with them. Once you have accurately identified all courses required for the major you're considering, ask yourself the following questions: Do the course titles and descriptions appeal to my interests and values? Do I have the abilities or skills needed to do well in these courses?

Be sure you know what academic standards need to be met to be admitted to the major. Some college majors are "impacted" or "oversubscribed," meaning that more students are interested in majoring in these fields than there are openings for them. Majors that tend to be oversubscribed are pre-professional majors that lead directly to a career (e.g., engineering, premed, nursing, or physical therapy). On some campuses, these majors are called "restricted" majors, meaning that departments restrict enrollment by limiting the number of students admitted to the major. Admission may be limited to students who earn a GPA of 3.0 or higher in certain introductory courses required by the major. In some cases, the department may rank students applying for the major according to their overall GPA, then proceed down the list and accept them in the order of their GPA until there are no more openings.

If you intend to major in a restricted field of study, be sure to keep track of whether you're meeting the acceptance standards of the major as you continue to complete courses and earn grades. If you're falling short of the academic standards of the major you hope to enter—despite working at your maximum level of effort and regularly using the learning assistance services available on campus—see an academic advisor about finding another major, particularly one that may be closely related to the restricted major you were hoping to enter.

Use your elective courses to test your interest in subjects that you're considering as possible majors. As its name implies, "elective" courses are courses you elect or choose to take. They come in two forms: free electives and restricted electives. *Free electives* refer to courses you are free to take that count toward your college degree but aren't required for general education or a particular major. *Restricted electives* are courses you must take to fulfill requirements in general education or a specific major, but you get to choose them from a restricted list (menu) of courses. For example, your campus may have a general education requirement in the social or behavioral sciences that stipulates you must take two courses in this field; however, you get to choose what those two courses are from a list of options (e.g., anthropology, economics, political science, psychology, or sociology). If you're considering one of these fields as a possible major, you can take an introductory course in that subject to test your interest in the subject while simultaneously fulfilling a general education requirement needed for graduation. This strategy allows you to use general education as the main highway to travel toward your final destination (a college degree) while using your restricted electives to explore side roads (potential majors) along the way. You can use the same strategy with your free electives.

Naturally, you don't have to use up all your electives for the purpose of exploring majors. See **Box 14.2** for other ways to use electives strategically and productively.

> "I took Biology to satisfy a distribution [general education] requirement and I ended up majoring in it."
>
> —Pediatrician

Box 14.2

Top Ten Suggestions for Making the Most of Your College Electives

Elective courses give you with academic freedom to take personal ownership and control of your coursework. By exercising this freedom responsibly and strategically will allow you to customize your college experience and maximize the impact of your college degree.

Listed below are ten recommendations for making effective use of your college electives. As you read them, note the strategies that most appeal to you and that you're most likely to put into practice.

1. **Complete a minor or build an area of concentration.** Electives can be used to pursue an additional field of study that complements and strengthens your major. (See p. 322 for further details.)

2. **Help you discover career interests.** Just as electives can be used to test your interest in a college major, they can be used to test your interest in a career. For instance, you could enroll in:
   - career planning or career development courses
   - courses that include internships or service learning experiences related to a career field you may be interested in (e.g., health, education, or business).

3. **Strengthen your skills in areas that would appeal to future employers.** Elective courses in foreign language, leadership development, and technology can supply you with skills that are attractive to employers. (See Chapter 15 for skills that are highly valued by today's employers.)

4. **Learn something you were always curious about.** If you've always wondered how members of the other sex think and feel, you could take a course on the psychology of men and women. If you've heard about a course that students talk about as being interesting, take that course and find out why.

5. **Stretch yourself to learn in different ways and develop new talents.** There are courses in the college curriculum on subjects you never experienced taken before, or never knew existed. These courses can supply you with an unprecedented opportunity to expand your knowledge base and skill set in ways that promote "growth mindset"—a key characteristic of successful people. (See Chapter 3, pp. 62–64, for more information on growth mindset.)

6. **Appreciate different diverse cultural viewpoints and enhance intercultural competence.** Electives may be taken that involve learning about cultural differences across nations (e.g., international relations) and within the United States (e.g., race and ethnicity).

7. **Develop practical life skills.** Courses in personal finances, marriage and family, or child development can provide you with skills for money management and effective parenting.

8. **Live a balanced, well-rounded life.** You can use your electives intentionally to cover all key dimensions of self-development, such as: emotional development (e.g., stress management), social development (e.g., social psychology), intellectual development (e.g., critical thinking), physical development (e.g., nutrition or self-defense), and spiritual development (e.g., world religions or death and dying).

> " I discovered an unknown talent and lifelong stress-reducing hobby."
>
> —An attorney talking about an elective ceramics course taken in college

9. **Make connections between different academic disciplines (subject areas).** *Interdisciplinary* courses are designed specifically to integrate two or more academic disciplines. For instance, psychobiology is an interdisciplinary course that integrates the fields of psychology (focusing on the mind) and biology (focusing on the body), enabling students to see how the mind influences the body and vice versa.

   Taking interdisciplinary courses that make connections between subjects to get a more complete understanding of personal or societal issues can be a stimulating intellectual experience. In addition, the presence of interdisciplinary courses on your college transcript may be attractive to future employers because "real world" job responsibilities and work challenges cannot be handled solely with the tools of a single major; they require the ability to integrate skills acquired from different fields of study.

10. **Develop broader perspectives on the human condition and the surrounding world.** Electives can be used strategically to gain progressively wider perspectives on yourself and the world around you, such as courses that provide a personal perspective (psychology), a societal perspective (sociology), a national perspective (political science), an international perspective (world geography), a global perspective (ecology), and a cosmological perspective (astronomy). (See Chapter 2, pp. 33–37 for more detailed information on these broadening perspectives.)

Your college catalog (bulletin) contains descriptions of all courses offered on your campus. Take some time to review these course descriptions and explore all the elective options available to you. Depending on your major, up to as many as one-third of your college courses may be electives. Take advantage of these free-choice courses to shape your college experience in a way that capitalizes on your personal interests, maximizes your personal growth, and enables you to reach your full potential.

Reflection 14.8

What strategies for selecting electives listed in Box 14.2 are you most likely to implement? Why?

> "Try not to take classes because they fit neatly into your schedule. Start by identifying classes that are most important to you and fit your schedule to accommodate them."
>
> —Katharine Brooks, *You Majored in What?*

Don't take your elective choices lightly or choose them merely based on scheduling convenience (e.g., to create a schedule with no early morning or late afternoon classes and no classes on Friday). Use your elective courses strategically to shape and create a college experience that is uniquely your own.

Choosing courses that best enable you to achieve your long-term educational and personal goals should take precedence over creating a schedule that leaves your Fridays free for three-day weekends.

Explore the possibility of completing a college minor in a field that complements your major. A college minor usually requires about half the number of credits (units) required for a major. Most schools allow students the option of completing a minor along with their major. Check your course catalog or consult with an academic advisor for college minors that may interest you.

If you have a strong interest in two different fields, a minor will allow you to major in one of these fields while minoring in the other. This enables you to pursue two fields of interest without having to sacrifice one for the other. Another advantage of a minor is that it can usually be completed with a major without delaying your time to graduation. In contrast, completing a double major may lengthen your time in college because of the extra time needed to complete all requirements for both majors.

Another way to complete a second field of study without increasing your time to graduation is by completing a "concentration" or "cognate area"—an academic specialization that requires even fewer courses to complete than a minor—e.g., four to five courses. Taking a cluster of courses in a field outside your major adds another specialization to your repertoire, which can strengthen your resume and your employment prospects; it also demonstrates your academic versatility and ability to acquire knowledge and skills in areas that may be missing or underemphasized in your major. For example, students majoring in the fine arts (e.g., music or theater) or humanities (e.g., English or history) can increase their employment options after graduation by taking a cluster of courses in fields such as mathematics (e.g., statistics), technology (e.g., computer science), or business (e.g., economics).

Myths about the Relationship between Majors and Careers

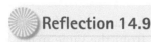
Reflection 14.9

Consider the following statement: "Choosing a major is a life-changing decision because it will determine what you will do for the rest of your life."

Would you agree or disagree?

Why?

Numerous misconceptions exist about the relationship between college majors and careers, some of which can lead students to make uninformed or unrealistic decisions about a major. Here are four common myths about the major–career relationship that you should be aware of and factor into your decisions about a college major and future career.

Myth 1. When you choose your major, you're choosing your career.

Although some majors lead directly to a specific career, most do not. Majors leading directly to specialized careers are often called pre-professional or pre-vocational majors; they include such fields as accounting, engineering, and nursing. However, the path from most college majors to a future career is not direct or linear. Students don't take a monorail ride straight from a specific major to a specific career tied directly to that major. For instance, all physics majors don't become physicists, all philosophy majors don't become philosophers, all history majors don't become historians, and all English majors don't become English teachers. Instead, these majors lead to a cluster or "family" of different career options.

> "Linear thinking can keep you from thinking broadly about your options and being open-minded to new opportunities.
>
> —Katharine Brooks, author, *You Majored in What?*

The truth is that for most students, their journey from college major to future career(s) is less like scaling a vertical pole and more like climbing a tree with multiple branches. As illustrated in **Figure 14.4**, the climb begins with the tree's trunk—

FIGURE 14.4: **The Relationship between General Education (Liberal Arts), College Majors, and Careers**

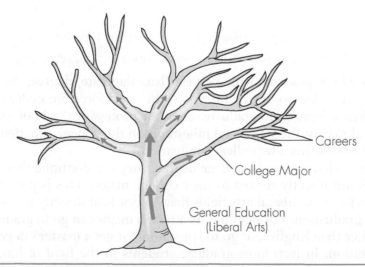

Careers

College Major

General Education
(Liberal Arts)

the foundation provided by general education (the liberal arts), which leads to separate limbs (choices for college majors), which, in turn, leads to different branches (various career paths or occupational options).

Note how different sets of branches (careers) grow from the same limb (major). Similarly, different career clusters or "career families" grow from the same major. An English major can lead to a variety of careers that involve writing (e.g., editing, journalism, or publishing), and a major in art can lead to different careers that involve visual media (e.g., illustration, graphic design, or art therapy).

Furthermore, different majors can lead to the same career. For instance, a variety of majors can lead a student to law school and a career as a lawyer; in fact, there's really no such thing as a "law major" or "pre-law major." Students with a variety of majors (or minors) can also enter medical school if they have a solid set of foundational courses in biology and chemistry and score well on the medical college admissions test.

Studies show that today's college graduates will change jobs ten times in the two decades following graduation and this rate of job changing rate is expected to escalate in the future. Surveys also show that only half of recent college graduates expect to be working in the same field that they're currently employed. In fact, the further along they proceed in their career path, the more likely it is that college graduates will be working in a field that's unrelated to their college major. These findings point to the following conclusion: Don't assume that your major *is* your future career, or that your college major automatically turns into your lifelong career. It is this mistaken belief that causes some students to procrastinate about choosing a major—they think they're making a lifelong decision and are afraid that they'll make the "wrong" decision and find themselves doing something they hate for the remainder of their lives.

Although it is important for students to think about how their current choice of a college major will affect their future career path, for most students, particularly those who are not majoring in pre-professional fields, deciding on a major and deciding on a career are not identical decisions made at the same time. Choosing a specific major is a decision that must be made by or before the end of the sophomore year; choosing a career (or careers) is a decision that can be made later.

> *Don't assume that choosing your college major means you're choosing what you will do for the rest of your working life. Deciding on a major and deciding on a career are not identical decisions must be made simultaneously.*

Myth 2. If you decide to continue your education beyond college graudation, you have to continue in the same field as your college major.

After college students graduate with a 4-year (baccalaureate) degree, they have two primary paths available to them: (a) enter the workforce immediately, and/or (b) continue their education in graduate school or professional school. (See **Figure 14.5** for a visual map of the stages and milestones in the college experience and the paths available to students after college graduation.)

Once students have earned a college degree, they can continue their education in a field that's not directly related to their college major. This is particularly true for students majoring in liberal arts fields that do not lead directly to a specific occupation after graduation. For example, an English major can go to graduate school in a subject other than English, or go to law school, or get a master's degree in business administration. In fact, most graduate students in the field of business (e.g., MBA-seeking students) were not business majors as undergraduates.

> "I intend on becoming a corporate lawyer. I am an English major. The reason I chose this major is because while I was researching the educational backgrounds of some corporate attorneys, I found that a lot were English majors. It helps with writing and delivering cases."
>
> — *College sophomore*

> "Things like picking majors and careers really scare me a lot! I don't know exactly what I want to do with my life."
>
> —*First-year student*

> "The first week of law school, one of my professors stressed the importance of 'researching, analyzing and writing.' I thought this was an interesting thing to say, because English majors learn and practice these skills in every class."
>
> —*English major attending law school*

FIGURE 14.5: A Snapshot of the College Experience and Beyond

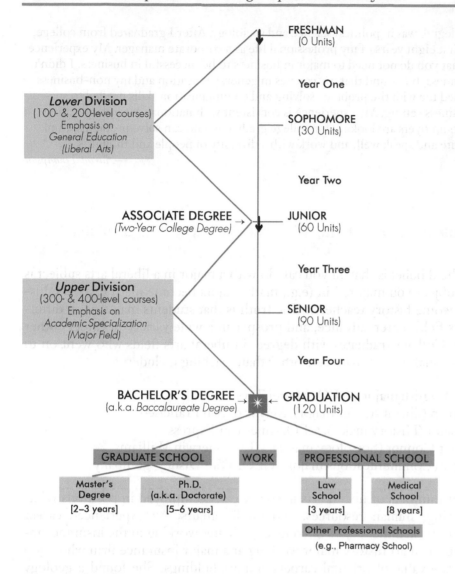

Notes

1. On average, about one-third of the courses required for a college degree are general education courses selected from the liberal arts curriculum. However, the number of required general education courses varies from campus to campus and can vary at the same campus depending on the student's major.

2. The word "freshman" originated in England in 1596, when every college student was a "fresh" (new) "man." Today, the term "freshman" is frequently being replaced by "first-year student" because this is a more gender-neutral term.

3. The term "baccalaureate" derives from "Bacchus"—the Greek god of wine and festive celebration, and "laurel"—a wreath made from the laurel plant that ancient Greeks draped around the neck of Olympic champions.

4. It often takes college students longer than four years to graduate due to a variety of reasons, such as working part-time and taking fewer courses per term, needing to repeat courses that were failed or dropped, or making a late change to a major and needing to fulfill additional requirements for the new major.

5. Graduate and professional schools are options for continuing to higher levels of education after completion of an undergraduate (college) education.

6. Students going to graduate school on a full-time basis can sometimes support themselves financially by working part-time as a teaching assistant (TA) or research assistant (RA). It's also possible for students to enroll in some graduate or professional school programs on a part-time basis while holding a full-time job.

7. The term "Ph.D." refers to "Doctor of Philosophy," in tribute to the ancient Greek philosophers (e.g., Socrates, Plato, and Aristotle). However, a Ph.D. can be earned in a wide variety of academic fields (mathematics, music, economics, etc.).

8. Compared with graduate school, professional school involves advanced education in more "applied" professions (e.g., pharmacy or public administration).

©Kendall Hunt Publishing Company

Myth 3. Because most college graduates are employed in business organizations or corporations, it's best to major in business.

Most college graduates end up working in business settings, so it's commonly believed that if you're going to work in a business, you should major in business. This belief likely explains why business is the most popular major among college students. However, most college graduates now working in business settings majored in fields other than business, and many CEOs of today's most profitable companies did not major in business. Certainly, if you have an interest in and passion for majoring in business, by all means major in business. However, don't choose a business major because you think it's the only major that will qualify you to be hired by, and succeed in, business organizations after graduating from college.

AUTHOR'S EXPERIENCE

My college degree was in political science and sociology. After I graduated from college, I spent the first eight years of my professional life as a corporate manager. My experience taught me that you do not need to major in business to be successful in business. I didn't major in business, but found that my courses in general education and my non-business major supplied me with the problem-solving and communication skills needed to succeed in a business setting. My experience is consistent with national surveys indicating that today's employers are looking for college graduates who can solve problems, think critically, write and speak well, and work with a diversity of people and thoughts.

—*Aaron Thompson*

Myth 4. If you major in a liberal arts field, the only career available to you is teaching.

A commonly held belief is that all you can do with a major in a liberal arts subject is to teach the subject you majored in (e.g., math majors become math teachers; history majors become history teachers). The truth is that students majoring in different liberal arts fields enter, advance, and prosper in a wide variety of careers other than teaching. College graduates with degrees in liberal arts fields who went on to achieve professional success in careers other than teaching include:

- Jill Barad (English major), CEO, Mattel Toys
- Willie Brown (liberal studies major), Mayor of San Francisco
- Ken Chenault (History major), CEO, American Express
- Christopher Connor (Sociology major), CEO, Sherwin Williams
- Robert Iger (Communications major), CEO, Walt Disney Company

> "I personally think there's going to be a greater demand in 10 years for liberal arts majors because when the data is all being spit out for you, options are being spit out for you, you need a different perspective in order to have a different view of the data ... someone who is more of a freer thinker."
>
> — Mark Cuban, businessman, 'Shark Tank' investor, and author of *How to Win at the Sport of Business*

Significant numbers of liberal arts majors are also employed in positions relating to marketing, human resources, and public affairs. An experienced career counselor once tracked the majors of college graduates working in the insurance industry. She found an art history major working at a major insurance firm whose job was to assess the value of oriental carpets and art holdings. She found a geology major working for an insurance company whose job was to evaluate beach properties and determine the odds that hurricanes or other natural phenomena will cause property damage. This former geology major spent much of her professional time traveling to beachfront communities to review new developments and assessing damages after hurricanes and other natural disasters.

It has also been found that the career mobility and career advancement of liberal arts majors working in the corporate world are comparable to business majors. Liberal arts majors are just as likely to advance to the highest levels of corporate leadership as majors in such pre-professional fields as business and engineering. The bottom line: If you have a passion for and talent in a liberal arts field, don't dismiss it as being "impractical," and don't be dismayed or discouraged by others who may challenge your choice by asking: "What are you going to do with a degree in that major?"

AUTHOR'S EXPERIENCE

My brother, Vinny, was a philosophy major in college. He came home one Christmas wearing a tee-shirt on which was printed the message: "Philosophy major. Will think for food." With his major in philosophy, my brother went to graduate school, completed a master's degree in higher education, and is now making a six-figure salary working as a college administrator. Looking back, his old tee-shirt should have read: "Philosophy major. Will think for money."

—*Joe Cuseo*

 Reflection 14.10

Look back at the four myths about the relationships between majors and careers. Which of them did you already know were not true? Which of these myths did you think were true?

Internet-Based Resources

For additional information related to the material covered in this chapter, consult the following websites.

Assessing Personality Types and Learning Preferences via the Myers-Briggs Type Indicator (MBTI)
http://www.humanmetrics.com/cgi-win/jtypes2.asp

Identifying and Choosing College Majors:
www.mymajors.com
https://www.princetonreview.com/college-major-search

Relationships between Majors and Careers:
https://uncw.edu/career/whatcanidowithamajorin.html

Careers for Liberal Arts Majors:
Liberal Arts Career Network (www.liberalartscareers.org/)

Chapter 14 Exercises

14.1 Quote Reflections

Review the sidebar quotes contained in this chapter and select two that you found to be especially meaningful or inspirational.

For each quote you selected, provide an explanation why you chose it.

14.2 Strategy Reflections

Review the strategies for *learning about different majors* on pp. 318–320. Select three you think are most important and intend to put into practice.

14.3 Reality Bite

Whose Choice Is It Anyway?

Ursula returned from a weekend visit and informed her parents of her plans to major in art or theater. After hearing about her plans, Ursula's parents exploded and insisted that she major in something "practical," like nursing or accounting, so that she could get a job after graduation. Ursula replied that she had no interest in these majors, nor did she feel she had the skills in science and math required by these majors. Her father shot back that he had no intention of "paying four years of college tuition for her to end up as a starving artist or unemployed actress!" He went on to say that if she wanted to major in art or theater she would "have to figure out a way to pay for college herself."

Reflection and Discussion Questions

1. If Ursula were your friend, what would you suggest she do?

2. Do you see any way(s) in which Ursula might pursue a major that's compatible with her interests and talents, while at the same time ease her father's concern about her ending up jobless after graduation?

3. Can you relate to this student's situation, or know of any students in a similar predicament?

14.4 Faculty Interview

Identify a faculty member on campus in the subject that you've chosen as your major or that you're considering to be your major. Make an appointment to speak with the faculty member during office hours for the purpose of learning more about that major. Let the faculty member know the purpose of your visit. During the interview, use the following questions but feel free to add or substitute questions of your own.

1. What initially *attracted* you to your academic field?

2. *When* did you decide to pursue a career in your academic field? Was it your *first* choice, or did you *change* to it from another academic area? (If you changed your original major, *why* did you change?)

3. What would you say is the most *enjoyable, exciting,* or *stimulating* aspect of your field of study?

4. What *skills, abilities,* or *talents* do you think are needed to succeed in your field of study?

5. Are there course requirements in your academic field that students often find to be *challenging*?

6. What personality *traits* or personal *interests* do you think would *"match up"* well with the type of work required in your academic field?

7. What *courses* or *out-of-class experiences* would you recommend to students to help them decide if your field is a good fit for them?

8. What *careers* are related to your academic field? (What careers do students majoring in your field tend to pursue after graduating?)

14.5 Developing a Long-Range Academic Plan for Course Work

This exercise is designed to help you design a detailed yet flexible, graduation plan that ensures you're making steady progress toward a college degree and not just piling up college credits. It may seem a bit overwhelming to develop a long-range plan at this stage of your college experience, so be sure to seek help from an academic advisor. This exercise is an opportunity for you to begin customizing your coursework and carve out a path to your educational future. Remember: an educational plan isn't something set in stone; it can change depending on changes in your academic and career interests. As you continue to follow or tweak this plan beyond the current academic term, continue to consult with your academic advisor.

Overview of Courses to Include in Your Plan

Your trip through the college curriculum will involve taking courses in the following three key categories:

1. *General education* courses that are required of all college graduates in all majors

2. *Required* courses that are required by your specific *major*

3. *Elective* courses that you choose to take

What follows are planning directions for each of these types of courses. By building these three sets of courses into your educational plan, you can design a pathway that lays out all your future coursework. Once these three key categories of courses are included in your plan, you will have created a compass to guide (not dictate) your educational future. As you gain more college experience, your specific academic and career interests are likely to change, which may change the specifics of your long-range plan. If you later change your mind about a course that was originally in your plan, you make that change without interfering with your educational progress by simply substituting another course from the same category. For instance, if your original plan was to take psychology to fulfill a general education requirement in the social and behavioral sciences and you decide later to take anthropology instead, you can make that switch smoothly because you already have a space reserved in your plan for completing the requirement in that category.

The purpose of this plan is not to restrict your academic freedom, but to supply you with guideposts that enable you to stay on track and moving in the right direction. Because this is a flexible plan, it's probably best to complete it in pencil or electronically so you can tweak it as needed.

Once you've created your plan, hold onto it, and keep an up-to-date copy of it throughout your time in college. Bring it with you when you meet with advisors and career development specialists, and come to these meetings prepared to discuss your progress on the plan as well as any changes you intend to make to it.

Part A. Planning for General Education

Step 1. Use your course catalog (bulletin) to identify the general education requirements for graduation. You're likely to find these requirements organized into general divisions of knowledge (humanities, natural sciences, etc.). Within each of these divisions, courses will be listed that fulfill the general education requirement(s) for that division. (Course catalogs can sometimes be tricky to navigate or interpret; if you run into any difficulty, seek help from your course instructor or an academic advisor.) You will probably be able to choose courses from a list of different options. Use this freedom of choice to select general education courses that capture your curiosity and are most relevant to your personal goals and career plans. You can use these courses not only to fulfill graduation requirements, but also to test your interest and talent in different fields—one of which may turn out to be your major (or minor).

Step 2. Identify courses in the catalog that you plan to take to fulfill your general education requirements and list them on the following form. Some of the courses you're taking this term may be fulfilling general education requirements, so be sure to list them as well.

Planning Grid for *General Education* Courses

Course Title	Units	Course Title	Units

Total Number of Units Required for *General Education* = _____

Part B. Planning for a College Major

The point of this portion of your educational plan is not to get you to commit to a major right now, but to develop a flexible plan that will allow you to reach a well-informed decision about your major. If you have already chosen a major, this exercise will help you lay out exactly what's ahead of you, confirm whether the courses required by your major are what you expected, and determine what other courses "fit" well with your interests and talents.

Step 1. Go to your college catalog and locate the major you've chosen or are strongly considering. If you're completely undecided, select a field that might be a possibility. To help you identify possible majors, peruse your catalog or go online to *www.mymajors.com*

Another way to identify a major for this exercise is to first identify a career you might be interested in and work backward to find a major that leads to this career. If you would like to use this strategy, the following website will guide you through the process: *https://uncw.edu/career/whatcanidowithamajorin.html*

Step 2. After you have selected a major, consult your college catalog to identify the courses required for that major. Your college may also have "major planning sheets" that list the specific course requirements for each major. (To see if these major planning sheets are available, check with your Advising Center or the academic department that offers the major you've selected.)

A college major will require all students majoring in that field to complete specific courses (e.g., all business majors are required to take microeconomics). Other required courses for a major may be chosen from a menu or list of options (e.g., "choose any three courses from the following list of six courses"). These courses are often referred to as "major electives." After reviewing the course descriptions of these major electives, select those that most interest you and are most relevant to your goals.

Note: You can "double dip" by taking courses that fulfill a major requirement and a general education requirement at the same time. For instance, if your major is psychology, you may be able to take a course in General or Introductory Psychology that counts simultaneously as a required course in your major and a required general education course in the area of Social and Behavioral Sciences.

Step 3. Identify courses that you will take to fulfill your major requirements and major electives and list them on the following form. Courses you are taking this term may be fulfilling some of these requirements or electives in the major you've selected, so be sure to list them as well.

Planning Grid for Courses in Your *Major*

Course Title	Units	Course Title	Units

Total Number of Units Required for Your *Major* = _____

Plan C. Planning Your Free Electives

After you've built general education courses and major courses into your educational plan, you're now ready to plan your *free electives*—courses not required for general education or your major but are needed to reach the total number of units required for a college degree. Free electives are courses that you're free to choose from any of those listed in the college catalog.

To determine how many free elective units you have, add up the number of course units that you need to take to fulfill your general education and major requirements, then subtract this number from the total number of units you need to graduate. The remaining number of course units represents your total number of free electives. When making choices about what free electives to include in your educational plan, consider the strategies suggested in **Box 14.2** (p. 321).

Planning Grid for Your *Free Electives*

Course Title	Units	Course Title	Units

Total Number of *Free Elective* Units = _____

Part D. Putting It Altogether: Developing a Comprehensive Graduation Plan

In the previous steps of this exercise, you built three key sets of college courses into your educational plan: general education courses, major courses, and free elective courses. Now you're ready to integrate these three sets of courses together into a comprehensive graduation plan.

Using the "Long-Range Graduation Planning Form" on pp. 331-335, enter the courses you selected to fulfill general education requirements, major requirements, and free electives. In the space provided next to each course, use the following shorthand notations to designate the course's category:

GE = *general education* course

M = *major* course

E = *elective* course

Notes:

1. If there are courses in your plan that fulfill two or more categories at the same time (e.g., a general education requirement and a major requirement), note both categories.

2. A college degree typically requires about 120 units, so to graduate in four years you should plan to complete at least 30 course credits each academic year. Keep in mind that you can take college courses in the summer as well as the fall and spring.

> *Unlike high school, taking summer courses in college doesn't mean you've fallen behind or need to retake a course you failed during the "normal" school year (fall or spring). Instead, summer term can be used in college to get ahead and shorten your time to graduation. Adopt the mindset that summer is a regular part of the college academic year and use that term to make progress toward completing your degree on time.*

3. If your campus offers a three-week May or January term, consider taking courses during these terms to get ahead and stay on track to graduate in four years.

4. Keep in mind that the course number indicates the year in college when the course is usually taken. Courses numbered in the 100s (or below) are typically taken in the first year of college, 200-numbered courses in the sophomore year, 300-numbered courses in the junior year, and 400-numbered courses in the senior year.

5. If you haven't yet decided on a major, focus on completing general education requirements during your first year of college. This will open more slots in your course schedule during your sophomore year, at which time you'll have a better idea about your major; you can then fill these open slots with courses required by your major. (Focusing on completing general education requirements during your first year also allows you to take courses in different subjects and test your interest in these subjects as possible majors.)

6. Be sure to check whether the courses in your plan have a *prerequisite*—a course that needs to be completed *before* you can enroll in the course you're planning to take. For example, before you can enroll in a literature course, you may need to complete a prerequisite course in writing or English composition.

7. Keep in mind that not all college courses are offered every term. College catalogs often do not contain information about when courses will be scheduled. If you're unsure about when a course will be offered, check with an academic advisor. Some colleges develop *a projected plan of scheduled courses* that shows the academic term(s) courses will be offered for the next few years. Ask an academic advisor if such a projected schedule of courses is available. If it is, request it and take advantage of it to develop an educational plan that not only includes *what* courses you intend to take, but also *when* you intend to take them. However, you don't have to take every course included in your long-range educational plan during the exact term when you originally planned to take. You can trade terms if it turns out that the course isn't offered during the term you were planning to take it, or if it's offered at a time that conflicts with another course you want to take that term.

9. Your campus may have a *degree audit program* that allows you to electronically track the courses you have completed and the courses you still need to complete a degree in your chosen major. If such a program is available, take full advantage of it.

Long-Range Graduation Planning Form

FRESHMAN YEAR

Fall Term

Course Title	Course Type General Ed. (GE), Major (M), Elective (E)	Course Units

Total Units = _____

Spring Term

Course Title	Course Type General Ed. (GE), Major (M), Elective (E)	Course Units

Total Units = _____

Summer Term

Course Title	Course Type General Ed. (GE), Major (M), Elective (E)	Course Units

Total Units = _____

SOPHOMORE YEAR

Fall Term

Course Title	Course Type General Ed. (GE), Major (M), Elective (E)	Course Units

Total Units = _____

Spring Term

Course Title	Course Type General Ed. (GE), Major (M), Elective (E)	Course Units

Total Units = _____

Summer Term

Course Title	Course Type General Ed. (GE), Major (M), Elective (E)	Course Units

Total Units = _____

JUNIOR YEAR

Fall Term

Course Title	Course Type General Ed. (GE), Major (M), Elective (E)	Course Units

Total Units = _____

Spring Term

Course Title	Course Type General Ed. (GE), Major (M), Elective (E)	Course Units

Total Units = _____

Summer Term

Course Title	Course Type General Ed. (GE), Major (M), Elective (E)	Course Units

Total Units = _____

SENIOR YEAR

Fall Term

Course Title	Course Type General Ed. (GE), Major (M), Elective (E)	Course Units

Total Units = _____

Course Title	Course Type General Ed. (GE), Major (M), Elective (E)	Course Units

Total Units = _____

Reflection Questions

1. What is the total number of course credits contained in your graduation plan? Does it equal or exceed the total number of credits needed to graduate from your college or university?

2. How many credits will you be taking in the following areas?

   a) General Education =

   b) Major =

   c) Free Electives =

3. Look over the courses required for the major you selected:

   a) Are there courses you were surprised or disappointed to see required? What were they?

   b) Are you still interested in majoring in this field?

   c) How likely is it that you will pursue the major you selected for this exercise?

4. What *challenges* or *obstacles* do you think might interfere with your ability to complete this educational plan? What campus *resources* might help you deal with these challenges or obstacles?

5. Did completing this long-range plan help you clarify your educational goals? Why or why not?

14.6 Developing a Co-Curricular Plan for Learning Experiences

Outside the Classroom

In addition to having an academic plan for your coursework, it's a good idea to have a plan for *experiential* learning—"hands-on" learning experiences that take place outside the classroom—either on campus (e.g., peer leadership positions) or off campus (e.g., service experiences, internships, or part-time employment). Learning opportunities available to you beyond the curriculum are known collectively as the *co-curriculum*. Co-curricular experiences complement your coursework, enhance the quality of your college education, and increase your employability. Keep in mind that co-curricular experiences are also resume-building experiences.

Ideally, by the time you graduate, you should have co-curricular experiences in each of the following areas:

- *Volunteer work* or *community service* that demonstrates social responsibility and allows you to gain "real world" experience

- *Leadership* and *mentoring* skills—for example, participating in leadership retreats, student government, peer mentoring, or serving as a student representative on college committees

- *Internships, work experience,* or *undergraduate research* in a field related to your major or career goals

- *Experiences with diversity*—for example, participating in multicultural clubs, organizations, or retreats

Step 1. Consult your *Student Handbook* or check with professionals working in the offices of Student Life (Student Development) and Career Development to locate co-curricular experiences in each of the above areas.

Step 2. Identify one campus program or opportunity in each of the above areas that interests you and note it on the planning form below.

Planning Grid for Co-Curricular Experiences

Volunteer Work/Community Service: _____

Leadership/Mentoring: _____

Diversity (Multicultural) Experience: _____

Internship, Work Experience, or Undergraduate Research Relating to Your Major or Career Goals: _____

Notes:

- Summer term is an excellent time of the year to build experiential learning into your educational plan without having to worry about time conflicts with your scheduled classes or doing it at the same time you're handling a full load of courses.

- Keep track of the specific skills you develop while engaging in co-curricular experiences and be sure to showcase them to future employers. Don't just list extracurricular activities on your resume, reflect on your out-of-class experiences, and be able to articulate what you learned from them. Identify the thinking processes you used (see **Box 8.4**, pp. 181-182) as well as the transferable skills and personal qualities you developed while engaging in these experiences (see Chapter 15, p. 352).

- Keep in mind that the professionals with whom you interact while participating in co-curricular experiences can serve as valuable references and sources of letters of recommendation to future employers, graduate programs or professional schools. (For strategies on requesting letters of recommendation, see Chapter 15, pp. 359-360.)

Reflection Questions

1. What *challenges* or *obstacles* do you think might interfere with your ability to complete your experiential learning plans? What campus *resources* might help you deal with these challenges or obstacles?

2. What people on or off campus could you *network* with to help you successfully navigate your experiential learning plans, or who might be a *mentor* for you?

Final Reminder:

Hold onto your curricular and co-curricular plans. Keep an up-to-date copy of them throughout your years in college. Bring these plans with you when you meet with academic advisors and career development specialists and come prepared to discuss your progress on these plans as well as changes you intend to make to them.

14.7 Making Connections between Major and Career

Steps:

1. Go to the following website: http://uncw.edu/career/WhatCanIDoWithaMajorIn

2. Select a major that you are currently interested in, or would like to explore, and review the careers related to the major you have selected.

3. Identify a career related to the major that most interests you, and answer the following questions:

   - What about the description of this career most appeals to you?

   - What level of education is required to enter this career?

   - Besides completing the level of education required to enter this career, what other work or learning experiences would increase your prospects for career entry and advancement?

Career Exploration, Preparation, and Development

FINDING A PATH TO YOUR FUTURE PROFESSION

It may be surprising to find a chapter on career development in a book written for first-term college students. Certainly, beginning college and beginning a career are events taking place at different points in time and are different life transitions. However, the process of exploring career options and developing career-entry skills should begin in the first year of college. Early career planning gives beginning college students a practical, motivational goal to strive for and gets them thinking about how the skills they are developing in college are relevant to their success beyond college. Thus, career planning is a form of *life* planning, and the sooner that college students start the process, the sooner they start gaining control of their future and start steering it in the direction they want it to go.

Acquire strategies that can be used during the first year of college and throughout the college experience to explore, prepare for, and enter a career that is compatible with your personal talents, interests, needs, and values.

 Reflection 15.1

Before digging into this chapter, take a moment to answer the following questions:

1. Have you decided on a career or are strongly considering one?

2. If yes, why have you chosen this career? (Was your decision strongly influenced by anybody or any experience?)

3. If no, what careers are you considering as possibilities?

The Importance of Career Planning

After completing your schooling, you will spend most of the remaining hours of your life working. In fact, the only other single activity you will spend more time doing is sleeping. Because such a sizable portion of your life is spent on your vocation, it's easy to see why your career can have such a strong influence on your personal identity and happiness. National and international surveys repeatedly show that being satisfied and engaged with one's work is one of the most important predictors of personal well-being.

Thus, choosing a career pathway is one of the most important choices you will make in your life; the earlier you start the process, the better. The need career planning is highlighted by a national survey of first-year college students, which revealed that almost 60% of them strongly agreed that it's important to be thinking about their career, but only 25% said they had a clear idea about how to achieve their career goals. Also, national surveys of career counselors and employers indicate that one key competency expected of college graduates is *career management*—the ability to identify and articulate personal skills, strengths, and experiences relevant to desired work positions and career goals, and to know what steps to take to pursue opportunities for employment and career advancement.

Even if you have decided on a career that you've been dreaming about since you were a preschooler, you still need to confirm this choice and may need to decide on a specific specialization within the career field you have chosen. For instance, if you're interested in pursuing a career in law, you will need to decide what branch of law you will practice (criminal law, corporate law, family law, etc.). You will also need to decide what employment sector or type of industry you would like to work in (e.g., nonprofit, for-profit, education, or government). Thus, whether you are currently certain or uncertain about your career plans, you still need to explore specific career options and develop a career preparation-and-development plan.

Planning a career pathway doesn't mean that the route you plan to take cannot be adjusted or modified. Career goals can change as you gather more experience, acquire new knowledge and skills, and discover different interests and talents. Making a tentative career plan doesn't mean that you are limiting your options, forfeiting flexibility, or locking yourself into premature plans about what you're going to do for the rest of your life. Instead, engaging in career planning is just mapping out a potential pathway that: (a) allows you to begin anticipating the type of future you'd like to create for yourself , (b) provides you with a sense of direction for getting there, and (c) starts moving you in the right direction.

Strategies for Career Exploration and Preparation

Reaching an effective decision about a career path involves four key steps:

1.

Awareness of *yourself*—gaining insight into your personal, interests, strengths, needs, and values

2.

Awareness of your *career options*—knowing what career choices are available to you

3.

Awareness of what career options provide the *best "fit"* for you—
knowing what career fields most closely match your personal interests, strengths, needs, and values

4.

Awareness of key *steps and strategies* needed to reach your career goal— knowing how to prepare for and gain entry into the career of your choice

In short, effective career planning begins with getting a deeper understanding of who you are, where you can go, where you want to go, and how to get there.

Step 1. Awareness of Self

The career goal you set for yourself says a lot about who you are and what you want in life. Thus, self-awareness is a critical first step in the process of career planning. You need to know yourself before you can know what career is best for you. Although this may seem obvious, self-awareness and self-discovery are often overlooked aspects of the career planning process. By deepening your self-awareness, you put yourself in a better position to choose a career goal and pursue a career path that's true to who you are and who you want to become.

For instance, deep awareness of your personal strengths can lead you to a career that allows you to use and capitalize on those strengths. National and international surveys show that employees who regularly use their strengths at work are more engaged at work, more enthusiastic about their work, and less likely to quit their job. Studies of individuals who demonstrate grit also reveal they are intrinsically interested in their work ("I love what I do") and value the work they do ("My work is important—both to me and to others."

> *Self-awareness is the first and most important step in the career planning process. Setting meaningful career goals and making effective career plans are built on a deep understanding of self.*

You can gain a deeper sense of self-awareness by asking yourself questions that stimulate introspection or self-examination. Introspective questions can launch you on an inner quest that leads to greater self-insight and self-discovery, which, in turn, can lead you to selecting a career that best reflects who you are and who you want to be. You can initiate this introspective process by asking yourself questions relating to your personal:

> "To love what you do and feel that it matters—how could anything be more fun?
> —Katharine Graham, former CEO of the Washington Post and Pulitzer Prize–winning author

- **Interests:** what you *like* to do
- **Talents (Strengths):** what you're *good* at doing
- **Needs:** what you find personally *satisfying* or *fulfilling*
- **Values:** what you believe is very *important* to do and is really *worth* doing

 Reflection 15.2

Complete the following sentences:

- My strongest interests are . . .
- My greatest talents or strengths are . . .
- What brings me the greatest sense of personal satisfaction and fulfillment is . . .

Another way to gain greater self-knowledge is by taking career self-assessment tests or inventories. These tests enable you to see how your personal characteristics (e.g., interests and values) compare with satisfied and successful professionals working in different careers. If your responses closely match the responses of satisfied and successful professionals in a particular career, this suggests that the career might be a good fit for you. Career interest inventories don't tell the whole story, but they are useful tools to have in your career planning toolbox. Strongly consider taking a career interest inventory and other types of career self-assessments.

In addition to your interests, another factor to consider when choosing a career are your needs. A *need* may be described as something stronger than an interest. When you do something that meets a personal need, you're doing something that is essential to your feeling satisfied and being motivated. Psychologists have identified several important human needs that vary in strength or intensity from person to person. **Box 15.1** contains descriptions of personal needs that are especially important to consider when making a career choice.

> I believe following my passion is more crucial than earning money. I think that would come itself eventually."
>
> —College sophomore responding to the question, "What are you looking for in a career?

Box 15.1

Personal Needs to Consider When Making a Career Choice

After reading about each need in this box, make a note indicating how strong that need is for you (high, moderate, or low).

1. **Autonomy.** The need to work independently without close supervision or control. Individuals with a high need for autonomy experience greater fulfillment working in careers that allow them to be their own boss, to have the freedom to make their own choices or decisions, and to be able to control their own work schedule. Individuals with a low need for autonomy are more satisfied with careers that are structured and involve working with a supervisor who provides direction, assistance, and frequent feedback.

> Our research [on happiness] indicates prosperity is not the most important factor. Personal freedom is more important, and it's freedom in all kinds of ways . . . political freedom and freedom of choice."
>
> — Ronald Inglehart, happiness researcher, University of Michigan

2. **Affiliation (Belongingness).** The need for social interaction, a sense of belonging, and the opportunity to collaborate or be of service to others. Individuals with a high need for affiliation experience greater fulfillment working in careers that involve teamwork and frequent interpersonal interaction with coworkers. Individuals low in this need are more likely to be satisfied working alone or in competition with others.

> To me, an important characteristic of a career is being able to meet new, smart, interesting people."
>
> —First-year student

3. **Achievement (Competence).** The need to experience challenge and a sense of personal accomplishment. Individuals with high achievement needs feel more fulfilled working in careers that push them to solve problems, to generate creative ideas, and to continually learn new information or master new skills. Individuals with a low need for achievement are likely to be more satisfied in careers that don't continually test their abilities or require them to stretch their skills to take on new tasks and different responsibilities.

> I want to be able to enjoy my job and be challenged by it at the same time. I hope that my job will not be monotonous and that I will have the opportunity to learn new things often."
>
> —First-year student

4. **Recognition.** The need for prestige, status, and respect from others. Individuals with high recognition needs are likely to feel more satisfied working in high-status careers that society perceives to be prestigious. Individuals with a low need for recognition feel comfortable working in careers they find personally satisfying or fulfilling, regardless of how impressive or enviable their job title may be.

continued...

5. Sensory Stimulation. The need to experience variety, change, and risk-taking. Individuals with high sensory stimulation needs are more likely to be satisfied working in careers that involve frequent changes of pace and place (e.g., travel), unpredictable events (e.g., work tasks that require them to think on their feet), and some degree of stress (e.g., working under pressure to meet deadlines). Individuals with a low need for sensory stimulation are likely to feel more comfortable working in careers that have structure, regular routines, predictable situations, minimal risk, and low stress.

> "For me, a good career is very unpredictable . . . I would love to do something that allows me to be spontaneous."
> —First-year student

Reflection 15.3

Which of the five needs listed in **Box 15.1** are strong needs for you?

What careers do you think would best match your strongest needs?

> "Don't expect a recluse to be motivated to sell, a creative thinker to be motivated to be a good proofreader day in and day out, or a sow's ear to be happy in the role of a silk purse.
> —Pierce Howard, author, The Owner's Manual for the Brain

AUTHOR'S EXPERIENCE

As a college junior, I had an eye-opening experience. I wish this experience had happened in my first year, but better late than never. When I made a career choice as a freshman, my decision-making process didn't involve critical thinking. I chose a major that I thought would lead to a prestigious career and pay me the most money. Although these aren't necessarily bad factors, I failed to use a systematic and reflective process to evaluate my career choice. In my junior year I asked one of my professors why he decided to get his Ph.D. and become a professor. He simply answered, "I wanted autonomy." This was an epiphany for me. He explained that when he reflected on what mattered most to him, he realized that he needed a career that offered independence. So, he began looking at career options that would allow him to be his own boss. After hearing his explanation, "autonomy" became my favorite word, and this story became a guiding force in my life. After going through a critical introspective process, I determined that autonomy was exactly what I desired and a professor is what I became.

—*Aaron Thompson*

In sum, four key personal characteristics should be considered when exploring and choosing a career: your talents, interests, values, and needs. As illustrated in **Figure 15.1**, these are the pillars that provide foundational support for making effective career choices and decisions. Ideally, you want to pursue a career that you're good at, interested in, passionate about, and that supplies you with a sense of pride, satisfaction, and fulfillment.

> "Set yourself earnestly to discover what you are made to do, and then give yourself passionately to the doing of it.
> —Martin Luther King, Jr., American clergyman, prominent leader in the African-American Civil Rights Movement, and winner of the Nobel Peace Prize

FIGURE 15.1: Foundational Personal Characteristics of Effective Career Choice

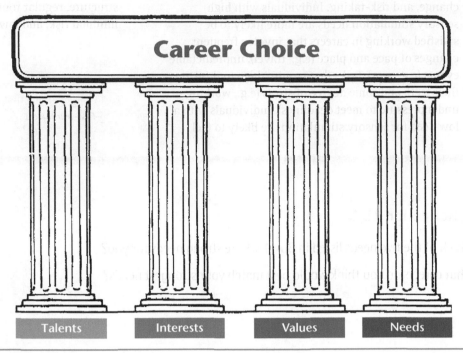

©Kendall Hunt Publishing Company

The opportunity to make money is certainly one factor to consider when choosing a career, but a good career decision involves considering factors other than what your starting salary. It's a decision that should involve deep awareness and careful consideration of what is meaningful and important to you. It's noteworthy that the word *vocation* derives from the Latin "vocatio" meaning "a calling." This suggests that a career should be more than a high-paying job; it should call out to you and call forth your true talents, interests, and values. In one study, employees who felt that their work was a calling agreed with the statement, ("my work is one of the most important things in my life") were found to miss three times fewer work days than employees who viewed their work as a "necessity of life" or "a stepping stone to other jobs."

Step 2. Awareness of Career Options

In addition to self-awareness and self-knowledge, effective career decision-making requires knowledge about your range of career options and the realities of the work world. If you were to ask people to name as many careers as they could, they would not come close to naming the 900 career titles listed by the federal government in its Occupational Information Network. More career choices are available today than at any other time in history. **Box 15.2** contains just a small sample of positions that didn't exist prior to the 21st century. They demonstrate how the nature of work in today's world is changing rapidly and how these changes are creating new career opportunities.

Box 15.2

Occupations that Didn't Exist Prior to the Turn of the 21st Century

1. App developer: When you hear "there's an app for that" it's because there are now professionals working in careers relating to the ever-growing number of mobile devices and mobile-device applications.

2. Market research data miner: Ever wonder how retailers know how to create customized advertisements especially for you? It's because of the increasing number of market-research data miners who collect data on consumer behaviors and predict trends that advertisers use to develop marketing strategies.

3. Educational or admissions consultant: Parents are now taking extra steps to ensure their children are accepted at the "right" school (from preschool to college). Educational and admissions consultants guide families through the application and interview process.

4. Millennial generation expert: It's now very common to find people from different generations working together in the same organization. Millennial generation experts help employers maximize the potential of their staff by providing advice on how to work with their youngest employees and mentor them for future success.

5. Social media manager: Businesses are making increasing use of social media to market and advertise their products and services. Social media manag-

ers specialize in targeting marketing messages to users of different social media sites.

6. Chief listening officer: Similar to social media managers, chief listening offices use social media to monitor consumer discussions and shares this information with marketing agents so they can design strategies that appeal to various segments of the population.

7. Cloud computing services: Most websites used every day by consumers can store incredibly large amounts of data. Data management specialists are employed by companies to accumulate and index tremendous volumes of information bytes—about a quadrillion!

8. Elder care: Life expectancy is increasing, and along with it, the need for individuals who possess the knowledge, skills, and compassion to serve the elderly, their families, and the agencies and companies that provide care for senior citizens.

9. Sustainability expert: For environmental and economic reasons, companies are now seeking ways to minimize their carbon emissions. This has created a demand for professionals with expertise in the science of sustainability and the ability to develop cost-effective "green" business practices.

10. User experience designers: These professionals do exactly what their titles suggest: they create experiences for consumers through technology. Using current technology, they create color, sound, and images by using tools such as HTML, Photoshop, and CSS.

Strategies for Gaining Awareness of Your Career Options

Capitalize on career information resources. Listed below are some of the best sources of information about careers. The primary place on campus where you can find these sources is your Career Center. In addition to helping you assess your career interests and abilities, the Career Center is the place where you can learn about the nature of different careers and find out about career-related work opportunities available to you while you're in college. The College Library is another campus resource where you can find a wealth of reading material on careers, both in print and online.

Dictionary of Occupational Titles (DOT) (available at www.occupationalinfo. org). The largest printed resource on careers; it contains concise definitions of more than 17,000 jobs and includes information on:

- Work tasks typically performed in different careers
- Background experiences of people working in different career positions that qualified them for the positions they hold

- Types of knowledge, skills, and abilities required by different careers
- Personal interests, values, and needs of individuals working in different occupations who report high levels of work satisfaction and success

Occupational Outlook Handbook (OOH) (available at www.bls.gov-/ooh). One of the most widely available and frequently used resources on careers. It contains descriptions of and information on approximately 250 positions, including work tasks and functions, work conditions, places of employment, training or education required for career entry and advancement, salaries and benefits, and sources for additional information about particular careers (e.g., professional organizations and governmental agencies associated with certain careers). A distinctive feature of this resource is that it also contains information about the *future employment outlook* for different careers.

Occupational Information Network (O*NET) Online (available at www.online.onetcenter.org). This is America's most comprehensive source of online information about careers. It contains up-to-date descriptions of almost 1,000 careers, plus lots of other career-related information similar to what you would find in the *Dictionary of Occupational Titles*.

Encyclopedia of Careers and Vocational Guidance (Chicago: Ferguson Press). As the name suggests, this is an encyclopedia of information on entry qualifications, salaries, and advancement opportunities for a wide variety of careers.

In addition to these general sources of information, your Career Development Center and College Library should have resources relating to specific careers or occupations (e.g., careers for English majors). You can also learn a great deal about different careers by simply reading advertisements for position openings in your local newspaper or online (e.g., www.linkedin.com, www.careerbuilder.com, and college.monster.com). When reviewing position descriptions, make special note of the tasks, duties, and responsibilities they involve and ask yourself whether these positions match up well with your personal talents, interests, needs, and values.

Participate in career planning and development workshops. Periodically during the academic year, your campus is likely to offer programs devoted to career exploration and career preparation (e.g., career exploration or career planning workshops sponsored by the Career Center). Research indicates that career development workshops are effective in helping students plan for and choose careers. Your Career Center may also organize career fairs on campus, at which professionals working in different career fields are seated at booths where you can visit with them and ask them questions about their careers. (See Exercise 15.7 at the end of this chapter for interview questions you can ask professionals about their careers.)

Take a career development course. Your college may offer career development courses for elective credit. These courses typically include self-assessments of career interests, information about different careers, and strategies for career preparation. Career planning needs to be done while you're enrolled in college, why not enroll in a career planning course that gives you college credit for doing it! Studies show that students who complete such a course report it had a positive impact on their career choice and career preparation.

You may also be able to explore your career interests in a writing or speech course that allows you to choose the topics you write or speak about. In any course where you have complete freedom to choose a topic to research, consider researching a career you may be interested in and make that the topic of your paper or presentation.

Another possibility for exploring careers through course work is to do an independent study on a career field you're exploring. Typically, an independent study involves an in-depth project that you select and research on your own after it's approved by the college. An independent study allows you to receive academic credit for an in-depth study of a topic of your choice without enrolling in a course that meets in class on a fixed schedule. It might be possible to use this independent study option to work on a project related to a career field you're exploring. To see if this independent study is available on your campus, check the college catalog or consult with an academic advisor.

Conduct information interviews. One of the best and most overlooked ways to get accurate information about a career is to interview professionals working in that career. Career development specialists refer to this strategy as *information interviewing*. Don't assume that working professionals lack the time or interest to speak with a student; most are open to being interviewed and many report that they enjoy helping students learn about their careers.

An information interview can provide you with inside information about what the career is really like because you're getting it directly from "the horse's mouth"—the person who is fully engaged in the career on a day-to-day basis. Information interviewing also helps you gain experience and self-confidence in interview situations, which can help you prepare for future job interviews. Also, during the interview, you may learn about employment opportunities that haven't been advertised. If you make a good impression on the persons you interview, they may suggest you contact them again after graduation to see if they have any position openings. If there is one, you might find yourself being the interviewee instead of the interviewer and end up being hired for your first job after college graduation.

Because interviews can supply you with valuable information about careers and provide possible contacts for future employment, we strongly encourage you to complete the information interview exercise (15.7) at the end of this chapter.

Shadow (observe) working professionals. In addition to reading about careers and interviewing professionals in different careers, you can also learn a lot about careers by observing professionals performing their daily duties in their place of work. The following two college-sponsored programs may be available on your campus either of which would allow you to observe working professionals:

- **Job Shadowing Program.** Students are given the opportunity to follow (shadow) and observe a professional performing typical job duties.
- **Externship Program.** An extended version of job shadowing that lasts for a longer time period (e.g., students observe a professional at work for 2-3 days).

Visit your Career Development Center to learn about what job shadowing or externship programs may be available on your campus. If no program is available for the career field you're exploring, consider reaching out to professionals in that career field and ask them if it might be possible to shadow them at work for short amount of time. This would be similar to asking someone for an information interview; instead of asking the person for an interview, you're asking if you could observe that person at work. In fact, at the end of an information interview, you could ask the person you interviewed if it might be possible to observe him or her at work.

Reflection 15.4

If you were to interview or observe a working professional in a career that interests you, what career would that be?

Information interviewing, job shadowing, and externships are three key ways to acquire inside information about a career. However, acquiring information about something is not the same thing as actually doing it. To get career-related work *experience*, you've got four major options:

- Internships
- Cooperative education programs
- Volunteer work or service learning
- Part-time work

These experiences augment academic learning and provide you with a deeper understanding of, and preparation for, your eventual career. Strongly consider building these forms of experiential learning into your career development plan.

Get an internship. In contrast to job shadowing and externships—which involve observing someone at work—an internship engages you in the work itself and allows you to perform career-related work duties. A distinguishing feature of internships is that students can receive academic credit or financial compensation for the work they do. Usually, an internship involves a total of 120 to 150 work hours, which may done at the same time that students are enrolled in courses, or at a time of the year when they're not taking classes (e.g., summer internship).

A key advantage of an internship is that it enables college students to escape the classic catch-22 trap they often run into when interviewing for their first career position, which goes something like this: The interviewer asks the college graduate, "What work experience have you had in this field?" The graduate has to say: "I haven't had any work experience because I've been a full-time student." You can avoid this catch-22 scenario *after* graduating from college by completing an internship *before* graduating from college. Participating in at least one internship while you're enrolled in college will enable you to beat the "no experience" rap after graduation and distinguish yourself from many other college graduates. Surveys show that employers prefer to hire college graduates who have completed internships. Research also shows that students with internships are more likely to acquire career-relevant work skills while in college and find immediate employment after college.

Typically, internships are available to college students during their junior or senior year; however, some campuses offer internships for first- and second-year students. Check with your Career Center if this option may be available to you. You can also pursue internships on your own by consulting published guides that list available career-related internships and provide information on how to apply for them (e.g., *Peterson's Internships* and the *Vault Guide to Top Internships*). You can also find internships on websites such as www.internships.com or www.vaultreports.com. Lastly, information on internships may also be available at the local chamber of commerce in your hometown, or in the city where your college is located.

> "Give me a history major who has done internships and a business major who hasn't, and I'll hire the history major every time."
>
> —*William Ardery, senior vice president, Investor Communications Company*

If your college offers a cooperative education (co-op) program, take advantage of it. Co-op programs are like internships but involve work experiences that last longer than one academic term and often require students to stop their coursework temporarily to participate in the program. However, some co-op programs (often called "parallel co-ops") allow students to continue to take classes while working part time at the co-op position. Typically, no academic credit is awarded to students who participate in co-op programs; instead, they are paid and their co-op experience is officially noted on their college transcript.

Co-ops are usually only available to juniors or seniors, but you can begin to explore co-op programs now by visiting the Career Center to see if co-op programs are available in a career field that you're pursuing or considering. If you find one, build it into your educational plan because it can provide you with authentic and extensive career-related work experience.

The value of co-ops and internships is strongly supported by research, which shows that students who have these experiences:

- Are more likely to report that their college education was relevant to their career
- Receive higher evaluations from employers who recruit them on campus
- Have less difficulty finding a position following graduation
- Are more satisfied with their first career position after they graduate
- Earn higher starting salaries

National surveys also show that when employers are asked to rank various factors they consider important when hiring new college graduates, internships and cooperative education programs receive the highest ranking. Furthermore, employers report that when full-time positions open up in their organization or company, these positions are typically offered first to their former interns and co-op students.

Use volunteer work and community service experiences to explore career options and gain work experience. Volunteer service not only gives you the opportunity to serve your community, it also gives you the chance to explore different work environments and gain work experience in career fields relating to your area of service. For example, volunteer service performed for different age groups (children, adolescents, or the elderly) and in different work environments (hospital, school, or laboratory) provides you with firsthand, resume-building experiences and opportunities to test your interest in careers related to these age groups and work environments. Volunteer experience also enables you to network with professionals who can serve as personal references and provide you with letters of recommendation. Furthermore, if these professionals are impressed with your service, they may hire you on a part-time basis while you're still in college or on a full-time basis after you graduate.

To get an idea of the range of career-related service opportunities available to you, see www.afsusa.org. You can also get volunteer experience by enrolling in service-learning courses that integrate service learning experiences into the class (e.g., through course assignments that involve you in service experiences and ask you to reflect on these experiences by writing papers or making class presentations).

Another way to gain class-related work experience is by enrolling in a course that includes a *practicum* or *field work*. For instance, if you're interested in working with children, courses in child psychology or early childhood education may offer opportunities at a local preschool or at a daycare center on campus.

Lastly, it might be possible to get career-relevant learning experiences by volunteering to help a campus office or a faculty member. Volunteering to help a faculty member as a research assistant or teaching assistant can be particularly valuable if you intend to go to graduate school. If you have a good relationship with faculty members in an academic field that interests you, consider asking those professors if they need some assistance with their teaching or research responsibilities. You might also check out your professors' websites to find out what type of research projects they're working on; if any of these projects interest you or relate to a career path you're considering, contact the professor about the possibility of volunteering your assistance. Volunteer work done for a professor could lead to making a joint presentation with the professor at a professional conference or may even result in your name being included as a contributing coauthor on an article published by the professor.

AUTHOR'S EXPERIENCE

I was once advising two first-year students, Kim and Christopher. Kim was thinking about becoming a physical therapist and Chris was thinking about becoming an elementary school teacher. To help Kim get a better idea if physical therapy was the career for her, I suggested that she visit a hospital near campus to inquire about the possibility of doing volunteer work in the physical therapy unit. As it turned out, the hospital needed volunteers; she decided to volunteer and absolutely loved it. Kim's volunteer experience convinced her that a physical therapist is what she wanted to be. Energized by her volunteer experience, she went on to complete a degree in physical therapy and is now a professional physical therapist.

Similarly, I suggested to Chris that he test his interest in becoming an elementary school teacher by visiting some local schools to ask if he could volunteer as a teacher's aide. One of the schools did need his services, and Chris volunteered there as a teacher's aide for ten weeks. About two weeks into his volunteer experience, he came into my office to tell me that the kids were just about driving him crazy and he was no longer interested in becoming a teacher! He finished up his ten-week volunteer commitment, but changed his major from education to communication and ended up working in the broadcasting industry.

Kim and Chris were the first two students I advised to get involved in volunteer work to test their career interests. Because their volunteer experiences proved to be so useful in helping them identify or modify their career path, I continued to advise all my students to try to get volunteer experience relating to the career they were considering.

—*Joe Cuseo*

 Reflection 15.5

If you have participated in volunteer experiences, did you learn anything about yourself from these experiences that might influence your career plans? Did you any acquire skills that you could list on your resume or mention in a future job interview?

Use part-time work for career development purposes. Even if you're going to college full-time and only working part-time, your part-time work experiences can (and should) be used as career development experiences. Part-time work can provide you with opportunities to develop job skills and personal qualities that are likely to be relevant to any future career you decide to pursue (e.g., customer relations skills, organizational skills, and ability to work effectively with coworkers from diverse backgrounds and cultures). It's also possible that work you do in a part-time position while in college may turn into a full-time position after college—as the following story illustrates.

AUTHOR'S EXPERIENCE

While enrolled in college, a former student of mine (Matt), an English major, worked part-time for an organization that provides special assistance to mentally challenged children. As soon as he completed his college degree, the organization offered Matt a full-time position, which he accepted. While working full-time at this position, Matt decided to go to graduate school part-time and eventually completed a master's degree in special education. This degree qualified him for a promotion to a more advanced position. Moral of the story: Part-time work done in college can sometimes lead to, and open up, future career opportunities.

—*Joe Cuseo*

You may also be eligible to work part-time on campus through your school's work-study program. Work-study jobs are done in a variety of settings on campus (e.g., Financial Aid Office, Library, Public Relations Office, or Computer Services Center) and they can be arranged so they don't conflict with your course schedule. Just like off-campus work, on-campus work can provide you with valuable career exploration and resume-building experiences, and the professionals for whom you work can also serve as excellent references and sources of letters of recommendation to future employers. To see whether you are eligible for your school's work-study program, visit the Financial Aid Office. If you don't qualify for work-study jobs, ask about other forms of campus employment that may be available.

There's no substitute for gaining knowledge about careers than through direct, hands-on learning experience in actual work settings—such as internships, volunteer services, and part-time work. These firsthand experiences represent the ultimate career "reality test." They allow you to experience careers as they really are—as opposed to the often glamorized but unrealistic way they're portrayed in TV programs and the movies.

> "As entertainment, TV shows are great. As reality, they fall a little short. So enjoy your TV and movies, but don't make career decisions based on them.
>
> —Katharine Brooks, author of *You Majored in What? Mapping Your Path from Chaos to Career*

> A key characteristic of effective goal setting is to set goals that are realistic. In the case of career goals, getting firsthand experience in actual work settings allows you to get a realistic view of what work is really like in a career that you're considering—before committing yourself to that career.

In short, getting real-life work experience during college has five powerful career benefits:

- You get an accurate picture of what work in a field is really like
- You get to test your interests and skills for certain types of work
- You strengthen your resume by your academic (classroom) learning with experiential learning
- You make contacts with people who can serve as personal references and write letters of recommendation for you
- You network with employers who may hire you or refer you to other positions after you graduate.

In addition, by getting work experience *early* in college, you become a more competitive candidate for internships and part-time positions that you may apply for later in your college experience. Take your part-time work experiences seriously, learn as much as you can from them, and build relationships with the people you work for and with. These are the people who can provide you with future contacts, personal references, and job referrals.

To find work opportunities that relate to your career interests, use all resources available to you, including campus resources (e.g., the Career Development Center and Financial Aid Office), local resources (e.g., Chamber of Commerce), and personal contacts (e.g., family and friends). Also, don't forget that almost three of every four jobs are obtained through personal relationships, a.k.a. "networking." So be sure to take advantage of all networking opportunities available to you, including online tools such as LinkedIn (www.linkedin.com)—the professional version of Facebook, and Meetup.com—an online service that organizes groups of people with similar personal and occupational interests.

Reflection 15.6

1. Have you had part-time work experiences that may contribute to your future career plans, or provided you with skills you can include on your resume?

2. If you could get work experience in any career field right now, what would it be?

Step 3. Awareness of Career Options that Provide the Best "Fit" for You

As has been emphasized throughout this chapter, a factor that should carry great weight in the career decision-making process is the match between your career choice and your personal strengths, interests, needs, and values. Because a career decision is an important life decision, considerable thought should be given to how that choice will affect your long-term life satisfaction and happiness. The ideal career choice should lead you to the following future-life scenario: You wake up on workdays and hop out of bed enthused and excited about going to work. When you're at work, you're so engaged in your work that time seems to fly by, and before you know it, the day's over. After work, you feel good about the work you've done and how well you did it. For this ideal scenario to become (or even approach) reality, you need to pursue a career that's "in sync" with your *strengths*— what you do well, your *interests*—what you like to do, and your *values*—what you feel proud doing.

Effective career decision-making also involves identifying all personal factors that should be factored into the decision and determining how much weight (influence) each of these factors should carry. A good career decision is based on considerations other than whether the career is currently "hot" (in demand) and lucrative (high starting salary). You may include these factors but should go beyond them to consider how the career will affect different aspects of your "self" (social, emotional, physical, etc.) at different stages of your life (young adulthood, middle age, and late adulthood). In addition to how much money you will make, your career will affect your personal life, how well you're able to balance the demands of work and family, and how your work impacts the lives of others. In short, an effective career choice is a choice not only about how you will earn a living, but also about how you will live your life.

> "Success is getting what you want. Happiness is wanting what you get."
>
> — Dale Carnegie, author of the best-selling book, *How to Win Friends and Influence People* and founder of *The Dale Carnegie Course*—a worldwide program for business based on his teachings

> "More people today have the means to live, but no meaning to live for."
>
> — *Viktor Frankl, Austrian neurologist, psychiatrist, and Holocaust survivor*

Reflection 15.7

Answer the following questions about a career you're considering or have chosen:

1. Why are you attracted to this career? (What led or caused you to become interested in the first place?)

2. Would you say that your interest in this career is driven primarily by *intrinsic* motivation—something "inside" of you, such as its compatibility with your personal abilities, interests, needs, and values? Or, would you say that your interest in the career is driven mainly by *extrinsic* motivation—something "outside" of you, such as earning a high income, holding a prestigious job title, or meeting the expectations of others (e.g., family or friends)?

3. If money weren't an issue and you could earn a comfortable living working in a career other than the one you've chosen or are considering, would you continue to pursue it?

(Complete exercise 15.6 at the end of this chapter to get an idea about careers that best match your personal characteristics and life goals.)

Step 4. Awareness of the Major Steps Needed to Reach Your Career Goal

Whether you are keeping your career options open or have already decided on a career, you can start right now to take steps toward successful career entry by using the following strategies.

Self-Monitoring: Watching and Tracking Your Skills and Attributes

Keep in mind that the *academic* skills you learn in college are also *professional* skills you will use after college. In other words, learning skills become earning skills. When you engage in academic tasks—such as note-taking, reading, writing papers, and taking tests—you're developing career-relevant skills—such as active listening, analysis, synthesis, critical thinking, and problem solving, as well as managing time and meeting deadlines.

What matters more to employers than the name of the major that appears on a student's diploma are the skills and personal qualities that student can bring to the workplace. You can start building these skills and qualities through effective *self-monitoring*—watching (monitoring) and tracking the specific skills you're developing during your college experience. Skills are habits, and like any other habit that is repeatedly practiced, skill development can be so gradual and subtle (like watching grass grow) that it's easy not to notice how much growth has taken place. For this reason, career development specialists recommend that you consciously and consistently keep track of the skills you're using so you remain aware of their development and can articulate them to future employers.

One way to track your developing skills is by keeping a *learning journal*, in which you reflect on the academic tasks and assignments you've completed along with the skills you developed while completing them. This journal should also include skills you develop outside the classroom, such as those acquired through co-curricular experiences, leadership development programs, volunteer service, and part-time jobs.

Because skills are actions, it's best to note them in your journal as *verbs*. You're likely to find that the action verbs you record will be similar to the work-related skills that employers seek from job candidates. **Box 15.3** contains a sample of action verbs representing skills acquired in college that correspond to skills required for successful performance in almost all careers.

Box 15.3

Transferable Skills Relevant to Successful Career Performance

The list below contains a sample of flexible skills that spell success in any career. As you engage in learning experiences throughout your years in college, track and note your development of these (and other) skills, either inside or outside the classroom.

advise	create	initiate	present	sequence
assemble	delegate	measure	produce	summarize
calculate	design	motivate	research	supervise
coach	evaluate	negotiate	resolve	synthesize
coordinate	explain			

In addition to tracking the skills you're learning, keep track of the positive traits and attributes you're developing. Although skills are best recorded as *verbs* because they represent actions that can be performed in positions you apply for, personal attributes are best recorded as *adjectives* because they describe who you are and what positive qualities you can bring to those positions. **Box 15.4** below identifies examples of personal traits and attributes that contribute to successful performance in any career.

Box 15.4

Personal Traits and Attributes Relevant to Successful Career Performance

As you proceed through college, make note of these and other personal attributes or character traits you are developing and be ready to articulate them to future employers.

collaborative	conscientious	considerate	curious	dependable
determined	energetic	enthusiastic	ethical	flexible
imaginative	industrious	loyal	observant	open-minded
organized	patient	persuasive	positive	precise
prepared	productive	prudent	punctual	reflective
sincere	tactful	team player	thorough	thoughtful

 Reflection 15.8

Look back at the transferable skills and personal attributes listed in **Boxes 15.3** and **15.4**. Underline or highlight those that you think are most relevant to the career(s) you're considering.

AUTHOR'S EXPERIENCE

One day after class I had a conversation with a student of mine (Max). He told me he was considering a future career in the music industry. He went on to add that to help pay for college, he was working part-time as a disc jockey at a night club. I asked him what it took to be a good disc jockey, and in less than 5 minutes of talking about his part-time work, we discovered that there were numerous career-relevant skills embedded in his job than he ever realized. Each night he worked, he was responsible for organizing 3–4 hours of music; he had to read the reactions of his audience (customers) and adapt or adjust his selections to their musical tastes; he had to arrange his selections in a sequence that varied the pace and tempo of music he played throughout the night; and he had to continually research and update his music collection to track the latest trends in hits and popular artists. His job also required him to deliver public announcements, which enabled him to overcome his fear of public speaking.

Although we were just having a short, friendly conversation after class about his part-time work, Max ended up reflecting on and identifying multiple skills he was developing on the job. We both agreed that it would be a good idea for him to get these skills down in writing so he could use them as selling points for future jobs in the music field, or any other line of work he might choose to pursue.

—*Joe Cuseo*

Embedded in your work inside and outside the classroom are transferable skills and personal qualities that are applicable to multiple careers. Tracking these skills and qualities and articulating them to potential employers is as important to securing employment after college as the name of the school and major on your college diploma.

Career Readiness

Career readiness refers to the attainment and demonstration of requisite competencies that broadly prepare college graduates for a successful transition into the workplace. Being ready or prepared to succeed in today's workplace is what employers seek from new employees. Based on extensive research among employers, the National Association of Colleges and Employers has identified key competencies associated with career readiness, which may be organized into three general categories: (1) *professional* skills, (2) *problem-solving* skills, and (3) *people* skills. By the time you graduate, employers expect that you developed most or all of the following competencies associated with these skills.

1. Professional Skills

* *Professionalism/Work Ethic*: Exhibit personal accountability and effective work habits, such as punctuality, work productively with others, manage time, and understand the impact of non-verbal communication; display integrity and ethical behavior; act responsibly with the interests of the larger community in mind; and be able to learn from mistakes.
* *Career Management*: Able to identify and articulate personal skills, strengths, and experiences relevant to desired positions and career goals; identify areas where professional growth is required; able to navigate and explore job options, take steps needed to secure employment opportunities, and know how to self-advocate for career advancement.

* *Oral/Written Communication*: Articulate thoughts and ideas clearly in written and oral form to people inside and outside the organization; good public speaking skills and ability to express ideas effectively; capable of writing and editing memos, letters, and complex technical reports.
* *Digital Technology*: Able to adapt to new and emerging technologies, and use digital technologies effectively and ethically to solve problems, complete tasks, and achieve goals.

(Strategies for developing these professional skills are included in this chapter as well as chapters 4 and 9.)

2. Problem-Solving Skills

* *Inquiry* skills: able to ask important questions, gather information and data, and apply information and data to handle work-related challenges.
* *Critical* thinking: use sound reasoning to analyze issues, solve problems, and make decisions.
* *Creative* thinking: ability to think innovatively and generate original ideas.

(Strategies for developing skills relating to problem solving, critical thinking, and creative thinking are included in chapter 8.)

3. People Skills

* *Collaboration/Teamwork*: Able to work in teams, negotiate differences, and manage conflict; capable of building partnerships with diverse co-workers and customers.
* *Global/Intercultural Fluency*: Respecting, valuing, and learning from diverse cultures, races, ages, genders, sexual orientations, and religions; demonstrate openness, sensitivity, inclusiveness, and ability to interact with various groups of people while appreciating and accommodating individuality.
* *Leadership*: Empowering others and capitalizing on their strengths to share work, delegate work, and achieve common goals; use interpersonal skills to coach and develop others; able to assess and manage one's own emotions and the emotions of others, and use empathy to support and motivate others.

(Strategies for developing "people skills," intercultural competency, and leadership potential are included in chapters 9 and 10.)

It's noteworthy that employers rate recent college graduates much lower in each of above skills than graduates rate themselves (see **Figure 15.2**). Thus, your ability to track, develop, and articulate these skills will distinguish yourself from other college graduates and increase your prospects for employment and advancement in your chosen career.

FIGURE 15.2

Competency	% of Employers That Rated Recent Grads Proficient*	% of Students Who Considered Themselves Proficient**
Professionalism/Work Ethic	42.5%	89.4%
Oral/Written Communications	41.6%	79.4%
Critical Thinking/Problem Solving	55.8%	79.9%
Teamwork/Collaboration	77.0%	85.1%
Leadership	33.0%	70.5%
Digital Technology	65.8%	59.9%
Career Management	17.3%	40.9%
Global/Intercultural Fluency	20.7%	34.9%

Source National Association of Colleges and Employers (NACE)

AUTHOR'S EXPERIENCE

I have hired numerous employees throughout my career and have found that applicants who projected strong personal and intercultural competencies were often the most qualified candidates. In many cases, this was true even when these candidates did not have as much professional experiences as other applicants. Although it may appear seem unusual to place more emphasis on competencies than experience, there's a good reason for this approach. I find that employees with strong personal and intercultural competencies work very effectively with colleagues, are great problem solvers, take initiative, and are able to think creatively and analytically. The contributions these employees made to the organization were positive and long-lasting and related more to their levels of personal competency than to their years of professional experience.

—*Michele Campagna*

Self-Marketing: Packaging and Presenting Your Skills, Strengths, and Attributes

Studies show that students who convert their college diploma into a successful career have two things in common: personal initiative and a positive attitude. They don't take a passive approach to finding employment, assuming they're owed a position or that a good position will fall into their lap because they possess a college degree. Instead, they take an active role involved in the job-search process by making a conscious effort to reflect on, document, and communicate their strengths to potential employers.

National surveys show that employers rank job applicants' *attitude* as the number one factor in making hiring decisions. In fact, they rate this factor higher in importance than reputation of the applicant's school, the applicant's prior work experience, and recommendations the applicant has received from former employers.

Unfortunately, however, many college students think that it's the degree itself—the credential or piece of paper—that will get them the career they desire. Graduating from college with a diploma in hand may make you a more competitive job candidate, but you still must compete with other candidates by packaging and sell-

"Man who stand on hill with mouth open will wait long time for roast duck to drop in.

—*Confucius, Chinese philosopher*

"Life just doesn't hand you things. You have to get out there and make things happen.

—*Emeril Lagasse, award-winning American chef, cookbook author, and TV celebrity*

ing your strengths and skills. A college diploma doesn't work like a merit badge or passport that's flashed to gain automatic access to a prosperous career. Your college education will open career doors for you, but it's your attitude, initiative, and effort that enable you to step through those doors and into a successful career.

One way to convert your college degree into gainful employment is by viewing yourself (a college graduate) as a product and viewing employers as potential customers who may be interested in purchasing your product (your skills and attributes). As a first-year student, it could be said that you are in the early stages of the process of developing your product. At this stage of your college experience, you begin the product-development process by tracking and recording your skills and attributes, so that by the time you graduate, you'll have a finished and attractive product that employers should be interested in purchasing. As career development specialist, Katharine Brooks puts it: "While no one is comparing you to a tube of toothpaste, you *are* selling yourself to an employer who likely has many candidates to choose from, and is sometimes just as confused and overwhelmed as you are in the toothpaste aisle. So it's your responsibility to make sure they consider you first."

By developing an effective self-marketing package and sharing it with employers, they get a clear idea of what you can bring to the table and do *for them*. Listed below are ways in which you can package and market your personal skills, qualities, and achievements to prospective employers.

> "The bottom line for most employers is 'Will this person fit in our environment?' One of the keys to marketing yourself is to make a connection, to get out of your mindset and into your audience's."
>
> —Katharine Brooks, author, *You Majored in What? Mapping Your Path from Chaos to Career*

Course Transcript

A course transcript is a listing of all courses you enrolled in and the grades you received in those courses. There are two particular pieces of information included on your college transcript that can strongly influence employers' hiring decisions, or admissions committee decisions about accepting students to graduate or professional school: (a) the grades you earned in your courses and (b) the types of courses you completed.

Simply stated, the better the grades you earn in college, the better your employment prospects are after college. Research on college graduates indicates that there is a positive relationship between their grades in college and:

- the prestige of their first job
- their total earnings (salary and fringe benefits)
- their job mobility (ability to change jobs or positions).

This relationship between college grades and greater career advantages holds true for students at all types of colleges and universities, regardless of the school's reputation or prestige.

Co-Curricular Experiences

Participation in student clubs, campus organizations, and other types of co-curricular activities are forms of experiential learning that can complement classroom-based learning and contribute to career readiness. A sizable body of research supports the power of these experiences for promoting career success. Co-curricular experiences that are especially valuable for promoting career development and career success are those that:

- Allow you to develop leadership and mentoring skills—such as participating in leadership retreats, student government, college committees, peer mentoring, or peer tutoring.
- Enable you to interact with others from diverse ethnic and racial groups—for instance, involvement in multicultural or international clubs and organizations.

- Relate to your academic major or career interests—for example, being an active member of a student club associated with your college major or intended career field.

Don't forget that co-curricular experiences are also resume-building experiences that serve as evidence of your involvement with, and commitment to, your campus and local community. Be sure to make these experiences visible to prospective employers. Also, remember that the campus professionals with whom you interact while participating in co-curricular activities (e.g., the director of student activities or dean of students) can serve as personal references and provide you with letters of recommendation to prospective employers, graduate schools, or professional schools.

Personal Resume

A resume may be described as a listed or bulleted summary of your most important accomplishments, skills, and credentials. (It derives from the French word, résumé, which means summary or outline.) Even if you haven't yet accumulated enough experiences to construct a fully developed resume, you can begin building a "skeletal resume" that contains key headings or basic categories (the skeleton) that you will eventually fill in ("flesh out") with your future experiences and accomplishments. A template for a skeletal resume is provided in **Box 15.5**, p. 359.

In your *letter of application* for a position, you can elaborate on the experiences contained in your resume, particularly those experiences that are relevant to the specific tasks and responsibilities called for by the position.

> "Writing my resume was a real ego booster—I've actually done stuff!
>
> —College student

Portfolio

Unlike a resume, which simply lists your experiences, a portfolio contains actual products or samples of your work. The word "portfolio" is commonly used to refer to a collection of artwork that professional artists put together to showcase or advertise their artistic ability. However, the term *portfolio* has broader meaning—it refers to a collection of any material that depicts a person's skills and talents or demonstrates the person's educational and personal development. For example, a college student's portfolio could include items such as:

- Outstanding papers, exam performances, research projects, or lab reports
- Work samples and photos from study-abroad experiences, service-learning experiences, or internships
- Video footage of oral presentations or public performances
- Performance evaluations and letters of recommendation or commendation received from professors, student development professionals, or employers

©Kendall Hunt Publishing Company

The ritual of burning completed coursework in high school is not recommended in college. Instead, save your best work and include it in a portfolio.

As a first-year student, you can begin the process of portfolio development by saving your best work and performances, including those relating to classes, co-curricular experiences on campus, and volunteer service or work experience off campus. You can store these performance products in a traditional portfolio folder or save them on your computer as an electronic portfolio. You could also create a website and upload them there. By starting now, you should eventually have a well-stocked collection of materials that showcase your skills, talents, and achievements.

Box 15.5

Skeletal Resume

The outline below can be used as a template or blueprint to organize and plan your career-development experiences. (If you have already created a resume, this template may be used to identify and include categories that may be missing from your current one.)

NAME
(First, Middle, Last)

Current Addresses: *Permanent* Addresses:
E-mail address   E-mail address
Phone number   Phone number
EDUCATION: Name of College or University, City, State
              Name of Degree Name (Associate of Arts, Bachelor of Science, etc.)
              College Major
              GPA
              Graduation Date

WORK EXPERIENCE
Position title; city and state of employment; start and stop dates (begin the list by starting with the most recent experiences)
Bulleted list of skills used or developed at work

VOLUNTEER (COMMUNITY SERVICE) EXPERIENCES
(Include a bulleted list of key kills used or developed while engaging in these experiences.)

NOTABLE COURSEWORK
(e.g., leadership, interdisciplinary and intercultural courses; study-travel courses)

CO-CURRICULAR EXPERIENCES
(e.g., student government or peer leadership)
Include a bulleted list of key skills used or developed while engaging in these experiences)

PERSONAL COMPETENCIES AND POSITIVE QUALITIES
(List as bullets, particularly competencies and qualities relevant to the position for which you're applying)

HONORS AND AWARDS
(Include those received in college, prior to college, and outside of college)

PERSONAL INTERESTS
(Include hobbies and recreational activities that are not reflected in your schoolwork or job experiences, particularly those that may be relevant to the position for which you're applying)

Reflection 15.9

What do you predict will be your best work products in college—those that you would most likely showcase in a portfolio? Why?

Letters of Recommendation (Letters of Reference)

Letters of recommendation represent another key component of your self-marketing package. You can improve the quality of the recommendations you receive by giving careful thought to (a) who will serve as your references, (b) how to approach your references, and (c) what information to provide your references. Specific strategies for doing so are provided in **Box 15.6**.

Box 15.6

The Art and Science of Requesting Letters of Recommendation: Effective Strategies and Common Courtesies

1. **Select recommendations from people who know you well and have witnessed your best work.** Think about individuals with whom you've had an ongoing relationship, who know you by name, who have observed your best performances, and who are aware of your strongest skill sets. Good candidates for letters of recommendation are instructors who you've had for more than one course, an academic advisor who you see often, or an employer who has witnessed your work habits over an extended period of time.

2. **Seek a balanced blend of letters from people who have observed you in different settings or situations.** Important settings where people may have seen you in action include:
   - The classroom—where a professor has observed and evaluated your academic performance
   - On campus—where a student life professional is familiar with your contributions to a club or organization
   - Off campus—where professionals not associated with your college have witnessed you perform volunteer service, part-time work, or an internship

3. **Pick the right time and place to make your request.** First, ask the person if he or she would be willing to write a letter of recommendation for you. Don't approach the person with the form in your hand; this sends the message that you're presuming the person will say yes or are pressuring the person to say (which isn't the most socially sensitive message to send

someone whom you're about to ask a favor.) Also, be sure to make your request in a place where the person can give full attention to your request (e.g., the person's office rather than in a busy hallway or in front of a classroom full of students), and give the person ample time to complete the recommendation (e.g., two or more weeks before its due date).

4. **Provide your references with a fact sheet about yourself.** Include your experiences and achievements, both inside and outside the classroom. A personal fact sheet will make your letter writers' job much easier by giving points to focus on; it will also make your recommendations stronger by enabling them to cite specific, concrete examples of your experiences and accomplishments. On your fact sheet, be sure to include high grades you may have earned in certain courses, as well as volunteer services, leadership experiences, awards or forms of recognition, and special interests or talents that relate to your academic major and career goals. Your fact sheet is the place where you can "toot your own horn" without being conceited. You're not boasting or showboating; you're just highlighting your strengths at a time and place where it's appropriate (and important) to do so.

5. **If your letter of recommendation is to be mailed, provide your references with a stamped, addressed envelope.** This is a simple courtesy that makes the letter writer's job easier and demonstrates your social sensitivity.

6. **Waive your right to see the letter.** You may have the option to waive (give up) your right to see the letter of recommendation. If you are confident that you will

continued...

receive a good recommendation, waive your right to review it. This shows confidence in the person writing the letter and assures the person reading the letter that you don't intend to inspect or screen it before sending it out.

7. **Follow up with a thank-you note.** Send this note at about the time your letter of recommendation should be sent. Sending a thank-you note is the sensitive thing to do because it expresses your appreciation to the letter writer; it's also the smart thing to do because if the letter hasn't been sent, your thank-you note will serve as a gentle reminder that the letter should be sent soon.

8. **Let your references know the outcome of your application.** If you have or have not been offered the position or been admitted to the school to which you applied, let your references know. This is the courteous thing to do. It's also the smart thing to do because your references are likely to remember your courtesy, which should increase their willingness to write any additional recommendations you may need.

 Reflection 15.10

At this point in your college experience, have you met anyone on campus who could serve as a future reference, or write a letter of recommendation for you?

If yes, what position does that person hold on campus?

If you haven't found anyone yet, who do you think might be future candidates?

Networking

Would it surprise you to hear that 80% of jobs are never advertised? This means that the jobs you see listed in a classified section of the newspaper and posted in a Career Development Center or employment center represent only 20% of available openings at any given time. Almost one-half of all job hunters find employment through people they currently know or previously met, such as friends, family members, and casual acquaintances.

What these findings suggest is that when it comes to locating position openings and finding gainful employment, *who* you know can be as important as *what* you know or how good your resume looks. Consequently, it's important to expand the circle of people who are aware of your career interests and qualifications. These people may know, or may come in future contact with employers who are looking for somebody with your career interests and qualifications.

Personal Interview

A job interview is your opportunity to make a positive in-person impression on a potential employer. Naturally, the very first impression you'll make will be your physical appearance, including how you're dressed. If you're unsure about what to wear, consult a professional on campus, such as a career counselor or academic advisor.

You can also make a strong impression during an interview by showing that you've done your homework. Come prepared with knowledge about yourself *and* knowledge about the organization offering the position. Bring a list of your strongest selling points to the interview and be ready to speak about them when the opportunity arises. Be especially ready to mention things that: (a) you would like the interviewer to know that's not on your resume and (b) might distinguish or differentiate you from other candidates. One simple, yet memorable way to separate yourself from the competition is to share personal experiences that are uniquely your own and which are relevant to the roles or responsibilities of the position, particularly personal stories relating to a problem or challenge you faced, how you handled it, and what you learned from it.

You can demonstrate knowledge of the organization by doing some web-based research on it, and if possible, on the people who are likely to be interviewing you. In advance of the interview, try to acquire as much information as possible (online and in print) about the organization and who works there.

To prepare for questions that may be asked of you during the interview, ask a career development professional on campus for common interview questions, or research them on the Internet (for example, go to https://job-hunt.org/job_interviews/smart-interview-answers.shtml). You might also speak with college seniors who have participated in job interviews with campus recruiters to get an idea about questions they were frequently asked. Once you begin participating in interviews, make note of the questions you have been asked and come ready to answer those in future interviews. Besides being asked general interview questions that may apply to any position (e.g., "Where do you see yourself in five years?"), you will likely be asked specific questions relating to your particular qualifications and personal experiences. If a question is asked about you in one interview, there's a good chance it will be asked again in future interviews. Consequently, as soon as you complete an interview, reflect on the questions you were asked and jot them down before they slip your mind. Consider developing an index-card catalog of those questions, writing the question you were asked on one side and your prepared response on the reverse side.

In addition to preparing for questions that will be asked of you during an interview, you should come to the interview prepared with questions to ask the interviewer—about the position and the organization. Taking time to do so shows that you're genuinely interested in both the position and the organization offering it. Furthermore, if you come to the interview with knowledge of your audience (the organization) and knowledge of yourself (your personal attributes and relevant experiences), you're well positioned to connect these two forms of knowledge and answer the most important interview question you'll be asked: "What can *you* do for *us?*"

Lastly, remember to send a thank you note to the people who interviewed you. This showcases your social intelligence and strengthens their memory of you—which, in turn, should strengthen your chances of being hired.

> "Strong interviewing skills rely on your knowledge of yourself, the position, field, and/or organization you're seeking, and your ability to quickly establish a relationship.
>
> —Katharine Brooks, author, *You Majored in What?*

Internet-Based Resources

For additional information on career exploration, preparation, and development, see the following websites:

Identifying Positive Attributes & Personal Values:
www.viacharacter.org
Developing a Personalized Career Plan:
https://www.mappingyourfuture.org/planyourcareer/
Career Descriptions and Future Employment Outlook:
www.bls.gov/bls/occupation.htm
Internships:
www.internships.com
http://www.vault.com/internship-programs
Position Openings and Opportunities:
www.indeed.com
www.rileyguide.com
Resume Writing and Job Interviewing:
https://www.livecareer.com/

Chapter 15 Exercises

15.1 Quote Reflections

Review the sidebar quotes contained in this chapter and select two that you found to be especially meaningful or inspirational.

For each quote you selected, provide an explanation why you chose it.

15.2 Strategy Reflections

Review the strategies for *gaining awareness of your career options* on pp. 343-350. Select three you think are most important and intend to put into practice.

15.3 Reality Bite

Career Choice: Conflict and Confusion

Josh is a first-year student whose family has made a great financial sacrifice to support his college education. He deeply appreciates their support and wants to pay them back as soon as possible. Consequently, he's looking at careers that pay the highest starting salaries immediately after graduation. Unfortunately, none of these careers seem to match Josh's natural abilities and personal interests. He's now feeling conflicted and worried. He knows he'll have to decide soon because careers with high starting salaries involve majors that have many specific course requirements, so if he expects to graduate in four years, he'll have to start taking those courses next semester.

Reflection and Discussion Questions

1. Do you see any way that Josh might balance his desire to pay back his family as soon as possible with his desire to pursue a career that's compatible with his personal interests and talents?

2. What questions or factors do you think Josh should consider before he makes his decision about a career?

3. Can you relate to Josh's story, or do you know of students in a similar predicament?

4. If you were Josh, what would you do?

15.4 Gaining Self-Awareness of Personal Interests, Talents (Strengths), and Values

No one is in a better position to know who you are and who you want to become than *you*. An effective way to gain deeper self-awareness and self-knowledge is through self-questioning. By asking yourself questions that cause you to pause and dive deeper into your inner qualities and characteristics, you can gain greater self-insight, which, in turn, can lead you to choose a career path that's true to you.

Respond honestly and thoughtfully to the following questions about your personal interests, strengths, and values. As you read each question, briefly note what thought(s) come to mind about yourself.

> "In order to succeed, you must know what you are doing, like what you are doing, and believe in what you are doing."
>
> —*Will Rogers, Native-American humorist and actor*

Personal Interests

1. What topics tend to stimulate your curiosity and intrigue you?

2. What types of activities or experiences are you able to engage in for long periods of time without losing your interest or focus of attention?

3. When time seems to "fly by" for you, what are you usually doing?

4. When your mind begins to wander, where does it usually take you?

5. What do you really look forward to doing or get most excited about doing?

6. What are your favorite hobbies or pastimes?

7. When you're with friends, what do you spend most of your time talking about or doing?

8. What has been your most stimulating or enjoyable learning experience?

9. If you've had previous work or volunteer experience, what jobs or tasks did you find most interesting?

10. What do you like to read?

11. When you open a newspaper or log onto the Internet, where do you tend to go first?

12. When you daydream or fantasize about your future, what do you see yourself doing?

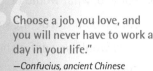

"Choose a job you love, and you will never have to work a day in your life."

—Confucius, ancient Chinese philosopher

Based on your responses to the above 12 questions, identify a career that appears to be most compatible with your personal *interests*.

Briefly explain why you think this career seems to match up well with your interests.

Personal Talents (Strengths)

1. What would you say is your greatest talent or strongest ability?

2. What are your most advanced or well-developed skills?

3. What seems to come naturally or easily to you that comes harder to others?

4. What would you say has been your greatest accomplishment or achievement in life thus far?

5. What about yourself are you most proud of, or take most pride in doing?

6. When others compliment you, what is it usually for?

7. If others come to you for help, advice, or assistance, what is it for and why do you think they come to you?

8. What would your closest friend(s) say is your best quality, trait, or characteristic?

9. What's one thing you have achieved or accomplished that gave you the feeling you might have a special talent for doing it?

10. On what types of learning tasks or activities have you experienced the most success?

11. In what courses or subjects have you earned the highest grades?

12. If you've received awards or other forms of recognition, what were they for and why did you receive them?

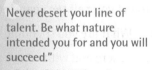

"Never desert your line of talent. Be what nature intended you for and you will succeed."

—Sydney Smith, 18th-century English writer and defender of the oppressed

Based on your responses to the above 12 questions, identify a career that appears to be most compatible with your personal *talents* or *strengths*.

Briefly explain why you think this career seems to match up well with your talents and strengths.

Personal Values

1. What matters most to you?

2. If you were to single out one thing you really stand for or believe in, what would it be?

3. What would you say are your highest priorities in life?

4. When you do something that makes you feel proud, or makes you feel good about yourself, what is it that you're usually doing?

5. If there were one thing in the world you could change, improve, or make a difference in, what would it be?

6. When you have extra spending money, what do you usually spend it on?

7. When you have free time, what do you usually spend it on?

8. For you, what would be "living the good life" or "living the dream"?

9. How would you define success? (What would it take for you to feel that you were successful?)

10. How would you define happiness? (What would it take for you to be happy?)

11. Do you have any heroes or anyone you admire, look up to, or believe has set an example worth following? (If yes, who and why?)

12. Would you rather be thought of as:

   a) smart

   b) wealthy

   c) creative

   d) caring?

Rank from 1 to 4, with 1 being the highest. Why did you rank #1 highest?

> "Do what you value; value what you do."
> —*Sidney Simon, author of* Values Clarification *and* In Search of Values

Based on your responses to the above 12 questions, identify a career that appears to be most compatible with your personal *values*.

Briefly explain why you think this career seems to match up well with your values.

15.5 Connecting Your Personality Type to Career Clusters

Your Career Center of the AchieveWORKS Personality assessment suggests career clusters that seem to align with your personality type. Which of these career clusters appeals most to you?

15.6 Visualizing Your Ideal Career

Project yourself ten years into the future and visualize what your ideal career and ideal life would be.

1. What are you spending most of your time doing during your typical workday?

2. Where and with whom are you working?

3. How many hours are you working per week?

4. Where are you living?

5. Are you married? Do you have children? How does your work influence your social life or family situation?

15.7 Conducting an Information Interview

One of the best ways to acquire accurate information about a career is by interviewing a working professional in that career. This career exploration strategy is known as an *information interview*. An information interview enables you to: (a) get up-to-date information on a career from someone involved the career, (b) expand your professional network, and (c) gain confidence in interview situations that can help you prepare for actual job interviews in the future.

Steps in the Information Interview Process

1. Select a career you may be interested in pursuing. Even if you're currently keeping your career options open, pick a career that might be a possibility. (You can use the resources cited on pp. 343-344 of this chapter to find information

about different careers, or by going to *myplan.com*.) Once you've selected a career, do some research on it to prepare for the interview.

2. Find someone in the career you've selected and set up an information interview with that person. To locate possible interview candidates, consider family members, friends of family members, and family members of your friends. Any of these people may be working in a career you're considering, or they may know someone who is. The Career Development Center on your campus, as well as the Alumni Association or the Rotary Club (a leadership and professional service organization in your local community) may also be able to connect you with professionals who you can interview.

3. Once you have identified a potential interview candidate, send that person a short letter or e-mail to ask about the possibility of scheduling an interview . Mention that you would be willing to conduct the interview in person or by phone—whichever would be more convenient. (If you don't hear back within a reasonable period—e.g., 4-5 days—send a follow-up message. If you don't receive a response to the follow-up message, find another candidate.)

4. Once you've set up the interview, consider asking some or all of following questions during the interview. (Feel free to add or substitute questions of your own.)

   * How did you decide on your career?

   * What steps did you take to locate your current position?

   * What personal qualifications or prior experiences enabled you to enter your career?

   * What would you recommend that first-year students do to begin preparing for a career in your field?

   * How would someone find out about openings in your career field?

   * How does someone advance in your career?

   * During a typical workday, what tasks and responsibilities take up most of your time?

   * What personal skills or qualities do you think are critical for success in your career?

   * Who are the type of people you typically work with and for?

   * Are females and members of diverse ethnic groups well represented in your career? (This may be an especially important question to ask if you're a member of an ethnic, racial, or gender group that is underrepresented in the career you have selected for this interview.)

   * What aspects of your work do you find most satisfying or fulfilling?

   * What are the most difficult or frustrating aspects of your work?

   * Are there any moral issues or ethical challenges that tend to arise in your field of work?

   * Do you see the nature of work changing in your field now or in the near future?

   * Does your career supply you with sufficient personal time outside of work to strike a healthy work-life balance?

   * If you had to do it all over again, would you choose the same career?

   * Would you recommend that I speak with someone else to obtain additional information or a different perspective on your career field? (If the answer is "yes," you may follow up by asking: "May I mention that you referred me?") (It's always a good idea to obtain more than one perspective before making any important decision, including a career decision.)

5. Take notes during the interview. Not only will this help you remember what was said, it also shows the person you're interviewing that you value the ideas he or she is sharing and that those ideas are noteworthy (worth taking notes on).

6. If the interview goes well and you're excited about the possibility of pursuing that career, consider asking if it might be possible to observe or shadow the person at work.

7. Send a thank-you note to the person within a week following the interview.

Self-Assessment Questions

After the interview, take a moment to reflect on the experience and answer the following questions:

1. What did you hear that impressed you about the career?

2. Did you hear anything that distressed (or depressed) you about the career?

3. What was the most useful piece of information you took away from the interview?

4. Based on the information you gathered during the interview, did your interest in the career increase, decrease, or remain the same?

5. Are you still interested in pursuing a career in this field? Why?

15.8 Creating a Skeletal Resume

Review the headings of a skeletal resume described on p. 359.

1. Under each heading, list any experiences or skills that you've already acquired.

2. Under each heading, add experiences or skills you plan to acquire during your college years.

3. Review the experiences and skills you entered under each heading and identify work products you might include in a personal portfolio that would showcase those experiences and skills. (See p. 357 for samples of work products that could be included in a portfolio.)

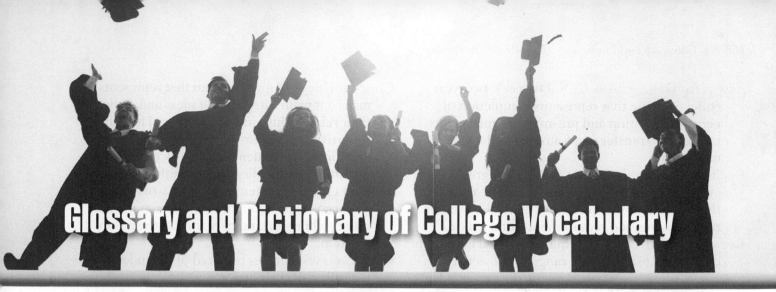

Glossary and Dictionary of College Vocabulary

Academic Advisors: faculty or professional staff who advise college students on course selection, help them understand college procedures, and guide their academic progress toward completion of a college degree.

Academic Affairs: unit or division of the college that deals primarily with the college curriculum, course instruction, and campus services that support academic success (e.g., library and learning center).

Academic Calendar: the scheduling system used by a college or university to divide the academic year into shorter terms (e.g., semesters, trimesters, or quarters).

Academic Credits (Units): how students receive credit for courses completed in college. The amount of academic credits awarded typically is determined by the number of hours the class meets each week (e.g., a course that meets for three hours per week counts for three credits).

Academic Discipline: a field of study (biology, psychology, philosophy, etc.).

Academic Dismissal: dismissing a student from college because the student's cumulative GPA does not meet a minimum standard (e.g., 2.0).

Academic Probation: a period (usually one term) given to students whose grade point average does not meet the college's minimum requirement for graduation (e.g., less than 2.0) to improve their grades. If the student's grades improve to the point where they meet or exceed the college's minimum GPA requirement, probation is lifted; if not, the student may be academically dismissed from the college.

Academic Standing: where a student stands academically (cumulative GPA) at a given point in the college experience (e.g., after one term or one year).

Academic Support Center: place on campus where students can strengthen their academic performance by receiving personal assistance from learning specialists and peer tutors.

Academic Transcript: an official list of all courses a student has enrolled in, the grades received in those courses, and the student's grade point average.

ACE Military Credit: credit granted toward a college degree based on previous military experience (Army, Navy, Air Force, Coast Guard, Department of Defense, or Marine Corps).

Active Involvement (a.k.a. Engagement): the amount of *time* a student devotes to learning in college and the degree of personal *effort* or *energy* (mental and physical) the student puts into the learning process.

Advanced Placement (AP) Tests: tests designed to measure knowledge and skills mastered in high school. If a student scores high enough on an AP test, college credit is awarded in the subject area tested, or the student can take an advanced college course in the subject area.

Analysis (Analytical Thinking): a form of higher-level thinking skill that involves breaking down information, identifying its key parts or underlying elements, and detecting the parts that are most important or relevant.

APA Style: a style of citing references in a research report or term paper adopted by the American Psychological Association (APA), which is most commonly used in academic fields that comprise the Behavioral Sciences (e.g., Psychology and Sociology) and Natural Sciences (e.g., Biology and Chemistry).

Aptitude: ability to do something well or having the potential to do it well.

Associate Degree (A.A./A.S. Degree): two-year college degree that represents completion of general education and pre-major requirements needed for transfer to a four-year college or university.

Bachelor's (Baccalaureate) Degree: degree awarded by four-year colleges and universities that represents completion of general education requirements and requirements for a major.

Breadth Requirements: required general education courses that span a wide range of subject areas.

Career Advancement: working up the career ladder to higher levels of authority and socioeconomic status.

Career Development Center: key campus resource where students learn about the nature of different careers and acquire strategies for locating career-related work experiences.

Career Development Courses: college courses that typically include self-assessment of career interests, information about different careers, and strategies for career preparation.

Certificate: credential received by students at a community college or technical college that signifies completion of a vocational or occupational training program and qualifies them for a specific job or occupation.

Citation: an acknowledgment of an information source used in a written paper or oral report.

Co-curricular Experiences: student learning and development that takes place outside the course curriculum.

Collaborative Learning: two or more students working interdependently as a team toward a common goal, in which they support each other and take equal responsibility for helping the team move toward its shared goal.

College Catalog (a.k.a. College Bulletin): an official publication of a college or university that identifies its mission, curriculum, academic policies and procedures, and the names and educational background of its faculty.

Communication Skills: skills necessary to comprehend and express ideas effectively (e.g., reading, writing, speaking, listening, and multimedia skills).

Commuter Students: college students who do not live on campus.

Concentration: a cluster of approximately three courses in the same subject area.

Concept (Idea) Map: a diagram that represents or maps out main categories of ideas and depicts their relationships in a visual–spatial format.

Cooperative Education (Co-op) Program: program in which students gain work experience relating to their college major, either by stopping their course work temporarily to work full-time in the co-op position, or by continuing to take classes while working part-time in the co-op position.

Core Courses: courses required of all students, regardless of their major.

Counseling Services: personal counseling provided on campus by professionals with expertise in promoting students' self-awareness and self-development, particularly with respect to social and emotional issues.

Cover (Application) Letter: letter written by an applicant applying for an employment position or admission to a school.

Cramming: packing a large amount of study time into one study session immediately before an exam.

Creative Thinking: a form of higher-level thinking that generates unique ideas, strategies, or work products.

Critical Thinking: a form of higher-level thinking that involves making well-informed evaluations and judgments.

Cross-registration: a collaborative program offered by two colleges or universities that allow students enrolled at one institution to register for and take courses at the other institution.

Culture: a distinctive pattern of beliefs and values learned by a group of people who share the same social heritage and traditions.

Cum Laude: graduating "with honors" (e.g., achieving a cumulative GPA of 3.3).

Cumulative GPA: a student's grade point average based on grades for all courses completed.

Curriculum: the total set of courses offered by a college or university.

Dean: a college or university administrator who is responsible for running a unit of the college (e.g., Dean of Fine Arts).

Dean's List: a list of students who achieved an outstanding GPA during a particular academic term (e.g., 3.5 or higher).

Developmental Education Courses (a.k.a. Transitional Courses): noncredit courses in reading, writing, or mathematics that students must complete before being able to take college credit–earning courses.

Distance Learning: courses taken online rather than in person.

Diversity: the variety of groups that comprise the human species (humanity).

Diversity Appreciation: valuing the experiences of different groups of people and willingness to learn from their experiences.

Diversity (Multicultural) Courses: courses designed to promote diversity awareness and appreciation of multiple cultures.

Doctoral Degree: an advanced degree obtained after completion of the bachelor's (baccalaureate) degree, which typically requires 5 to 6 years of full-time study in graduate school, including completion of a thesis or doctoral dissertation.

Documentation: references used to support or reinforce points made in a written paper or oral presentation.

Double Major: a bachelor's degree in two majors that students earn by meeting course requirements in both fields of study.

Drop/Add: the process of changing an academic schedule by dropping courses or adding courses to a student's original schedule.

Electives: courses that students elect (choose) to take.

Ethnic Group (Ethnicity): a group of people who share the same culture.

Experiential Learning: out-of-class experiences that promote learning and development.

Faculty: the collection of instructors on campus whose primary role is to teach courses offered in the college curriculum.

FAFSA (Free Application for Federal Student Aid): a form prepared annually by current and prospective college students (undergraduate and graduate) to determine their eligibility for student financial aid from the federal government.

Fine Arts: a division of the liberal arts or general education curriculum that focuses largely on artistic expression and appreciation of artistic expression, seeking answers to such questions as: What is beautiful? How do humans express and appreciate aesthetic (sensory) experiences, imagination, and creativity?

Free Electives: courses that students choose to enroll in, which count toward a college degree, but are not required for general education or an academic major.

Freshman Fifteen: a phrase commonly used to describe the average 15-pound weight gain that some students experience during their first year of college.

Full-time Student: a student enrolled in at least 12 units of coursework during an academic term.

General Education Curriculum: a collection of courses designed to equip students with a broad base of knowledge and transferable skills needed for success in any major or career.

Grade Points: number of points earned for a course, which is calculated by multiplying the course grade by the number of credits carried by the course.

Grade Point Average (GPA): translation of students' letter grades into a numeric system, in which the total number of grade points earned in all courses is divided by the total number of course units.

Graduate Assistant (GA): a graduate student who receives financial assistance to pursue graduate studies by working in a university office or for a college professor.

Graduate Record Examination (GRE): a standardized test for admission to graduate schools, similar to how SAT and ACT tests are used for admission to undergraduate colleges and universities.

Graduate School: education pursued after completing a bachelor's degree.

Graduate Student: student who has completed a four-year (bachelor's) degree and is enrolled in graduate school to obtain an advanced degree (e.g., Master's or Ph.D.).

Grant: money received to pay for college that does not have to be repaid.

Greek Life: a term referring to fraternities (usually all male) and sororities (usually all female).

Hazing: a rite of induction to a social or other organization, most commonly associated with fraternities.

Health Services: on-campus services that treat students experiencing physical illnesses or injuries and educate students on matters relating to health and wellness.

Higher Education: formal education beyond high school.

Higher-Level Thinking: thinking at a higher or more complex level than merely acquiring factual knowledge or memorizing information.

Holistic (Whole Person) Development: development of the total self, which includes intellectual, social, emotional, physical, spiritual, ethical, and vocational development.

Honors Program: a special program of courses and related learning experiences designed for students who have demonstrated exceptionally high levels of academic achievement.

Humanities: division of the liberal arts curriculum that focuses on the human experience, human culture, and questions relating to the human condition, such as: Why are we here? What is the meaning or purpose of our existence? How should we live? What is the good life? Is there life after death?

Humanity: common elements of the human experience shared by all human beings.

Hypothesis: an informed guess that might be true, but still needs to be tested to confirm or verify its truth.

Impacted Major: a college major in that has more students interested in it than there are spaces for it; thus, students must formally apply and qualify for admission to the major by going through a competitive screening process.

Independent Study: a project in which students receive academic credit for in-depth study of a topic of their choice by working independently under the guidance of a faculty member rather than enrolling in a classroom-based course.

Information Interview: an interview with a professional currently working in a career to obtain inside information about what the career is really like.

Information Literacy: the ability to access, retrieve, and evaluate information.

Intellectual (Cognitive) Development: acquiring knowledge, learning skills, and the ability to think at a higher level.

Intercultural Competence: ability to appreciate and learn from human differences and interact effectively with people from diverse cultures.

Interdisciplinary: courses or programs designed to help students integrate knowledge from two or more academic disciplines (fields of study).

International Student: a student attending college in the United States who is a citizen of another nation.

International Study (Study Abroad) Program: a program in which domestic students take courses at a college or university in a foreign country, typically for one term during the sophomore or junior year.

Internship: work experience related to a college major for which students receive academic credit and, in some cases, financial compensation.

Interpret: to draw a conclusion and support that conclusion with evidence.

Inter-term (a.k.a. January Interim or Maymester): a short academic term, typically running 3-4 weeks, during which students enroll in only one course or subject that is studied intensively.

Job Shadowing: a program that allows a student to follow (shadow) and observe a professional during a typical workday.

Leadership: ability to influence people in a positive way (e.g., motivating peers to do their best), or the ability to produce positive change in an organization or institution (e.g., improving the quality of a school, business, or political organization).

Learning Community: a program in which the same group of students takes the same block of courses together during the same academic term.

Learning Habits: the usual approaches, methods, or techniques a student uses to learn.

Liberal Arts: the component of a college curriculum that embodies the essential knowledge and skills needed to lead a productive, meaningful, and fulfilling life.

Lifelong Learning: learning how to learn and to learn continuously throughout life.

Living-Learning Environment: on-campus student residence designed to integrate student learning experiences into the living environment (e.g., in-residence study groups, tutoring, and student development workshops).

Lower-Division Courses: courses taken by college students during their freshman and sophomore year.

Magna Cum Laude: graduating with "high honors" (e.g., achieving a cumulative GPA of 3.5).

Major: the academic field students choose to specialize in while in college.

Master's Degree: degree obtained after completion of the bachelor's (baccalaureate) degree that typically requires two or three years of full-time study in graduate school.

Matriculation: the process of initially enrolling in or registering for college (the term derives from the medieval word, *matricula*—a list or register of persons belonging to a society or community).

Mentor: someone who serves as a role model and guide for another person, helping that person (mentee or protégé) reach educational, occupational, or personal goals.

Merit-Based Scholarship: money awarded to students based on academic performance or achievement that does not have to be repaid.

Metacognition: thinking about how you are thinking while you are thinking.

Midterm: the midpoint of an academic term.

Minor: a field of study designed to complement and strengthen a college major, which usually requires 6-8 courses.

MLA Style: a style of citing references adopted by the Modern Language Association (MLA) that is commonly used in academic fields that comprise the Humanities and Fine Arts (e.g., English and Philosophy).

Mnemonic Device (Mnemonic): a memory improvement method for retaining and recalling information (e.g., an acronym or rhyming pattern).

Multicultural Center: place on campus designed for interaction among and between members of diverse cultural groups.

Multidimensional Thinking: a form of higher-level thinking that involves taking multiple perspectives or vantage points.

Multiple Intelligences: the theory that humans display intelligence and mental ability in a variety of ways (e.g., social intelligence and emotional intelligence).

Natural Sciences: a division of the liberal arts curriculum that focuses on the systematic observation of the physical world and underlying explanations of natural phenomena, asking such questions as: "What causes the physical events that take place in the natural world?" "How can we predict and control natural events?"

Need-Based Scholarship: money awarded to students based on financial need that does not have to be repaid.

Netiquette: applying principles of social etiquette and interpersonal sensitivity to online communication.

Nonresident Status: out-of-state students who typically pay higher tuition than in-state students because they are not residents of the state in which their college is located.

Nontraditional Students (a.k.a. Re-entry Students): students who do not begin college immediately after high school.

Online Resources: resources for searching and locating information, which include online card catalogues, Internet search engines, and electronic databases.

Oral Communication Skills: ability to speak in a clear, confident, and articulate manner.

Orientation: an educational program experienced by students before their first term in college that is designed to help them make a smooth transition to higher education.

Oversubscribed (a.k.a. Impacted) Major: a major that has more students interested in it than there are openings for it.

Paraphrase: restating or rephrasing information in your own words.

Part-Time Student: a college student who enrolls in fewer than 12 units during an academic term.

Part-to-Whole Study Method: a study strategy that involves taking material to be learned, dividing it into smaller parts, and studying these parts in short, separate sessions in advance of an exam; then, on the day before the exam, all the previously studied parts are reviewed as a whole.

Pass/Fail (Credit/No Credit) Grading: a grading option offered in some courses where students can choose to receive a grade of "pass" (credit) or "fail" (no credit), rather than a letter grade (A–F).

Persuasive Speech: an oral presentation intended to persuade the audience to agree with a certain position by presenting sound arguments and supporting evidence.

Phi Beta Kappa: a national honor society that recognizes outstanding academic achievement of students at four-year colleges and universities.

Phi Theta Kappa: a national honor society that recognizes outstanding academic achievement of students at two-year colleges.

Placement Tests: tests administered to new students upon entry to a college or university that are designed to assess their basic academic skills (e.g., reading, writing, mathematics) and place them in courses that are neither beyond nor below their level of skill development.

Plagiarism: intentional or unintentional use of someone else's work without acknowledging it, thus giving the impression that it's your own work.

Portfolio: a collection of work materials or products that showcases skills and talents or demonstrates educational and personal development.

Postsecondary Education: formal education that takes place after secondary (high school) education.

Pre-professional Coursework: undergraduate courses that are required or strongly recommended for gaining entry into professional school (e.g., medical school or law school).

Prerequisite Course: a course that must be completed before a more advanced course can be taken.

Prewriting: an early stage in the writing process where the focus is on generating ideas, rather than expressing or communicating ideas to someone else.

Primary Sources: information obtained from firsthand sources or original documents.

Process-of-Elimination Method: test-taking strategy for multiple-choice exams that involves eliminating or "weeding out" choices that are clearly wrong until the best possible answer is identified.

Professional School: education pursued after a bachelor's degree in a school that prepares students for an "applied" profession (e.g., Pharmacy, Medicine, or Law).

Proficiency Tests: tests given to college students before graduation that are designed to assess whether they can perform certain academic skills (e.g., writing) at a level high enough to qualify them for college graduation.

Proofreading: final stage of editing one's own work that focuses on detecting mechanical errors relating to referencing, grammar, punctuation, and spelling.

Quarter System: a system for scheduling courses in which the academic year is divided into four quarters (fall, winter, spring, and summer terms), each of which lasts approximately 10–11 weeks.

Recall Test Questions: questions that require test-takers to generate or produce the correct answer on their own (e.g., essay questions), as opposed to questions that ask them to select an answer from answers provided to them (e.g., multiple-choice or true-false questions).

Recitation (Reciting): a study strategy that involves recalling and speaking aloud information to be remembered without looking at it.

Recognition Test Question: test questions that require test-takers to select or choose a correct answer from answers provided to them (e.g., multiple-choice, true–false, and matching questions), as opposed to questions requiring them to produce answers on their own (e.g., essay test questions).

Reference Letter (a.k.a. Letter of Recommendation): a letter written on behalf of a student who is applying for employment, admission to graduate or professional school, or admission to special campus programs (e.g., honors program or peer mentoring program).

Registrar's Office: campus office that maintains college transcripts and other official records associated with student coursework and academic performance.

Research Skills: ability to locate, access, retrieve, organize, and evaluate information from a variety of sources, including libraries and technology-based (computer) systems.

Resident Assistant: undergraduate student (sophomore, junior, or senior) whose role is to help new students adjust successfully to residence hall life and enforce residential-life rules.

Resident Director: student development professional in charge of residential (dormitory) life to whom resident assistants report.

Resident Status: in-state students who typically pay lower tuition than out-of-state students because they are residents of the state in which their college is located.

Residential Students: students who live on campus or in a housing unit owned and operated by the college.

Restricted Electives: courses that students choose to take from a restricted set or list of possible courses that have been specified by the college.

Resume: a list of an individual's credentials, accomplishments, skills, and awards.

Rough Draft: an early stage in the writing process during which the writer's major ideas are expressed without close attention to the mechanics of writing (e.g., punctuation, grammar, or spelling).

Scholarly: a criterion or standard for evaluating the quality of an information source; typically, a source is considered "scholarly" if it has been peer reviewed by a panel or board of impartial experts in the field before being published.

Secondary Source: a publication that relies or builds on a previously published source (e.g., a textbook that draws its information from previously published research studies or journal articles).

Self-Assessment: the process of reflecting on and evaluating personal characteristics, such as one's personality traits, personal interests, or learning habits.

Self-Monitoring: maintaining self-awareness of what you're doing and how well you're doing it.

Self-Regulation: adjusting learning strategies to meet the specific demands of the subject being learned (e.g., using different strategies when learning math than when learning history).

Semester System: a system for scheduling courses in which the academic year is divided into two terms (fall and spring) that are approximately 15–16 weeks long.

Semester (Term) GPA: GPA calculated for one semester or academic term.

Senior Seminar (Capstone) Course: course designed to put a "cap" or final touch on the college experience, helping seniors tie ideas together in their major and make the transition from college to post-college life.

Service Learning: a form of experiential learning in which students serve or help others while also acquiring skills that enable them to strengthen their resumes and explore potential careers.

Sexually Transmitted Infections (STIs): a group of contagious infections spread through sexual intercourse.

Shadow Majors: students who have been admitted to their college or university but have not yet been admitted to their intended major.

Shallow (Surface) Learning: an approach to learning in which a student's study time is spent repeating and memorizing information in the exact form in which it has been presented, rather than transforming it into words that are personally meaningful.

Social and Behavioral Sciences: a division of the liberal arts or general education curriculum that focuses on the observation of human behavior, individually and in groups, asking such questions as: What causes humans to behave the way they do? How can we predict, control, or improve human behavior?

Socially Constructed Knowledge: knowledge that is built up through interaction and dialogue with others.

Student Activities: co-curricular experiences offered outside the classroom that are designed to promote student learning and involvement in campus life.

Student-Designed Major: an academic program offered at some colleges in which a student works with a college representative or committee to develop a personally customized major that is not officially listed in the college catalog.

Student Development Services (Student Affairs): division of a college or university that devoted to student issues relating to social and emotional adjustment, student involvement in campus life outside the classroom, and student leadership development.

Student Handbook: an official college publication that identifies student roles and responsibilities, violations of campus rules and policies, and co-curricular opportunities,(e.g., student clubs, campus organizations, and student leadership positions).

Summa Cum Laude: graduating with "highest honors" (e.g., achieving a cumulative GPA of 3.8 or higher).

Summer Session: courses offered during the summer between spring and fall terms, which typically run for 4–6 weeks.

Syllabus: an academic document that outlines course requirements, attendance policies, grading scale, course topics, test dates, and assignment due dates, as well as information about the instructor (e.g., office location and office hours).

Synthesis: a form of higher-level thinking that involves integrating (connecting) smaller, separate pieces of information into a more comprehensive and coherent whole.

Teaching Assistant (TA): a graduate student who receives financial assistance to pursue graduate studies and earns this financial assistance by teaching undergraduate courses, leading course discussions, and helping professors grade papers or conduct labs.

Test Anxiety: a state of emotional tension that can weaken test performance by interfering with concentration, memory, and ability to think at a higher level.

Test-Wise: using characteristics of the test question itself (such as its wording or format) to increase your chances of choosing the correct answer.

Theory: a body of conceptually related concepts and general principles that helps organize, understand, and apply knowledge that has been acquired in a field of study.

Thesis Statement: a one- to three-sentence statement contained in the introduction to a paper, which serves as a summary of the key point or main argument the writer intends to make and support with evidence.

Transfer Program: two-year college program that provides general education and pre-major coursework to prepare students for successful transfer to a four-year college or university.

Transferable Skills: skills that can be transferred or applied across different subjects, careers, and life situations.

Trimester System: a system for scheduling courses in which the academic year is divided into three terms (fall, winter, and spring) that are approximately 12–13 weeks long.

Undeclared: students who have not declared (committed to) a college major.

Undergraduate: student enrolled in a two-year or four-year college.

Upper-division Courses: courses taken by college students during their junior and senior years.

Visual Aids: charts, graphs, diagrams, or concept maps designed to improve learning and memory by organizing information into a picture or image.

Visualization: a memory improvement strategy that involves creating a mental image or picture of what is to be remembered, or by imagining it in a familiar site or location.

Vocational (Occupational) Development: exploring career options, making wise career choices, and developing skills for career success.

Vocational/Technical Programs: community college programs that train students for an occupation or trade and immediate employment in that trade or occupation after completing a one-year certificate program or a two-year associate degree (e.g., Associate of Applied Science).

Volunteerism: committing personal time to help others without receiving financial compensation or academic credit.

Waive: to give up one's right to access information (e.g., waiving the right to see a letter of recommendation).

Wellness: a state of optimal health that promotes peak performance and positive well-being by balancing and integrating different dimensions of the "self" (body, mind, and spirit).

Withdrawal: dropping a class after the drop/add deadline, which results in the student receiving a "W" for the course and no academic credit.

Work-Study Program: a federal program that supplies colleges and universities with funds to provide on-campus employment for students in financial need.

Writing Center: a campus support service where students receive assistance at different stages of the writing process (e.g., collecting and organizing ideas, or composing a first draft.)

Index